Raphael Cohen-Almagor in this thoughtful and sensitive study tackles the most complex and controversial of all constitutional guarantees: The free speech principle. Following the footsteps of John Stuart Mills he probes dilemmas and offers guidelines that political theorists, politicians, judges and journalists will have good reason to ponder.

Geoffrey Marshall, former Provost of Queen's College, Oxford

The Scope of Tolerance

One of the dangers in any political system is that the principles that under-lie and characterize it may, through their application, bring about its destruction. Liberal democracy is no exception. Moreover, because democracy is a relatively young phenomenon, it lacks experience in dealing with pitfalls involved in the working of the system – the "catch" of democracy.

The Scope of Tolerance is an interdisciplinary study concerned with the limits of tolerance, this "democratic catch", and the costs of freedom of expression. Rights are costly, and someone must pay for them. We can and should ask about the justification for bearing the costs, weighing them against the harms inflicted upon society as a result of a wide scope of tolerance. While recognizing that we have the need to express ourselves, we should also inquire about the justifications for tolerating the damaging speech and whether these are weighty enough.

This book combines theory and practice, examining issues of con-tention from philosophical, legal and media perspectives, and covers such issues as:

- Media invasion into one's privacy
- Offensive speech
- Incitement
- Hate speech
- Holocaust denial
- Media coverage of terrorism.

This book is essential reading for anyone who has research interests in political theory, extremism, and free speech.

Raphael Cohen-Almagor teaches at the Department of Communication, and Library and Information Studies at the University of Haifa, and is the Director of the Centre for Democratic Studies. Between 1997 and 2000 he was a member of the Israel Press Council. He is the author of a number of books, including *The Boundaries of Liberty and Tolerance* (1994), *The Right to Die with Dignity* (2001), *Speech, Media and Ethics* (2001, paperback 2005), and *Euthanasia in The Netherlands* (2004).

Routledge studies in extremism and democracy

Series Editors: Roger Eatwell
University of Bath
and
Cas Mudde
University of Antwerp-UFSIA

This new series encompasses academic studies within the broad fields of "extremism" and "democracy". These topics have traditionally been considered largely in isolation by academics. A key focus of the series, therefore, is the (inter-)*relation* between extremism and democracy. Works will seek to answer questions such as to what extent "extremist" groups pose a major threat to democratic parties, or how democracy can respond to extremism without undermining its own democratic credentials.

The books encompass two strands:

Routledge Studies in Extremism and Democracy includes books with an introductory and broad focus which are aimed at students and teachers. These books will be available in hardback and paperback. Titles include:

Understanding Terrorism in America
From the Klan to al Qaeda
Christopher Hewitt

Fascism and the Extreme Right
Roger Eatwell

Racist Extremism in Central and Eastern Europe
Edited by Cas Mudde

Routledge Research in Extremism and Democracy offers a forum for innovative new research intended for a more specialist readership. These books will be in hardback only. Titles include:

1 **Uncivil Society?**
   Contentious politics in Post-Communist Europe
   Edited by Petr Kopecky and Cas Mudde

2 **Political Parties and Terrorist Groups**
   Leonard Weinberg and Ami Pedahzur

The Scope of Tolerance

Studies on the costs of free expression and freedom of the press

Raphael Cohen-Almagor

Routledge
Taylor & Francis Group

LONDON AND NEW YORK

First published 2006
by Routledge
2 Park Square, Milton Park, Abingdon, Oxon OX14 4RN

Simultaneously published in the USA and Canada
by Routledge
270 Madison Ave, New York, NY 10016

Routledge is an imprint of the Taylor & Francis Group

Transferred to Digital Printing 2005

© 2006 Raphael Cohen-Almagor

Typeset in Baskerville by Wearset Ltd, Boldon, Tyne and Wear

British Library Cataloguing in Publication Data
A catalogue record for this book is available from the British Library

Library of Congress Cataloging in Publication Data
A catalog record for this book has been requested

ISBN 0-415-35757-8 (hbk)
ISBN 0-415-35758-6 (pbk)

In memory of
Professor Gary Schwartz
and
Dr Rafi Livni
who were taken prematurely

Contents

Series editors' preface

For much of the "short twentieth century", history was characterized by the clash of great ideologies, internal violence and major wars. Although most catastrophic events took place outside the Western world, Europe and the USA were not immune from the turmoil. Two world wars and a series of lesser conflicts led to countless horrors and losses. Moreover, for long periods Western democracy – especially in its European form – seemed in danger of eclipse by a series of radical forces, most notably communist and fascist.

Yet by the turn of the 1990s, liberal democracy appeared destined to become the universal governmental norm. Dictatorial Soviet communism had collapsed, to be replaced in most successor states by multi-party electoral politics. Chinese communism remained autocratic, but in the economic sphere it was moving rapidly towards greater freedoms and mercerization. The main manifestations of fascism had gone down to catastrophic defeat in war. Neo-fascist parties were damned by omnipresent images of brutality and genocide, and exerted little appeal outside a fringe of ageing nostalgics and alienated youths.

In the Western world, political violence had disappeared, or was of minimal importance in terms of system stability. Where it lingered on as a regularly murderous phenomenon, for instance in Northern Ireland or Spain, it seemed a hangover from the past – a final flicker of the embers of old nationalist passions. It was easy to conclude that such tribal atavism was doomed in an increasingly interconne. ed "capitalist" world, characterized by growing democratic norms and forms of multi-level governance that were transcending the antagonism and parochialism of old borders.

However, as we move into the new millennium there are growing signs that extremism even in the West is far from dead – that we celebrated prematurely the universal victory of democracy. Perhaps the turn of the twenty-first century was an interregnum, rather than a turning point? In Western Europe there has been the rise of "extreme right" and "populist" parties, such as Jean-Marie Le Pen's Front National, which pose a radical challenge to existing elites – even to the liberal political system.

In the USA, the 1995 Oklahoma mass bombing has not been followed by another major extreme right attack, but there is simmering resentment towards the allegedly over-powerful state among well-armed militias and other groups. More generally across the West, new forms of green politics, often linked by a growing hostility to globalization–Americanization, are taking on more violent forms (the issue of animal rights is also growing in importance in this context).

In the former Soviet space, there are clear signs of the revival of "communist" parties, often masquerading as "socialists" or "social democrats", whose allegiance to democracy is (in varying degrees) debatable. In Latin America there remain notable extremist movements on the left, though these tend not to be communist. This trend may well grow both in response to globalization–Americanization and to the (partly linked) crises of many of these countries, such as Argentina. This in turn increases the threat to democracy from the extreme right, ranging in form from paramilitary groups to agro-military conspiracies.

The rise of Islamic fundamentalism has been an even more notable feature of recent years. This is not simply a facet of Middle Eastern politics, where insurgent opposition in post-2003 war Iraq and elsewhere threaten American dreams of universalizing democracy. It has had an impact within some former Soviet republics, where the old nomenklatura have used the Islamic threat to maintain autocratic rule. In countries such as Indonesia and India, Muslims and other ethnic groups have literally cut each other to pieces. More Al-Qaeda bombings of the 2002 Bali-type threaten economic ruin to Islamic countries which attract many Western tourists.

It is also important to note that growing Islamic fundamentalism has had an impact within some Western countries. The terrorist attacks on the World Trade Center and elsewhere in the USA on 11 September 2001 are perhaps the most graphic illustration of this impact. But in democracies generally, the rise of religious and other forms of extremism pose vital questions about the limits of freedom, multiculturalism, and tolerance. This is especially the case in ones which have experienced notable Islamic immigration and/or which face the greatest threat of further terrorist attack, many of which have witnessed the growth of domestic Islamophobia.

Democracy may have become a near-universal shibboleth in the West, but its exact connotations are being increasingly challenged and debated even in its heartland. As long as the "evil empire" of communism existed, democracy could in an important sense define itself by the "Other" – by what it was not. It did not have overt dictatorial rule, censorship, the gulags, and so on. But with the collapse of its great external foe, the spotlight has turned inward (although Islam is in some ways replacing communism as the "Other"). Is (Western) liberal democracy truly democratic? Can it defend itself against terrorism and new threats without undermining the very nature of democracy?

These general opening comments provide the rationale for the *Routledge Series on Extremism and Democracy*. In particular, there are three issues that we seek to probe in this series:

- Conceptions of democracy and extremism
- Forms of the new extremism in both the West and the wider world
- How democracies are responding to the new extremism.

Raphael Cohen-Almagor's book raises points relevant to all three of these issues. He begins by citing Karl Popper, who in his classic work *The Open Society and its Enemies* argues that: "Unlimited tolerance must lead to the disappearance of tolerance". The point can easily be seen today by a brief visit to the Internet, which over the last decade has been extensively used by groups and individuals who have demanded their right to freedom of expression in order to disseminate pornography, Holocaust denial, racism and miscellaneous forms of extremism.

Political philosophers, such as John Stuart Mill, have paid surprisingly little attention to the issue of when it is legitimate to restrict freedom. Moreover, constitutionally speaking, there have been notably different answers to the conundrum. On the one hand, the American first Amendment prohibits the curtailment of "the freedom of speech, or of the press". On the other hand, the (West) German Basic Law (1949) adopted a "militant" (*streitbare/Wehrhafte*) conception of democracy, which allowed for the banning of non-democratic parties, as well as other restrictions such as the proscription of Hitler's *Mein Kampf*. However, in practice these are "ideal-types" rather than descriptions of the workings of the respective systems. For example, since 9/11 the US has adopted a variety of new laws and policies that challenge its historic constitutional commitment to freedom of speech.

Cohen-Almagor, therefore, adopts an approach based on specific case studies. Focusing on the US, Israel, Canada, and the UK, he takes examples concerning five broad issues: i) the media invasion of privacy; ii) offensive speech; iii) incitement; iv) hate speech and Holocaust denial; and v) media coverage of terrorism. Using an interdisciplinary approach combining philosophical, legal, and media studies perspectives, and combining a mastery of the secondary literature with insights from interviews conducted with experts in relevant fields, Cohen-Almagor probes the question of when it is legitimate to restrict freedom.

Princess Diana died in a car crash, after being chased by *paparazzi* across Paris. Was this the tragic ending to a symbiotic relationship between a beautiful personality who secretly craved publicity? Or was it more the extreme result of the invasion of privacy which the media regularly inflict on a variety of people who are of no interest in themselves, but whose lives have taken on dimensions which make them of interest to a media hungry for "human interest stories" (such as the victims of Al-Qaeda's murderous attacks on 9/11)?

The American Civil Liberties Union (ACLU) has (in)famously defended the rights of groups like the Ku Klux Klan and National Socialist Party not only to publish extremist views, but also to hold rallies which were clearly designed to offend. Is there a right for such groups to march through Jewish areas, such as Skokie in Illinois? And does the issue change if it seems that the purpose of the rally is not simply to put across a message by gaining media publicity, but actually to provoke a violent response?

The religious ultra-nationalist member of the Israeli Knesset, Meir Kahane, engaged in provocative visits to Arab villages and openly called Palestinians "dogs", a "malignant disease" who "multiply like fleas". Does a democrat have to defend the right to make such statements? Should the media report them? And what are the media's responsibilities when the "dogs" fight back with weapons rather than words? Cohen-Almagor cites Walter Laqueur, who has argued that if terrorism is propaganda by deed, then the success of terrorism is strongly related to the media coverage it receives. Would 9/11 have had a similar impact had the media not published pictures of the symbolic fall of the Twin Towers (over and over again)?

Cohen-Almagor proposes four factors which we should take into account when considering restricting freedom: i) the content of the expression; ii) the manner of the expression; iii) the intention of the speaker, and iv) the circumstances in which the expression occurs. Of these, he sees the first and last as the most important. Cohen-Almagor does not accept the naïve view that speech can do no harm, accepting that rights can be costly and that someone must pay for them. Nevertheless, he presents an argument which – in mature democracies at least – justifies prohibiting free speech in only exceptional cases. Even racist or "hate speech", which has become increasingly proscribed in Western democracies, is not seen as necessarily beyond the pale. Cohen-Almagor argues that whilst people cannot choose the colour of their skin or "race", such speech should no more be banned than statements about abortion or a person's sexual orientations and other matters of choice.

Wide-ranging and provocative, this work sets out arguments which are of vital importance to policy-makers as well as to academics.

Roger Eatwell and Cas Mudde
Bath and Antwerp
April 2005

Acknowledgments

This book is the result of research and thinking conducted during the past decade. I would like to thank friends and colleagues who conversed with me on pertinent questions and who read parts or the entire book. First and foremost I feel fortunate for having had the opportunity to communicate and exchange ideas with Geoffrey Marshall, formerly Provost of Queen's College, Oxford, and a great constitutional scholar, who read drafts of each and every chapter, and commented and criticized with his usual precision and sharpness. Geoffrey, an inspiring teacher and colleague, died while I was completing the book, and he will be sorely missed. He was one of the wittiest and sharpest personalities I have ever met.

Other people who have read and commented on one or more chapters are Rick Abel, Larry Alexander, Valerie Alia, Eric Barendt, Isaiah Berlin (who is also sorely missed), Jerry Cohen, David Feldman, Ken Karst, Iddo Landau, Roderick A. Macdonald, Joe Magnet, Dick Moon, Steve Newman, Georg Nolte, Jack Pole, Robert Post, Michel Roy, Stephen Scheinberg, Danny Statman, Hillel Steiner, Wayne Sumner, Eugene Volokh, Richard Warman, Jim Weinstein, and Conrad Winn.

I also express gratitude to the following people for providing me with information and pertinent material: Harry Abrams, Aharon Barak, Michael Ben-Yair, Ian Binnie, Ilan Bombach, Louise Bourgeois, Jane Britten, Guy Caron, Dan Caspi, Ronald Cohen, Peter de C. Cory, Dalia Dorner, Martin Freeman, Mark J. Freiman, Mike Gasher, Edward Greenspon, Tessa Hale, Frank Iacobucci, Mota Kremnitzer, Sam Lehman-Wilzig, Neil Malamuth, Yigal Marsel, Herbert Marx, David Matas, Eliyahu Matza, Mayo Moran, Brian Mulroney, Moshe Negbi, Ross Perigoe, Christian Pihet, Jerrold M. Post, Marc Raboy, Enn Raudsepp, Elyakim Rubinstein, Bob Rupert, Noam Solberg, Mel Sufrin, Anne Taylor, Yaakov Tirkel, Stefan Verhulst, Gabi Weimann, Yitzhak Zamir, and Amir Zolti.

I acknowledge with gratitude the generous support of the University of Haifa Research Authority and Faculty of Humanities, the Canadian government, the British Council, the Israel Association for Canadian Studies, the Fulbright Foundation, and Johns Hopkins University. I am also most grateful to the Rockefeller Foundation for providing me with a residency fellowship in the most tranquil and picturesque Villa Serbelloni in Bellagio, arguably the most perfect place one could imagine for thinking and deliberating.

Last but not least, I express my deep gratitude to Eli Dunker, Keren Eyal, Dareen Jaacob, Jeannette E. Pierce, Grace Yaacob, and Tali Yanai for their excellent research assistance, and to my family for their love, understanding, support, and enduring patience.

An early version of Chapter 1 was published in Antonio Punzi (ed.), *Rawls*, special issue of *Rivista Internazionale di Filosofia del Diritto* (2004). An early version of Chapters 4 and 5 was published in *International Journal of Politics and Ethics*, 2(2 and 3) (2002): 101–117 and 189–209 (two parts). An early, shorter version of Chapter 6 was published in Raphael Cohen-Almagor (ed.), *Liberal Democracy and the Limits of Tolerance: Essays in Honour and Memory of Yitzhak Rabin* (Ann Arbor: University of Michigan Press, 2000), pp. 79–98. An early, much shorter and very different version of Chapter 7 was published in *Review of Constitutional Studies*, 6(1) (2001): 79–100. A different version of Chapter 8 was published in *Canadian Journal of Communication*, 30(3) (2005). An early version of Chapter 9 was published in *Canadian Journal of Communication*, 25(2) (2000): 251–284. My gratitude is granted for permissions to use the material.

The book is dedicated to two friends who died much too early. Gary Schwartz of UCLA School of Law, and Rafi Livni, who was a physician in several Israeli hospitals, were people who readily contributed to the well-being of their respective societies. Their lives' projects were cut unexpectedly, and the world lost two humanitarians who cared more for others than for themselves. I miss them and cherish their memories.

Raphael Cohen-Almagor
JHU, Baltimore

Introduction

> Unlimited tolerance must lead to the disappearance of tolerance. If we extend unlimited tolerance even to those who are intolerant, if we are not prepared to defend a tolerant society against the onslaught of the intolerant, then the tolerant will be destroyed, and tolerance with them.
>
> Karl Popper *The Open Society and Its Enemies*

In many democracies, freedom of expression and freedom of the media are guaranteed by the same constitutional provision. Section 2(b) of the Canadian Charter of Rights and Freedoms holds that everyone has the following fundamental freedoms: "freedom of thought, belief, opinion and expression, including freedom of the press and other media of communication".[1] The First Amendment to the American Constitution prohibits the abridgement of "the freedom of speech, or of the press".[2] The British courts tend to treat freedom of speech and freedom of the press as interchangeable terms.[3] In turn, Article 5 of the German *Grundgesetz*[4] covers press and broadcasting freedom, as well as the right enjoyed by everyone to disseminate opinions freely.[5]

This book is about the limits of tolerance and the costs of freedom of expression. The concept of tolerance and its legitimate scope lies at the center of analysis. It considers problematic expressions that require society to pay a certain price if tolerated. The analysis includes discussions

---

1 Part 1 of the Constitution Act, 1982, being schedule B to the Canada Act 1982 (UK), 1982, c.11.
2 http://caselaw.lp.findlaw.com/data/constitution/amendment01/.
3 See, for instance, *A.G.* v. *Guardian Newspapers (no. 2)* [1990] A.C. 109. See also E. Barendt, "Press and broadcasting freedom: does anyone have any rights to free speech?", *Current Legal Problems*, 44 (1991): 64–65.
4 *Basic Law for the Federal Republic of Germany* (Bonn: Press and Information Office of the Federal Government, 1994). Cf. D. P. Kommers, *The Constitutional Jurisprudence of the Federal Republic of Germany* (Durham: Duke University Press, 1997); G. H. Fox and G. Nolte, "Intolerant democracies", *Harvard International Law Journal*, 36(1) (1995): 32–34.
5 In Israel, no specific law guarantees freedom of speech or of the press.

on media invasion into one's privacy, offensive speech, incitement, hate speech and Holocaust denial, and finally media coverage of terrorism. The book's primary aim is to formulate precepts and mechanisms designed to prescribe boundaries to freedom of expression conducive to safeguard democracy. This interdisciplinary study combines theory and practice, examining the issues of contention from philosophical, legal, and media perspectives. Its methodology involved extensive literature survey (books, journal and newspapers articles, classified documents) as well as interviews with experts in media ethics, constitutional law, and political extremism in Israel, the United Kingdom, Canada, and the United States.

The "democratic catch"

Democracy in its modern, liberal formation is a young phenomenon. It was crystallized only after World War I. Viscount James Bryce wrote in 1924: "Seventy years ago ... the approaching rise of the masses to power was regarded by the educated classes of Europe as a menace to order and prosperity. Then the word Democracy awakened dislike or fear. Now it is a word of praise."[6] The idea that governments would be elected through popular vote alarmed and frightened the nineteenth-century decision-makers. Now we are so accustomed to the idea of democracy that we tend to forget how young and fragile it is.

Indeed, one of the dangers in any political system is that the principles that underlie and characterize it may, through their application, bring about its destruction. Democracy, in its liberal form, is no exception. Moreover, because democracy is a relatively young phenomenon, it lacks experience in dealing with pitfalls involved in the working of the system. This is what I call the "catch" of democracy.[7] The freedoms the media enjoy in covering events are respected as long as they do not imperil the basic values that underlie democracy. Freedom of speech is a fundamental right, an important anchor of democracy, but it should not be used in an uncontrolled manner.

Like every young phenomenon, democracy needs to develop gradually, with great caution and care. Since democracies lack experience, they are uncertain with regard to the appropriate means to be utilized in order to fight down explicit antidemocratic and illiberal practices. Abundant literature exists about the pros of democracy, the value of liberty, the virtue of

---

6 J. Bryce, *Modern Democracies* (London and New York: Macmillan, 1924), Vol. I, p. 4.

7 R. Cohen-Almagor, *The Boundaries of Liberty and Tolerance* (Gainesville: University Press of Florida, 1994); *Speech, Media, and Ethics: The Limits of Free Expression* (Houndmills and New York: Palgrave-Macmillan, 2005).

tolerance.[8] Liberal thinkers wish to promote liberty and tolerance; urge governments not to apply partisan considerations that affirm principally their own interests and conceptions; seek ways to accommodate different conceptions of the good,[9] to reach compromises by which democracy will respect variety and pluralism. Much less in comparison was written in the field of political theory about the intricate issue of the appropriate scope of tolerance.

Persons, as moral agents, have their conceptions of a moral life, and accordingly determine what they deem to be the most valuable or best form of life worth leading. A conception of the good involves a mixture of moral, philosophical, ideological, and religious notions, together with personal values that contain some picture of a worthy life. One's conception of the good does not have to be compatible with moral excellence. It does not mean a conception of justice. The assumption is that a conception of the good comprises a basic part of our overall moral scheme and that it is public insofar as it is something we advance as good for others as well as for ourselves. Consequently, we would want others to hold the conception for their sake. But when that desire is based on coercion, it cannot be said to be moral because people are no longer autonomous to decide on their way of life. They are then forced to follow a scheme which they do not consider to be a conception of the good life.

In the United States, the American Civil Liberties Union (ACLU), among other organizations, has supported the rights of racist and anti-Semitic organizations, most notoriously the Ku Klux Klan and the American National Socialist Party, to speak, to demonstrate, to march, and to organize.[10] In their defense of radical political groups, the ACLU and others have not claimed that the words, pictures, and symbols of such

---

8 See, for instance, S. Mendus (ed.), *Justifying Toleration* (Cambridge: Cambridge University Press, 1988); D. Heyd (ed.), *Toleration: An Elusive Virtue* (Princeton: Princeton University Press, 1996); J. Horton and S. Mendus (eds), *Toleration, Identity and Difference* (Houndmills: Macmillan, 1999); S. Mendus (ed.), *The Politics of Toleration* (Edinburgh: Edinburgh University Press, 1999); T. M. Scanlon, *The Difficulty of Tolerance* (Cambridge: Cambridge University Press, 2003); C. McKinnon and D. Castiglione (eds), *The Culture of Toleration in Diverse Societies* (Manchester and New York: Manchester University Press, 2003).

9 Of course the autonomy principle may have to be subordinated to the harm principle. Thus, for instance, democracies may infringe the thief's autonomy in order to protect others' property. See J. Raz, *The Morality of Freedom* (Oxford: Clarendon Press, 1986), pp. 134–135; R. Cohen-Almagor, *The Boundaries of Liberty and Tolerance*, Chapter 3.

10 See *Collin* v. *Smith*, 578 F.2d 1197 (7th Cir.) cert. denied 439 U.S. 915 (1978). *Village of Skokie* v. *National Socialist Party of America*, 69 Ill. 2d 605, 373 N.E.2d 21 (1978). For further deliberation, see A. Neier, *Defending My Enemy* (New York: E. P. Dutton, 1979).

groups have no negative consequences.[11] The constitutional protection accorded to the freedom of speech is not based on a naïve belief that speech can do no harm but on the confidence that the benefits society reaps from the free flow and exchange of ideas outweigh the costs society endures by allowing reprehensible and even dangerous ideas. Free speech activists acknowledge that the racist and anti-Semitic images and discourse of these groups can inflict damage on the targeted individuals, can harmfully corrupt the level and nature of civic discourse, and can at times increase the probability of violent and unlawful acts being committed against people on account of their race or religion. Yet the admission of speech's causal propensities and harmful consequences has not lessened the strength of the Free Speech Principle. That is because the free speech rights of Nazis and the Ku Klux Klan are not a consequence of the ineffectualness or the harmlessness of their utterances. The Nazis and their ilk have free speech rights not because what they say is harmless, but despite the harm they cause by what they say.[12]

Rights and costs

However, as Frederick Schauer rightly points out, we need to recognize that rights are costly, and that someone must pay for them.[13] In the liberal framework, the concept of "rights" is understood in terms of a need that is perceived by those who demand it as legitimate and, therefore, the state has the responsibility to provide it for each and every citizen. Rights are primary moral entitlements for every human being. In this context one could differentiate between rights that guarantee certain goods and services, like the right to welfare and to healthcare, and rights that protect against certain

---

11 On the free speech rights of the Ku Klux Klan and other radical organizations, see *Brandenburg* v. *Ohio*, 395 U.S. 444 (1969); *Forsyth County* v. *Nationalist Movement*, 505 U.S. 123 (1992); *R.A.V.* v. *City of St. Paul*, 505 U.S. 377 (1992). See also *United States* v. *Hayward and Krause* 6 F. 3d 1241 (7th Cir. 1993) and *U.S.* v. *Juveniles J.H.H., L.M.J and R.A.V.* 22 F. 3d 821 (8th Cir. 1994) in which the court held that some forms of expression, like cross burning, used to intimidate, are harmful and damaging to others and, as such, do not enjoy the protecting cover of speech in the constitutional sense. On the other hand, see *Virginia* v. *Black*, 123 S. Ct. 1536 (2003), which declared the Virginia crossburning statute unconstitutional because it discriminated on the basis of content and viewpoint. For critique of this highly controversial opinion, see S. G. Gey, "A few questions about cross burning, intimidation, and free speech", Florida State University College of Law, *Public Law Research Paper*, No. 106 (February 2004).

12 Cf. F. Schauer, "The cost of communicative tolerance", in Raphael Cohen-Almagor (ed.), *Liberal Democracy and the Limits of Tolerance* (Ann Arbor: University of Michigan Press, 2000), p. 29.

13 *Ibid.*, pp. 32–33.

harm or guarantee certain liberties, like the right to freedom of expression and to exercise choice.[14] This book concentrates attention on the latter.

Another pertinent distinction is between an individual's rights with regard to the state or government and an individual's rights with regard to his or her fellow citizens. Rights, conceived to be legitimate, that must be met by the state (e.g., the right to life, to shelter, and to associate), justify taking political actions to fulfill them. Rights regarding other individuals who act illegitimately justify the use of coercive measures against those individuals either by concerned citizens (right to self-defense, to privacy, or to protect one's property) or by the state.[15]

The claim that citizens have rights that the state or the government is obligated to guarantee does not mean that the state may not, under certain circumstances, override these rights. Citizens have a right to freedom of expression, but the state can limit that right in order to prevent a threat to public order, the security of the state, or third parties in need of protection (such as children). If it is the case that public security is decreased because of the harmful exercise of the Free Speech Principle, then it is quite possible that the rhetoric of rights will not suffice to justify the protection of the questionable speech. Then the strength or scope of the rights recognized ought to be decreased.

Once we recognize that rights have costs, we can and should ask about the justifications for bearing the costs, weighing them against the harms inflicted upon society as a result of a wide scope of tolerance. While recognizing that as humans we have the need to express ourselves and, therefore, suppressing speech in itself is a form of damage, we should also inquire about the justifications for tolerating the damaging speech and whether these are weighty enough. We should examine how serious is the "democratic catch" and whether it might seriously harm a certain group of people or endanger democracy.

14 Cf. R. Cohen-Almagor, *Speech, Media, and Ethics*, p. xiii.
15 For further discussion on the concept of rights, see R. Dworkin, *Taking Rights Seriously* (London: Duckworth, 1977); R. J. Pennock and J. W. Chapman (eds), *Human Rights* (New York: New York University Press, 1981); L. W. Sumner, *The Moral Foundation of Rights* (Oxford: Clarendon Press, 1989); M. Freeden, *Rights* (Minneapolis: University of Minnesota Press, 1991); H. Steiner, *An Essay on Rights* (Oxford: Blackwell, 1994); A. Gewirth, *The Community of Rights* (Chicago: University of Chicago Press, 1996); P. M. Sniderman et al., *The Clash of Rights* (New Haven and London: Yale University Press, 1996); A. S. Brett, *Liberty, Right and Nature* (Cambridge: Cambridge University Press, 1997); R. Dagger, *Civic Virtues* (New York: Oxford University Press, 1997); M. H. Kramer, N. E. Simmonds and H. Steiner, *A Debate over Rights: Philosophical Enquiries* (Oxford: Clarendon Press, 1998); M. J. Perry, *The Idea of Human Rights: Four Inquiries* (New York: Oxford University Press, 1998); S. Walker, *The Rights Revolution* (New York: Oxford University Press, 1998); J. R. Rowan, *Conflicts of Rights* (Boulder: Westview Press, 1999); M. Ignatieff, *The Rights Revolution* (Toronto: House of Anansi Press, 2000); W. A. Edmundson, *Introduction to Rights* (Cambridge: Cambridge University Press, 2004).

Underlying premises

The underlying premises of this book are: first, free expression is a fundamental right and value in democracies. It is the freedom of the individual
to realize herself, to form a worldview and an opinion by giving flight to
her spirit. It is the freedom of the individual and the community to bring
truth to light through a struggle between truth and falsity. The underlying
assumption is that truth will prevail in a free and open encounter with
falsehood. Furthermore, freedom of expression is necessary for keeping
the vitality of beliefs. It is the freedom to exchange opinions and views in a
spirit of tolerance, with respect to the autonomy of every individual, and
to persuade one another in order to strengthen, secure, and develop the
democratic regime. Freedom of expression is crucial to indicate causes of
discontent, the presence of cleavages, and possible future conflicts.[16]

The second premise holds that – generally speaking – there is a need to
strike a balance between the right to freedom of expression and the
harms that might result from a certain speech. It is argued that the right
to exercise free expression does not include the right to do unjustifiable
harm to others.[17] Indeed, one of the four key principles of the Society of
Professional Journalists' Code of Ethics is to minimize harm. It says,
"ethical journalists treat sources, subjects and colleagues as human beings
deserving of respect". The Code further instructs journalists to show compassion for those who may be affected adversely by news coverage and to
avoid pandering to lurid curiosity, maintaining that the "pursuit of the
news is not a license for arrogance".[18]

Third, democracy and free media live and act under certain basic
tenets of liberty and tolerance from which they draw their strength and
vitality and preserve their independence. Two of the most fundamental
background rights underlining every democracy are respect for others
and not harming others.[19] They should not be held secondary to considerations of profit and personal prestige of journalists and newspapers. Journalists should see people as ends and not as means – a Kantian

16 A. Barak, "Freedom of expression and its limitations", in R. Cohen-Almagor,
   The Boundaries of Liberty and Tolerance, op. cit., pp. 89–93; T. I. Emerson, *Toward
   a General Theory of the First Amendment* (New York: Random House 1966), esp.
   pp. 5–15.
17 Canadian Charter of Rights and Freedoms, section 1; *R. v. Keegstra* [1990] S.C.J.
   No. 131; *Canadian Human Rights Commission* et al. v. *Taylor* et al. 75 D.L.R. (4th)
   [1990]; *R. v. Butler* [1992] 1 S.C.R. 452.
18 See Ontario Press Council, *24th Annual Report* (Toronto, Ontario, 1996), p. 79.
19 R. Dworkin, "Liberalism", in *A Matter of Principle* (Oxford: Clarendon Press,
   1985): 181–204; *ibid., Taking Rights Seriously* (London: Duckworth, 1976); R.
   Cohen-Almagor, *The Boundaries of Liberty and Tolerance, op. cit.* For further
   reading and analysis, see R. L. Abel, *Speaking Respect, Respecting Speech* (Chicago
   and London: University of Chicago Press, 1998).

deontological approach.[20] We respect others as autonomous human beings who exercise self-determination to live according to their life plans; we respect people as self-developing beings who are able to expand their inherent faculties as they choose, that is, to develop the capability they wish to cultivate, not every capability that they are blessed with. In turn we respect people in order to help them realize what they want to be. Each individual is conceived as a bearer of rights and a source of claims against other persons, just because the resolution of the others is theirs, made by them as free agents. To regard others with respect is to respect their right to make decisions regardless of our opinions of them. We simply assume that each of us holds that our own course of life has intrinsic value, at least for the individual, and we respect the individual's reasoning, so long as he or she does not harm others. We respect the individual's rights as a person even we have no respect for his or her specific decisions and choices.[21]

Fourth, indeed, the role of the media is not merely to report what "is there" and to "further truth". Along with the power the media possess come responsibilities of the media to their audience, their profession, and the democracy that enables their functioning.[22] The establishment of powerful press empires in the Western world feeds the debate on social responsibility. The debate on ethical boundaries to media coverage is very lively, revolving around the questions *what* to report, in what priority and in accordance to what standards, as well as *how* to report.[23] It is possible,

20 I. Kant, *Foundations of the Metaphysics of Morals* (Indianapolis: Bobbs-Merrill Educational Publishers, 1969).

21 In his comments Steve Newman suggests a distinction between respecting a person for who the person is, and respecting a person as an abstract bearer of rights. I may respect an agent as a bearer of rights, but I do not necessarily respect her opinion on a given subject. And if I come to the conclusion that all her moral judgments are equally flawed, I might lose respect for her as a person; yet this will not affect my respect for her status as a bearer of rights.

22 I have developed this argument in R. Cohen-Almagor, *Speech, Media and Ethics: The Limits of Free Expression.* For discussion on the basis of free expression theory and its limits, see K. Greenawalt, *Speech, Crime and the Uses of Language* (New York: Oxford University Press, 1989); Home Office, *Report of the Committee on Privacy and Related Matters* (June 1990), Cm 1102; Sir David Calcutt, *Review of Press Self-Regulation* (London: Her Majesty's Stationary Office, January 1993), Cm 2135.

23 A. Belsey and R. Chadwick (eds), *Ethical Issues in Journalism and the Media* (London and New York: Routledge, 1992); H. Holmes and D. Taras (eds), *Media, Power and Policy in Canada* (Toronto: Harcourt Brace Jovanovich, 1992); N. Russell, *Morals and the Media* (Vancouver: UBC Press, 1995); V. Alia, B. Brennan and B. Hoffmaster (eds), *Deadlines and Diversity: Journalism Ethics in a Changing World* (Halifax, Nova Scotia: Fernwood, 1996); R. Lorimer and J. McNulty, *Mass Communication in Canada* (Ontario: Oxford University Press, 1996); A. Siegel, *Politics and the Media in Canada* (Toronto: McGraw-Hill Ryerson, 1996); J. Winter, *Democracy's Oxygen: How Corporations Control the News* (Montreal: Black Rose Books, 1997); R. A. Hackett and Y. Zhao, *Sustaining Democracy? Journalism and the Politics of Objectivity* (Toronto: Garamond Press,

for instance, to report the activities of hate-mongers without directly reporting their malicious diatribes.

Outline

This is the third book in a trilogy that started with *The Boundaries of Liberty and Tolerance*,[24] and continued with *Speech, Media and Ethics: The Limits of Free Expression*.[25] The first chapter provides the theoretical underpinnings of the book, discussing the scope of tolerance and its moral reasoning. Tolerance is not to be equated with indifference, nor can it be considered as indifference, for the doer *does* have strong reservations regarding the conduct. Furthermore, tolerance could not be equated with the concept of neutrality;[26] it assumes that the agents are partial regarding the phenomenon at hand.

I discuss the Millian[27] and Rawlsian[28] theories on tolerating the intolerant, and then criticize consequentialism, arguing that we need to ponder the *ethical* question of the constraints of tolerance in addition to consequences. I then discuss the distinction between *moral* overriding principles and general overriding principles, explaining that we could speak of tolerance only when the principles that convince us to adhere to tolerance are moral in nature. Acts of tolerance, carried out solely on prudential grounds, are not to be considered as tolerance in the genuine sense of the word as understood here. Only those people who tolerate others out of respect are conceived as tolerant beings. The essay further provides a distinction between two forms of tolerance: *latent* and *manifest*.

Much of the discussion in this book addresses the role of media. The discussion focuses on the way journalists conceive the ethical notions of accountability and responsibility, and whether media ethics exist at all in the "real world" of writing and reporting. Is ethical journalism visible in fiercely competitive markets where the prime motivation is to sell?

1998); M. Kieran, *Media Ethics* (London: Routledge, 1998); R. Cohen-Almagor, "Ethical boundaries to media coverage", *Australian Journal of Communication*, 26(2) (1999): 11–34; A. D. Gordon and J. M. Kittross, *Controversies in Media Ethics* (New York: Longman, 1999); J. Rosen, *What Are Journalists For?* (New Haven: Yale University Press, 1999); D. Taras, *Power and Betrayal in the Canadian Media* (Ontario: Broadview Press, 1999); D. Pritchard, *Holding the Media Accountable* (Bloomington: Indiana University Press, 2000); K. Sanders, *Ethics and Journalism* (Thousand Oaks: Sage, 2003).

24 Gainesville: The University Press of Florida, 1994.

25 Houndmills and New York: Palgrave-Macmillan, 2001, 2nd edn 2005.

26 Cf. R. Cohen-Almagor, "Between Neutrality and Perfectionism", *Canadian Journal of Law & Jurisprudence*, VII(2) (1994): 217–236.

27 J. S. Mill, *Utilitarianism, Liberty, and Representative Government* (London: J. M. Dent, 1948, Everyman's edition).

28 J. Rawls, *A Theory of Justice* (Oxford: Oxford University Press, 1971).

Generally, the journalist is assumed to answer the following questions: first, is what the journalist reports, analyzes or criticizes of any interest to the public? Second, does the journalist deal fairly with the subject? Namely, does the journalist take all the important aspects of the issue into full consideration? Issues related to social responsibility that need to be addressed concern the journalist's commitments to the public, and whether he or she must observe certain rules that stem from his or her view of society and the role of the media within it. A related issue is whether these notions are stagnant or in flux.

Chapter 2 is the first of five chapters (2, 3, 7, 8, 9) that were enriched by a fieldwork in Britain, the United States, and Canada during which I interviewed some prominent lawyers, judges, policy-makers, media professionals, and scholars. Chapters 2 and 3 canvass the issue of speech that intrudes on people's privacy.[29] Privacy is central to liberal thought – as a right the state guarantees to protect from interference by others or by the state itself. In Western democracies, privacy is generally seen as a state of being or a right enjoyed by an individual. Privacy is considered basic to a free and open society and crucial for individual development. It facilitates spontaneity and insulates the individual from social pressure to conform.[30] However, when news is becoming entertainment, private lives can be unkindly exposed to obtrusive publicity. Then speech under the guise of "the public's right to know" might become very costly for the individuals involved.

After explicating the underpinning concepts for ethical and legal analysis of privacy I go on to discuss two specific case studies: England and Canada. Thus, in Chapter 3 I explore the intricate relationships Princess Diana had with the media, and then examine the Quebec *Les Editions Vice-Versa Inc.* v. *Aubry*.

The remainder of the book in one way or another is related to the limitations imposed on free expression or press freedom by security or public order considerations. Chapters 4 and 5 supplement the discussion on privacy, dealing with the related issue of speech that offends sensibilities of a given group. This is a neglected issue that did not receive ade-

29 Possibly the most classic text on privacy is the path-breaking article of S. Warren and L. D. Brandeis, "The right to privacy", *Harvard Law Review*, 4 (1890): 289–320. See also the discussions of J. Rosen, *The Unwanted Gaze* (New York: Random House, 2000), pp. 43–45; J. DeCew, "Privacy", in E. N. Zalta (ed.), *The Stanford Encyclopedia of Philosophy* (summer 2002), available at http://plato.stanford.edu/archives/sum2002/entries/privacy; William A. Edmundson, "Privacy", in M. P. Golding and W. A. Edmundson (eds), *The Blackwell Guide to the Philosophy of Law and Legal Theory* (Oxford: Blackwell Publishing, April 2004).
30 F. Olsen, "Privacy", in Edward Craig (ed.), *The Routledge Encyclopedia of Philosophy* (London: Routledge, 1998), p. 691.

quate attention.[31] To what an extent could the Offense to Sensibilities Argument serve as possible grounds for limiting free expression? The task is truly problematic because of the difficulty in assessing emotional and psychological offense. At the same time, we acknowledge that some expressions under certain circumstances might hurt no less than physical harms. Offense to sensibilities can be devastating, stripping people of their sense of human dignity.[32] Thus, we must invest more efforts in understanding the concept of offense. The pertinent questions are: under what conditions should the Offense to Sensibilities Argument take precedence over the Free Speech Principle? What criteria should be examined when we are asked to evaluate the severity of the offense? Who should be asked to assess the severity of the offense?

The study first introduces the theme of boundaries to freedom of expression. It proceeds by an examination of Israeli law and, more specifically, of the main Supreme Court cases in which the Offense to Sensibilities Argument was raised, formulating some ground principles for the evaluation of offense. Chapter 5, in turn, applies the formulated principles to analyze Rabbi M. K. Meir Kahane's visits to Arab villages. It serves as a case in point when the Offense to Sensibilities Argument may provide justified grounds for curtailing free expression. The Argument will take precedence over free expression only in cases where severe and direct damage is inflicted upon the emotional system of individuals or a target group under circumstances in which the individuals or target group cannot avoid being subject to the offensive expression. Psychologists should be consulted to assess the severity of the offense.

After speaking of offense, it is natural to speak of harm. Chapter 6 discusses the costs of free expression in a specific context: Israel after the signing of the Oslo Accords in September 1993, which widened the split between the political "left" and "right" in Israel. The only Jewish democracy in the world was forced to acknowledge the "democratic catch" and to deal with its harsh consequences on 4 November 1995. On that tragic day, Prime Minister Yitzhak Rabin was assassinated in the main square of Tel Aviv. The study argues that incitement (or instigation) should be excluded from the protection of the Free Speech Principle.

The discussion is opened by an examination of the Attorney General's proposal to the media not to broadcast incitement. I argue that it is in the interest of the media, of the people and of the government to have the

---

31 Still, some good discussions are Joel Feinberg's *Offense to Others* (New York: Oxford University Press, 1985); K. Greenawalt's, *Fighting Words: Individuals, Communities, and Liberties of Speech* (Princeton: Princeton University Press, 1995), and A. Ellis's "Offense and the liberal conception of the law", *Philosophy & Public Affairs*, 13(1) (Winter 1984).

32 The term "dignity" is derived from the Latin noun *dignitas*, which means: (a) worthiness, merit; (b) greatness, authority; and (c) value, excellence.

media free of government directives. I proceed by analyzing examples of incitement prior to Prime Minister Rabin's assassination that required intervention but where insufficient measures were taken to forestall them or to punish the individuals involved. The essay concludes by providing an analysis of a Supreme Court decision, *Rabbi Ido Elba* v. *State of Israel*, which explicitly condemned racist incitement and held that such incitement should not be treated mercifully.

Chapters 7, 8 and 9 consider two of the most problematic issues relating to the scope of tolerance and costs of free expression: hate speech and terrorism. It is first argued that we need to be aware of the harms involved in hate speech. Hate speech is designed to promote abhorrence on the basis of race, religion, national origin or ethnicity. Many democracies are aware of the danger entailed in hate propaganda and fight against it by various means: education, increasing awareness, recruitment of the media, and by passing laws that expressively prohibit its dissemination. Each country should devise its own mechanisms to combat hate.

Germany enacted criminal and civil laws that protect against insult, defamation, and other forms of verbal assault, such as attacks on a person's integrity or honor, damage to one's reputation, and disparaging the memory of the dead. Section 130 of the *Penal Code* prohibits the production, storage or use of documents inciting hatred against part of the population or against groups determined by nationality, race, religion, or ethnic origin.[33] The Austrian *Verhetzung*, Section 283 of the *Criminal Code* – incitement to hostile action, punishes whoever publicly induces or incites – in a manner likely to endanger public order – the commission of a hostile act against a church or religious community existing in the State or against a group determined by appurtenance to such a church or religious community, race, nation, ethnic group or state. The same law also prohibits a person from ridiculing members of one of such groups in a contemptuous fashion, or from insulting them in a manner that offends their human dignity.[34] Article 266(b) of the Danish *Penal Code* outlaws statements "threatening, insulting or degrading a group of persons on account of their race, color, national or ethnic origin or belief".[35] In the

---

33 StGB art 130 (F.R.G.) (*Penal Code*). Translation by F. Kubler in "How much freedom for racist speech? Transnational aspects of a conflict of human rights", *Hofstra Law Review*, 27 (1998): 340–345. For further discussion on hate speech regulation in Germany, and also France, see J. Q. Whitman, "Enforcing Civility and Respect: Three Societies", *Yale Law Journal*, 109 (2000), 1279.

34 Cf. European Monitoring Centre on Racism and Xenophobia, *EUMC Study on Anti-Discrimination Legislation in EU Member States, Austria* (Vienna, 2002), p. 12; http://eumc.eu.int/.

35 J. Weinstein, "Hate speech, viewpoint neutrality, and the American concept of democracy", in T. R. Hensley (ed.), *The Boundaries of Freedom of Expression and Order in American Democracy* (Kent: Kent State University Press, 2001), p. 169.

Netherlands Section 137 of the *Criminal Code* dictates it is a criminal offense to "deliberately give public expression to views insulting to a group of persons on account of their race, religion or conviction or sexual preference". In Sweden, the *Freedom of the Press Act* (Chapter 7, Article 4) prohibits the expression of contempt for a population group "with allusion to its race, skin colour, national or ethnic origin, or religious faith". In Australia, Section 3 of *Racial Hatred Act 1995* prohibits public behaviour that is likely "to offend, insult, humiliate or intimidate another person or group of people" if the act is done because of the race, colour or national or ethnic origin of the other person or a group.[36] In Israel, Amendment No. 20 (1986) of the *Penal Code* makes "incitement to racism" a criminal offense.[37] And the 1965 British Race Relations Act made "incitement to racial hatred" an offense in circumstances where the accused intended to incite racial hatred against any section of the public distinguished by color, race, nationality, or ethnic or national origins and the language used was threatening, abusive or insulting and was likely to stir up racial hatred.[38]

The aims of Chapter 7 are to detail the history of hate speech in Canada, to argue that Holocaust denial is a form of hate speech, to analyze how it was treated by the courts and by the media, and to voice an opinion as to how we should treat different manifestations of hate. Courts interpret the law whereas the media follow their own principles of free speech, the public's right to know, objectivity, and the pursuit of truth. Hate-mongers and terrorists well understand the power of the media, and often utilize the media to achieve their goals, at the expense of democracy. Ernst Zündel in particular exploited the media's eagerness to sell and to achieve high ratings. It is argued that the media should not cooperate with hate-mongers by providing them an uncontrolled platform for disseminating their ideas. This is not to say that the media should fail to report the conduct of hate-mongers. Instead, it is argued that media coverage of hate speech should be cautious, sensitive to the interests of the group under attack, and responsible. Acknowledging the "democratic catch", the free media should assist democracy that enables their functioning in fighting down enemies of democracy.[39]

36 W. Sadurski, *Freedom of Speech and Its Limits* (Dordrecht: Kluwer, 1999), p. 179.
37 Sections 144 (A–E) of the *Penal Code*, Amendment No. 20 (1986). See also R. Cohen-Almagor, *The Boundaries of Liberty and Tolerance*, Chapter 13.
38 Section 6 of the *Race Relations Act*. See also R. Cohen-Almagor, *The Boundaries of Liberty and Tolerance*, p. 270, note 25, and p. 281, note 26. For argument against the supposed public interest served by the hate speech laws, see S. Braun, *Democracy Off Balance: Freedom of Expression and Hate Propaganda Law in Canada* (Toronto: University of Toronto Press, 2004).
39 For further discussion, see W. Kinsella, *Web of Hate: Inside Canada's Far Right Network* (Toronto: HarperCollins, 1995); S. Newman (ed.), *Constitutional Politics in Canada and the United States* (New York: State University of New York Press, 2004).

As for terrorism, there have been many instances in which media coverage of terrorist events has been problematic, to the point of even cooperating with terrorists against the government. During terrorist events, the media tend to exaggerate and accelerate political successes and failures. Experienced movements learn to anticipate such cycles so they can minimize the damage associated with government success and seize the opportunities that emanate from official failures.[40] The concluding two chapters open by mentioning some of the most troubling episodes, arguing that a zero sum game exists between democracy and terror: any gain for the one is a loss for the other. I discuss pertinent questions: is it prudent to hold live interviews with terrorists during dramatic events? What are the effects of repeating the same story again and again? What is the prime role of the media, to tell the truth or act responsibly while considering the possible consequences of their coverage?

The closing chapter reflects on the FLQ crisis in October 1970, arguably the most problematic event of all, showing that some organs of the French media cooperated with the terrorists because they felt sympathy with the FLQ's basic premise, and did not really perceive them as terrorists. The crisis escalated rapidly into a state of national emergency after the killing of one of the hostages, and the War Measures Act was invoked. It is argued that some segments of the media played a significant role in provoking the authorities to such a dramatic action. I close by proposing some ethical guidelines for responsible media coverage of terrorist incidents.[41]

The FLQ study benefitted from a review of previously undisclosed 1970 Cabinet records concerning the FLQ and the kidnapping of James Cross

40 G. Wolfsfeld, *Media and Political Conflict: News from the Middle East* (Cambridge: Cambridge University Press, 1997), p. 114. For discussions on terrorists' memoirs and writings, see D. C. Rapoport, "The international world as some terrorists have seen it: a look at a century of memoirs", and B. Cordes, "When terrorists do the talking: reflections on terrorist literature", both in D. C. Rapoport (ed.), *Inside Terrorist Organizations* (London: Frank Cass, 2001), pp. 32–58, 150–171; M. Stohl, "The Myths and Realities of Contemporary Political Terrorism", in M. Stohl (ed.), *The Politics of Terrorism* (New York and Basel: Marcel Dekker, 1988), pp. 1–19; K. G. Barnhurst, "The literature of terrorism", in A. Odasuo Alali and K. Kelvin Eke (eds), *Media Coverage of Terrorism* (Newbury Park: Sage, 1991), pp. 112–137; R. P. J. M. Gerrits, "Terrorists' perspectives: memoirs", in D. L. Paletz and A. P. Schmid (eds), *Terrorism and the Media* (Newbury Park: Sage, 1992), pp. 29–61; J. M. Post, E. Sprinzak and L. M. Denny, "The terrorists in their own words: interviews with 35 incarcerated Middle Eastern terrorists", *Terrorism and Political Violence*, 15(1) (2003): 171–184.
41 For a recent useful study that brings together sixty-nine journalists, government officials, and scholars to examine reporting and policy-making during periods of war and terror, see S. Hess and M. Kalb (eds), *The Media and the War on Terrorism* (Washington, DC: Brookings Institution Press, 2003).

and Pierre Laporte. This information was made public only recently. In certain instances, information has been removed in accordance with various sections of the *Access to Information Act* (e.g., section 14, information that would be injurious to the conduct of federal–provincial affairs), but I was allowed to look at more than 200 pages of relevant records showing the sense of urgency the government felt during and immediately after the October crisis.[42] The major bulk of deliberations dealt with questions of law and order, means to combat terrorism, police powers and responsibilities, mobilization of troops into Quebec and their withdrawal, intelligence resources, and ways to deal with separatism. The files show there was a real fear that things might get out of control to the point of insurrection. For three weeks, the government had been forced to concentrate on virtually nothing but the FLQ. The files further show that members of the government were very dissatisfied with the media's role in the crisis and sought ways to regulate them. Prime Minister Pierre Elliott Trudeau and his cabinet were aware of the media's power and of the need to publicize their own views in order to mobilize public support for their decisions.

The new data shed interesting light on how the government perceived the role of the Canadian Broadcasting Corporation (CBC). The data provide insight on the deliberations revolving around whether or not to broadcast the FLQ manifesto. The documents also present direct quotations from Prime Minister Trudeau's views on the role of the media during the crisis, as well as quotations of other senior public officials. There are illuminating discussions on censorship and media regulation, and suggestions to amend the existing laws to promote the integration of Canada. The documents also testify about the efforts that were made to calm the heads of the media organizations after the invocation of the War Measure Act on 16 October 1970.

---

42 I am most grateful to Ciuineas Boyle, Coordinator, Access to Information and Privacy, for the valuable assistance.

1 The scope of tolerance and its moral reasoning

> This is true liberty, when free-born men,
> Having to advise the public, may speak free,
> Which he who can, and will, deserves high praise;
> Who neither can, nor will, may hold his peace:
> What can be juster in a state than this?
>
> Euripid *Hicetid*

Introduction

Liberal philosophers are hesitant when addressing the question of the proper boundaries of free expression. A perusal of the writings of John Milton,[1] John Stuart Mill,[2] John Dewey,[3] and John Rawls[4] indicates that tolerance and freedom are regarded as values, virtues, as the right lofty ideals for developed and humane societies. These and other philosophers wish to discuss principles, not the exceptions to them.[5] This is not to say that they do not acknowledge the need to place limits on tolerance and freedom when speech is concerned, but usually their discussion is devoted to the placement of principles and these are (in the context of democracy) tolerance and freedom. Relatively little attention is paid to the clarification of

---

1 J. Milton, *Areopagitica: A Speech for the Liberty of Unlicensed Printing* (Cambridge: Deighton, Bell & Co., 1973). Milton writes (p. 35): "And though all the winds of doctrine were let loose to play upon the earth, so Truth be in the field, we do injuriously by licensing and prohibiting to misdoubt her strength. Let her and falsehood grapple; who ever knew Truth put to the worse, in a free and open encounter?"
2 J. S. Mill, *Utilitarianism, Liberty, and Representative Government* (London: J. M. Dent & Sons, 1948), Everyman's Edition, and "Law of libel and liberty of the press", in G. L. Williams (ed.), *John Stuart Mill on Politics and Society* (Glasgow: Fontana, 1976): pp. 143–169.
3 J. Dewey, *Freedom and Culture* (New York: G. P. Putnam's Sons, 1939).
4 J. Rawls, *A Theory of Justice* (Oxford: Oxford University Press, 1971).
5 Cf. G. Newey, "Tolerance as a virtue", in J. Horton and S. Mendus (eds), *Toleration, Identity and Difference* (Houndmills: Macmillan, 1999): pp. 38–64.

the exceptions to the principles and to the outlining of boundaries. Several explanations can be suggested to explain this tendency; some are time-bound or specific to a historical–cultural context, others are more general in nature, touching upon the roots of liberal outlook.

Among all philosophers, John Stuart Mill is most associated with the themes of tolerance and liberty. *On Liberty*, published in 1859, is probably quoted more than any other writing in praise of freedom and tolerance. A close examination of the book shows that it deals with the boundaries to free expression in a rather hasty manner, two or three times throughout the book, when one of the limitations is mentioned only in a footnote. The most well-known limitation relates to incitement statements and is illustrated by a short discussion about an excited mob gathering outside the corn-dealer's home:

> ...even opinions lose their immunity when the circumstances in which they are expressed are such as to constitute their expression a positive instigation to some mischievous act. An opinion that corn-dealers are starvers of the poor, or that private property is robbery, ought to be unmolested when simply circulated through the press, but may justly incur punishment when delivered orally to an excited mob assembled before the house of a corn-dealer, or when handed about among the same mob in the form of a placard.[6]

Instead of a systematic discussion of the boundaries to free expression, Mill provided an *ad hoc* proposal as a solution to a special case. Mill lived in an era in which it was customary to write in a decisive style. Writers expressed their opinions in a self-confident manner, without the hair-splitting and meticulousness engaged in today. The thinking was that for the ideas to be understood correctly, they must be presented in an acute and clear language. More specifically in regard to Mill, he was an elitist who did not trust the masses much. He doubted their ability to understand complex messages, and asked that the people understand the general principles. To this end, it was first and foremost necessary to generate the principles. Once these had been absorbed and understood it would be possible to discuss the exceptions to the principles. This is why there is an emphasis in his writings on the principles of tolerance and freedom, and the exceptions to them appear so seldom.

In his *Autobiography*, Mill portrayed *On Liberty* as a philosophical essay containing *one* truth.[7] In the Introduction to *On Liberty*, Mill described truth as being embodied in *one* single principle. The masses (or rather, *even* the masses) could understand one single principle. Notice the language he adopted:

6 J. S. Mill, *Utilitarianism, Liberty, and Representative Government*, p. 114.
7 J. S. Mill, *Autobiography* (Oxford: Oxford University Press, 1971), p. 150.

The object of this Essay is to assert *one very simple principle*, as entitled to govern absolutely the dealings of society with the individual in the way of compulsion and control, whether the means used be physical force in the form of legal penalties, or the moral coercion of public opinion. That principle is, that the sole end for which mankind are warranted, individually or collectively, in interfering with the liberty of action of any of their number, is self-protection...[8]

Indeed, readers of Mill's books cannot avoid the feeling that the number "one" was Mill's favorite. This language that was intended to emphasize one principle repeated itself in an early article in which Mill sought to anchor freedom of expression. In the article "Law of Libel and Liberty of the Press", he wrote:

There is *one case*, and *only one*, in which there might appear to be some doubt of the propriety of permitting the truth to be told without reserve. This is when the truth, without being of any advantage to the public, is calculated to give annoyance to private individuals.[9]

It does not matter that Mill actually thought that there was more than one principle for restricting the search for truth, as I show elsewhere.[10] It was important to emphasize that restrictions were absolutely exceptional. In most cases people should adhere to the Free Speech Principle, in service of truth.

Jeremy Bentham and Mill's father, James Mill, who molded John Stuart's thinking to a great extent, also adopted a similar language that emphasized a single principle. They suggested an understanding of governments' actions by focusing on one simple principle: people will always act in accordance with their interests and, of all interests, the utilitarian interest rules supreme. People wish to increase gains, to enrich happiness and to decrease pain.[11]

In the twentieth century it was John Rawls who influenced liberal philosophy more than any other philosopher. His book, *A Theory of Justice*, is considered by many as one of the few books that will earn a prominent

---

8 J. S. Mill, *Utilitarianism, Liberty, and Representative Government*, pp. 72–73 (emphasis mine, RCA.).

9 J. S. Mill, "Law of libel and liberty of the press", in G. L. Williams (ed.), *John Stuart Mill on Politics and Society*, pp. 160–161 (emphasis mine, RCA.).

10 R. Cohen-Almagor, "Why tolerate? Reflections on the Millian Truth Principle", *Philosophia*, 25(1–4) (1997): 131–152.

11 For further discussion, see C. W. Everett, *Jeremy Bentham* (London: Weidenfeld & Nicolson, 1966); H. L. A. Hart, *Essays on Bentham* (Oxford: Clarendon Press, 1982); J. Dinwiddy, *Bentham* (Oxford: Oxford University Press, 1989); R. Cohen-Almagor, "Ends and means in J. S. Mill's *On Liberty*", *The Anglo-American Law Review*, 26(2) (1997): 141–174.

place in the philosophical literature and be remembered along with the writings of John Locke, Immanuel Kant, Karl Marx and John Stuart Mill. Rawls renewed the discussion of contractarianism and enriched the world of philosophy at large with a fresh breath of originality and wisdom. However, Rawls dedicated only six pages to the discussion on general boundaries to tolerance and liberty (action and speech), which do not do justice to this intricate topic.[12]

The Rawlsian theory is grounded on two main principles: the equal liberty principle and the difference principle.[13] When Rawls deals with the question of whether or not to tolerate the intolerant, he supposes that it becomes dangerous to tolerate some intolerant action and some intolerant speech when they cause significant harm that threatens the fabric of equal liberty. He implicitly appeals to the idea that rights are limited and liberty rights potentially conflict with other rights, such as rights to security, peace and order. The main thrust of the discussion on this issue is very simple: we should tolerate the intolerant as long as we can afford it. We should tolerate the intolerant as long as they are weak, when they cannot endanger the fabric of democracy. Rawls pursues a line of argument that avoids addressing *why*, ethically speaking, beyond expedient reasoning, we must act with tolerance toward those that are intolerant as long as they do not pose a risk to our existence.[14]

The Rawlsian argument

Rawls's reasoning goes like this: he explains that his concept of justice is independent from and prior to the concept of goodness in that its principles limit the conceptions of the good that are permissible. His ideal polity would not be congenial toward those who believe that their personal conception of the good involves forcing others to abide by it. It would exclude some beliefs, such as those that entail coercion of others. The justification for excluding controversial beliefs lies in the social role of justice, which is to enable individuals to make mutually acceptable to one another their shared institutions and basic arrangements. This justification is accompanied by an agreement on ways of reasoning and rules for weighing evidence that govern the applications of the claims of justice. Thus, for instance, Rawls argues that liberty of conscience is limited by the common interest in public order and security, and that this limitation itself is derivable from the contract point of view.[15] Hence, Rawls does not exclude religious groups with strong beliefs who may demand strict

12 J. Rawls, *A Theory of Justice*, at 216–221.
13 *Ibid.*, pp. 150–161, 175–183.
14 See also A. Fish, "Hate promotion and freedom of expression", *Canadian Journal of Law & Jurisprudence*, 2(2) (1989): 111–137, esp. 136–137.
15 J. Rawls, *A Theory of Justice*, p. 212.

conformity and allegiance from their members, but he could not endorse the formation of a theocratic state, for some people lack such intensity of religious belief. The limitation of liberty is justified only when it is necessary for liberty itself, to prevent an invasion of freedom that would be still worse.[16] No particular interpretation of religious truth can be acknowledged as binding upon citizens generally, nor can it be agreed that there should be a single authority with the right to settle questions of theological doctrine.[17]

Rawls emphasizes: "Justice does not require that men must stand idly by while others destroy the basis of their existence".[18] Since we should not forgo the right of self-protection, the question, in Rawls' view, is whether the tolerant have a right to curb the intolerant when they are of "no immediate danger to the equal liberties of others".[19]

Rawls elucidates the question by providing an example, arguing that if an intolerant sect appears (Rawls does not say how) in a well-ordered society (i.e., a society that accepts his two principles of justice), the others should keep in mind the inherent stability of their institutions. The liberties of the intolerant may persuade them to a belief in freedom. Rawls explains that this persuasion works on the psychological principle that those whose liberties are protected by and who benefit from a just constitution will, other things being equal, acquire an allegiance to it over a period of time. He maintains, "So even if an intolerant sect should arise, provided that it is not so strong initially that it can impose its will straightaway, or does not grow so rapidly that the psychological principle has no time to take hold, it will tend to lose its intolerance and accept liberty of conscience."[20]

Rawls's assumption is that it is for society's benefit to allow broad scope for tolerance and encounter such a phenomenon because it would strengthen the beliefs of its members in the face of the threat. But, Rawls warns, we should be sure that the force of the threat is not too great. Hence, as previously stated, tolerance should take place as long as it is safe for it to win over the threat, and not at all events. If the threat seems serious, then justification for intolerance might be in order.[21]

16 *Ibid.*, p. 215.
17 *Ibid.*, p. 217.
18 *Ibid.*, p. 218.
19 *Ibid.*
20 *Ibid.*, p. 219.
21 Similar argument is made by Alasdair MacIntyre, who explicates that toleration should be extended to the exponents of any and every point of view, provided that they "do not threaten the security, order and harmony of society". Not only may the state not attempt to impose any one view, but no one else may either. What is excluded, explains MacIntyre, is coercion, especially coercive violence or the threat of coercive violence. See A. MacIntyre, "Toleration and the goods of conflict", in Susan Mendus (ed.), *The Politics of Toleration* (Edinburgh: Edinburgh University Press, 1999), p. 138.

Rawls concludes that the freedom of the intolerant should be restricted only when the tolerant sincerely and with reason believe that their security and that of the institutions of liberty are in danger. Knowing (how do we know?) the inherent stability of a just constitution, members of a well-ordered society have the confidence to limit the freedom of the intolerant only in the special cases (how do we define "special cases"? What constitutes a "special" case, or makes a case "special"?) when it is necessary for preserving equal liberty itself.[22]

There are many difficulties with this line of blurred argument, which is quite striking bearing in mind the detailed, painstaking reasoning that is so powerfully espoused in the rest of the book. More importantly, it seems that Rawls simply missed the point. Instead of discussing the *ethical* question of the constraints of tolerance, he largely shifted the discussion to the practical consideration of the magnitude of the threat. Rawls pursued a line of reasoning that avoided the philosophical issue, which is the essence of the question of what we may consider as constraints on tolerance and liberty. He said that we should adhere to tolerance in order to preserve equal liberty, but he did not explain from an ethical perspective why we should withhold tolerance in order to preserve equal liberty. Rawls preferred to concentrate on considerations of circumstances and the extent of the threat. From a philosopher of the stature of Rawls, I would have expected a more sturdy exposition than saying that we should adhere to tolerance as long as it is likely to win over the threat. After all, we do not in general think that we should leave free or tolerate harmful acts until they get to the rather drastic point of threatening the fabric of equal liberties. We prohibit many liberties just because they cause damage, sometimes even if they are trivial and nowhere serious enough to be a threat to any system of rules or liberty.

Now, the Rawlsian theory is applicable to well-ordered societies, i.e., to just liberal democracies. What about unripe democracies that are not so well ordered?[23] Well, here the confusion grows. Rawls did not say how those societies should deal with intolerant challenges. We may assume that he would not have expected liberal persuasion to work on the "psychological principle", simply because this principle is yet to be crystallized. And obviously, to wait till the tolerant sufficiently believe that their security might be in danger might be an imprudent policy, leaving the tolerant with little or no democracy. The Rawlsian conceptualization is so vague, so general, that we are left with limited tools for thinking when coming to prescribe the boundaries of tolerance.

---

22 J. Rawls, *A Theory of Justice*, p. 220.
23 By unripe democracies I refer to democracies with a totalitarian past (countries in South America), democracies that live under severe stress (Israel), and democracies that face both predicaments (South Africa).

Consequentialism

Rawls's theory of justice has inspired liberal thinking. Arguably, his line of reasoning on the question of tolerating the intolerant contributed to the very fashionable consequentialist approach. As Jerry Cohen suggests,[24] nothing follows from any of Rawls' principles of justice except in the light of factual claims about consequences of policies. Consequential reasoning is popular among justices and philosophers, especially in the United States. What is striking about this approach is that consequentialists are willing to endure the costs of offensive speech *now* because of speculative fears of the consequences of restriction. Hence, American liberals justify the Skokie decision of the Illinois Supreme Court which permitted the Nazis to march in the Jewish neighborhood,[25] saying that it helped the cause of fighting racism in the United States and increased the awareness of the general public regarding the Holocaust, yet at the same time they show little or no consideration of the actual harm that might have been inflicted on the Holocaust survivors of Skokie if the Nazis had taken the option granted them to exercise (or rather to abuse) their First Amendment right and march through this Jewish suburb of Chicago. Liberals warn that if we restrict speech, this might lead to an increasing tendency towards law and order legislation (Anthony Skillen)[26]; to the creation of undergrounds (Norman Dorsen)[27]; abuse of power on part of the government (Thomas Scanlon,[28] Frederick Schauer)[29]; or to a less tolerant society (Lee Bollinger).[30] Tolerance is needed to advance ourselves, to develop reasoned discussion and arguments, and to progress society.

Furthermore, not only is very little attention given by some of these philosophers (Skillen, Dorsen) to the actual harm that is inflicted upon people by the speech, but philosophers who do acknowledge the harm that might result from the speech in question are also not terribly concerned to explain the circumstances and conditions that constitute exceptions to free speech. Like Rawls's, their terminology is obscure and the discussion disappointing. For instance, Scanlon in "A theory of freedom of expression" does acknowledge the harmful effects of certain forms of speech and devotes the last two pages of his essay to the "near catastrophe" exception to the Free Speech

24 In his comments on this chapter.
25 *Village of Skokie* v. *The National Socialist Party of America* 373 N.E. 2d 21 (1978).
26 A. Skillen, "Freedom of speech", in K. Graham (ed.), *Contemporary Political Philosophy* (Cambridge: Cambridge University Press, 1982), pp. 139–159.
27 N. Dorsen, "Is there a right to stop offensive speech? The case of the Nazis at Skokie", in L. Gostin (ed.), *Civil Liberties in Conflict* (London: Routledge, 1988), pp. 122–135.
28 T. M. Scanlon, "Freedom of expression and categories of expression", *University of Pittsburgh Law Review*, 40(3) (1979): 519–550. Reprinted in *The Difficulty of Tolerance* (Cambridge: Cambridge University Press, 2003).
29 F. Schauer, *Free Speech: A Philosophical Enquiry* (New York: Cambridge University Press, 1982).
30 L. C. Bollinger, *The Tolerant Society* (Oxford: Clarendon Press, 1986).

Principle. However, Scanlon fails to explain adequately what exactly he means by this.[31]

In 1979 Scanlon wrote a second article, which supplements and accommodates the first essay of 1972. Here Scanlon speaks of a "good environment" for expression, explaining that the central interest (especially of the audience) is in having a good environment for the formation of one's beliefs and desires.[32] Yet Scanlon does not address the question of how we should behave when society is saturated with constant threats and offensive language that create a poor environment for the democratic forces to work – if we resort to Rawlsian terms – on the psyche of people and generate tolerant behaviour in regard to unpopular views. Some may argue that the environment in Israeli society after the signing of the Oslo Accords in September 1993 was a poor environment indeed, even a bad environment, entailing constant incitement against the government and especially against Prime Minister Rabin. At the same time, the incitement was not strong enough to destroy Israeli democracy. In this context we should understand the flurry of calls to "get rid" of Rabin. The forces working for tolerance and stability apparently were not strong enough to overcome the forces of intolerance and destruction (the "democratic catch"). On the other hand, it was a perfectly conducive environment for the crystallization of Yigal Amir's beliefs and for the formation of his understanding of the right ways available to him to further his ends, as well as the means designed to forestall the peace process. On 4 November 1995, Amir assassinated Prime Minister Rabin (see Chapter 6).

Indeed, generally speaking, liberals (many of whom are consequentialists) prefer to speak of the general rules – liberty, tolerance (Alf Ross,[33] Alexander Meiklejohn,[34] Franklin Haiman,[35] Fred Schauer, Lee Bollinger), rights (Hugo Black,[36] Aryeh Neier[37]), equality (Ronald Dworkin),[38] truth (John Stuart Mill),[39] justice (John Rawls, Chaim Perelman[40]). They feel less comfortable addressing the issue of exceptions.

31 T. M. Scanlon, "A theory of freedom of expression", in R. M. Dworkin (ed.), *The Philosophy of Law* (Hong Kong: Oxford University Press, 1977), pp. 153–171. Reprinted from *Philosophy & Public Affairs* (1972).

32 T. M. Scanlon, "Freedom of expression and categories of expression", esp. p. 527.

33 A. Ross, *Why Democracy?* (Cambridge: Harvard University Press, 1952).

34 A. Meiklejohn, *Political Freedom* (New York: Oxford University Press, 1965).

35 F. S. Haiman, *Speech and Law in a Free Society* (Chicago and London: University of Chicago Press, 1981).

36 H. L. Black, "The Bill of Rights", *New York University Law Review*, 35 (1960): 865–881.

37 A. Neier, *Defending My Enemy* (New York: E. P. Dutton, 1979).

38 R. M. Dworkin, *A Matter of Principle* (Oxford: Clarendon Press, 1985).

39 J. S. Mill, *Utilitarianism, Liberty, and Representative Government* (London: J. M. Dent, 1948, Everyman's Edition).

40 C. Perelman, *Justice* (New York: Random House, 1967); *Justice, Law and Argument: Essays on Moral and Legal Reasoning* (Dordrecht: Reidel, 1980).

Fred Lawrence writes that "any definitive attempt to distinguish a purely consequentialist approach to free expression from a purely non-consequentialist theory is doomed to failure".[41] I think that at least David Kretzmer and Justice Eliyahu Matza will disagree with this statement. In his 1987 article, Kretzmer offers moral reasoning which could be termed "principled" (as opposed to consequentialist), calling to exclude racist speech from the protection of the Free Speech Principle.[42] In turn, Justice Matza in the *Ido Elba* case (discussed in Chapter 6) opined that racist incitements hurt the character of the State of Israel as a Jewish democratic state, further arguing that the State of Israel was founded upon general as well as Jewish moral values and it could not afford, nor could it consent, for the sake of its integrity and future, to treat the foul phenomenon of racist incitement mercifully.[43] Both Kretzmer and Matza assert that the very nature of racist expressions provides justifiable grounds to deny their protection.

I personally do not advocate this standpoint. I am not convinced that attacks on one's race are more offensive than attacks on certain beliefs, such as one's beliefs on abortion, euthanasia or pornography. In the United States, physicians performing abortions have been murdered by "pro-life" activists.[44] While acknowledging that one cannot be held responsible for one's race in the way that one is responsible for one's ethical convictions, I still do not see why dignity or equal respect and concern are more at stake in one case and not in another. I also do not think that racism is more of a moral or political issue than pornography or issues that concern life and death. All are grave issues that affect the shape and character of society. Sometimes (but not at all times) racist expressions should be excluded from the protection of the Free Speech Principle, for instance when it is calculated to harm a designated group of people who cannot avoid being exposed to the serious offense which could be equated to physical harm (like the Jews at Skokie[45] and see the

41 F. M. Lawrence, "The collision of rights in violence-conducive speech", *Cardozo Law Review*, 19(4) (1998): 1333–1346.
42 D. Kretzmer, "Freedom of speech and racism", *Cardozo Law Review*, 8 (1987): 445–513.
43 Criminal File 2831/95. *State of Israel* v. *Ido Elba*, especially paras. 24 and 61 (Hebrew).
44 For interesting pertinent free-speech cases, see *Planned Parenthood of the Columbia/Willamette Inc.* et al. v. *American Coalition of Life Activists*, U.S Court of Appeals for the Nine Circuit (21 May 2002); *Planned Parenthood of the Columbia/Willamette Inc.* et al. v. *American Coalition of Life Activists*, U.S Court of Appeals for the Nine Circuit (28 March 2001); *Planned Parenthood of the Columbia/Willamette Inc.* et al. v. *American Coalition of Life Activists*, No. 95-1671-JO, 41 F.Supp.2d 1130 (16 March 1999). The Supreme Court denied a write of certiorari, 123 S.Ct. 2637 (2003). See also http://www.adl.org/poisoning_web/anti_abortion.asp.
45 R. Cohen-Almagor, *Speech, Media and Ethics* (New York and Houndmills: Palgrave-Macmillan, 2005), Chapter 1.

discussion in Chapter 5), but we should not outlaw racist provocations merely because of their content without regard to the speakers' intentions and the given circumstances.

Having said that, elsewhere I offered a principled outlook regarding the disqualification of lists.[46] It is one thing to express an opinion and quite another to pass laws that transform democracy into an antidemocratic entity. Greater scope for free expression should be allowed than for the freedom to be elected and enjoy the capacity of passing laws. The power to legislate could immediately transform a society from a democracy, which allows the expression of detestable opinions, to a society that imposes uniformity and coercion. *Ergo* I offer an ethical perspective explaining why we should withhold tolerance when antidemocratic movements that resort to violence wish to be elected for parliament. On this issue my view differs significantly from those of John Rawls, Thomas Scanlon, and Frederick Schauer, among other philosophers. While they prefer to concentrate their discussions on the practical consideration of the magnitude of the threat, I address the ethical question of the constraints of tolerance. The fundamental question is ethical rather than practical. Hence, as a matter of moral principle, violent parties which act to destroy democracy or the state should not be allowed to run for parliament.[47]

Some countries have learned the lessons of history and enacted such laws. For instance, Article 21(2) of the German Basic Law holds that political parties seeking "to impair or do away the free democratic basic order or threaten the existence of the Federal Republic of Germany shall be unconstitutional".[48] Twice the Federal Constitutional Court upheld this law to ban parties: in 1952 when it banned the neo-Nazi Socialist Reich Party, and in 1956 when it ruled the Communist Party unconstitutional.[49] In turn, Sections 1 and 3 of the Austrian *Verbotsgesetz* (literally: "Prohibition-Law"),[50] passed in May 1945, prohibited the National Socialist German Workers Party (Nazi Party) and subjected anybody who still

---

46 R. Cohen-Almagor, *The Boundaries of Liberty and Tolerance* (Gainesville: University of Florida Press, 1994), esp. Chapter 11.
47 See R. Cohen-Almagor, *Speech, Media and Ethics*, Chapter 3. For further critique of consequentialism, see S. Scheffler (ed.), *Consequentialism and Its Critics* (Oxford: Oxford University Press, 1988); S. Scheffler, *The Rejection of Consequentialism* (Oxford: Clarendon Press, 1994); A. Haworth, *Free Speech* (London and New York: Routledge, 1998), pp. 53–82.
48 *Basic Law for the Federal Republic of Germany* (Bonn: Press and Information Office of the Federal Government, 1994).
49 Socialist Reich Party Case, 2 BVerfGE 1 (1952), and Communist Party Case, 5 BVerfGE 85 (1956). See also D. P. Kommers, *The Constitutional Jurisprudence of the Federal Republic of Germany* (Durham: Duke University Press, 1997), pp. 12, 218–222, 224.
50 StGBl 13/1945.

belonged to that party, or who acted for it or its aims, to capital punishment, which was later abolished. Section 1 holds:

> The NSDAP ["Nationalsozialistische deutsche Arbeiterpartei", i.e. National Socialist Workers' Party], its armed forces ["Wehrverbände": SS, SA, NSKK, NSFK), its organizations and affiliated formations and all national socialist organizations and institutions are declared disbanded; their re-establishment is prohibited. Their capital has fallen to the republic.

Section 3 further instructs: "It is prohibited for anybody to engage in activities for the NSDAP or its goals, also outside this organization".[51]

An important note has to be made in this connection. One could argue that in a sense principled reasoning is also consequentialist: those who criticize consequentialism think that permitting certain expressions (Kretzmer, Matza) or practices like running for parliament might result in harmful consequences. But then everything is consequential and the point becomes trivial. The starting point of principled argumentation is moral. We offer some guidelines as a matter of principle, not necessarily out of fear of the consequences. I think that, as a matter of principle, a democratic parliament has no place for those who wish to destroy the parliament or the state by violent means. Acknowledging the "democratic catch", democracy should not allow violent movements scope to further their aims via legislation. Undoubtedly these movements do not accept the basic principles that underlie every democratic society, i.e., the principles of respect for others and not harming others. Those who betray these principles should not enjoy the capacity to use them in the name of liberal tolerance and freedom to undermine the legal basis of democracy. Hence on this matter we need not resort to the method of balancing, weighing one against the other free speech considerations and public order or security. We can state categorically that just as we see democracy and terrorism as counterforces that negate one another and which could not co-exist, so we should view democratic parliament and violent movements whose members aim at the destruction of democracy as mutually exclusive.

It seems that what unites liberal philosophers on this issue is the fear of sliding down the slippery slope, namely that deciding on exceptions to the principles of tolerance and liberty might open the door to further exceptions.[52] Indeed, setting boundaries is not easy. The task is difficult and sisyphean, requiring us to define the exceptions narrowly without opening

---

51 European Monitoring Centre on Racism and Xenophobia, *EUMC Study on Anti-Discrimination Legislation in EU Member States, Austria* (Vienna, 2002), p. 11, available at http://eumc.eu.int/.
52 Cf. E. Volokh, "The mechanisms of the slippery slope", *Harvard Law Review*, 116 (2003): 1026.

the door for different interpretations. Furthermore, any proposed restriction is bound to be controversial, because liberals are united in their opinion about the importance of tolerance and liberty but there is no consensus about the exceptions to those principles. One who proposes a certain restriction to tolerance and liberty might be considered illiberal by others claiming that the restriction is too sweeping, too dangerous. Therefore liberals are often reluctant to address this ungrateful task.

Liberals are also lacking confidence as to the right course of action. As explained in the Introduction, the democratic phenomenon as we know it today is relatively young and therefore suffers from inherent deficiencies. From a historical perspective, democracy is merely an infant. It lacks the experience of dealing with those who wish to exploit tolerance and liberty in order to bring the destruction of democracy.

Democracy is conceived in positively charged terms, as the preferred form of governance. When a concept is elevated to a value, a positive thing that is an ideal for humanitarian and advanced societies, as in the works of John Dewey and other philosophers, it is very difficult to set limits to it.[53] Liberals feel uncomfortable with the task of setting boundaries because of the sincere desire to be as democratic and liberal as possible, to show that democracy tolerates everything, or almost everything, and that in this it is different from other forms of governing. The problem is that many liberals do not acknowledge that democracy is *not* essentially different from other governing forms in one critical characteristic: any form of governing is characterized by the fact that the foundations that make it up are also those that can bring about its destruction. This is easy and clear to comprehend when we deal with governing forms that are based on coercion. When capable, the oppressed people will try to break free from their chains. This rationale – that the foundations that underlie the system are also those that can bring about its destruction – is true for democracy as well. Democracy that is based on tolerance without proper boundaries endangers its existence. Freedom is not lawlessness, and tolerance is not anarchy. We must prescribe the foundations of democracy. We must acknowledge "the democratic catch".[54]

Tolerance, of course, is not to be equated with apathy or indifference. Tolerance is composed of three main components: (1) a strong disapproving attitude toward a certain conduct, action or speech; (2) power or authority to curtail the disturbing conduct; and (3) moral overriding principles which sway the doer not to exert his or her power or authority to

---

53 J. Dewey, *Freedom and Culture*, esp. p. 127. See also P. Nicholson, "Toleration as a moral ideal", in J. Horton and S. Mendus (eds), *Aspects of Toleration* (New York: Methuen, 1985), pp. 158–173.

54 For further discussion, see R. Cohen-Almagor (ed.), *Liberal Democracy and the Limits of Tolerance* (Ann Arbor: University of Michigan Press, 2000), esp. pp. 1–2.

curtail the said conduct. From this formulation it is clear that tolerance cannot be considered as indifference, for the doer *does* have strong reservations regarding the conduct. He or she cares greatly about the issue, but nevertheless applies self-restraint. Tolerance could not also be equated with the concept of neutrality because neutrality is perceived as a specific requirement of justice and, in this respect, its meaning is akin to that of impartiality. As stated, tolerance, on the other hand, assumes that the agents are very partial regarding the phenomenon they consider.

I now turn to discuss the moral grounds of tolerance and then provide a distinction between two forms of tolerance: latent and manifest.

Moral overriding principles

I see it as crucial to speak of *moral* overriding principles as distinct from general overriding principles. Let me explain the difference by considering two examples:

1   Ronny is notoriously unpunctual. Every appointment that he makes is qualified by the remark, "I'll be there on time, give or take half an hour; what's half an hour among friends?" Now Ronny has a relatively new girlfriend, Sasha. As ever, Ronny has been late for their previous meetings and has found that, unlike his other friends, Sasha strongly resents his behavior and qualifications. She wants to see him on time, period. She has also warned him that she will break off with him if he comes late to their next meeting.

   Ronny is on his way to meet Sasha. He departs his home early, quite certain that this time Sasha will be happy. He is going to be in Sasha's place earlier than expected. Then Sasha will realize that the relationship means a great deal to him. On his way he passes through the park and he sees two teenagers attacking a girl, stripping her clothes and about to rape her. Ronny has grave reservations about rape; he detests such a violent, gross behavior. Moreover, he is a big lad, in a perfect shape, and with powerful arms. He knows that he could overcome those two teenagers if he embarked on a fight with them. However, he also knows that it will take him some time to subdue them, and consequently he will be late, yet again, for his date. Sasha has clearly told him that she has no interest in hearing further apologies, explanations and excuses, however perfectly logical and convincing these might be. She will not tolerate any late arrival. Ronny continues on his walk and allows the rape.

2   The second example has to do with the decision of the anti-Nazi allies not to bomb Auschwitz. In 1944 the allies knew what was going on in the extermination camps; they knew the exact location of the camps, and had the bombers to bomb the railroads. Nevertheless, they failed to do it because they used their bombers for other purposes, because

they did not want to kill civilians and victims of the Nazis, or for other reasons deemed to be substantial.

The question before us is the following: could we say that Ronny, in the first example, and the allies, in the second, were tolerant toward the detestable conduct in question? If we do, then we imply two things: that the term "tolerance" is *not* value loaded and could be used with regard to what is conceived to be a negative behavior; and that any overriding considerations will do to characterize not putting into effect authority or power to forestall a most detestable conduct.

To my mind, this usage of the term "tolerance" in these examples and in any like context is unconvincing. We cannot be said to tolerate something because of *any* reason that comes to mind. Ronny and the decision-makers in the allies' headquarters cannot be said to have behaved indifferently, because Ronny had strong feelings against rape and the allies presumably had strong feelings against mass murder. Ronny was not tolerant, because the overriding principle that he employed – not to be late to his date – was not moral. Rather it was a partisan, egoistic, convenient consideration that served him better. I tend to think the same about the allies' policy during World War II not to bomb the Nazi death camps. Both Ronny and the allies did not tolerate transgressions against humans; they were simply preoccupied with other matters.[55]

That is to say that the overriding considerations that are applied by the tolerators should be directly connected to the phenomena that outrage them. Actors can be said to behave in a tolerant fashion only when they apply moral considerations that are relevant to the detested phenomena, convincing them to exhibit restraint. In the above examples, restraint was the result of lack of action but the behavior was repugnant.

The following section offers a distinction that conceives tolerance as a matter of personal attitude, as well as of institutions and laws. I discern different levels of latent and manifest tolerance in accordance with the efforts the tolerator invests in performing acts of toleration. This distinction is concerned with different ways in which tolerance exhibits itself, and explains the scope of tolerance. Before I begin the analysis, a note on terminology is in order. The term "latent" is used to convey the notion of something hidden, as opposed to open and expressed. Both forms of tolerance, the manifest as well as the latent, are understood to be intentionally exercised by conscious agents. I argue that degrees of manifest

55 For further deliberation about the concept of tolerance, see the following excellent collections: J. Horton and S. Mendus (eds), *Aspects of Toleration* (New York: Methuen, 1985); S. Mendus and D. Edwards (eds), *On Toleration* (Oxford: Clarendon Press, 1987). See also S. Mendus, *Toleration and the Limits of Liberalism* (London: Macmillan, 1989). For discussion of tolerance between people, see M. Walzer, *On Toleration* (New Haven and London: Yale University Press, 1997).

tolerance can be distinguished, and that the latent form of tolerance is significant, although it is not expressed openly. Latent tolerance is significant to the tolerator, and to the overall notion of toleration that is upheld in society.[56]

Latent and manifest tolerance

I have contended that tolerance is composed of a disapproving attitude and one or more principles that override that disapproval. The disapproval may be latent or manifest. If it is manifest it can take several forms, ranging from a lenient attitude to strong disapproval. The lenient attitude, in relation to freedom of expression, urges that every idea should be heard as long as it does not coerce other people, and hence that every manifest form of disapproval should not abridge the right to free speech in any way. The manifest strong disapproval involves objections to an opinion but nevertheless believes in its right to be heard.

A very lenient view argues that respect for others requires respect for everyone, whoever they may be, as well as respect for any opinion a person may wish to hold, however distasteful it may be. Every opinion has the right to compete with other opinions. A less lenient attitude might convey counter-arguments or deeds designed to fight the disapproved opinion and persuade the public to take sides against the disliked views. Disapproval may also take the form of manifest protest against these views, usually after any hope of trying to influence the agent to moderate her conduct has been lost. Yet the overriding principles restrict the freedom of the tolerator to exercise suppression. Let us examine this range of attitudes in detail.

In the first instance, during a debate we may think there is a point in trying to change the other's mind by exchanging views. As tolerators we are willing to face the other person, whose ideas or behavior we strongly resent; nevertheless, we respect the other's right to hold and preach them. We may even come to a debate determined to convince the other, and simultaneously not be averse to changing our views. Condescension is not at work in such instances, nor is opportunism or indifference. This sort of tolerance is distinct from indifference because the agent does care about the other's conduct and preferences. Indeed, this is the real essence and meaning of the idea of tolerance, and it may be entitled *strong manifest tolerance*.

A weaker manifest tolerance occurs when we are willing to confront the other but come with a different purpose in mind; not so much to influence the other participants (the gap between the views might be too wide and unbridgeable) but rather to influence the audience, in the hope of scoring more points than our opponent.

56 The following discussion draws upon Chapter 2 of my book *The Boundaries of Liberty and Tolerance.*

A still weaker form of manifest tolerance is when we tolerate the
conduct of others, but are not willing to negotiate with them or do anything which might help the others convey their views. Thus, on some occasions, we may tolerate an opinion but not be willing to share the same
platform with our opponent for fear that so doing might legitimize the
other's views. Another means of seeking to withhold another's views of
legitimization is by walking out of the room whenever unpopular views are
being expressed.

For instance, in early October 2001 the Russian politician Vladimir
Zhirinovsky came to a NATO meeting in Ottawa, and began his inflammatory remarks by denying involvement of anyone other than the USA in the
terrorist raid of 11 September 2001, claiming that the Americans bombed
their own World Trade Centre and the Pentagon in order to have a
reason for their imperialist globalization policies. "The United States is
responsible", Zhirinovsky said, "All the terror has been organized by the
United States. Osama (bin Laden) had nothing to do with it."[57] Zhirinovsky also claimed that without a doubt it was Israel that brought down
the Tupolov airplane of the Siberian Airlines over the Black Sea on 4
October. Seventy-eight passengers and crew, most of them Israeli Russians,
were killed in this tragedy. The Ukrainian government admitted that it
mistakenly brought down the plane by firing a missile during military
training. Zhirinovsky, however, said that Israel caused this tragedy for
political gains. Were I present in the audience, I would have walked out.
Zhirinovsky does not deserve an attentive audience when making such
unfounded allegations.

It should be noted that the act of walking out is not the result of losing
interest. I often attended halls that were crowded with people at the
beginning of talks and were quite empty towards the end. The discussion
here is about an act of protest, designed to de-legitimize the speech in
question. My reaction to Zhirinovsky's diatribe might prompt other
people to do the same, but even if this is not the case, at least I will not
confer legitimacy on his speech by my presence. In any event, I reiterate
that walking out from a Zhirinovsky-like speech is not because I have lost
interest; as a Jew and an Israeli I greatly care about what he, and people
like him, say.

More recently, Linda Ronstadt dedicated a song ("Desperado") to
liberal film-maker Michael Moore and his controversial documentary
Fahrenheit 9/11, which criticizes President George W. Bush and the costly
US-led war in Iraq. About a quarter of the 4,500 people in the audience
were said to have left in anger. They, however, accompanied their protest
by more explicit actions: spilling drinks, shouting, tearing down posters,

57 M. Cook, "U.S. orchestrated terrorist attacks: Russian charges notorious radical
    preaches anti-U.S. conspiracy theory", *The Ottawa Citizen* (8 October 2001),
    p. A9.

and demanding their money back.[58] These actions together exhibited explicit intolerance. Indeed, Ronstadt was escorted out of the hotel after the performance, and a spokesperson for the casino said that she will not be welcomed back.

However, let us focus only on the act of walking out in protest. Whether this form of action can still be considered as an act of tolerance may be reasonably questioned. It may be argued that it cannot, since such a practice is incompatible with the activity of rational debate or discussion, and also a way of life in which people normally refrain from listening to opposite views cannot be considered an open society or one in which freedom of speech flourishes. However, these arguments ignore the concomitant effect of legitimization when an opinion is allowed a free hearing. Walking out on opposed views rather than rebutting them does not necessarily demonstrate little feeling for freedom of speech. It may imply that "we don't want any part of what is said", that the gap between the views cannot be narrowed, and that we see no point in intellectual discussion because the entire fabric of pre-suppositions and values is different or even contradictory.

Therefore, we may fight for the other's right to be heard, and at the same time fight to curtail the influence of the disliked views, in order not to do anything which could be interpreted as giving those views equal status. Plausibly a tolerator may respect the other's right to voice opinions, yet think that some defensive measures should be taken to diminish their influence. These measures can include warnings and prevention of legitimization.

Finally, in an even weaker type of manifest tolerance a person tolerates speech and argues for the right of distasteful views to be heard, but opposes the right of the propagators of these views to stand for elections. The argument that may be advocated here is that a liberal society should allow the pursuit of every concept and value, whatever they may be (provided that they do not inflict harm upon others), but no requirement says that every view should be allowed to gain institutional legitimization. Society can endure any opinion, but no obligation exists that a parliament should represent each and every view. Harmful and discriminatory opinions could be allowed to be pronounced, but they may have no place in the House of Representatives;[59] they deserve no legitimization by democracy to help them develop and attract more people. This attitude shows a *qualified* tolerance, for it denies the right to equal respect. Some paths to

---

58 Reuters, "Singer Linda Ronstadt ejected by Las Vegas Casino", *New York Times* (19 July 2004).
59 See R. Cohen-Almagor, "Disqualification of Lists in Israel (1948–1984): retrospect and appraisal", *Law & Philosophy*, 13(1) (1994): 43–95, and "Disqualification of political parties in Israel: 1988–1996", *Emory International Law Review*, 11(1) (1997): 67–109.

exercise freedom and autonomy are denied because the overriding principle includes considerations of safety, either of the entire democratic
framework or of some parts of the community.[60]

Thus far I have considered manifest ways of expressing disapproval. But
a different sort of disapproval is latent – that is, not expressed publicly.
The clash between the negative attitude toward a conduct and an overriding principle of, say, the belief in mutual respect does not necessarily have
to be manifested. A person may disapprove of a view and do nothing to
show this attitude. This is still a form of tolerance, for it contains the
ability to understand those who differ from oneself, or of respecting their
rights and liberties despite the fact that their opinions or conduct rouse
the tolerator against them. We may feel contempt for an opinion, yet
decide that out of respect for the persons who express it, whom we appreciate, we had better remain silent. We may even assist such persons in
spreading their views by renting a public space for their meetings. Thus,
for instance, on 30 September 1999 the Vancouver Public Library rented a
meeting room to Doug Christie and the Canadian Free Speech League.
Christie is known as a "free speech champion" who defends white
supremacists, anti-Semites, and neo-Nazis. The meeting attracted the
former head of the British Columbia Ku Klux Klan, the Ontario web-
master for racists, and other notorious figures. The public purse incurred
an estimated expense of $30,000 to provide security and policing for the
event,[61] this in the name of free speech and tolerance (Chapter 7 elabo-
rates on hate speech in Canada).

The latent position is a form of tolerance because a definite attitude
opposes a conduct, some ability to protest exists, and overriding principles
are held which make us refrain from exercising liberty and ability to
restrain that conduct. Can it be counted as significant? What is the
meaning of this tolerance when the tolerator resents a conduct but does

60 In his comments on a draft of this chapter, Geoffrey Marshall wrote that refus-
    ing someone the right to stand in an election seems to involve an infringement
    of the Free Speech Principle since it is depriving him of the right to argue that
    he should be elected. If speeches are disorderly and harmful in the sense of
    being incitatory, they should presumably be penalized and prevented either in
    an election campaign or in the legislature. The corollary would be that if they
    are not incitatory or otherwise criminal they should be permissible in both. In
    my articles on disqualification of political parties in Israel, cited *supra*, I took a
    different stance. Steve Newman commented that he has doubts whether such
    restrictive legislation really saves democracy. In his opinion, strong laws will not
    substitute for good character – if we're going to have a democracy. Newman
    thinks we need to trust the people to do the right thing, and we must never
    stop working to educate the people and inculcate democratic values. Newman
    has in mind his own country, Canada. I have my own doubts as to whether what
    he says is true for less ripe democracies like, say, Argentina and Israel, or for
    democracies with a troubled racist history like Germany.
61 D. Matas, *Bloody Words* (Winnipeg: Bain & Cox, 2000), p. 107.

nothing to manifest resentment? While we recognize that latent tolerance cannot be regarded as indifference, we still could argue that when tolerance is latent then silence prevails, and consequently we cannot distinguish it from indifference. However, when citizens adopt a tolerant attitude, the latent form included, they *do* have an opinion. The issue at hand does matter to them, and this attitude may have an impact on society, on the people's norms and general attitude toward a disliked group. A tolerated group may gain something from the lack of interference on the part of the tolerator. For example, ethnic minorities which are out of favor with the government may yet live in a tolerant atmosphere. Polls may detect the prevalent notions under the surface and give an indication of future policies regarding the tolerated, sometimes with regard to related concerns as well.

This point takes us to the further argument, that latent tolerance does not necessarily stay latent. A trigger might transform it into a manifest form of tolerance. And even if such a transformation does not take place, latent tolerance is valuable because it is significant to the tolerator. It indicates to tolerators the relationship of their priorities to those of the society in which they live. It is vital to any conception of self, society or value. Latent tolerance, therefore, counts because of its contribution to shaping a frame of mind, a set of values, and the establishment of priorities. This contribution, I suggest, cannot easily be ignored.

One final comment is relevant. Tolerance may evolve from two main sources: expediency, in terms of self-interest, and respect for others as human beings. I exclude the first from being considered as a tolerant act, because tolerance is concerned mainly with consideration for others. Having said that, when persons adopt overriding principles that support positions in favor of granting equal rights to groups which are discriminated against in society, they might be inclined to adopt latent tolerance and make marginal improvements on behalf of that discriminated group, rather than trying to rebel against society. This is merely a sociological observation. This is, in a way, a case of self-interest, but this reason for tolerance differs from the "pure" cases of self-interest because the main reason in tolerating the other, or in tolerating a conduct, is still respect for the other's rights. This rather diluted form of tolerance is the result of societal constraints.

Conclusion

Putting up with people or activities does not necessarily mean that the agent is a tolerant person. People can perform acts of toleration on prudential grounds, but this does not necessarily make them tolerant beings. When we genuinely tolerate persons or conduct we do it *not* in order to maintain or ensure stability, tranquility or any other desired value, but rather because we respect others as human beings who should enjoy the ability to exercise choice and lead their lives as free, autonomous people, so long as they do not harm others. The consequences of tolerance may as well be peace and order in society, but the emphasis and reasoning are totally different.

2 The right to privacy: part I

The hand should not necessarily be the quickest organ in one's body when one is writing.

Raphael Cohen Almagor

Introduction

This and the following chapters probe the issue of privacy. When news is becoming entertainment (infotainment) and private stories become public spectacle, individual lives can be mercilessly exposed to the glaring spotlight of unwanted publicity. In delineating the boundaries of intrusion, distinctions are made between children and adults; between public figures and ordinary citizens; between people who choose to live in the spotlight and ordinary citizens who stumble into the public forum; and between ordinary citizens doing something of public significance and those who do not. In the next chapter I specifically discuss two episodes: the tragic death of Princess Diana and the Quebec *Charter of Human Rights and Freedoms* and Chapter III of the *Civil Code of Quebec [1994]* that were invoked in a recent Supreme Court case, *Les Editions Vice-Versa Inc.* v. *Aubry*. Siding with the Court's majority in this case it is asserted that the public's right to know does not allow scope to magazines to take photos of people to decorate their covers without the individuals' consent.

With due appreciation for the liberal inclination to provide wide latitude to freedom of expression, we must also acknowledge the "democratic catch" and the need for prescribing the scope of tolerance. The right to free expression and free media, supplemented and strengthened by the concept of the public's right to know, does not entail the freedom to invade individual privacy without ample justification.[1] The media should

1 See Section 8 of the Canadian Charter of Rights and Freedoms, and Article 17 of the International Covenant on Civil and Political Rights: "No one shall be subjected to arbitrary or unlawful interference with his privacy, family, home or correspondence, nor to unlawful attacks on his honour and reputation." UNTS No. 14668, Vol. 999 (1976).

adopt some social responsibility standards to retain some credibility in the eyes of the public.[2]

Free expression does not include the right to do unjustifiable harm to others.[3] Indeed, one of the four key principles of Sigma Delta Chi, the Society of Professional Journalists' Code of Ethics, is to minimize harm. It says, "ethical journalists treat sources, subjects and colleagues as human beings deserving of respect". The Code further instructs journalists to show compassion for those who may be affected adversely by news coverage, and to avoid pandering to lurid curiosity, maintaining that the "pursuit of the news is not a license for arrogance".[4]

Privacy

Privacy is commonly understood as insulation from observability, a value asserted by individuals against the demands of a curious and intrusive society.[5] It is intimately associated with our most profound values, our understanding of what it means to be an autonomous moral agent capable of self-reflection and choice. Its violation is demeaning to individuality and an affront to personal dignity.[6] Jean Cohen contended that a constitu-

---

2 Cf. Commission on Freedom of the Press (Hutchins Commission), *A Free and Responsible Press* (Chicago: University of Chicago Press, 1947); R. W. McChesney and J. C. Nerone (eds), *Last Rights: Revisiting Four Theories of the Press* (Urbana and Chicago: University of Illinois Press, 1995), esp. pp. 77–124. See also D. Caspi, "Between enlightened authoritarianism and social responsibility – on media and politics", in R. Cohen-Almagor (ed.), *Israeli Democracy at the Crossroads* (London: Routledge, 2005).
3 Canadian Charter of Rights and Freedoms, section 1; *R. v. Keegstra* [1990] S.C.J. No. 131, 3 S.C.R. 870; *Canadian Human Rights Commission* et al. v. *Taylor* et al. [1990] 3 S.C.R. 892, 75 D.L.R. (4th); *R. v. Butler* [1992] 1 S.C.R. 452.
4 Founded in 1909 as Sigma Delta Chi, the Society of Professional Journalists (SPJ) is the US's largest and most broad-based journalism organization. SPJ is a not-for-profit organization made up of more than 10,000 members dedicated to encouraging the free practice of journalism; stimulating high standards of ethical behavior; and perpetuating a free press. Sigma Delta Chi's first Code of Ethics was borrowed from the American Society of Newspaper Editors in 1926. In 1973, Sigma Delta Chi wrote its own code, which was revised in 1984 and 1987. The present version of the Society of Professional Journalists' Code of Ethics was adopted in September 1996. http://spj.org/awards/SDX98/rules.htm#society; http://spj.org/ethics/ethics.pdf. See also Ontario Press Council, *24th Annual Report* (Toronto, Ontario, 1996), p. 79.
5 R. C. Post, "The social foundations of privacy: community and self in the common law tort", *California Law Review*, 77 (1989): 957.
6 A. Etzioni, *The Limits of Privacy* (New York: Basic Books, 1999), p. 191. James Q. Whitman argues that privacy is an aspect of personal dignity within the continental tradition. For a useful discussion on privacy, especially in Germany and France, see his "The two Western cultures of privacy: dignity versus liberty", *Yale Law Journal*, 113 (2004); *idem*, "Enforcing civility and respect: three societies", *Yale Law Journal*, 109 (2000): 1279–1398.

tionally protected right to personal privacy is indispensable to any modern conception of freedom,[7] whereas Avishai Margalit asserted that the institutions of a decent society must not encroach upon personal privacy.[8] However, when opening today's newspapers, especially the tabloids, one can read many details that concern very private aspects of the other.

There is a strong link between media and entertainment. As a result, the media at large, and the sensational media in particular, prefer to intrude on private matters at the expense of analyzing social, cultural, scientific, and political matters. We witness gossip and a tendency to popularize the news; the tabloids around the globe have specialized in character assassinations and incidents of intrusion on privacy. The large sensational narratives are taking so much space that they drive out discussion about politics.

According to the Angus Reid polling firm, two out of three Canadians think the media are guilty of sensationalizing scandals, and more than one-third (35 percent) have actually boycotted certain media because of their extensive intrusive reporting. Almost two-thirds (65 percent) feel reporting delves too deeply into the personal lives of public figures.[9] In the United States, public opinion polls show that Americans are appropriately agitated about invasions of privacy.[10]

This phenomenon, of course, is not uniquely North American. In today's world the leaders of democracies and celebrities are continuously watched, even hounded. Political leaders and public figures live in a media bubble where their movements are likely to be observed. Their public faces can almost never be taken off, and their private lives can be mercilessly exposed to the glaring spotlight of unwanted publicity. The willingness of public figures to have themselves aired demonstrates both the seductiveness and the reach of the media.[11]

In a public lecture delivered at Columbia University in 1995, The Right Honourable Brian Mulroney spoke of the costs of free expression. He said that the personal abuse by the media that leaders suffer nowadays has become an unfortunately high – but necessary – price for them to pay for the privilege of service in democracies. He maintained that politicians are not the only ones tracked by the media, or by individuals masquerading as journalists: they are only the most numerous and the most visible. Prime

7 J. L. Cohen, "Rethinking privacy: the abortion controversy", in J. Weintraub and K. Kumar (eds), *Public and Private in Thought and Practice: Perspectives on Grand Dichotomy* (Chicago: University of Chicago Press, 1997), p. 137.
8 A. Margalit, *The Decent Society* (Cambridge: Harvard University Press, 1996), p. 201.
9 "Most of us feel reporters pry too much into lives of public figures", *Globe and Mail* (10 October 1998), p. C3.
10 A. Etzioni, *The Limits of Privacy, op. cit.*, p. 2.
11 D. Taras, *The Newsmakers: The Media's Influence on Canadian Politics* (Ontario: Nelson Canada, 1990), p. 235.

Minister Mulroney called for responsibility and accountability by the media as they fulfill their "indispensable roles as vigorous critics and faithful chroniclers of our lives and times".[12]

Public figures v. ordinary citizens

In this context it is important to distinguish between public figures and ordinary citizens. Public figures are more susceptible to media invasion of their privacy. Justices L'Heureux-Dube and Bastarache of the Canadian Supreme Court said:

> it is generally recognized that certain aspects of the private life of a person who is engaged in a public activity or has acquired a certain notoriety can become matters of public interest. This is true, in particular, of artists and politicians, but also, more generally, of all those whose professional success depends on public opinion.[13]

Ordinary citizens are usually of no interest to the public and therefore do not, generally speaking, attract media attention. For example, ordinary people attending a funeral are not usually photographed. In the first instance, there should be a very good reason to send a photographer to a funeral to take such pictures (such as when covering a funeral of a hostage killed by terrorists), and the photographer is then obliged to ask for permission prior to taking the photos. Celebrities and politicians who attend funerals might be photographed, and usually this conduct does not raise any controversy. Politicians attend those funerals as part of their public responsibilities, and celebrities not only don't mind the presence of the camera; often they welcome it.

Having said that, some standards of decency should be maintained. For many years some organs of the media have exhibited poor taste by speculating that some dead celebrities are alive (the most notable examples being Elvis Presley[14] and Marilyn Monroe[15]). They excelled themselves by

12 The Right Honourable Brian Mulroney, public speech delivered at Columbia University, New York (20 March 1995).
13 *Les Editions Vice-Versa Inc.* v. *Aubry* [1998] 1 S.C.R. 591, Section IV of their judgment, at 616.
14 J. Mennie, "They love him tender; Quebecers more likely to believe Elvis Presley's still alive, poll says", *The Gazette* (Montreal, Quebec) (1 November 1991), p. A7; J. Stock, "Making a mint by keeping Elvis alive; can any serious investigator honestly believe Elvis Presley is still alive?", *South China Morning Post* (Hong Kong) (16 August 1992), p. 4; "Special: some people are desperate to prove that Elvis Presley is still alive", *The Advertiser* (26 March 1992); L. Frydman, "Elvis death hoax", http://www.elvispresleynews.com/article1045.html; Starlight, "Elvis alive and well in Ohio?", http://www.elvispresleynews.com/article1150.html.
15 I. Haysom, "Marilyn Monroe is alive and well", *Ottawa Citizen* (7 September

grossly claiming that one known celebrity, alive and kicking, had actually died. They repeatedly alleged that Paul McCartney had died in an automobile accident outside London in November 1966 and was secretly replaced under very mysterious circumstances by a double.[16] It does not matter that McCartney has a family and continues to produce songs and to hold concerts; the tale has become one of the cult stories associated with the Beatles.[17] I have always wondered what McCartney himself thinks about this. How does he feel about the allegations that he actually died, and that an imitator (he himself) took his place and exploits McCartney's reputation? In the summer of 1997 I contacted a senior editor in the British press and through him, asked Sir Paul for a response. After a while the editor returned to me, saying that Sir Paul had no interest in commenting on the issue. Maybe the story is to his advantage, making him some sort of a legend during his lifetime – literally, greater than life. Apparently, he does not take offense at being described as a phony imitator. Other celebrities might regard such an innovation differently.

In any event, public figures have experience in dealing with the media, and can gain access to present their side of the story, to voice their content or discontent, and to respond to allegations and gossip. Now let us turn to another interesting question: are the media entitled to intrude on private matters of public officials when these matters do not directly concern their work and office?

If, for instance, a public figure known and respected for preaching family values, decency among couples and honesty in marriage, is found to be betraying his wife, the media have a right to break the news and bring the issue to public attention. The public is entitled to know that the person who speaks so eloquently about family values does not espouse those values at home.[18] The issue is different when the public figure has made his reputa-

---

1996), p. B5. See also L. Frydman, "Elvis death hoax", http://www.elvispres-leynews.com/article1045.html.

16 J. Marks, "No, No, No, Paul McCartney is not dead", *New York Times* (2 November 1969), p. D13; "Beatle spokesman calls rumor of McCartney's death 'rubbish'", *New York Times* (22 October 1969), p. 8; J. Phillips. "McCartney 'death' rumors", *Washington Post* (22 October 1969), p. B1; "McCartney Ballad: 'So Long Paul'", *Washington Post* (1 November 1969), p. C6.

17 The Israel military radio station, Galei Zahal, for more than two decades repeatedly ran shows hosted by their music expert, Yoav Kutner, who was making this claim. See http://web.sadna.co.il/icexcellence2/website/topbar/advisory.html.

18 In his comments on this chapter, Eric Barendt says that he is unsure that the public is always entitled to know that someone who supports family values, and poses as married with wife and children on his election address, has had, or even is currently having, an affair. That does not mean that his views are less entitled to respect and discussion. The argument that the press makes that it is always right to expose hypocrisy is, in Barendt's view, too crude. Rod Macdonald elucidates this issue by providing two examples. First, suppose that a speaker makes a claim about family values and goes on to say how difficult it is

tion in other spheres, unrelated to his family life, and the conduct in his private life does not affect his public duties. Most broadsheet papers would not cover the infidelity story, while most of the popular press would probably publish the story in the name of the public's right to know. Most broadsheet papers don't consider as valid the argument that if a person is betraying the closest person to him or her, i.e. the spouse, then that person might also cheat on other matters in which he or she is less personally involved. Interestingly, the Israeli media have hardly ever exposed infidelity stories. They believe that the confines of the bedroom should remain intact. At most, they hint about such affairs without specifically identifying the adulterer. The only infidelity affair that became public during the 1990s was connected with Benjamin Netanyahu, and the details of this episode were revealed by Netanyahu himself in a primetime public television broadcast.[19]

What about sexual orientations of public officials? Many of us believe that sexual orientation is both immaterial and irrelevant to virtually all public sectors. Still, for a significant proportion of the population, having a homosexual or bisexual orientation is immoral.[20] Some would see the "right" and "normal" sexual orientation as a necessary qualification for holding public office. Personally, I do not conceive this view as persuasive enough to allow intrusion on one's privacy. I am not aware of a single study that substantiates the claim that homosexuals are less capable than heterosexuals to carry out public responsibilities. However, others would resort to practical reasoning and argue that homosexual candidates should disclose their sexual orientation because otherwise they might subject themselves to blackmailing and to other pressures that might compromise their performance.

In August 2004, New Jersey Governor James E. McGreevey announced his resignation following an affair with a man that had left him vulnerable to "false allegations and threats of disclosure".[21] Golan Cipel, McGreevey's former lover, threatened to publicize his affair with McGreevey and to file

to live to this standard and that we should not be judgmental about those who do not or cannot meet it. In this case, Barendt seems to have a point. Second, suppose that a speaker says that family values include integrity and honesty in communication with one's spouse. Here, the media are entitled to reveal his extra-marital affairs. Where one's personal life is being held out as a reflection of the claim being made, then the media may be justified in inquiring into one's personal life. A case in point is Gerry Hart's presidential campaign and the revelations about his love life.

19 S. Spero, "Bibi's 'personal problem'", *Jerusalem Post* (19 January 1993), p. 6; See also   http://www.jewishsf.com/content/2-0-/module/displaystory/story_id/4041/edition_id/72/format/html/displaystory.html.

20 Forty-three percent of Americans still believe that being gay is immoral. See S. Goldenberg, "Gay in the USA", the *Guardian* (15 July 2003). For further discussion, see http://health.yahoo.com/centers/sexual_health/524.html.

21 M. Powell and M. Garcia, "N.J. Governor resigns over gay affair", *Washington Post* (13 August 2004), p. A1; "'My truth is that I am a gay American'", *Washington Post* (13 August 2004), p. A06.

a sexual harassment lawsuit against him if the Governor refused to pay him $5 million to quash the suit. Governor McGreevey saw this as extortion and decided to step down, explaining that the affair had left him "vulnerable to rumors, false allegations and threats of disclosure" and compromised his "ability to govern".[22]

Acts of infidelity (whatever the gender of the couple involved, although when the partners belong to the same gender the story becomes juicier) necessitate resorting to lies, and these might necessitate cover-ups and misconduct. Information about such allegations that some parts of the public – even a small part – deem relevant, should be made available. The person who wishes to have information about a candidate's marital infidelity can be understood as saying that, in a democracy, the determination of the nature of a public office and its qualifications are as important to him or her as this personal preference is important to the adulterer.[23] This is not a mere matter of curiosity. As the McGreevey example shows, such acts might compromise the ability to govern.

For this reason I cannot agree with Dennis Thompson, who argues that citizens do not need to know about the drinking habits of an official because the alleged effects can be discovered by observing his actions on the job.[24] Alcohol, like drugs, might affect a person's judgment, and people should be aware that their representative has a soft spot for certain drinks and/or drugs that might cloud the ability to make delicate decisions. Furthermore, some people would like to know about such a habit before electing or nominating someone for a responsible position. Many people don't have the time and energy to inquire about such habits themselves and they trust the media to disclose this information, upon obtaining it, to the public. Many people would not like to take the risk and discover that their representative is drunk at a moment of crisis – then it might be too late. In this context, a former president of Israel, Ezer Weizman, disclosed many years after the 1967 Six Day War that the Chief of Staff at that time, Yitzhak Rabin, collapsed on the eve of the war and asked Weizman to replace him. Weizman was his deputy at the time. He refused, Rabin collected himself, and led the Israeli army to victory. Later

22 G. Thrush and J. Riley, "New Jersey governor quits, citing his adulterous affair with man", *Baltimore Sun* (13 August 2004), p. A1; L. Mansnerus, "New Jersey Governor resigns, disclosing a gay affair", *New York Times* (13 August 2004); "The Governor's secret", *New York Times* (13 August 2004); http://www.app.com/gsbr/; http://abcnews.go.com/wire/US/ap20040814_544.html. For further discussion, see K. L. Karst, "Myths of identity: individual and group portraits of race and sexual orientation", *UCLA Law Review*, 45 (1995): 265.

23 Cf. F. Schauer, "Can public figures have private lives?", in E. F. Paul, F. D. Miller Jr and J. Paul (eds), *The Right to Privacy* (New York: Cambridge University Press, 2000), pp. 293–309.

24 D. F. Thompson, "Privacy, politics, and the press", in J. R. Rowan and S. Zinaich, Jr (eds), *Ethics for the Professions* (Belmont: Wadsworth, 2003), p. 395.

it also became public that Rabin had a drinking problem.[25] The Israeli public deserved to know all this before the outbreak of the 1967 fateful war, and before Rabin was elected to further high positions.

Yet I wish to refrain from the sweeping generalization that *everything* is relevant. Some boundaries need to be introduced. A major consideration in coming to decide the confines of privacy is any consequences of the official's action on the political/social process. In all the examples pointed *supra* – infidelity, hidden sexual preferences, addiction problems – those kinds of behaviour might affect the official's performances and ability to function. But is this the only consideration?

Suppose a public official beats his wife in bed as part of their sexual fore-play. If this is done with the wife's consent, then this fact should not be revealed to the public. I don't think it likely that consenting violence might affect his public behavior. The case is different if the wife does not consent to the beating. Then it is just another version of domestic violence. Should this be revealed to the public? Now, if you focus all attention on the effect this behavior might have on the official's public conduct, it might be argued quite persuasively that domestic violence has no bearing on performing one's duties. The wife can complain to the police, and then there will be repercussions against the beater. But it is difficult to argue that this repugnant behavior might instigate cover-ups, commonly used to hide infidelity stories that might have an effect on a person's conduct.

It might be argued that if a certain behavior goes against the majority's norm, then that behavior needs to be exposed. I don't find the argument of majorities and minorities convincing. The majority may hold a norm which at another point of time may seem to be repugnant. Such, for instance, was slavery in North America. In current times, the majority of people in one democracy or another may think homosexuality is repugnant. At another point in time homosexuality may have been conceived of as normal – indeed, in Greek and Roman times homosexuality was considered differently.[26] Majority opinion should not be considered as grounds for invasion of privacy.

My argument is that domestic violence should be exposed in public because the public needs to be aware of such behavior, whether or not it has a bearing on the instigator's public duties. One of the basic foundations of liberal democracy is not to harm others. Any action which causes physical harm to individuals or groups, for any reason other than self-protection, ought to be curtailed.[27] When this underpinning is broken, the

---

25 E. Weizman, *On Eagles' Wings* (New York: Macmillan, 1976), pp. 211–212. Weizman told me this story in detail in a lengthy private interview about the Six Day War in 1986. Rabin declined the invitation for interview.

26 Cf. C. A. Williams, *Homosexuality: Ideologies of Masculinity in Classical Antiquity* (New York: Oxford University Press, 1999).

27 Cf. R. Cohen-Almagor, *Speech, Media, and Ethics: The Limits of Free Expression*, esp. Chapter 1.

public has the right to know. Violence against women is vile, goes against the underlying values of democracy, and should be fought against and curtailed. Violence against weak parties is something wrong. It is wrong *qua* unjustified violence, even if no one is aware of its existence.

One may suggest a different line of reasoning, based on law, arguing that the media should report all transgressions of law and refrain from reporting on matters that are within the confines of law. The scope of reporting should coincide with the confines of law. I find this reasoning too simplistic, and unconvincing. Law and ethics overlap to one extent or another, but they do not overlap completely. There are controversial issues that are illegal yet some may argue that the media should not report; and conversely there are many issues that are within the confines of the law that the media should report.

A public official may smoke marijuana in the weekends for his own pleasure. This conduct is illegal in Israel as well as in other countries. Yet I am not sure whether the media should report this to the public. Marijuana can be useful for certain medical purposes. Many who smoke this soft drug argue that it does not affect them more than cigarettes do. Media professionals may take different stances on this issue.

On the other hand, infidelity is one example of a legal issue that the media, at least sometimes, should report, in accordance with the above line of argument. Addiction is another. A third example concerns the taking of actions that might compromise the conduct of a public official, yet are within the law.

When Ezer Weizman was the President of Israel, it was reported that for many years he received substantial sums of money from Edouard Seroussi, a millionaire friend who wanted to support the Weizman family. The issue was brought before Attorney General Elyakim Rubinstein to investigate what, if anything, Weizman gave in return, and whether to pursue charges against the president on the grounds that bribery might have been involved. Rubinstein decided to close the case. Rubinstein possibly made the right decision; it may indeed have been that Weizman did not give his business friend any favors in return. Yet this conduct is questionable, and the public certainly had the right to be informed about the special relationship between the president and the affluent businessman.[28]

Public figures v. ordinary citizens who stumble into the public forum

Another pertinent distinction is between public figures who choose to live in the spotlight, and ordinary citizens who stumble into the public forum. On occasion, people fall unintentionally into the spotlight, under

---

28 E. Arbel, "Weizman should resign", *The Jerusalem Post* (16 February 2000), p. 8; http://www.knesset.gov.il/lexicon/eng/weitzman_ez_eng.htm. I invited Attorney General Elyakim Rubinstein to comment on the issue, but he declined.

circumstances that are not under their control. They may, for instance, commit a significant public act, like saving a family from a fire, or rescuing a public figure from danger. They might become victims in a criminal or terrorist attack. The media should publish the heroic deed of the individual, but should refrain from intruding into his or her private life that is of no importance to the public unless there are countervailing interests weighty enough to warrant such interference.

The media have a strong appetite for tragic stories, being eager to highlight the dramatic aspects with little or no sensitivity to the victims. One painful story is of the massacre of fourteen women in Montreal in December 1989. During the days that followed, there was what one writer describes as "a savage hunt" for gossip from neighbors and friends, and the ravaged faces of mourners. Information on the victims was gleaned from every possible source, invading people's privacy in the pursuit of a story. The killer's mother had to go into hiding, and her private life was reported in minute details taken from divorce papers.[29] The fact that her son was a killer legitimized crossing all ethical borders. In another case, a Canadian woman and her child were killed during a skyjacking in Malta in November 1985. When the husband returned to Canada, a "milling crowd of reporters, photographers and TV cameramen" met him at the airport. The man told them that they were not invited to the funeral.[30] After this episode, it was said that the encounter prompted soul-searching in the newsrooms as editors weighed the news value of the event against the human grief and pain involved.[31]

In this context, it should be noted that the CBC's *Journalistic Standards and Practices* holds: "An individual's right to privacy is cherished in Canada ... The invasion of an individual's privacy is repugnant. Privacy in its broadest sense means being left alone. It means protecting an individual's personal and private life from intrusion or exposure to the public view."[32]

---

29 R. D. Crelinsten, "Victims' perspectives", in D. L. Paletz and A. P. Schmid (eds), *Terrorism and the Media* (Newbury Park: Sage, 1992), p. 217.

30 *Ibid.*, p. 219.

31 For review of other disturbing episodes in which the media hinder activities of security forces and have even cooperated with terrorists, see Chapters 8 and 9.

32 See also Section VI of the Statement of Principles for Canadian Daily Newspapers, Canadian Daily Newspapers Publishers Association, adopted in April 1977: "Every person has a right to privacy. There are inevitable conflicts between the right to privacy and the public good or the right to know about the conduct of public affairs. Each case should be judged in the light of common sense and humanity." Quoted in N. Russell, *Morals and the Media* (Vancouver: UBC Press, 1995), pp. 123, 199. For further discussion, see S. L. Borden and M. S. Pritchard, "Conflict of interest in journalism", in M. Davis and A. Stark, *Conflict of Interest in the Professions* (New York: Oxford University Press, 2001), pp. 73–91; J. Lichtenberg, "Truth, neutrality, and conflict of interest", in J. R. Rowan and S. Zinaich, Jr (eds), *Ethics for the Professions* (Belmont: Wadsworth, 2003), pp. 379–386.

Let us consider another example of an individual who stumbles into the limelight in different circumstances. Suppose John performs a brave act by saving the life of his president. John is a quiet citizen who has never before attracted public attention, and literally overnight becomes the center of media concern. One tabloid newspaper decides to reveal to the public who John, the brave savior, is. The editor assigns a diligent reporter to the job who, after a few days, returns with sensational news: John leads a double life. During the day he is a working man, who has a wife and three kids whom he supports; and during the evening he is secretly active in the gay community of San Francisco. The editor decides to publish the story in the name of the pursuit of truth and the public's right to know. He does not ask for John's consent. His justification for this publication is that the public has a right to know who saved the life of the president, especially as John can serve as a role model for the gay community, where members are usually portrayed as "sissies", incapable of conducting such acts of bravery. Following the publication, John's wife sues for divorce.

Here, John's private life was clearly immaterial to the act of saving the president's life. His privacy, which he strove so hard to protect, should have been safeguarded. The "role model" argument is unconvincing. Surely the gay community would rather identify with someone who is proud of his identity – not with John, who did his utmost to hide his sexual preferences in the closet. Accountable media should think about the consequences of reporting, and not remain oblivious to the issue, "*que sera sera*, whatever will be will be". Human life is not a cheap commodity to be played with, and sensational news should not be conceived as a trump to outweigh decency and respect for people. John should settle his private life with his wife and his friends. It is not a matter for the media to intrude upon. If this is the media's conduct, people like John will think twice before making acts of bravery, not wanting to be coerced into paying the possible price of intrusion. They would rather stay away from the limelight and continue to lead their quiet, peaceful lives and forego good citizenship.

A good real-life example in this context, with significant differences, is the Oliver Sipple story. Sipple was the ex-marine who, on 22 September 1975, knocked a gun out of the hands of Sara Jane Moore, a would-be assassin of then American President Gerald Ford. Shortly after the incident it was revealed by the media that Sipple was active in the San Francisco gay community, a fact that had not been known to Sipple's parents, brothers and sisters, who thereupon broke off relationships with him. His entire life was shattered as a result of this publication. The good deed he had done brought about extremely harmful consequences for Sipple.[33] Sipple filed a petition against the press to the California Supreme Court,

---

33 See R. Cohen-Almagor, *The Boundaries of Liberty and Tolerance*, pp. 113–115. I have changed my mind regarding the affair since the publication of my book in 1994.

arguing that the publication exposed him to contempt and ridicule, causing him great mental anguish, embarrassment, and humiliation. However, his motion was declined. The court held that there was a legitimate public interest in his private life, and that in San Francisco Sipple did not make a secret of his sexual orientation.[34] The court discounted the fact that Sipple's family in the Midwest knew nothing about his Californian life. Sipple eventually decided to end his life and committed suicide.[35]

Sipple's private life was immaterial to the act of saving the president's life. However, this story is different from the above example of John in two substantive respects. First, unlike John, Sipple was open about sexual preferences and did not strive to hide them. He marched in gay parades on several occasions, and was involved in gay public affairs. His friendship with another prominent gay man was well-known and publicized in gay newspapers; his homosexual association and name had been reported in several gay magazines. Apparently, Sipple's community activities were well-known by hundreds of people in a variety of cities, including New York, Dallas, Houston, San Diego, Los Angeles, and San Francisco.[36] Unlike the quiet John, Sipple did not make a secret of his being gay. The court said that Sipple conceded that "if anyone would ask, he would frankly admit that he was gay".[37] Therefore, the court quite rightly concluded that "since appellant's sexual orientation was already in public domain", and since the newspaper articles about Sipple's private life did no more than give further publicity to matters which he left open to the public eye, "a vital element of the tort was missing rendering it vulnerable to summary disposal".[38]

The court further considered the incentive for the publications in question and concluded that they were not motivated by a morbid and sensational prying into Sipple's private life but rather were prompted by legitimate political considerations, namely "to dispel the false public opinion that gays were timid, weak and unheroic figures and to raise the equally important political question whether the President of the United States entertained a discriminatory attitude or bias against a minority group such as homosexuals".[39]

---

34 *Sipple* v. *Chronicle Publishing Co.* et al. No. A011998, 201 Cal. Rptr. 665 (Cal. App. 1st, 13 April 1984).
35 J. Q. Whitman, "The two Western cultures of privacy: dignity versus liberty", *Public Law & Legal Theory Research Paper Series*, No. 64, Yale Law School (2003), p. 61, later published in *Yale Law Journal*, 113 (April 2004). Whitman does not find the intrusion into Sipple's life justifiable. Similar reasoning is espoused by J. Rosen, *The Unwanted Gaze* (New York: Random House, 2000), pp. 47–48.
36 *Sipple* v. *Chronicle Publishing Co.* et al. No. A011998, at 669.
37 *Ibid.*
38 *Ibid.*
39 *Ibid.*, at 670.

Since Sipple did not try to hide his being gay, he may serve as a role model for his community. As stated, Sipple participated in gay parades, so we can assume that he wished to promote gay rights. Here, an opportunity presented itself to do so forcefully. One can assume that Sipple would be quite happy to widely publicize the event, and his sexual identity, so as to reach the eyes of all but his close family. Furthermore, Gerald Ford refrained from promptly thanking Sipple for his selfless, heroic act, and there was speculation that this was due to his view on homosexuality. The *Los Angeles Times* explained the newsworthiness of the publication by saying:

> the intimation that the President … had refrained from expressing normal gratitude to an individual who perhaps had saved his life raised significant political and social issues as to whether the President entertained discriminatory attitudes toward a minority group, namely, homosexuals.[40]

While I find the *Sipple* decision justified, I cannot endorse the Supreme Court decision in the *Hill* case. In 1952, James Hill, his wife and their five children involuntarily became the subjects of a front-page story after being held hostage by three escaped convicts in their own home in Pennsylvania. During the nineteen hours of the ordeal, the convicts had treated the family courteously and did not molest them. However, the event made a deep impression on the family, especially on Mrs Hill, and shortly thereafter the family moved to Connecticut. They discouraged all efforts to keep them in the public spotlight through magazine articles or appearances on the media.[41]

Two years later, a play titled *The Desperate Hours* opened on Broadway, based on Joseph Hayes' novel published in the spring of 1953 under the same title. Unlike the Hills' experience, the family of the story suffered brute violence in the hands of the convicts. The play was set in Indianapolis, but *Life* magazine in a feature story about the play, decided to photograph the actors in the former home of the Hill family and to describe the play, with all its terror, as a re-enactment of what had happened to the Hills. The article intended to, and did, give the impression that the play mirrored the Hills' experience. This was false. The *Life* story was devastating to the family. Mrs Hill suffered a psychiatric breakdown. Mr Hill said he could not understand how *Life* could publish such a story without at least checking with him its truth. "It was just like we didn't exist", he said, "like we were dirt."[42]

---

40 *Ibid.*, at 670, note 2.
41 *Time Inc.* v. *Hill*, 385 U.S. 374 (1967), 1 Media l. Rep. 1791, at 378.
42 A. Lewis, "The right to be let alone", in C. L. LaMay (ed.), *Journalism and the Debate Over Privacy* (Mahwah: Lawrence Erlbaum, 2003), p. 64.

The Hill family sued the publisher, Time Inc., for invasion of privacy. A jury awarded them $50,000 compensatory and $25,000 punitive damages. Upon further appeal, damages were reduced to $30,000 compensatory damages without punitive damages, and Time Inc. further appealed to the Supreme Court which eventually, in a five to four decision, reversed the judgment. Speaking for the majority, Justice Brennan relied on *New York Times* v. *Sullivan*[43] to hold that the Constitution delimits a State's power to award damages for libel in actions brought by public officials against critics of their official conduct. Factual error, content defamatory of official reputation, or both, are insufficient for an award of damages for false statements unless actual malice, "knowledge that the statements are false or in reckless disregard of the truth", is alleged and proved.[44] This was not the case here, and therefore the Court decided for *Life*.

I find this reasoning unconvincing. As Justice Harlan noted in his partial dissent, there is a vast difference in the state interest in protecting individuals like the Hills from irresponsibly prepared publicity, and the state interest in similar protection for public officials. In *Sullivan*, the Court acknowledged public officials to be a breed from whom hardiness to exposure to charges, innuendoes, and criticisms might be demanded, and who voluntarily assumed the risks involved.[45] But the Hills stumbled into the spotlight in most unfortunate circumstances. They did whatever they could to avoid public exposure, thus the state interest in encouraging careful checking and preparation of published material is far stronger than in *Sullivan*. A state should be free to hold the press dutiful of making reasonable investigations of the underlying facts and limiting itself to "fair comment".[46] Justice Harlan concluded by saying that the First Amendment cannot be thought to insulate all press conduct from review and responsibility for harm inflicted. He appropriately observed that sanctions against such conduct should be employed when it creates a severe risk of irremediable harm to individuals involuntarily exposed to it and powerless to protect themselves against it. Harlan further noted, quite rightly, that a constitutional doctrine which relieves the press of even this minimal responsibility would ultimately harm the best interest of the press.[47] The public would lose its faith in it.

Justice Fortas, in his dissent, said the following compelling and quite moving words, with which I agree fully:

> The courts may not and must not permit either public or private action that censors or inhibits the press. But part of this responsibility

43 376 U.S. 254 (1964), 84 S. Ct. 710.
44 *Time Inc.* v. *Hill*, at 388.
45 *Ibid.*, at 408.
46 *Ibid.*, at 409.
47 *Ibid.*, at 409–410.

is to preserve values and procedures which assure the ordinary citizen that the press is not above the reach of the law – that its special prerogatives, granted because of its special and vital functions, are reasonably equated with its needs in the performance of these functions. For this Court totally to immunize the press – whether forthrightly or by subtle indirection – in areas far beyond the needs of news ... would be no service to freedom of the press, but an invitation to public hostility to that freedom.[48]

Fortas maintained that the Court cannot and should not refuse to permit under state law the private citizen who is aggrieved by assaults, which are not protected by the First Amendment, to recover compensatory damages for recklessly inflicted invasion of his rights.[49] The scope of tolerance should not be extended to such insensitive, inconsiderate, intrusive, and harmful promotion of plays which disrespects the victims involved.

Furthermore, I find Justice Douglas' concurring opinion with the majority staggering in its crudeness. For him, public interest in "news" and free speech rule supreme. He paid no consideration to the issue of coercion, i.e. the distinction made here between voluntary and involuntary stepping into the limelight. Douglas argued that in this case a private person was catapulted into the news by events over which he had no control (referring to the appellant, Mr Hill), and henceforth he and his activities would be in the public domain. For Douglas, privacy ceased when Mr Hill's life ceased to be private, even though he was coerced into the event that caused the unfortunate publicity. Justice Douglas reinforced his position by expressing fear that "once we narrow the ambit of the First Amendment, creative writing is imperiled and the 'chilling effect' on free expression ... is almost sure to take place".[50]

I fail to understand how liberals like Douglas can have so much sympathy with the First Amendment, emphasizing "chilling effects" on future hypothetical speech and the importance of "creative writing" that has destructive effect on people, and at the same time have so little sensitivity to real people who come before the court hurt and devastated.[51] Liberals like Douglas are more worried about possible costs to free expression than the costs forced upon people here and now.

48 *Ibid.*, at 420.
49 *Ibid.*
50 *Ibid.*, pp. 401–402. For further discussion, see M. B. Nimmer, "The right to speak from times to time: First Amendment theory applied to libel and misapplied to privacy", *California Law Review*, 56 (1968): 935.
51 For further deliberation on involuntary celebrities, see L. M. Friedman, "The one-way mirror: law, privacy, and the media", *Stanford Public Law and Legal Theory Working Paper Series*, No. 89 (March 2004), forthcoming in *Washington University Law Quarterly*.

Intruding into the private lives of previously well-known figures

Another unhappy story concerns William James Sidis. He was a famous child prodigy in 1910. His name and prowess were well-known due to the efforts of his father, who developed complex ideas on child training. When young Sidis was three-and-a-half years old, he could use a typewriter. By the time he was five, Sidis was able to read, write, and speak English, was an expert accountant, and had begun to study French and Latin. He wrote a textbook on anatomy and another on English grammar. At the age of eight Sidis entered high school, and in six weeks he had completed the math-ematical course and begun writing an astronomy book. Then he also plunged into the study of German and Russian. Boris, the proud father, took care to issue bulletins to the press detailing all these (and other) achievements. The press followed William and praised Boris for the so-called "successful" implementation of his "advanced" theories. At the age of eleven, Sidis lectured to distinguished mathematicians, on four-dimensional bodies, at Harvard. At sixteen he graduated from Harvard College, amid considerable public attention. He was declared to be, according to the *New York Times*, "the most learned undergraduate that has ever entered the Cam-bridge institution".[52] Since then, however, his name appeared in the press only sporadically as Sidis sought to live as unobtrusively as possible, until *The New Yorker* published quite an unflattering article about him in 1937.

The New Yorker did features on past personalities under the title "Where are they now?" The article on Sidis was printed with the subtitle "April fool", playing on the fact that William was born on 1 April. The reporter described Sidis's early accomplishments and the wide attention he received, then recounted his general breakdown and the revulsion that Sidis felt for his former life of fame. The article described how Sidis tried to conceal his identity, his chosen career as an insignificant clerk, his enthusiasm for collecting streetcar transfers and for studying the history of a certain American-Indian tribe, and his proficiency with an adding machine. The untidiness of Sidis's room, his curious gasping laugh, his manner of speech, his wary eyes, and other personal habits were com-mented upon at length. The article portrayed William's lodgings, "a hall bedroom of Boston's shabby south end" and the man at the age of thirty-nine, "large, heavy . . . with a prominent jaw, a thickish neck, and a reddish mustache".[53] The article ended by saying that the little boy who lectured in 1910 on the fourth dimension to a gathering of learned men was expected to grow up to be a great mathematician, a famous leader in the world of science but, in the words of Sidis himself, "I was born on April Fools' Day".[54]

---

52 "Sidis could read at two years old", *New York Times* (18 October 1909), p. 7.
53 J. L. Manly, "Where are they now? April fool!", *The New Yorker* (14 August 1937), pp. 22–26.
54 *Ibid.*, p. 26.

Sidis sued for violation of privacy. The issue at hand was not whether the article was true. Sidis, who so desperately wanted to be let alone and to live his life away from the public eye, was exposed in a cruel fashion. The court recognized that, saying "the article is merciless in its dissection of intimate details of its subject's personal life", maintaining that the article may be fairly described as "a ruthless exposure of a once public character, who has since sought and has now been deprived of the seclusion of private life".[55]

However, despite the sympathy for Sidis, Judge Clark found for the defendant, saying that "Everyone will agree that at some point the public interest in obtaining information becomes dominant over the individual's desire for privacy".[56] Notice the language: Clark is recruiting "everyone" for this assignment of trumping the plaintiff's privacy. I hasten to think that there would be quite differences of opinion among "everyone" regarding the exact point at which public interest in obtaining information becomes dominant. This point is not clarified in the judgment. Clark maintained, "At least we would permit limited scrutiny of the 'private' life of any person who has achieved, or has had thrust upon him, the questionable and indefinable status of a 'public figure'."[57] Indeed, "thrust upon him" is the correct phrase, as William was a child, incapable of independent autonomous decision-making, when he became a public figure due to the endless efforts of his father to push him into the spotlight. When he was able to break free and to stand on his own, Sidis opted for anonymity. The court essentially says that once a public figure, always a public figure. There is no escape. Even if you want to be forgotten, you cannot. You owe to the public the right to inform them about major developments in your life, however tragic and personal those might be. The fact that Sidis never made a decision to become a public figure, and when he was able to control his life he chose the exact opposite of being one, was insignificant for the court.

In 1937, Sidis had not been a public figure for some time. He was not a retired public official who still might have been held accountable for past actions. He was not a celebrity who relished the limelight – quite the opposite. Sidis did whatever he could to sink into oblivion. Intruding on his privacy in the name of popular curiosity was unjustified and unethical. Granted, there was public interest in Sidis. The public is interested in many things, including state security, official secrets, capturing Osama Bin-Laden, the sexual behavior of supermodels and politicians, and how much money one's neighbor earns. This does not mean that the media should provide all data of interest. The court's decision was erroneous

---

55 *Sidis* v. *F-R Publishing*, 113 F2d 806 (2nd Cir., 22 July 1940), at 807–808.
56 *Ibid.*, at 809.
57 *Ibid.*

and damaging. Four years after the court decision, Sidis died unemployed and destitute.[58]

I would like to take issue with another statement made by Clark. He wrote:

> Regrettably or not, the misfortune and frailties of neighbors and "public figures" are subjects of considerable interest and discussion to the rest of the population. And when such are the mores of the community, it would be unwise for a court to bar their expression in the newspapers, books and magazines of the day.[59]

This is a very dangerous path to follow. Courts are not salons of beauty contests, and popular standards are not necessarily the standards that they should aspire to follow. Courts are places where individuals come to seek justice, to voice grievances, to speak up against what they conceive as maltreatment. Sometimes, it is incumbent upon the courts to do the thankless job of going against the stream, to lead their communities to a different path, recognizing that the old path was unfair, unjust or simply wrong. In a racist, misogynistic or homophobic community, where the norms are discriminatory, individuals who are exploited and abused should feel free to approach the courts to seek justice *contra* existing bigoted norms. In a community where sensationalism and prying rule supreme, individuals should be reassured that the courts may take a different stance on privacy and secure their right to live away from the public eye, even though the public may be eager to see nude photos of Claudia Schiffer, Ariel Sharon or Princess Diana.[60]

Now, if the person stumbles into the public forum prefers to remain in the public eye and to harvest more attention by further deeds or expressions, then he or she is no longer a private citizen and should accept the pros and cons involved in public life. But many of them may wish to regain their privacy and return to normal life. With regard to these people, the media should refrain from intruding into their private lives and should respect their privacy, especially when exposure of certain details could harm one or more of the people involved.[61]

58 A. Lewis, "The right to be let alone", *op. cit.*, p. 64.
59 *Sidis* v. *F-R Publishing*, at 809.
60 For further deliberation on another interesting case, see *Luther and Dorothy Haynes* v. *Alfred A. Knopf* 8 F.3d 1222 (7th Cir. 1993). The case involves a suit against a best-selling author on the ground that his book libeled the plaintiffs and invaded their right to privacy. Most of the facts depicted in the book were not contested. The Hayneses' claimed that they have been a respectable couple for two decades and that the book, by describing events that took place almost thirty years ago, damages the reputation they built so hard. The court (Posner J.) protected the author's right to tell a story which raises "profound social and political questions" (at 38).
61 Section IIB(b) of the Quebec Press Council's *The Rights and Responsibilities of the Press* (2nd edn, 1987) holds: "Media and journalists should distinguish between

In *Shulman*, the court balanced privacy and press freedom in the commonplace distressing context of a car accident. The plaintiffs, the mother and son of the Shulman family, were injured when their car overturned and trapped them inside. A medical transport and rescue helicopter came to their assistance, accompanied by a cameraman working for a television producer. The cameraman filmed the plaintiffs' extrication from the car, the flight nurse and medic's efforts to provide them medical care, and their transport to hospital. The nurse wore a microphone that picked up her conversations with other rescue workers, as well as with Ms Shulman. This videotape and sound track were edited and subsequently broadcast, months later, on a documentary show called *On Scene: Emergency Response* (29 September 1990). The plaintiffs, who consented neither to the filming and recording nor to the broadcasting, alleged that the television producers thereby intruded into their privacy and gave unwanted publicity to very private moments of their lives at a most tragic time.

Ms Shulman was left paraplegic as a result of this accident. She did not know her rescue had been recorded, and was never asked for her consent to broadcast the event. She found out about it on the night of the broadcast, and was shocked that she had been exploited in such an intrusive manner. Ms Shulman later explained:

> I think the whole scene was pretty private. It was pretty gruesome, the parts that I saw, my knee sticking out of the car. I certainly did not look my best, and I don't feel it's for the public to see. I was not at my best in what I was thinking and what I was saying and what was being shown, and it's not for the public to see this trauma that I was going through.[62]

The trial court granted summary judgment for the producers on the ground that the events depicted were newsworthy, and therefore their activities were protected under the First Amendment. Not much attention was paid to the highly offensive conduct of the television producers, their lack of sensitivity, and their gross and egregious intrusion of the victims' privacy. After all, patients' conversations with medical care providers in course of treatment, especially emergency treatment, carry a traditional and legally well-established expectation of privacy.[63]

The Court of Appeal reversed the decision, finding triable issues of fact existed as to Ms Shulman's claim for publication of private facts, and legal error on the trial court's part as to both plaintiffs' intrusion claims. The trial court had erred in applying a complete defense of newsworthiness

matters of public interest and public curiosity. The publication of information concerning the private life of individuals is acceptable only to the extent that it is in the public interest."

62 *Shulman* et al. v. *Group W. Productions*, No. S058629, 18 Cal.4th 200, 955 P2d 469 (1998), at 212.

63 *Shulman* et al. v. *Group W. Productions*, at 234.

where balancing was proper, weighing, one against the other, privacy claims and media freedom. Agreeing with some of the Court of Appeal's analysis, the Supreme Court of California concluded that summary judgment was proper as to the plaintiffs' cause of action for publication of private facts, but not as to their cause of action for intrusion.[64] The Court explicated that the state may not intrude into the proper sphere of the news media to dictate what they should publish and broadcast, but neither may the media play tyrant to the people by unlawfully spying on them in the name of newsgathering.[65]

The broadcast material was lurid and sensational in emotional tone, and intensely personal in content. The plaintiffs could reasonably expect privacy in the interior of the helicopter, which served as an ambulance. No one had told them of the presence of the cameraman, and in their agony and confusion they should not be expected to think about this issue. No one bothered to ask them for their consent. The Court said: "we are aware of no law or custom permitting the press to ride in ambulances or enter hospital rooms during treatment without the patient's consent".[66] Furthermore, as the Court rightly recognized, the Shulmans were entitled to a degree of privacy in their conversations with the rescue team. The public has no legitimate interest in witnessing casualties' disorientation and despair, nor does it have any legitimate interest in knowing their personal and innermost thoughts immediately after sustaining severe injuries, while they struggle with what the impact on their lives is going to be. By placing a microphone on the nurse, amplifying and recording what she said and heard, "defendants may have listened in on conversations the parties could reasonably have expected to be private".[67] Arguably, the last thing an injured victim should have to worry about while being saved from a wrecked car is that a television crew may be recording the event for the possible edification and entertainment of viewers. The Court said: "fundamental respect for human dignity requires the patients' anxious journey be taken only with those whose care is solely for them and out of sight of the prying eyes (or cameras) of others".[68] The conduct of journalism does not depend, as a general rule, on the use of secret devices to record private conversations.[69]

64 See *Miller* v. *National Broadcasting Co.*, 187 Cal. App.3d 1463, 232 Cal. Rptr. 668 (1986), which stated two elements for intrusion: (1) into a private place, conversation or matter (2) in a manner highly offensive to a reasonable person.
65 *Ruth Shulman* et al. v. *Group W. Productions*, at 242.
66 *Shulman* et al. v. *Group W. Productions*, at 232.
67 *Ibid.*, at 233.
68 *Ibid.*, at 238.
69 *Ibid.*, at 239. For further discussion on the use of deception, see R. P. Bezanson, "Means and ends and food lion: the tension between exemption and independence in newsgathering by the press", *Emory Law Journal*, 47 (1998): 895. For a different point of view, unconvincingly justifying ABC's conduct, see R. A. Smolla, "Privacy and the First Amendment right to gather news", *George Washington Law Review*, 67 (1999): 1122, 1129–1130.

Conclusion

Democracy has an interest in protecting the privacy and tranquility of the home. That interest has been recognized by the American[70] and Israeli[71] Supreme Courts in several decisions. In *Mapp* v. *Ohio*, the Court referred to the right to privacy, conceived as being no less important than any other right carefully and particularly reserved to the people as "basic to free society".[72] Justice Frankfurter wrote in one of his prominent rulings: "Homes are sanctuaries from intrusions upon privacy and of opportunities for leading lives in health and safety".[73] Similar reasoning was enunciated by Justices Black and Brennan. Justice Black held that a person's home is "the sacred retreat to which families repair for their privacy and their daily way of living", "sometimes the last citadel of the tired, the weary, and the sick", wherein people "can escape the hurly-burly of the outside business and political world".[74] In turn, Justice Brennan said:

> Preserving the sanctity of the home, the one retreat to which men and women can repair to escape from the tribulations of their daily pursuits, is surely an important value. Our decisions reflect no lack of solicitude for the right of an individual "to be let alone" in the privacy of the home.[75]

Here Brennan echoed what Warren and Brandeis had written in their classic article where they spoke of the right to be let alone and of privacy, referring to the "precincts of private and domestic life" as sacred.[76]

70 Cf. Justice Douglas in *Public Utilities Commission* v. *Pollack* 343 U.S. 451, 467 (1952). See also *Boyd* v. *United States* 116 U.S. 616 (1886); *Stanley* v. *Georgia*, 394 U.S. 557, 89 S. Ct. 1243, 22 L.Ed.2d 542 (1969); *City of Wauwatosa* v. *King* 182 N.W. 2d 530, 537 (1971). See also West's Legal News, "Supreme court denied Certiorari in anti-abortion demonstrators' picketing case", *West's Legal News* 3061, 1995 WL 910586 (19 October 1995).

71 H.C. (High Court of Justice) 456/73. *Rabbi Kahane* v. *Southern District Police Commander* (was not published); Shamgar J'.s judgment in F.H. 9/83. *Military Court of Appeals* v. *Vaaknin*, P.D. 42 (iii), 837, 851; H.C. 2481/93. *Yoseph Dayan* v. *Police Chief District of Jerusalem*.

72 367 U.S. 643, 81 S. Ct. 1684 (1961), at 656.

73 *Martin* v. *City of Struthers* 319 U.S. 141, 153 (1943). See also my discussion in *Speech, Media and Ethics*, Chapter 2.

74 *Gregory* v. *City of Chicago*, 394 U.S. 111, 125, 118, 89 S.Ct. 946, 953–954, 950, 22 L.Ed.2d 134 (1969).

75 *Carey* v. *Brown* 447 U.S. 455, 471 (1980). In *Rowan* v. *United States Post Office Department*, 397 U.S. 728, 737, 90 S. Ct. 1484, 25 L.Ed.2d 736 (1970), Chief Justice Burger stated that the concept that "a man's home is his castle" into which not even the king may enter, has lost none of its vitality. For further discussion, see R. Cohen-Almagor, *Speech, Media, and Ethics: The Limits of Free Expression*, Chapter 2; R. J. Arneson, "Egalitarian justice v. the right to privacy?", in E. F. Pail, F. D. Miller Jr. and J. Paul (eds), *The Right to Privacy*, pp. 91–119.

76 S. Warren and L. D. Brandeis, "The right to privacy", *Harvard Law Review*, 4 (1890): 289–320.

However, the US Supreme Court has not yet fashioned a general rule striking a balance between our competing interests in preserving personal privacy and in unfettered publication of truthful information.

In the next chapter I wish further to probe the issue of privacy versus free speech and the public's right to know by considering two episodes: one took place in England; the other in Canada. Both will shed further light on the costs of free expression, and help us prescribe the scope of tolerance.

3   The right to privacy: part II

The pen is crueler than the sword.
(Correspondence between John le Carre and Salman Rushdie *Harper's Magazine*, February 1998)

Introduction

Having laid the conceptual framework of analyzing the right to privacy, and discussed legal and ethical principles pertinent to addressing this right when it clashes with free expression and the public's right to know, this chapter now highlights two specific prominent case studies, English and Canadian.

I should explain the rationale for choosing these two case studies. Diana's complicated relationships with the British media and the *Aubry* case in Canada have attracted attention in the respective countries. In a way, the two stories exemplify the two different cultures: British and French-Quebec. The British media give less credit to privacy than their French counterparts. The two episodes also supplement one another and exemplify the public–private distinction when the media intrude on people's privacy. The Diana story is different from the Canadian *Aubry* case in several aspects. Diana was a celebrity and Aubry a private person; Diana was constantly reported in the newspapers whereas Aubry's photograph was used only once for artistic and commercial purposes. No one coerced Diana to cooperate with the media. She voluntarily and quite happily made the private public, whereas Aubry was involuntarily recruited to decorate a magazine cover. Diana's case evoked public moral outrage whereas Aubry's case was minor by comparison, involving violation of the law. Diana tried to avoid going to courts whereas the *Aubry* case was resolved by the courts. Diana's case is far more complicated, involving many intricate issues: the use of the media to blunt royal power, and the ability (or inability) to sustain privacy when one party encourages media coverage and utilizes the media for private purposes. In addition, there is the further consideration of children (William and Harry) as a protected class of people.

However, there are also similarities between the two cases: both raise a host of legal and ethical considerations; both were *not* cases of photojournalism – instead, the attractive images of both Diana and Aubry were splashed on journals' covers with the purpose to increase sails of newspapers; the privacy of both women was intruded upon without their consent; both felt that they were exploited by the media to advance the media's own partisan interests. Both cases illustrate the need to outline boundaries to free expression and free press.

The first case study is essentially concerned with one of the most intrusive forms of reporting: gossip. Gossip is about events that are of little social value but are of interest to the public. Reporting of these events feeds the voyeuristic needs of many of us, to various extents. Many of us enjoy learning the details of what is thought to be unattainable by the common people – if I cannot be like the "beautiful people", at least I would like to know about their lifestyle: what living in a castle with servants is like; the pros and cons of living with three wives; what it is like to be an idolized rock star; what a famous basketball player eats for breakfast; why he chose to divorce his wife. Many of these gossip events can be quite banal. For instance, millions of women are pregnant around the globe at any given time, and the media usually do not regard this as newsworthy. However, it might attract public interest if the concerned woman is a soap opera star or a leading actress in one of the commercial comedy series. Many viewers of *Melrose Place* would be very interested in knowing that their favorite character is actually pregnant in her private life. They would begin to ponder and speculate about various questions: will the character she acts out in the series become pregnant as well? Will the series' producers try to conceal her pregnancy? Will the star finally get married? Will a replacement be found in case the pregnancy does not fit the producers' plans? Will they decide, God forbid, to terminate the filming of the series during the advanced months of pregnancy? These are top priority questions for captive followers of the series.[1]

Gossip is not supposed to be stripped of ethics either. People's honor must be dealt with carefully, and the boundaries of decorum must be maintained. Pure voyeurism might cause unjustified harm to celebrities and their families, and often this attitude does not add to a paper's reputation.

In Israel, the gossip columns adopted some ethical standards in reporting about celebrities and public figures. They never report about their children, believing children should be left out of the public scene and

---

1 For further discussion, see R. Cohen-Almagor, *Speech, Media, and Ethics* (Houndmills and New York: Palgrave-Macmillan, 2005), Chapter 5. See also C. Edwin Baker, "Autonomy and informational privacy, or gossip: the central meaning of the First Amendment", *Social Philosophy and Policy*, 21(2) (July 2004): 215–268, esp. 260–267.

their privacy should be maintained. Gossip reporters never 'out' homosexuals who prefer to remain "in the closet", and they would never publish material that might bring about the breakdown of families. Consequently, they may say that a minister, or a senior public official, or a famous singer is having extramarital affair, but they will keep that person's name anonymous.

The British press has been constantly under public scrutiny during the past two decades. At the end of the 1980s there was a growing uneasiness with regard to its functioning. It was decided to set up an inquiry committee to consider the behaviour of the press and to suggest remedies. In particular, the issue of privacy was in the forefront of concern. The first report of June 1990 concluded with the view that "the press should be given one last chance to demonstrate that non-statutory self-regulation can be made to work effectively. This is a stiff test for the press. If it fails, we recommend that a statutory system for handling complaints should be introduced."[2] However, both the 1990 Calcutt Report and the earlier Younger Report[3] recommended that no general tort of invasion of privacy be introduced.[4]

The press failed the test, and in January 1993 a second report was issued by Sir David Calcutt QC, arguing that the Press Complaints Commission (PCC) was not an effective regulator of the press.[5] Sir David maintained that the PCC did not:

> hold the balance fairly between the press and individual. It is not the truly independent body, which it should be. As constituted, it is, in essence, a body set up by the industry, and operating a code of practice devised by the industry and which is over-favourable to the industry.[6]

---

2 Home Office, *Report of the Committee on Privacy and Related Matters* (London: Her Majesty's Stationary Office, June 1990), Cm 1102, at 73. Sir David Calcutt Report.
3 Younger Report, Cmnd. 5012 (1972), para. 659.
4 Privacy is protected in Art. 12 of the UN Declaration of Human Rights and Art. 17 of the International Covenant on Civil and Political Rights as well as in Art. 8 of the European Convention on Human Rights. Cf. M. J. Beloff, "Politicians and the press", in J. Beatson and Y. Cripps (eds), *Freedom of Expression and Freedom of Information* (Oxford: Oxford University Press, 2002), p. 76.
5 In the United States, the mere idea of establishing of a body like the British Press Complaints Commission would set a firestorm of debate. The absolute language of the First Amendment, "Congress shall make no law respecting an establishment of religion, or prohibiting the free exercise thereof; or abridging the freedom of speech, or of the press", is taken almost literally. Cf. P. Meyer, *Ethical Journalism* (Lanham: University Press of America, 1987), pp. 3–16.
6 Sir David Calcutt QC (January 1993) *Review of Press Self-Regulation* (London: Her Majesty's Stationary Office), Cm 2135, at xi.

Accordingly, the report recommended the replacement of the self-regulatory body of the press with a statutory regime designed to ensure that privacy "is protected from unjustifiable intrusion, and protected by a body in which the public, as well as the press, has confidence".[7]

Although Sir David thought that his recommendations were "designed to make a positive contribution to the development of the highest standards of journalism, to enable the press to operate freely and responsibly, and to give it the backing which is needed, in a fiercely competitive market, to resist the wildest excesses",[8] the government did not accept his coercive recommendations, preferring to tolerate the conduct of the press. The feeling was that the formation of a statutory regime might hinder freedom of expression and the right of the public to know. However, the proprietors who formed the PCC out of necessity, fearing possible governmental intervention, understood after Princess Diana's death that it was up to them to make the necessary accommodations, otherwise voices for governmental regulations might be reheard – possibly with greater public support.

Princess Diana and the British media

The London tabloids compete in the same market, and design themselves to a particular slice of the market: people who want an easy read, unsophisticated entertainment, provision of the news with good portions of gossip, sports, pictures, and humour. This is arguably the most competitive market in the print industry worldwide. Soon enough, publishers of tabloids realized that Princess Diana was their best sales-promoter. Her picture on the front page could prompt people to buy their paper instead of another. Diana became the most photographed person in the world. In fact, Diana set an historical precedence that will be very difficult to beat regarding the number of her photos that were published on journal and magazine covers. The tabloids were willing to pay enterprising and shameless photographers millions of dollars for capturing Diana in her private moments – the more private, the better. Tapes of Diana's intimate telephone conversations were leaked to the media, she was watched by spy agencies, and journalists dissected her every move. Ex-lover James Hewitt betrayed her trust and published a humiliatingly juicy and detailed account of their affair for a very nice sum of money. According to one report, the widely circulated photo of Diana embracing boyfriend Dodi al-Fayed netted the photographer more than $3.2 million

7 Calcutt, 1993, at xiv.
8 Calcutt, 1993, at 63. I asked Sir David to grant me an interview during the summer of 1997 but he refused, saying that he had shifted his interests to other spheres.

– an incentive that drove paparazzi to break any ethical boundary in the book in search of a quick fortune.[9]

On 31 August 1997, the Princess of Wales was killed in a shocking road accident in Paris. Princess Diana and her lover were trying to escape some paparazzi photographers who were racing after their car.[10] Princess Diana was exceptional among celebrities because she insisted upon continuing to live as normal a life as possible despite the constant surveillance to which she was subjected (in her words, "to sing openly", a way of living that the Royal family did not appreciate so much but the paparazzi adored). Princess Diana understood the power of the media, and frequently used them and manipulated them for her own advantage. One can say that Diana confused public interest with public prurience.

Although the paparazzi made her life very difficult in her later years, Princess Diana never filed a complaint against newspapers (under Section 8, Harassment, of the Code of Practice).[11] Even after her private pictures were taken in a gym and subsequently published in the *Daily Mirror* (7 November 1993), she chose not to complain and elected to resolve the matter through conciliation.[12] The court was therefore denied an opportunity to consider the limits of publicity when it comes to photos taken in a private place. One may speculate that the newspaper would almost certainly have argued that the Princess was not averse to publicity

---

9 C. J. Sykes, *The End of Privacy* (New York: St Martin's Press, 1999), p. 190.

10 The princess, her companion, Dodi al-Fayed, and the car's driver, Henri Paul, all died following the crash, which was survived by bodyguard Trevor Rees-Jones, the only occupant of the limousine wearing a seatbelt. The inquest revealed that Henri Paul was drunk and had alarming amounts of drugs in his blood, and as a result caused the accident.

11 *The Oxford English Dictionary* defines "harassment" as to trouble, worry, make repeated attacks on.

12 In August 1996, the Princess of Wales obtained an injunction restraining a named freelance press photographer from coming within 300 metres of her, wherever she might be, because of fear of harassment; and there have been cases where injunctions have been obtained to restrain publication of photographs taken of the Princess and other members of the royal family in intimate settings by means of telephoto lenses, etc. The general rule is that the taking of photographs cannot in itself be controlled (except where it is likely to cause a breach of the peace), unless the interference with the subject's life is so significant that it amounts to serious and probably intentional harassment. See H. Fenwick and G. Phillipson "Confidence and privacy: a re-examination", *Cambridge Law Journal*, 55(3) (November 1996): 447–455. In *Hellewell* v. *Chief Constable of South Yorkshire* [1995] 1 WLR 804, Laws J. said that if someone with a telephoto lens were to take from a distance and with no authority a picture of another engaged in some private act, his subsequent disclosure of the photograph would amount to a breach of confidence and the law would protect a right of privacy, although the name accorded to the cause of action would be breach of confidence (at 807).

and had colluded with the press in the past, permitting herself to be photographed in swimwear and disclosing her private feelings to journalists.[13] However, surely the issue of consent does make a difference. Diana did not grant permission for anyone to take photos of her exercising in the fitness centre.

To a large extent Diana's image was built by the media, which in turn used her to sell newspapers. You need two to tango, and the two – Princess Diana and the media – were eager to dance. Starting in 1991, she began recording the story of her life and her troubled marriage for journalist Andrew Morton, who took pains to conceal Diana's actual involvement until after her death. Indeed, Diana seems to have approached her revelations in Morton's book almost as a form of therapy, pouring out her vulnerabilities and very private episodes to the journalist's tape recorder. Largely as the result of her own revelations, the public came to know that Diana had seriously considered calling off the wedding two days before the occasion when she discovered Charles planned to give Camilla Parker-Bowles an inscribed bracelet.[14] The book revealed the drugs Diana took, which psychologists and spiritualists she consulted, the size of her waist (which had shrunk from twenty-nine inches on her engagement to twenty-three inches on her wedding day),[15] her bulimia nervosa,[16] her post-natal depression,[17] and her constant arguments with Charles. The book expressed Diana's bitter suffering by saying that her friends referred to the acronym POW (Princess of Wales) as meaning "Prisoner of War".[18]

Morton's book further testified to Diana's various suicide attempts, including the January 1982 attempt by throwing herself down a flight of steps. Diana was three months' pregnant with Prince William at that time. Charles, who apparently stood there, dismissed her plight and carried on with his plan to go riding.[19] Diana suffered severe bruising around her stomach. Luckily the fetus was not injured.

Indeed, the book depicts Prince Charles in a very cold light. It thus reveals that during a visit to California, Diana fainted in public. When she recovered, Charles told her bluntly that if she was going to faint she should have done so in private,[20] as if we humans prepare or plan to faint. The book described in detail Diana's dreadful loneliness, her therapies, and her various emotional turmoils. Her depressions, panics, and grief were meticulously shared, documented, and reported. Throughout her

---

13 R. Wacks, *Privacy and Press Freedom* (London: Blackstone Press, 1995), pp. 2–3.
14 A. Morton, *Diana: Her True Story* (New York: Simon and Schuster, 1992), pp. 3, 63–64.
15 *Ibid.*, p. 59.
16 *Ibid.*, pp. 3, 67.
17 *Ibid.*, p. 80.
18 *Ibid.*, p. 135.
19 *Ibid.*, p. 73.
20 *Ibid.*, p. 92.

final years, she confided details of her married life and her romances to close journalists, often with the expectation that the stories would be published on the front pages of the newspapers. And as she came to resent the press, she appeared on BBC's *Panorama* program to discuss her failing marriage. The program was watched by twenty-one million people in Britain and millions more around the world.[21] Princess Diana admitted her affair with James Hewitt, opening virtually every aspect of her life to scrutiny. Diana even publicly portrayed how she told her sons that she and Charles were splitting up and about how she and her sons discussed their father's relationship with her rival, Camilla Parker-Bowles, who was the third person in her marriage to Charles.[22]

Princess Diana was struggling against a far superior opponent, the Royal Court. She led a confusing double life where she was celebrated by the public but watched in doubtful and often jealous silence by her husband and the rest of his family. Within the royal family, Diana was seen as an outsider and a problem. Diana was tactile, emotional, and spontaneous. For a white-gloved, stiff-upper-lip institution, she was a threat.[23] Soon enough Diana realized that her main, perhaps only, asset was the media. While her face graced the cover of a million magazines and the public sang her praises, her husband and his family rarely gave her a word of encouragement, congratulation or advice. The media did. In this sphere she was able to compete against the Royal Court, and win. Diana wondered: how can all these people want to see me? And then "I get home in the evening and lead this mouse-like existence. Nobody says 'Well done'." She had this incredible dichotomy in her mind.[24]

In her relationship with the media, Diana knew what a good picture was and supplied the photos that were printed all over the world and helped newspapers to increase their sales. She attracted widespread public attention and provided endless stories for the reporters and photographers who followed her. What she did not understand is that she could not choose which pictures should be taken and which not, or which photographers could accompany her during her trips and which should not follow her. Princess Diana was disgusted and appalled by the behavior of the unscrupulous paparazzi photographers who made their living by recording her private moments. The famous dictum, 'The Englishman's home is his castle' was transformed, where Diana was concerned, to 'her castle is our homework' – or rather, 'our golden peepshow'. Apparently, Diana failed to recognize to the end that when she opened the door for the media they would enter in force, to make the most of this opportunity to make some profit.

21 K. Sanders, *Ethics and Journalism* (London: Sage, 2003), p. 79.
22 C. J. Sykes, *The End of Privacy*, p. 191.
23 A. Morton, *Diana: Her True Story, op. cit.*, p. 138.
24 A. Morton, p. 112.

And Diana did open the door to document her most private moments. Robin Esser, Consultant Editor of the *Daily Mail*, argued that Princess Diana was obsessive about her image. It was not rare for her to phone the paper's royal reporter a few times a week, sometimes a few times a day. Princess Diana spoke to him on the phone regularly every week from 1995 to 1997.[25] Charles Moore, Editor of the *Daily Telegraph*, said that Princess Diana was regularly in touch with senior people in the paper, like himself, the royal affairs reporter, and another senior member who was close to the royal family.[26] When Diana was vacationing in St Tropez with her two sons, each morning they would appear on the beach where they cavorted willingly in full view of the photographers. The resulting pictures of the princess in a bathing suit were devoured by much of the world press. Reportedly, the paparazzi were so grateful for her cooperation that they sent her a hundred red roses. Not coincidentally, public attention completely overshadowed her ex-husband's birthday party for Camilla Parker-Bowles. She had trumped her rival by sacrificing her privacy. Furthermore, as her romance with Dodi al-Fayed intensified, Diana tipped off photographers about her "secret" rendezvous. She passed information to fashion photographer Mario Brenna about their whereabouts, enabling him to shoot rolls of film showing Diana and Dodi frolicking together in the surf. She also let photographer Jason Fraser know the exact time and locations along the French and Italian coasts where she and Dodi would be sailing. The results were seemingly intimate shots of the couple romping together on a jet ski.[27]

Following Princess Diana's tragic death, many people in England called for a re-examination of the tension between the right to freedom of expression and the right to privacy. Lord Wakeham, Chairperson of the Press Complaints Committee, declared immediately after Princess Diana's funeral (6 September 1997) that the PCC would need to ponder ways to protect the privacy of Princes William and Harry so that they would not have to go through the agonizing experiences that their mother lived almost daily after she became the Princess of Wales.[28] Lord Wakeham said

25 Interview with Mr Esser (20 October 1997).
26 Interview with Mr Moore (21 October 1997).
27 C. J. Sykes, *The End of Privacy*, p. 191.
28 After Princess Diana's funeral, as part of the soul-searching, the *Guardian* contemplated the idea of appointing an "external" ombudsman, in addition to the Readers Editor. In the *Guardian* system, the Readers Editor is the first person to whom complaints are referred. He will adjudicate, and if he thinks it is a substantial complaint he will ask the reporter for response. The Editor cannot tell him what he should write. He cannot be sacked by the Editor. At the same time he is a staff member. The external ombudsman will be paid by the Guardian Group, but is not a staff member. He may write everything that he wants and, according to the planned scheme, the *Guardian* will publish his words in a prominent place in the paper. Interview with Mr Alan Rusbridger, Editor of the *Guardian* (28 October 1997).

he was "extremely concerned" about what would happen as the Princes reached the age of sixteen,[29] conceding that the PCC's Code of Practice might change after consultation with editors.[30] Lord Wakeham's statement followed the pledge made by Earl Spencer, Princess Diana's brother, during her funeral. The outraged Earl committed himself to protecting her children from the media, not allowing them "to suffer the anguish that used regularly to drive you [Diana] to tearful despair".[31] Of course, all the people concerned realize that it is not enough to join the Press Council and to subscribe to its Code of Practice. Although almost all newspapers in England subscribe to the Code, this is often more lip service.[32] Clearly, the tabloids still often betray it in their publications.[33]

It should be added that civil actions and prosecutions are easier under the UK Protection from Harassment Act (1997). This law makes it a criminal offense, punishable by imprisonment, for a person knowingly and unreasonably to pursue "a course of conduct which amounts to harassment of another". The test of constructive knowledge is whether "a reasonable person in possession of the same information" would think the course of conduct amounted to such harassment.[34] Harassment includes causing alarm or distress, and civil actions for damages may also be pursued.[35]

29 Clause 12 of the PCC Code of Practice holds that children under sixteen should not be interviewed or photographed on subjects involving their personal welfare without the consent of a parent or other adult responsible for them. For further discussion, see Lord Wakeham's speech at St Bride's Institute (23 August 1995), in *Moving Ahead* (Press Complaints Commission, 1995).
30 A. Boshoff, "Curbs on press to protect Princes", the *Daily Telegraph* (8 September 1997), p. 1.
31 "Earl Spencer's Funeral Address", the *Sunday Telegraph* (7 September 1997), p. 2.
32 However, it is noted that the *Daily Mail* incorporated the Code of Practice into its journalists' contracts, and there were cases in which journalists were dismissed for breaching the Code. In one incident, a reporter was dismissed because he did not identify himself as a journalist. Interview with Mr Robin Esser, Consultant Editor of the *Daily Mail* (20 October 1997).
33 Shortly after Princess Diana's tragic death, Rupert Murdoch had an interview during which he was asked whether he had any regrets regarding the conduct of his papers during Princess Diana's life. His answer was that the only regret he had was that he needed to pay too much money for the paparazzi photos. Interview with Martin Bell MP (21 October 1997).
34 Protection from Harassment Act 1997, section 1(2).
35 Cf. D. Pannick, "Resist pressure for a rushed law", *The Times* (9 September 1997), p. 33. It should also be noted that Section 8 (ii) of the PCC Code of Practice holds: "*Unless their enquiries are in the public interest,* journalists should not photograph individuals on private property ... without their consent; should not persist in telephoning or questioning individuals after having been asked to desist; should not remain on their property after having been asked to leave and should not follow them" (my emphasis, RCA). Section 18 defines the term "public interest" as: "i) Detecting or exposing crime or a serious misdemeanour. ii) Protecting public health and safety. iii) Preventing the public from being misled by some statement or action of an individual or organization."

On 8 September 1997, three daily newspapers, the *Mirror*, the *Sun*, and the *Independent*, announced that they would no longer use paparazzi pictures of Princes William and Harry in the first step to agreeing to tighter self-regulation. The *Mirror* said it "will now work swiftly with the Press Complaints Commission to protect these boys from intrusive paparazzi pictures".[36] Andrew Marr, Editor of the *Independent*, declared that "we will never again publish any pictures of the princes in a private situation and we will be more sparing of pictures of the princes and other members of the royal family in other situations as well".[37] Associated Newspapers, publishers of the *Daily Mail*, *Mail on Sunday*, and London's *Evening Standard*, declared that any use of paparazzi pictures would have to be cleared with Lord Rothermere, the proprietor, who in turn proclaimed that there would be a ban on "all intrusive pictures except where they are considered necessary".[38] Max Hastings, Editor of the *Standard*, said: "There can be few British journalists who did not spend some hours this weekend brooding about privacy after Lord Spencer's vengeful contribution ... Some members of the newspaper trade have behaved like animals, and it is strongly in the public interest that they should be deterred from doing so."[39]

Because of the public sensitivity following the death of Princess Diana, the tabloids indeed honoured the privacy of young Princes William and Harry for as long as they were at school. Eton is a relatively big, open place, yet no pictures of the two young boys were taken at school. The only photos that were released were those issued by the Palace.

Privacy of children is usually respected far more by the media than is the privacy of adults. Children are conceived as being more vulnerable and sensitive, and rightly so. This is not to say that the media do not report stories about children. Of course they do. Maltreatment of children is of public interest. The media take it upon themselves to protect weak third parties. The media have reported measures to prevent youth

---

36 K. Ahmed, "Editors bar snatched pictures of Princes", the *Guardian* (9 September 1997), p. 2.

37 *Ibid.*

38 *Ibid.*

39 *Ibid.* For an interesting American case involving a paparazzo who made a career of photographing Jacqueline Kennedy Onassis and her children in public places and whose intrusions were enjoined by the courts, see *Galella* v. *Onassis*, 487 F.2d 986 (2nd Cir. 1973); *Galella* v. *Onassis*, 533 F.Supp. 1076 (S.D.N.Y. 1982). Galella entered the children's private school and bribed service personnel to be kept apprised of family's movements. He was fined $120,000, but the fine was suspended when Galella agreed to pay Onassis $10,000 in legal fees and to promise never again to photograph her. For further discussion on this case and anti-paparazzi laws in the United States, see R. A. Smolla, "Privacy and the First Amendment right to gather news", *George Washington Law Review*, 67 (1999): 1106–1116, 1123.

suicide;[40] at the same time, suicide cases of youth and children have been reported, sometimes in an irresponsible manner that might provoke the thought of suicide in the minds of vulnerable young people.[41] If the children's conduct is conceived as news story, then children will also be photographed.

Children who take part in wars and other hostilities often appear in the media. For instance, Palestinian children who throw stones at armed soldiers are photographed, and with good reason. The public should know that children are in the frontline, fighting with stones against armed men. Such photos inform the public of the Palestinian determination, of the balance of power between the two sides, of the sensitivity (or lack thereof) that both sides to the conflict show regarding the use of children in the battlefield. The media love David versus Goliath stories, and in such instances one photo is better than a thousand words. Furthermore, the children *want* to be shown; their parents, on the whole, encourage them to risk their lives, and the Palestinian leaders who orchestrate the hostile events are quite eager to have such photos taken and published. A photo showing a child throwing stones at Israeli tank serves both Palestinian propaganda and the national interest. You may argue that the children are abused politically and are subjected to a system of cynical manipulation that is working against their basic interests not to be harmed. Still, the media have a vested interest in covering the story and showing their pictures.

The most recent controversy that relates to Diana, more than six years after her death, took place in the United States when CBS broadcast photos of the princess as she lay dying after the car accident. It was the first time a major media outlet had published pictures of the injured princess. Although photographs taken of Diana in the wreckage of her limousine a few minutes after it crashed on 31 August 1997 have been known to exist for years – and were presented to national newspapers in

---

40 L. Tevet, "Prevention kits to fight teenage suicides", *Haaretz* (Israeli daily) (4 June 2004); News release, "Rock and Dhaliwal announce funding for cross-Canada tour to prevent youth suicide", *Health Canada* (15 September 2000), at www.hc-sc.gc.ca.

41 See R. Chesshyre, "Why another young man took his life", the *Daily Mail* (6 November 2001); M. Woolf, "Doctors get help to spot suicidal young men", the *Independent* (21 March 1999), p. 4. On the impact of the media especially on young people, see R. D. Goldney, "The media and suicide: a cautionary view", *Crisis*, 22(4) (2001): 173–175; M. S. Gould, "Suicide and the media", *Science of Suicide Prevention – Annals of NY Academy of Sciences*, 932 (2001): 200–224; J. Pirkis and R. Warwick Blood, "Suicide and the media", *Crisis*, 33(4) (2001): 146–154; Editorial, "Influences of the media on suicide", *British Medical Journal*, 325 (2002):1374–1375; D. L. Zahl and K. Hawton, "Media influences on suicidal behaviour: an interview study of young people", *Behavioural and Cognitive Psychotherapy*, 32 (2004): 189–198; R. Cohen-Almagor, *Speech, Media and Ethics*, Chapter 6.

Britain on the day after the accident – none has been openly published, though they may be found on websites. The network insisted that the pictures – which showed an unconscious Diana being treated by a doctor as she lay slumped in the back of a car in the Alma road tunnel in Paris – were not graphic or exploitative.[42]

The British press expressed front-page outrage, while Prime Minister Tony Blair called the broadcast of the grainy black-and-white images "distasteful". Still, a spokeswoman for the CBC proclaimed: "We stand by the report".[43] I question the wisdom of that decision. For me, it is appalling not only that CBS' *48 Hours Investigates* decided to show these private photos of the Princess in her very last moments, but also that they did not acknowledge their mistake. It seems that the CBS network, anxious to outdo its commercial rival NBC (which one month earlier had broadcast tapes recorded by the princess about her married life and confrontation with her rival Camilla Parker-Bowles in the early 1990s), decided to show those photos in order not to fail behind their competitor. NBC had achieved viewing figures of seventeen million with its two-part programme.[44]

Les Editions Vice-Versa Inc. v. Aubry

So far, Quebec is the only province in Canada to have enacted quasi-constitutional provisions[45] about privacy for the private sector.[46] The Quebec Charter of Human Rights and Freedoms holds that "Every person has a right to the safeguard of his dignity, honour and reputation", and that "Every person has a right to respect for his private life".[47] In turn, Chapter III of the *Civil Code of Quebec [1994]* holds:

42　"Anger at CBS use of Diana photos", www.CBSnews.com (22 April 2004).

43　*Ibid.*

44　S. Bates and G. Younge, "US viewers to see pictures of dying Diana", the *Guardian* (22 April 2004), http://www.guardian.co.uk/uk_news/story/ 0,3604,1200277,00.html.

45　Rod Macdonald notes in his comments on this chapter that it is accurate to characterize these two documents as "quasi" constitutional because, even though they take precedence over other legislation unless excluded, they are in no way entrenched as against subsequent Parliamentary activity.

46　The first legislation designed to protect privacy in the private sector was enacted in 1993 with the *Loi de protection des renseignements personnels dans le secteur privé*. For examination of existing legislation, international laws and initiatives relating to privacy and freedom of information as well as voluntary codes of conduct for Canadian businesses to ensure the safety of their clients' personal information see Media Awareness Network: Media Issues – Privacy, http://www.media-awareness.ca; http://www.screen.com/mnet/eng/issues/ priv/laws/laws.htm.

47　Quebec Charter of Human Rights and Freedoms, R.S.Q., c C-12.

35. Every person has a right to the respect of his reputation and privacy. No one may invade the privacy of a person without the consent of the person or his heirs unless authorized by law.

36. The following acts, in particular, may be considered as invasions of the privacy of a person:

1   entering or taking anything in his dwelling;
2   intentionally intercepting or using his private communications;
3   appropriating or using his image or voice while he is in private premises;
4   keeping his private life under observation by any means;
5   using his name, image, likeness or voice for a purpose other than the legitimate information of the public;
6   using his correspondence, manuscripts or other personal documents.[48]

Both statutory provisions were invoked in *Les Editions Vice-Versa Inc.* v. *Aubry*.[49] The case was concerned with Ms Aubry, who brought an action in civil liability against a photographer and the publisher of a magazine dedicated to the arts, for taking and publishing a photograph showing her, then aged seventeen, sitting on the steps of a building. The photograph was published without her knowledge and consent. *Les Editions Vice-Versa* sold 722 copies, and the photograph was drawn to Aubry's attention by a friend who bought a copy of the magazine. Aubry sued for damages in the amount of $10,000, half as compensatory damages and the other half as exemplary damages. The trial judge recognized that the unauthorized publication constituted a fault, and ordered the *Vice Versa* magazine to pay her $2,000.[50] The majority of the Court of Appeal for Quebec affirmed this decision, saying that the unauthorized publication of the photograph constituted an encroachment of her anonymity, which is an essential element of the right to privacy. Even in the absence of bad faith,

48 Chapter III, "Respect of reputation and privacy", *Civil Code of Quebec [1994]*. It is argued that the Quebec privacy laws are too broad, having unintended effects on historical research because they impede the development of access to archival holdings. See J. Burgess, "The right to privacy in the private sector: what is at stake for historians and historical research", Canadian Historical Association Newsletter (Summer 1998): 26–27. Rod Macdonald disagrees with this position, saying that no Quebec decision that he is familiar with has ever used the Charter to impede archival access. Privacy laws respecting the disclosure of nominative information do impede certain kinds of contemporary research, but that is not history.
49 *Les Editions Vice-Versa Inc.* v. *Aubry* [1998] 1 S.C.R. 591.
50 Eric Barendt notes that in libel, damages are presumed to flow from publication of defamatory statement, and the same principle perhaps should apply to invasion of privacy. Rod Macdonald adds that there is also an analogy to the tort of trespass to land, where you don't have to prove actual damages to recover.

the dissemination of Aubry's photo without her knowledge and consent was wrongful. The magazine then appealed to the Supreme Court.

The majority of the Court, *per* L'Heureux-Dube, Gonthier, Cory, Iacobucci and Bastarache J. J., dismissed the appeal, holding that the right to one's image is an element of the right to privacy under the Quebec Charter. One of the purposes of the Charter is to protect people from compulsion or restraint. If the purpose of the right to privacy is to protect a sphere of individual autonomy, it must include the ability to control the use made of one's image. In this case, the appellants were liable *a priori*, because the photograph was published when the respondent was identifiable. The artistic expression of the photograph could not justify the infringement of the right to privacy it entails. The majority of the Court maintained:

> An artist's right to publish his or her work is not absolute and cannot include the right to infringe, without any justification, a fundamental right of the subject whose image appears in the work. It has not been shown that the public's interest in seeing this photograph is predominant. In these circumstances, the respondent's right to protection of her image is more important than the appellant's right to publish the photograph of the respondent without first obtaining her permission.[51]

The minority of the Court, *per* Lamer C. J. and Major J., accepted the appeal. Lamer C. J. wrote that mere infringement of a right or freedom does not necessarily constitute fault. This case cannot be resolved "merely by relying upon the respondent's right to her image or the appellant's freedom of expression; the rights concerned must also be balanced".[52] Lamer C. J. acknowledged that the right to privacy "certainly includes a person's right to his or her image", and he agreed with his colleagues that the right to one's image is "primarily a personality right, an interest of an extrapatrimonial nature".[53] Consequently, the dissemination of Aubry's

---

51 *Les Editions Vice-Versa Inc.* v. *Aubry* [1998] 1 S.C.R. 591. In his comments on this essay, Joe Magnet argues that *Aubry* is a property type case following a well-established property law doctrine in Canada as to the ownership of the image. Magnet thinks that the privacy aspect in this case, while interesting, is a side issue. Rod Macdonald elucidates the point by referring to a famous 1973 court case involving a comedian, Yvon Deschamps, whose image was used by an automobile company in an advertising campaign without his consent. Cf. judgment of Rothman J. in *Deschamps* v. *Renault Motors* (1977), Cahiers de droit 937 (Quebec Superior Court, 1972). For a brief description of the case, see J. E. C. Brierley *et al.*, *Quebec Civil Law* (Toronto: Emond Montgomery, 1993), pp. 156–157.

52 *Les Editions Vice-Versa Inc.* v. *Aubry* [1998] 1 S.C.R. 591, at 604.

53 *Ibid.*, at 605.

image constituted a violation of her privacy and of her right to her image. Lamer C. J. said that "in the abstract" to appropriate another person's image without her consent to include in a publication constitutes a fault. He also thought, and I concur, that a reasonable person would have been more diligent and would at least have tried to obtain Aubry's consent to publish her photograph. Furthermore, Lamer C. J. said, and I agree, that the appellant did not do everything necessary to avoid infringing the respondent's rights.[54]

So why did Lamer C. J. and Major J. accept the appeal? Because, in their opinion, there was no evidence of damage. The respondent's statement that her classmates laughed at her did not in itself constitute sufficient evidence of prejudice, as it did not provide any information about how she felt. Nor was there any evidence that Ms Aubry had become a "well-known figure", or that the instant proceedings and the media coverage they received increased her notoriety.

I side with the majority in this case. The majority court also resorted to the balancing method, weighing, one against the other, the right to information and the right to privacy. They acknowledged that a photograph of a single person can be "socially useful" because it serves to illustrate a theme. But that does not make it acceptable if it infringes the right to privacy. The majority did not consider it appropriate to adopt the notion of "socially useful" for the purposes of legal analysis. The artistic expression of the photograph, which was alleged to illustrate contemporary urban life, could not justify the infringement of the right to privacy it entailed.[55] As the justices said, since the right to one's image is included in the right to respect for one's private life, it is manifest that every person possesses a protected right to her image. This right arises when the subject is recognizable. Consequently there is a breach of the person's right to her image, and therefore fault when the image is published without permission.

In the name of the public's right to know, magazines should not send photographers onto the streets to take photos of people to decorate their covers without the people's consent. It is one thing to publish a group photograph, when none of the faces is identifiable, and quite another to zoom in on one person and circulate his or her photo. It is one thing to take a photo of a public place where people are depicted *en masse*, and quite another to use a public place as a background for showing a person who is the true subject of the photo. Justices L'Heureux-Dube and Bastarache noted these differences in their judgment. They wrote that public interest prevails when a person appears in an incidental manner in a photograph of a public place. An image taken then can be regarded as an anonymous element of the scenery, even if it is technically possible to

54 *Ibid.*, at 605.
55 *Ibid.*, at 618.

identify certain individuals. Since "the unforeseen observer's attention will normally be directed elsewhere, the person 'snapped without warning' cannot complain. The same is true of a person in a group photographed in a public place."[56] Such a person cannot object to the photograph's publication if he or she is not the principal subject.

In the case at hand, I do not see any reasonable justification or legitimate purpose in invading anyone's privacy without that person's consent. The arguments for freedom of expression and freedom of information in this context are simply not persuasive. No harm would have been done if the photo of Aubry had been replaced with a photograph of another young, beautiful woman who had consented, or even was paid, to appear on the magazine's cover. There are enough women who would be delighted to do it. The issue of prior knowledge and consent of those photographed are not immaterial. Of course, if consent is granted then no problem arises. However, people should enjoy the freedom to remain anonymous if they so desire. For Aubry, this was not an abstract issue but a concrete contravention of her right to privacy. Her friends and peers at school teased her, and she felt humiliated. I side with the majority, who thought that a teenager's damages are the logical, direct and immediate consequence of the fault, and that Aubry's sensitivity and the possibility of "being teased by her friends are eminently foreseeable".[57]

Furthermore, young Ms Aubry did not do anything that is of public interest. She was just sitting in a shopping mall. There is a difference between a person who does something of public significance and a person who, say, strolls the streets. If a man, for instance, is polishing a new public sign or symbol, then that person, who is totally unknown to the public, might be photographed not because of who he is, but rather because of what he does. In December 2001, newspapers around the world showed workers cleaning and shining the Euro signs, posted in order to promote awareness of the new currency in Europe. Even in this instance I would urge photographers to ask the workers whether they mind that their faces will be shown in public newspapers while they polish the Euro yellow shining signposts.

Chief Justice Lamer argued in his dissent that Aubry's statement that "people laughed at me" did not in itself constitute sufficient evidence of damage, because it did not provide any information about how she felt.[58] But surely no one would like to be laughed at. This statement shows that Aubry felt that the dissemination of her photo was wrong, and that it did cause her moral prejudice. As the Court of Quebec held, to learn through teasing by friends that her picture had been published in a prestigious magazine without her even knowing that her picture had been taken and

---

56 *Ibid.*, at 617.
57 *Ibid.*, at 620.
58 *Les Editions Vice-Versa Inc.* v. *Aubry*, para. 32 in Lamer C. J.'s judgment.

without her authorization merits compensation for the humiliation, discomfort and upset suffered as a result of the invasion of Aubry's privacy. The majority of the Supreme Court adopted this opinion, thinking that there was sufficient evidence regarding the discomfort and upset felt by Aubry as a result of the publication.[59]

Another issue concerns the commercial aspect of this affair. The magazine used Aubry's photo because its editors thought that her looks would attract people's eye and the magazine's sales would be increased. It was therefore only fair that Aubry should have her share in the business.

Cases like that of Aubry are different from cases involving public officials and celebrities. Diana had no say in having her photograph taken and then published when she was appearing in public places. This was a price she had to pay for being "Queen of Hearts", and one should bear in mind that Diana had gained a lot in terms of publicity and fame. She protested against the taking of unauthorized private photos. Thus, consent is required to publish photos of ordinary citizens that are taken in both public and in private spheres, whereas where public officials and celebrities are concerned, consent is required only when photos are taken in the private sphere.

Conclusion

Individuals should be allowed to define themselves and to decide how much of themselves to reveal or to conceal in different situations. As Jeffrey Rosen notes, privacy is a form of opacity, and opacity has its values. We need more shades, more blinds and more virtual curtains. By respecting the boundaries between public and private speech and conduct, a liberal state can provide sanctuary from the invasions of privacy that are inevitable in social interactions.[60] The right of ordinary people to the protection of their image is more important than the right to publish photographs without obtaining permission.

Quite recently in the UK there have been some interesting cases regarding the scope of privacy under the UK Human Rights Act 1998 (which came into effect on 2 October 2000), which incorporates the

---

59 *Les Editions Vice-Versa Inc.* v. *Aubry*, paras. 614–618, 621–622 of the majority judgment delivered by L'Heureux-Dube and Bastarache J. J. Rod Macdonald added that the flaw in Lamer's argument is that it implicitly denies that the invasion of privacy can be a tort *per se*, like trespass to land. Macdonald maintained that to date the private law has been much more solicitous of protecting the integrity of land than it has the integrity of people.

60 J. Rosen, *The Unwanted Gaze* (New York: Random House, 2000), pp. 223–224. For a critique of this book, see R. C. Post, "Three concepts of privacy", *Georgetown Law Review*, 89 (2001): 2087–2098.

European Convention on Human Rights (ECHR).[61] Article 8 of the ECHR has been used in a whole range of contexts, from phone tapping[62] to the use of medical records in court; from the rights of children whose parents have been deported to the right to have records altered.[63] It was held in a case brought by the ex-news reader Anna Ford, who was photographed through a long-distance lens on a beach, that she had no reasonable expectation of privacy in a public place, and that if she wore a bikini in public she could not object to being photographed.[64]

An American case that comes to mind is that of *De Gregorio* v. *CBS*.[65] It

61 Article 8 of the *ECHR* provides: "1. Everyone has the right to respect for his private and family life, his home and his correspondence. 2. There shall be no interference by a public authority with the exercise of this right except such as is in accordance with the law and is necessary in a democratic society in the interests of national security, public safety or the economic well-being of the country, for the prevention of disorder or crime, for the protection of health or morals, or for the protection of the rights and freedoms of others."

62 The leading US court decision on phone tapping is *Bartnicki* et al. v. *Vopper*, 532 U.S. 514 (2001), where the Supreme Court ruled in a six–three decision that someone cannot be held liable in court for publishing or broadcasting the illegally intercepted contents of telephone calls or other electronic communications. Breyer, J., joined by O'Connor, J., concurring, argued that (a) the radio broadcasters had acted lawfully up to the time of final public disclosure, and (b) the information publicized involved a matter of unusual public concern. Breyer further expressed the view that the Supreme Court's holding did not imply a significantly broader constitutional immunity for the media, and ought not to be extended beyond the circumstances presented in the case at hand. Rehnquist, Ch. J., joined by Scalia and Thomas, J. J., dissenting, expressed the view that the Supreme Court's decision diminished the purposes of the First Amendment by chilling the speech of millions who relied upon electronic technology to communicate each day.

63 M. J. Beloff, "Politicians and the press", in J. Beatson and Y. Cripps (eds), *Freedom of Expression and Freedom of Information*, p. 82.

64 I am grateful to Geoffrey Marshall for this piece of information. For further discussion on privacy and English law, see Sir Brian Neill, "Privacy: a challenge for the next century", in B. S. Markesinis (ed.), *Protecting Privacy* (Oxford: Oxford University Press, 1999), pp. 1–28. See also *Naomi Campbell v Mirror Group Newspapers Ltd*, where it was held that, in order for the media to conform with Art. 8 of the *European Convention on Human Rights*, they should respect information about aspects or details of the private lives of celebrities and public figures that they legitimately chose to keep private, certainly "sensitive personal data" under the 1998 Act, unless there was an overriding public interest duty to publish consistent with Art. 10(2) of the Convention. Striking the balance between Art. 8 and Art. 10 of the Convention and having full regard to s.12(4) of the 1998 Act, the court held that Campbell was entitled to £3,500 remedy of damages for breach of confidence after the paper revealed her treatment for drug addiction. Cf. *Campbell v Mirror* [2002] EWHC 499 (QB) QBD (Morland J.) 27/3/2002. http://www.cs.mdx.ac.uk/staffpages/cgeorge/PrivacyIssues.doc.

65 *Carl De Gregorio* v. *CBS Inc.*, 473 N.Y.S.2d 922, Supreme Court of New York (14 March 1984).

concerned a news broadcast entitled "Couples in love in New York", which showed briefly the plaintiff, a married man, walking hand-in-hand with an unmarried female co-worker on a city street. When De Gregorio noticed that he was being filmed he demanded that the TV crew destroy the film, advising the production manager that he was married and that his female friend was engaged to be married. Therefore, it would not "look good" to have a film of them holding hands shown on television. The manager ignored his plea, a five-second segment of the plaintiff and his friend was included in the footage, and subsequently De Gregorio sued CBS alleging invasion of privacy, intentional infliction of emotional distress, *prima facie* tort, and defamation.

The court ruled that plaintiff's five-second appearance on the broadcast without speaking or being identified by name was merely an incidental use and, thus, could not form the basis for liability under the civil rights statute; the fact that the defendant may have earned a profit from the broadcast did not alter its right to depict matters of public interest. Moreover, since there was no false representation in the broadcast, constitutional principles of freedom of the press precluded any redress for the film clip.[66]

As a matter of law, the court judgment may have been the right one. However, the behavior of the TV crew was ethically flawed. The broadcast included numerous shots of couples walking down Fifth Avenue holding hands, romantically walking through Central Park, or embracing in other public places. Upon the explicit request of De Gregorio not to include him in the film, the film manager should have complied with the request. There was enough material without this specific scene. Furthermore, showing the plaintiff and his friend was not a crucial news item. It was no news at all. In the name of free speech, free press and the public's right to know, the CBS crew had no qualms in potentially harming two individuals for no good cause or reason. The couple should have been left alone to settle their own affairs, as well as their affairs with their respective partners, in private, away from the public eye.

The two fundamental background rights underlining every democracy are respect for others and not harming others.[67] They should not be held secondary to considerations of profit and personal prestige of journalists and newspapers. Media freedom does not entail, nor does it protect, the taking of unlimited measures designed to increase the sales of a newspaper or promote the ratings for certain broadcasts.

Journalists should see people as ends and not as means – a Kantian

---

66 *Ibid.*
67 R. Dworkin, "Liberalism", in *A Matter of Principle* (Oxford: Clarendon Press, 1985), pp. 181–204; *idem, Taking Rights Seriously* (London: Duckworth, 1976); R. Cohen-Almagor, "Between neutrality and perfectionism", *Canadian Journal of Law & Jurisprudence*, VII(2) (1994): 217–236.

deontological approach.[68] When reporting in the name of the people's right to know, media professionals should be careful not to cause unjustified harm to others. These instances should be distinguished from incidents where the harm is justified. For instance, when a person acts corruptly, and there is evidence to prove it, the media are allowed, and even obliged, to look into the issue and bring it to public scrutiny. This is what is meant when calling the media "the watchdog of democracy".[69]

68 See I. Kant, *Foundations of the Metaphysics of Morals* (Indianapolis: Bobbs-Merrill Educational Publishers, 1969). For further discussion, see J. Raz, *Value, Respect, and Attachment* (Cambridge: Cambridge University Press, 2001), esp. pp. 140–151.

69 For further discussion on privacy, see Privacy Commissioner, *1997–98 Annual Report* (Ottawa, Ont., 1998); J. Black, B. Steele and R. Barney, *Doing Ethics in Journalism* (Boston: Allyn and Bacon, 1995), pp. 181–196; J. Jarvis Thomson, "The right to privacy", *Philosophy & Public Affairs*, 4(4) (1975): 295–314; C. Cumming and C. McKercher, *The Canadian Reporter* (Toronto: Harcourt Brace, 1994), pp. 387–390; P. Meyer, *Ethical Journalism* (New York: Longman, 1987), pp. 77–93; K. Sanders, *Ethics and Journalism, op. cit.*, pp. 77–92. See also http://strategis.ic.gc.ca/privacy. For a useful discussion on privacy at home, at work, in court, and in cyberspace, see J. Rosen, *The Unwanted Gaze, op. cit.*

4   Offense to sensibilities: part I

What is freedom of expression? Without the freedom to offend, it ceases to exist.

Salman Rushdie

Introduction

This and the following chapter discuss the issue of offense to sensibilities as possible grounds for limiting freedom of expression. This issue is constantly brought to the public agenda as, for example, in the recent limitation imposed in Israel on the playing of Richard Wagner's music by Israeli orchestras. The proposed thesis is as follows: the Offense to Sensibilities Argument will take precedence over free expression only in cases where profound and direct damage is inflicted upon the sensibilities of individuals or a target group under circumstances in which the individuals or target group cannot avoid being subject to the offensive expression. In every case, it is incumbent upon us to examine the content of the expression, the manner of the expression, the speaker's intentions, and the circumstances. Psychologists should be consulted concerning the severity of each offense.

The study has three parts. The first is a concise introduction to the theme of limits to free expression. The second deals with Israeli law and, more specifically, with the landmark court cases in which the issue of offense to the sensibilities of a given group was raised. The third part, articulated in Chapter 5, deals with the visits of the quasi-fascist member of Knesset Meir Kahane to Arab villages, and serves as a case in point when the Offense to Sensibilities Argument may provide justified grounds for limiting free expression.

Debatable expressions

Just as there is a need to set boundaries to free action, so there is a need to set boundaries to free expression.[1] Several costly categories of expression are excluded from the scope of tolerance and the protection of the Free Speech Principle.[2] These categories include purposefully made false statements of facts such as libel, defamation or fraud;[3] incitement;[4] expressions that threaten state security; hard pornography that makes use of minors and animals, and that involves rape;[5] copyright violations; and, to a lesser extent "fighting words"[6] and commercial speech (liberals believe in the free market of products, but many of them are not willing to have these freely promoted in the marketplace of ideas).[7] Also, certain symbolic

---

1 For discussion on the distinction between freedom of action and freedom of expression, see T. I. Emerson, *Toward a General Theory of the First Amendment* (New York: Random House, 1966); *idem, The System of Freedom of Expression* (New York: Random House, 1970); E. J. Eberle, "Hate speech, offensive speech, and public discourse in America", *Wake Forest Law Review*, 29 (1994), 1135, at 1193–1204.

2 For discussion regarding boundaries to free expression, see M. Glass, "Antiracism and unlimited freedom of speech: an untenable dualism", *Canadian Journal of Philosophy*, VIII (1978): 559–575; R. Amdur, "Harm, offense, and the limits of liberty", *Harvard Law Review*, 98 (1985): 1946–1959; K. Greenawalt, *Speech, Crime and the Uses of Language* (New York: Oxford University Press, 1989); S. Lee, *The Cost of Free Speech* (London: Faber and Faber, 1990); S. J. Heyman (ed.), *Controversies in Constitutional Law: Hate Speech and the Constitution* (New York and London: Garland Publishing Inc., 1996) and "Righting the balance: an inquiry into the foundations and limits of freedom of expression", *Boston University Law Review*, 78 (1998): 1275.

3 Cf. *Zauderer* v. *Office of Disciplinary Counsel*, 471 U.S. 626, 105 S.Ct. 2265, 85 L.Ed.2d 652 (1985); *Gertz* v. *Robert Welch, Inc.*, 418 U.S. 323, 94 S.Ct. 2997, 41 L.Ed.2d 789 (1974); *Beauharnais* v. *Illinois*, 343 U.S. 250, 72 S.Ct. 725, 96 L.Ed. 919 (1952). For further discussion on defamation in England and the United States, see Y. Akdeniz and H. Rogers, "Defamation on the Internet", in Y. Akdeniz, C. Walker and D. Wall (eds), *The Internet, Law and Society* (Harlow: Pearson Education Ltd, 2000), pp. 294–316.

4 *Brandenburg* v. *Ohio*, 395 U.S. 444, 89 S.Ct. 1827, 23 L.Ed.2d 430 (1969).

5 Cf. *New York* v. *Ferber*, 458 U.S. 747, 102 S.Ct. 3348, 73 L.Ed.2d 1113 (1982).

6 Cf. *Chaplinsky* v. *New Hampshire* 315 U.S. 568 (1942); *State of Nebraska* v. *Broadstone*, 233 Neb. 595, 447 N.W.2d 30 (20 October 1989); *State of Nebraska* v. *Groves*, 219 Neb. 382, 363 N.W.2d 507 (1 March 1985); *Jordan* v. *Burgoyne* [1963] 2 QB 744 (DC). See also K. Greenawalt, *Fighting Words: Individuals, Communities, and Liberties of Speech* (Princeton: Princeton University Press, 1995). Eric Barendt notes in his comments on this chapter that the fighting words doctrine has been reduced almost to vanishing point. Indeed, the doctrine now applies only in situations where there is a clear-and-present danger of a violent physical reaction in the concerned audience to such words.

7 For further discussion, see *Valentine* v. *Chrestensen* 316 U.S. 52 (1942); Justice Blackman in *Virginia State Board of Pharmacy* et al. v. *Virginia Citizens Consumer Council, Inc.*, et al. 425 U.S. 748 (1976). See also Justice Cheshin in High Court of Justice (H.C.) 606/93, *Kidum* v. *Broadcasting Authority*, P.D. (*Piskei Din*, Judg-

speeches conceived to be particularly hurtful are not always protected (in the United States, a man was convicted during the Vietnam war for burning draft cards).[8] In addition, words that incite for an uprising or for a violent revolution are controversial, outside the scope of the Free Speech Principle.[9]

Here I wish to focus on one category of debatable expression. The question is whether offense to sensibilities can serve as valid grounds for restricting free speech. This issue is complicated and troublesome and has many variations, from causing discomfort, through the causing of nervousness, feelings of disgust, insult or humiliation, violation of normative codes of culture and good taste, to causing psychological offense morally on a par with physical harm.[10] The elusiveness of the issue has caused jurists to throw away the proverbial baby with the bathwater, thereby failing to give it adequate attention. It is not enough to argue for protecting even the most offensive speech without ample discussion and clarification of the relevant criteria that we should ponder. Sweeping generalizations are not the answer for complicated questions.[11] This essay attempts to deal with the baby, focusing on the types of expression that hurt sensibilities.

Most cases in which the expression "offense to sensibilities" is used do not involve the type of behavior that causes emotional incapacity, a sort of assault on the person's sensibilities.[12] The reference here is to offense to sensibilities as possible grounds for restricting free expression only when it is an expression that might cause severe damage. The task of definition is truly problematic because of the difficulty in assessing emotional and psychological offense. At the same time, we acknowledge that certain expressions under certain circumstances might hurt no less than physical harm. An irreversible offense to the sensibilities of a person, which brings that person to a state of shock or constant dejection, is arguably more harmful than injury to one's arm or leg, or irreversible damage to one's kidneys.

ments, official publication of the judgments of the Israeli Supreme Court) 48 (2), 8, at 27–30; T. M. Scanlon, *The Difficulty of Tolerance* (Cambridge: Cambridge University Press, 2003), esp. Chapter 8.
8 *U.S.* v. *O'Brien* 391 U.S. 367 (1968). For a general discussion, see M. B. Nimmer, "The meaning of symbolic speech under the First Amendment", *UCLA Law Review*, 21 (1973): 29–62.
9 R. H. Bork, "Neutral principles and some First Amendment problems", *Indiana Law Journal*, 47(1) (1971): 1–35.
10 A. Ellis, "Offense and the liberal conception of the law", *Philosophy & Public Affairs*, 13(1) (1984): 7.
11 See, for instance, the unsatisfactory discussion of E. J. Cleary, "Silence coerced by law: a look at recent national and international efforts to silence offensive expression", *Washington and Lee Law Review*, 52 (1995): 1667.
12 See D. Statman, "Offense to religious sensibilities", in M. Mautner, A. Sagie, and R. Shamir (eds), *Multiculturalism in the Democratic and Jewish State* (Tel Aviv: Ramot, 1998), p. 136 (Hebrew).

While a person can live without a limb or a kidney, one might lose the taste for life if the offense to sensibilities is devastating and irreversible. In extreme cases, it can cause the victims to lose their human dignity. Thus, we must not avoid discussion on the Offense to Sensibilities Argument, but rather invest more efforts to set defensible criteria for restriction. Instead of being discouraged from the outset, we must make greater, more rigorous attempts to find sensible solutions.

It must be reiterated that offenses causing people mere discomfort are not of concern here. People are offended by almost everything. The intention is not to prohibit anything that might cause offense to anybody's sensibilities. For instance, a white woman holding hands with a black man might offend racists. Alternatively, a girl shouting commands might disturb the peace of mind of male misogynists, or someone who is homophobic might claim deep hurt by the mere suggestion of homosexuals as equal to others. Should we come to their assistance?

The definitive answer is "No". The discussion is about outrages or wounds to basic human dignity. People who adopt discriminatory ideologies and ideas, such as racism, are exploiting democratic mechanisms for the purpose of hurting others. The racist's and misogynist's so-called "offenses" lack normative power because their origins are morally deficient. The Offense to Sensibilities Argument is designed to promote the values that underlie liberal democracy – respect for others and not harming others – rather than to assist those who wish to undermine them.[13]

Thus, the first question is: will every offense to the sensibilities bring us to limit free expression? Clearly, we must shake off the neutral cloak, which holds that we must not discriminate between different conceptions of the good. There is good in the world; there is also evil in the world. The yardstick that guides our considerations is a moral one. Some opinions do not coincide with the moral rationale at the base of liberal democracy. Some forms of speech are pronounced with the aim of causing harm to others.

The second question to ask is: what is the extent of the offenses to be prohibited? Only those expressions that might cause the individual or the target group a profound offense, one that is real and deep, so much so as

---

13 Cf. J. S. Mill, *Utilitarianism, Liberty, and Representative Government* (London: J. M. Dent & Sons, 1948), Everyman's Edition; I. Kant, *Foundations of the Metaphysics of Morals*, trans: L. White Beck, with critical essays (Indianapolis: Bobbs-Merrill Educational Publishers, 1969); R. Dworkin, *Taking Rights Seriously* (London: Duckworth, 1977), and *A Matter of Principle* (Oxford: Clarendon Press, 1985); R. Cohen-Almagor, *Boundaries of Liberty and Tolerance; Speech, Media and Ethics: The Limits of Free Expression*. For further discussion on respect for people, see J. Raz, *Value, Respect, and Attachment* (Cambridge: Cambridge University Press, 2001), esp. pp. 124–139, 158–175.

to shatter the emotional structure of the victims, will be prohibited.[14] The offense should be so severe that it could be considered morally on a par with physical harm.

This brings us to the third question: is it possible to avoid exposure to the offense? If it is possible to avoid exposure to the offense at a minimal cost that brings about only a certain amount of discomfort, then the problematic expression should be protected. However, if we are dealing with an expression that the target group could not avoid, then there is room to consider whether the problematic expression should be excluded from the protection of the Free Speech Principle. In this sense, democracy would be obligated to restrict it. For example, it is justified to prohibit indecent advertisements on public boards in ultra-orthodox neighborhoods (such as B'nei Brak and Mea Shearim in Israel, or the Satmer and Chabad communities in New York). I will develop this argument further when analyzing the visits of Member of Parliament Meir Kahane to Arab villages immediately after his election to the Knesset in 1984.

The fourth and last question relates to the authority that will estimate the extent of the offense. We are dealing with a controversial and difficult issue to assess. Should we leave such a tangled problem of assessing the extent of offense to courts alone? Are justices the appropriate authority for assessing offense to the sensibilities, which has more to do with the framework of mind and human psyche? Here, justices are encouraged to ask the advice of psychologists who, despite the deficiencies of their profession, still seem to be better equipped than other professionals to assess offenses to the sensibilities. Surely, the decision should remain in the hands of justices, but they should not hesitate to turn to the advice of experts in order to gain a more comprehensive picture of the issue. Psychologists can shed a different light and provide justices with additional tools for assessment, analysis, and critique.

Let me proceed by examining how the Israel High Court of Justice has treated the issue of offense to sensibilities and how much weight has been given to such offense in limiting free expression. Obviously, I am examining the argument as it relates to limiting free expression, not *free action*. This is why court cases such as *Miteral* (possible offense to sensibilities of

---

14 Of relevance is the new British Protection from Harassment Act, section 7, which speaks in terms of causing alarm and distress. Although the Act was designed mainly against potential action by stalkers and such, it is being used in all sorts of disputes and the courts appear to accept that harassment can be brought about by speech. There has to be a repeated course of action, and it is a defense to show that one's allegedly harassing actions are reasonable. Geoffrey Marshall contended in his comments that it will presumably be possible to argue that it is reasonable to exercise one's free speech right under the Human Rights Act, and the courts will have to find criteria for balancing free expression where it alarms or distresses.

the religious public once the import of meat is privatized, thus enabling the extended import of non-Kosher meat to Israel)[15] and *Horev* (closing a major road in Jerusalem, Bar-Ilan, so as not to offend religious emotions and their way of life)[16] are not included in the framework of this discussion. Space will not allow me to examine *all* the petitions that have been brought before the High Court to limit free expression on the grounds of offense to sensibilities. The overview will, nevertheless, examine the major court decisions from the establishment of the state of Israel in 1948 until the present, outlining trends and developments in thinking.

Court cases

The German language offends the public's sensibilities

One of the first occasions on which the Offense to Sensibilities Argument was raised in Israel was in *Forum Film* v. *Censorship Council of Films and Plays*,[17] in 1960. The issue at hand was a pro-Israeli documentary film, entitled *Paradise in the Desert*, which was distributed with German commentary. At that time in Israel there was a significant public whose feelings were hurt when the soundtrack was in German. The Censorship Council stipulated that the commentary should be in Hebrew, not in German. Its claim was that "a film about Israel should not be presented in German" (p. 612 of the court judgment).

The court, in a short judgment written by Justice Moshe Zilberg, held that the Council represents different sectors of society. If it contends that German commentary is not appropriate for the content of the film, then the court is not willing to counter this decision and deem it unreasonable. Interestingly, the justices did not find it appropriate to examine and inspect the film itself. As Justice Zilberg noted, "we do not know exactly what is the content of this film" (p. 612). That is, the court made its decision without watching the film and without knowing its precise content. This serves as strong testimony to the power of censorship at that time.

In justifying the decision, Justice Zilberg said, "it is not appropriate and not in good taste that the commentary and explanations in it be given in the German language" (p. 613). Supporters of the decision would argue that this statement should be understood in its historical context – that is,

---

15 H.C. 3872/93 *Miteral Inc. v The Prime Minister and Minister of Religions*, P.D. 47 (5), 491. See also A. Kasher, "Offense to sensibilities and the public good in the Jewish Democratic State: philosophical comments on *Miteral*", *Law and Governing*, 2(1) (1994): 289–302 (Hebrew).

16 H.C. 5016/96, 5025/96, 5434/96 *Lior Horev and Others* v. *Minister of Transportation and Others* (Jerusalem, April 1997), esp. President Barak's opinion.

17 H.C. 260/60 *Forum Film* v. *Censorship Council of Films and Plays*, P.D. 15 (1), 611.

not long after the Holocaust. Liberals, on the other hand, would say that this was a harsh decision because it did not deal with a captive audience.[18] The public who were offended by the German language needed only to refrain from watching the film. Furthermore, it was quite farfetched to argue that the public might be offended merely by the knowledge that others were watching a film accompanied by German commentary.

Offense to public sensibilities (especially the Christian)

Twelve years later, in 1972, Amos Keinan's play *Friends Talk About Jesus*[19] was brought before the courts instead of the theater stage. Again, the argument of offense to sensibilities was raised in order to prohibit free expression, and again freedom of expression was overturned by illiberal use of the offense argument.

The Censorship Council did not permit the showing of the play because its content offended and scorned religious sensibilities in general, and Christian religious sensibilities in particular. The play included shameful and obscene expressions toward God, Jesus, and his mother, Mary. In one of the play's episodes, the crucified figure appeared as a picture in an art collection that was for sale with "nails coming apart". An old man who offered the picture for sale told an interested woman that "there was once a customer who was masturbating on it". The woman replied: "Mister, you excite me" (p. 813 of the opinion). It was further claimed that the play offended the sensibilities of most secular people, who respected the religious sensibilities of others and felt disgusted by the vulgar language. In addition, the play offended the sensibilities of bereaved parents who had lost their children in wars and hostilities (p. 815).

Amos Keinan, the playwright, petitioned the High Court of Justice. Justice Moshe Landau acknowledged that the play inflicted severe offense on Christian religious sensibilities (p. 813). In this regard, he mentioned article 149 of the Criminal Law (1936), which holds that "any person who publicizes any picture, painting, writing, or figure that might or is intended to desecrate religious emotions or faith of others ... will be accused of misdemeanor and be liable for one-year imprisonment" (p. 814). The play also referred to the Holocaust in a disgusting, offensive manner (p. 816). Justice Landau said: "It is not the subjective motive of the person who publicized the expression that is determinant for this article, but the impression that the publications are likely to arouse in the

18 On captive audience limitation on public discourse, see *Erznoznik* v. *City of Jacksonville* 422 U.S. 205, 209 (1975): restrictions on free speech are upheld when the degree of captivity makes it impractical for the unwilling viewer to avoid exposure.
19 H.C. 351/72 *Amos Keinan* v. *Censorship Council of Films and Plays*, P.D. 26 (2), 811–817.

heart of religious believers" (p. 815). Here, the offense to sensibilities overrides the Free Speech Principle:

> Even a playwright is not exempt from the obligation not to grossly hurt another's religious sensibilities. This obligation results directly from the obligation for reciprocal tolerance among free citizens holding different views, without which no democratic society as pluralistic as ours can exist. This obligation is so important that even the basic principle of freedom to express opinions must regress before it.

Justice Landau added that throughout the play, the use of certain words indicated dullness of sensibility and incredible rudeness. He called the play "a disgusting mixture of the desecration of the Christian faith and vulgarity" (p. 815).

Justice Moshe Etzioni agreed with his colleague. He wrote that after reading the play, there was no doubt in his mind that the Censorship Council's considerations were completely reasonable. The concern was not about offending a particularly sensitive group of people, but rather about inflicting offense on the public at large, both religious and secular. Quoting from another opinion of his (H.C. 124/70), he proposed the following test: "When we speak, for example, of offending the sensibilities of a religious public by using a word that has religious association, the appropriate test is the opinion and sensitivity of the majority, or of a considerable part of the public, not the polar opinions of an extreme minority" (p. 817).[20]

This test, however, raises the following question: why is offense to the sensibilities of a large public more substantial than offense to the sensibilities of a small public? Is the test utilitarian in essence? The scale used here to define a certain expression (in this case, a satire) as a prohibited offense to religious sensibilities is the emotions of the ones who are hurt. It is not at all taken into account that those who consider themselves offended by certain expressions can easily remain outside the theater. The court apparently sees itself as a protector of the public even when this public has the capability of protecting itself at a reasonable cost – by avoiding exposure to the slanderous and hurtful play.

The play, we may agree, is particularly vulgar, filled with blasphemy and obscenities that mock the said commercialization and kitsch of the church symbols. Thus, we may argue that the value of the expression in the play is very low. One may argue that a person who resorts to so many obscenities is lacking the ability to crystallize his own thoughts and express himself

20 H.C. 124/70 *Shemesh and Others* v. *the Company Registrar*, V 25 (1), 506 in which it was determined that there was no basis to prohibit the name of "West Wall Films" company despite the fact that it offended public sensibilities. See also D. Statman, "Offense to religious sensibilities", *op. cit.*, p. 180.

clearly. However, Amos Keinan is a talented writer who had previously demonstrated his ability to write good plays. He himself is aware that blasphemy tends to overshadow complex messages, and it is not clear that he wanted such a reaction. A play that is based on blasphemy testifies first and foremost to the shallowness of the author's message, and it undermines the understanding of complex messages. Therefore, showing a blasphemous and obscene play arguably harms the reputation of the playwright more than it harms the audience. Perhaps it is simply best to let the market forces determine the outcome. I would like to think that a play that includes no content other than vulgarity will attract limited audience and thus will not survive for long on the stage. The public can distinguish between a quality play and a shallow one and will be able to "vote with their feet". Prohibiting the showing of the play might do it service by arousing curiosity – as it is said, forbidden fruit tastes sweetest.

Offense to sensibilities of Holocaust survivors

A concern that is no less charged than religious emotions is that of the Holocaust, as addressed by the court in the case of *Noah Films* in 1975.[21] At issue in this case was *The Night Porter*, a fictional film that takes place in part during the Holocaust and includes vulgar erotic scenes. The Censorship Council initially granted permission to show the film, but retracted its decision once screening began. The reason given for this reversal was that "appeals were brought before the Council by various viewers, including Holocaust survivors, that the movie offended the sensibilities of the Jewish public" (p. 769) and might provoke, as the State Attorney noted, "unpleasant associations" among some Holocaust survivors (p. 770).

The court accepted the petition of Noah Films and permitted the screening of the movie – not so much because of the importance placed on free speech considerations, but due more to procedural considerations. Justice Alfred Witkon asserted that "the censorship institution is not favorable among us" (p. 762) and that providing permission is not something that "we give today, take tomorrow" (p. 762). Nevertheless, Witkon maintained that his opinion should not be interpreted as an outright rejection of the censorship institution. Abolishing censorship is a matter for the legislator, not for the courts (p. 763).

Justice Witkon further argued that the film was not problematic. Films about the Holocaust had been permitted for screening in the past. The content of the film carried anti-Nazi messages, and lacked any justification or forgiveness for "that sinful regime" (p. 672). It did include bold erotic scenes, but no one had requested that the film be banned because of its

21 H.C. 549/75 *Noah Films Inc, v. Censorship Council of Films and Plays*, P.D. 30 (1), 757.

pornographic content. Undisputedly, the film was a creative piece of a high standard, accepted worldwide.

Justice Meir Shamgar postulated an argument of procedural "natural justice" (p. 765) to overrule the Censorship Council's decision. Due to the fact that the license for showing the film was revoked without providing the petitioners with an opportunity to present their claims, the decision must be overruled. The petitioners had invested money and taken care of all the necessary arrangements to show the film. The harm involved in interfering with its business was thus especially significant here. As such, the upholding of procedural justice considerations relieved the court from examining the Council's reasons for censorship (p. 766).

President Shimon Agranat proposed a similar rationale, emphasizing two criteria for overruling the Censorship Council's decision: (1) the fact that the petitioners were not given an opportunity to present their claims, and (2) the problems entailed in retroactively curtailing the showing of a film following the inconsistency among Council members (pp. 766–771). The court decided that the prohibition of the film screening after it had been approved was invalid and illegal.

In this case, free expression was protected not because of its importance, but because the screening of the film was first approved and then annulled. This verdict, despite its liberal outcome, did not serve as an important anchor for the Free Speech Principle. Indeed, six years later, in 1981, the High Court of Justice found itself in a similar situation in the case of *Yaki Yosha*. Here too, the Censorship Council approved freedom of expression in art and then retracted its decision. However, whereas the judges in *Noah Films* considered the change of heart in a negative light, in *Yosha* the change in the ruling was accepted with understanding.

Offense to the sensibilities of bereaved families

An additional public whose sensibilities the court was requested to protect was the community of bereaved families. The *Yosha* case involved *The Vulture*, a fictional film with a harsh view of the commercialization of victims of Israeli wars. The film was initially given approval for screening, but after ᵣeceiving sharp criticism the Deputy Defense Minister approached the Minister of Interior Affairs, who in turn contacted the Censorship Council. Following this intervention by the Ministry of Defense, the Council then demanded that cuts be made in the film.[22] The High Court of Justice justified the request in the name of offense to sensibilities. It is plausible that because the petition was made this time by such a "sacred" institution as the Ministry of Defense, procedural justifications were not put forth to protect freedom of expression.

---

22 H.C. 243/81 *Yaki Yosha* v. *Censorship Council of Films and Plays*, P.D. 35 (3), 421.

Justice Landau, who wrote the Court judgment, opined that the Council decided to disallow the film *not* because of public pressure, but upon the independent decision of its members: "They noticed the public reaction, but the decision was theirs; each person based it on his or her own view and conscience" (p. 425). With all due respect, I disagree. The film earned a second review because of the critiques. Justice Landau contended that the bereavement of the families of those who died in Israel's wars was an extremely sensitive topic. If there were many who were deeply hurt by the way in which commemoration was presented in this film, then these people should be worthy of special tolerance and consideration. In his attempt to balance the feelings of the bereaved families against free expression, Landau explained, "the care we should treat their emotions is balanced against the feelings of disgust from any form of censorship" (p. 425). Accordingly, Landau did not find sufficient reason to contradict the Council's ruling, and the High Court of Justice confirmed the decision to cut several scenes from the film.

The Court was highly considerate of families who saw themselves hurt by the content of the film, and it belittled the emotions of other bereaved families that might have considered its screening of importance. Justice Landau mentioned that a member of a bereaved family came before the Council arguing that the film did not hurt the sensibilities of some families of those who had died in wars. Also mentioned were letters from bereaved families who supported the screening of the film (p. 423). That is to say, we are not dealing with a homogeneous public of bereaved families, but rather with a heterogeneous, non-cohesive community. Nevertheless, the Court decided to focus on those who considered themselves offended by the film, and diminished the importance of the feelings of other families who identified with the film's critique of the commercialization of bereavement. Again, the offense argument was utilized in an illiberal fashion.

Offense to public sensibilities and public order considerations

Five years later, in 1986, we witnessed a breakthrough in the Court as it pursued a liberal line of thinking. The case at hand, *Laor*, dealt with a play entitled *Efraim Returns to the Army*.[23] The Censorship Council refused its showing because it allegedly distorted reality was incitatory, and promoted a negative attitude toward the state by arousing disgust and contempt for the Israel Defense Forces (IDF) in general and the military presence in the occupied territories in particular. Last but not least, the play was considered to be offensive to the sensibilities. It was argued, *inter alia*, that the military was described in a distorted way by comparing it to the Nazi regime (p. 421).

---

23 H.C. 14/86 *Laor* v. *Censorship Council of Films and Plays*, P.D. 41 (1), 421.

Of all these reasons the Court examined the second, namely the inciting nature of the play. Yet Justice Aharon Barak assimilated the third reason in the second by his broader definition of the term "public order". Barak explained that it was within the Council's authority to deny the approval of the play if it thought that its showing might be harmful to public order. The definition of "public order" encompassed considerations of harm to state security, democratic government, public safety, morality, religious sensibilities, a person's good name, and due process of law (p. 430). Justice Barak explained that the "public order" test was consequential. The questions were not whether the play was of an adequate artistic quality, or whether it adequately portrayed the reality that it claimed to represent. Instead, "The question is whether the showing of the play – with whatever truth or distortions are included in it – might harm public order" (pp. 430–431).

That is, Justice Barak rejected the first reason proposed for not showing the play, namely, its distorting quality. For him, two issues were under examination: (1) What was the intensity of harm to public order that justified the Council's involvement? (2) What was the probability that the showing of the play might harm public order? Because "public order" became an all-encompassing term that also included considerations of morality and offense to religious sensibilities, the question regarding the intensity of offending religious sensibilities that might justify the involvement of the Council was lost in the overall discussion.

Barak argued that the Council did not have the complete and final say in the matter. As with every authority, the authority of the Censorship Council must be limited. Accordingly, it was authorized to prohibit plays that harmed public order, but it must balance public order considerations against freedom of expression. Free expression could be overturned only when the extent of harm to public order was grave and serious, and when there was *probability* that the harm would take place. Thus, the appropriate equation for balance is that in which "freedom of expression retreats only where the harm to public order is great, serious, and severe" (p. 435). This test is still accepted by the High Court of Justice.

As for this play, the Council did not prove that there was a probability of incitement and agitation. At most, there was a "bad tendency" for incitement and agitation (p. 440), and the Court did not consider the bad tendency test as a legitimate one.[24] Furthermore, it was determined that

---

24 See the harsh commentary of Justice Haim Cohen on the bad tendency test in Election Appeal 1/65 *Yeredor* v. *Chairperson of the Central Committee for the Elections to the Sixth Knesset*, P.D. 19 (3), 365. The roots of the test lie in *Gitlow* v. *N.Y.* 268 U.S.657 (1925). See also Justice Barak in H.C. 399/85 *Kahane* v. *Board of Directors of the Broadcasting Authority*, P.D. 41 (3), 255, at 308, and Election Appeal 3/84 2/84 *Moshe Neiman and Uri Avneri* v. *Chairperson of the Central Committee for the Elections to the Eleventh Knesset*, P.D 39 (2), 225, esp. at 311–318.

the distortion of facts and the offense to sensibilities did not in themselves justify the disqualification of the play. As Justice Barak stated:

> Only in exceptional cases can one establish that the showing of a theater play – designed naturally for a limited and sometimes selected audience that willingly comes to view the play – will result in a probability of harming public order. Mostly, it is difficult to establish more than a mere concern.

In a democratic society, this concern is not considered enough to undermine freedom of expression (p. 440).

Despite the all-encompassing definition of the term "public order", Justice Barak was still required to discuss the argument of the offense to the public's sensibilities. He devoted only one paragraph (no. 24) to this issue. In his opinion, democracy recognizes that there are offensive and hurtful expressions, but it does not prohibit them *tout court*. Barak wrote (p. 441):

> We live in a democratic society, in which this burning of the heart (resulting from offensive speech) is the heart of democracy. Its power is not in the recognition that I have the right to listen to pleasantries. Its power lies in recognizing that the other has the right to express opinions that are unpleasant and hurtful.

Barak added that the offense to sensibilities was present in only one part of the play and was repeated only a small number of times. Therefore, it did not appear that the offense to sensibilities was so severe as to justify undermining free expression (p. 441).

For Justice Barak, the appropriate consideration was not offense to sensibilities, but harm to public order. Ultimately, this verdict does not adequately address the question of whether grave and profound offense to the public's sensibilities may serve as grounds for limiting free expression. Focusing on maintaining public order – a rationale that is widely accepted, especially in England,[25] Germany,[26] and Israel – brought about a desirable liberal outcome, but at the same time left us with ambiguity as to the validity of the offense argument. Using this rationale, it is difficult to project what Barak's stand would be in a case where free expression is not

---

25 Cf. Feldman, *Civil Liberties and Human Rights in England and Wales* (Oxford: Clarendon Press, 1993); G. Marshall, "The control of civil disorder in Britain", in R. Cohen-Almagor (ed.), *Challenges to Democracy* (London: Ashgate, 2000), pp. 189–202; D. Feldman, "Protest and tolerance: legal values and the control of public-order policing", in R. Cohen-Almagor (ed.), *Liberal Democracy and the Limits of Tolerance:* (Ann Arbor: University of Michigan Press, 2000), pp. 43–69.

26 G. H. Fox and G. Nolte, "Intolerant democracies", *Harvard International Law Journal*, 36(1) (1995): 1–70; D. P. Kommers, *The Constitutional Jurisprudence of the Federal Republic of Germany* (Durham: Duke University Press, 1997).

limited to the theater, when there is severe offense to the public's sensibilities, but where the offense does not result in disturbing public order. Also unclear is what offense to sensibilities would be considered by Barak as severe enough to justify restricting free expression. It is clear that one part of a play does not in itself constitute a severe offense, but this does not provide a sufficient criterion for examining the validity of the offense argument.

Justices Shoshana Netanyahu and Yaacov Maltz joined the opinion of their colleague Barak. As Justice Netanyahu contended: "If this artistic climate persists, there might be room to consider the extent of harm to public order as well as the probability test" (p. 443). Thus far, however, she considered Israeli democracy as strong enough to stage "a corrupt and worthless play as the one before us" (p. 444). Likewise, Justice Maltz wrote that according to the probability test, there were insufficient grounds for the Council to conclude that the danger was severe and immediate (p. 445).

In sum, the court had very few qualms about interfering in the deliberations of an appointed body designed to critique plays, and practically took its place. Indeed, following this judgment, the responsibilities of the Council were effectively restricted to reviewing films only.

Offense to the sensibilities of the Christian public

In 1988, The Censorship Council prohibited the screening of the film *The Last Temptation of Christ* because it might offend the religious sensibilities of the Christian public, and also because its screening might cause damage to the state of Israel.[27] Here again, the court was required to protect the sensibilities of religious minorities, this time in relation to a film based on Nikos Kazantzakis's book and directed by Martin Scorsese. The film describes the life of Jesus since his days in Jerusalem, with his performance of miracle acts and preaching of Christianity, until his crucifixion. Jesus is portrayed in a human fashion, and is even depicted in erotic scenes. Various Christian organizations pressured the Council to prohibit its screening. A member of the Council, David Glass, who supported the decision to ban the film, said, "The side effect of the Council's decision will be arousing great sympathy among millions of Christians. In a time when we lack sympathy such a decision is good."[28]

Justices Shamgar, Barak, Levine, Goldberg, and Maltz unanimously accepted the petition of Universal City Studios, arguing that there was no room for the Council's decision. President of the Supreme Court

27 H.C. 806/88 *Universal City Studios* v. *Censorship Council of Films and Plays*, P.D. 43 (2), 22.
28 R. Shahor, "The Criminal Code is enough to deal with film producers or presenters", *Maariv* (Israeli daily) (19 October 1988), pp. 9–10.

Shamgar noted that the Council's authority was limited to prohibiting films that undermined public order and should not be used to prohibit films only because they offended morals. As Shamgar noted:

> we would not consider it correct today to disallow a play or a film only because it "offends good taste" . . . The court does not have the pretension of educating viewers of theaters or films in accordance with the justices' artistic taste. Such cultural paternalism is foreign to our conception.

Shamgar elucidated that "only a serious, considerable, and extreme offense can provide grounds for interfering with free expression" (p. 28), and that the test we must adopt is the *probability* test; we must balance public order considerations against free expression. Only "an extreme, gross and deep offense" (p. 30) would justify restricting free expression, providing that the likelihood of offense is great. In this case, there was not sufficient evidence for severe and exaggerated offense to the sensibilities of Christians, especially in light of the fact that the film has been screened throughout the Christian world (p. 32).

Justice Barak agreed with President Shamgar and added that cinematic expression was included in the framework of the Free Speech Principle; that the offense to religious sensibilities was a legitimate consideration contradicting free expression; that the film may have offended religious emotions, but not in a manner that exceeded the allowed boundaries or involved a captive audience. Those who did not watch the film were not exposed to the offense: "The offense we must take into consideration is that of a person who does not view the film, as no one is forced to view it". Accordingly, the offense perpetrated by the film failed to meet the requirements of being severe, serious and grave (p. 39). After all, any deviant opinion or criticism might annoy a certain group: "Those who hold contradictory beliefs might offend another's sensibilities. This is a reality of life that a democratic society must accept" (p. 39). We therefore must distinguish between a true offense to sensibilities and mere intolerance.

Justice Eliezer Goldberg joined his colleagues, holding that there was no reason to apply the probability test because the preceding test that examines the extent of offense (intensity and scope) was not fulfilled. In his opinion, the screening of the film would indeed offend a certain sector of the public who held Christian beliefs, a consideration that he did not take lightly. Still, the offense was not so severe as to damage the human spirit (p. 42).

Justice Yaacov Maltz found in the entire film only one segment that seemed to constitute extreme offense to Christian sensibilities. He considered whether he should make the screening of the film conditional on the censoring of that segment. On second thought, however, he concluded that the segment was insufficient to endanger public safety or public order (p. 42).

As in the *Laor* case, the focus of *Universal* was not on balancing offense to sensibilities against free expression, but on balancing public order considerations against free expression. As in *Laor*, freedom of expression won. Again, I have no argument with the judicial outcome, with which I agree, but the discussion on the offense argument was quite disappointing. It is unclear as to when the offense to sensibilities in itself may provide a criterion for limiting free speech, if at all. In this case, the Court was willing to consider the offense argument as a possible ground for limiting expression only if it endangered public order. Again, the Court evaded discussion on the validity of this problematic argument by itself, assimilating it instead into public order considerations.

Following *Universal*, retired Justice Haim Cohen was asked about the functioning of the Censorship Council. To this he replied:

> I think the Council should be annulled, because its functioning is not consistent with free speech. If someone thinks that a film includes slander or pictures of abomination or offense to religious sensibilities, then producers or presenters could be prosecuted under the criminal law, and this is sufficient. We punish retroactively and not proactively.[29]

Offense to sensibilities of the American government

A year later, in 1989, the court was required to address the sensibilities of the American government in the case of *Indor* v. *Mayor of Jerusalem*.[30] The petitioner had built a Yasser Arafat doll in front of the American consulate in Jerusalem. The doll was holding US flags in protest against the alleged close relationship between the PLO and the United States. The consulate requested the removal of the flags from the doll, claiming that this conduct was offensive to the US government as well as to the American flag. The Jerusalem Municipality was asked to exercise its authority according to the bylaw that enabled the mayor to prohibit a public display if it might offend the public's emotions.[31] This bylaw is a harsh example of the authority that the municipality possesses to ban expressions without set criteria. It provides an opportunity for arbitrary decisions based on the mayor's biased considerations. After all, the mayor is a political figure with a clear orientation and bias.

29 R. Shahor, "The Criminal Code is enough to deal with film producers or presenters", *Maariv* (19 October 1988), p. 10.
30 H.C. 953/89 *Indor* v. *Mayor of Jerusalem*, P.D. 45 (4), 683.
31 Jerusalem Bylaw (Sign-posts) 1980, sect. 21.

Justice Barak argued that the attachment of flags to the doll was not enough to create the probability of a severe, serious, and grave harm to the public's safety. This was a symbolic act that indeed might have offended some people, but there was no escape from suffering such offenses in a democratic and pluralistic society. As Barak wrote (p. 690):

> If every offense to sensibilities will allow restricting freedom of expression, we will end up without free expression. Thus, a democratic society that wants to protect both freedom of expression and public emotions must set an "endurance level" ... Only an offense to the public's sensibilities that passes this level will justify restricting free expression.

Indor's use of the American flag did not exceed the "endurance level" that was allowed in Israeli society. The symbolic speech under consideration was an offense that a democratic regime must "absorb" without proactively restricting free expression. Barak maintained that it was unclear as to whether the mayor had assessed the likelihood and severity of the offense to the public's well-being and emotions (p. 695).

Indeed, it is difficult to speak of the "sensibilities of the American government". It is a misplaced compliment to suggest that any government has emotions. Governments usually operate according to interests. Therefore, Barak's balancing method has no place here. It is difficult to assume that the Jerusalem Municipality meant to protect the emotions of a foreign government. The Court exhibited too much tolerance in regard to this absurd petition by allowing it the right to be heard.

People are entitled – some would say encouraged – to express opinions that might offend governments. If we accept the rationale of offending governments' sensibilities, then we should not screen *Midnight Express* for fear that it might offend the Turkish government;[32] we should not criticize the Argentinian government for its dictatorship; we should not discuss the murder of IRA members in Gibraltar to avoid embarrassing the British government; we should refrain from mentioning how the Swiss authorities treated Jews seeking asylum during World War II to avoid placing the Swiss government in an uncomfortable position, etc. It is most interesting that in *Indor*, the consulate in question is that of the United States, a country that cherishes the First Amendment to the constitution and generally exhibits the most tolerant attitude in the world toward freedom

---

32 In this regard, see *Federation of Turkish-American Societies Inc.* v. *American Broadcasting Companies* 620 F. Supp. 56 (10 October 1985), where the plaintiff sought an injunction against further distribution or showing of *Midnight Express* in the United States, and the award of compensatory and punitive damages. The court dismissed the complaint, holding that the First Amendment protects the offensive utterances fully as much as it protects the bland or uncontroversial.

of expression.[33] Yet the famous American tolerance was quite limited in this case.

Offense to radio listeners

An especially interesting case is that of *Kidum*.[34] "Kidum" is a company that deals with training students for the matriculation and psychometric exams, which condition acceptance to higher education institutions. It filed a petition against the Broadcasting General Director's decision to prohibit an advertisement, "Go Excel", on the grounds that the advertisement did not meet the required standards of "good taste". It was argued that the advertisement's slogan provoked a connotation of the curse "go fuck yourself" in Hebrew.[35] Article 6 in the regulations of the Broadcasting Authority says:

> The General Director of the Broadcasting Authority maintains the right not to broadcast any commercial that he thinks includes an offense to good taste or contradicts public order or harms the public.
> (p. 13 of the opinion)

It was maintained that the advertisement's slogan offended the sensibilities of listeners, who constituted a captive audience. Commercials are broadcast within various shows, or immediately before and after shows. Listeners who were interested in the show could not avoid hearing the vulgar commercial (p. 8).

In a two to one decision, the High Court accepted Kidum's petition. Justice Dalia Dorner argued that the respondents violated the petitioner's free speech. After declaring that freedom of speech held a special place with a superlative right, hence allowing for restrictions only in specific instances, Justice Dorner addressed the question whether commercial speech was protected under the Free Speech Principle, and what degree of protection was extended. In her opinion, commercial speech was part and parcel of free expression, and a component of free trade that characterizes a democratic society (paragraph 8, pp. 10–11).

Yet not all rationales of free expression apply to commercial expressions. Thus, for instance, the rationale of maintaining democratic procedures was deemed to apply only partially to commercial expressions. Therefore, it was possible to prohibit commercial expression that offended public emotions, provided that the extent of the offense was severe and considerable enough to justify such restriction (p. 14).

---

33 For discussion on the American position on a similar case, see *Boos* v. *Barry* 485 U.S. 312 (1988), 108 S.Ct. 1157.
34 H.C. 606/93 *Kidum (1981)* v. *Broadcasting Authority*, P.D. 48 (2), 8.
35 "Go excel" in Hebrew is *"lech titztayen"*. "Go fuck yourself" is *"lech tizdayen"*.

Justice Dorner was not convinced that the slogan "Go Excel" seriously offended public sensibilities. In her view, other no less offensive commercial items were broadcast on the airwaves. Furthermore, the petitioner's commercial clip that included the same slogan had been shown on television, and no petition had been made to stop it. Dorner remained unconvinced by the captive audience argument, thinking quite rightly that those who might be offended could avoid the offensive expression (paragraph 15, p. 16). The Broadcasting Authority did not adequately consider Kidum's right to free speech, and consequently failed to balance this right against the possible offense to listeners' sensibilities (paragraph 21, p. 17).

I would like to comment on one assertion made by Justice Dorner. While quoting President Shimon Agranat in the landmark *Kol Ha'am* decision,[36] she argued that freedom of expression enjoys the status of a "superlative right" (p. 9). I have always wondered about this sweeping wording of President Agranat that became popular in the language of the courts. In reality, free speech does not enjoy such a supreme status when it comes into conflict with other important values. Indeed, it should not categorically enjoy this supreme status. Freedom of expression is a most important right in democracies. Yet it has boundaries, and often there are times when the courts are required to balance it against other rights and liberties.

If we were to seriously hold that free speech has a *superlative* status from the outset, then free expression would have enjoyed a preferred position[37] as compared to other rights and liberties, and this is not the case. The balance is based on the particular circumstances, the conflicting values under consideration, and the damages and benefits that are expected. It would be right to abandon the sweeping and imprecise statement about "a superlative right" and instead use more precise descriptive language: freedom of expression is a basic value in modern Western democracies, an important and primal one that constitutes an essential layer of democracy. Yet we should not say that it enjoys *a priori* precedence in comparison to other values, such as the right to privacy, the right to personal security, the right to fair trial or the need to maintain state security. At times, balancing the scales may favor the conflicting interests, making it imperative that we examine each case separately.[38]

The most interesting and, I may say, strange opinion is that of Justice Mishael Cheshin. Cheshin opened his commentary with the famous

---

36 H.C. 73/53 87/53 *Kol Ha'am* v. *Minister of the Interior*, P.D. 7, 871.
37 On the American preferred position doctrine, see Justice Stone in *United States* v. *Carolene Products Co.* 304 U.S. 144 (1938), fn. 4. See also *Jones* v. *Opelika* 316 U.S. 584 (1942); *Murdock* v. *Pennsylvania* 319 U.S. 105 (1943); *Thomas* v. *Collins* 323 U.S. 516 (1945).
38 For further discussion, see A. Barak, "Freedom of expression and its limitations", in R. Cohen-Almagor (ed.), *Challenges to Democracy*, pp. 167–188.

quotation from Voltaire: "I disapprove of what you say but I will defend to the death your right to say it", and then maintained:

> Were we to ask Voltaire if he would protect till death the right of the petitioner to express the slogan "Go Excel" – while explaining to him well that we are dealing with freedom of expression – then he would have asked us to repeat the question: so far this is from what Voltaire intended.
>
> (paragraph 1, p. 18)

At this stage the reader might think that Justice Cheshin agreed with his colleague Dorner, but this was not the case. As becomes clear later in the judgment, Justice Cheshin actually supported the Broadcasting General Director's decision to curtail the advertisement of Kidum. Would Voltaire have agreed with Justice Cheshin's opinion? I doubt it.

Cheshin continued the explanation of his illiberal position by attempting to convince us that we were *not* actually dealing here with free expression. In his opinion, using the Free Speech Principle to protect the broadcasting of the slogan "Go Excel" was nothing but an inappropriate use of the notions of liberty (p. 19). He considered the issue at hand to be minor, insignificant, "truly trivial", not something worthy of an appeal to the High Court of Justice. If his opinion were to be heard, said Cheshin, "we would dismiss this appeal and free our time to deal with true liberties" (p. 19).

If we were indeed dealing with such a minor "truly trivial" issue, and assuming that Voltaire would have allowed it under the Free Speech Principle, then why would Cheshin not allow it as well? How does he align his illiberal outcome with his liberal Voltairian introduction? Cheshin contends that commercial advertisement is included within the boundaries of free expression, but that it has relatively inferior status and hence can be restricted by "limitations that one will not introduce when 'classical' freedom of expression is concerned" (p. 27). Thus, thinks the reader, this is where the heart of the matter lies: commercial expression is different from non-commercial expression. This is an accepted position by many jurists in the United States[39] and in other parts of the world,[40] especially as

39 A central judgment on this topic is *Central Hudson Gas & Electric Corp.* v. *Public Service Comm 'n*, 447 U.S. 557 (1980), esp. 566. See also W. Van Alystne, "Remembering Melville Nimmer: some cautionary notes on commercial speech", *UCLA Law Review*, 43 (1996), 1635; R. Post, "The constitutional status of commercial speech", The Nimmer Lecture, UCLA (2000), published in *UCLA Law Review*, 48(1) (2000). For opinions that downgrade the value of commercial expression, see S. Shiffrin, "The First Amendment and economic regulation: away from a general theory of the First Amendment", *Northwest University Law Review*, 78 (1983), 1212, esp. 1223–1251; *Posadas de Puerto Rico Assoc.* v. *Tourism Co.*, 478 U.S. 328, 340 (1986); *Board of Trustees* v. *Fox*, 109 S. Ct. 3028,

one compares the appropriate immunity level afforded to political expression with that afforded to commercial expression. This is, indeed, my own position. It is generally agreed that political expression enjoys greater immunity because it concerns the public at large, whereas commercial speech is aimed to advance economic partisan interests.[41]

However, Justice Cheshin directly addresses the question of whether free expression also protects commercial advertisement, and answers in the positive. Cheshin writes, in his figurative and poetic language: "We were born free, and free we will be able to speak and sing and publicize as we please" (p. 28). Again the reader is puzzled. So what is the crux of the matter?

In paragraph 21 of his reasoning, Cheshin finally begins to detail his logic, which consists of three layers. First, expressions that are rude and vulgar, curses and "other bad things that come from the mouth" will not be afforded protection. Second, commercial advertisement may be protected under the Free Speech Principle, but as a minor player in the kingdom of free expression (p. 29). Third, esthetic considerations are appropriate to assess when deciding whether to air commercial advertisements (paragraph 23, pp. 31–32). The slogan "Go Excel" brings us, by way of association, innuendo and sound connotation directly to a popular expression of obscenity, and undoubtedly this was the intention of Kidum in order to attract young audiences. Thus, the decision to prohibit airing of the slogan was within the discretion of the Broadcasting Authority and within the law, and there were insufficient grounds for the court to interfere (paragraph 24). After all, free expression is not equivalent to lawlessness in speech, and it does not protect the intention to offend: "We should stay away from bad smells – smell of smells and smell of talking" (paragraph 27, p. 33).

Justice Cheshin testified that he found it difficult to treat the case at hand as a free speech issue (paragraph 25). However, Kidum anchored its petition on free expression rights, and to this Cheshin responded: "We

3033 (1989); R. K. L. Collins and D. M. Skover, "Commerce and communication", *Texas Law Review*, 71 (1993), 697, esp. 710–726. Dissenting opinions are expressed by Justice Brennan in *Posadas* (minority opinion) and by D. F. McGowan, "A critical analysis of commercial speech", *California Law Review*, 78 (1990): 359–448; R. A. Smolla, "Information, imagery, and the First Amendment: a case for expansive protection of commercial speech", *Texas Law Review*, 71 (1993): 777–804.

40 E. Barendt, *Freedom of Speech* (Oxford: Clarendon Press, 1987), esp. pp. 54–63; 7805/77 X *& Church of Scientology* v. *Sweden*, 16 D. & R. 68; R. A. Shiner, "Freedom of commercial expression", in W. J. Waluchow (ed.), *Free Expression* (Oxford: Clarendon Press, 1994), pp. 91–134.

41 For an extended discussion, see C. E. Baker, *Human Liberty and Freedom of Speech* (New York: Oxford University Press, 1989), pp. 194–224; R. A. Shiner, *Freedom of Commercial Expression* (Oxford: Oxford University Press, 2003).

must be careful not to fall victim to the tyranny of free expression" (p. 32). For him, this was not the right context for dealing with this trivial, minor and non-esthetic language.

It seems that Justice Cheshin was torn between his commitment to free expression and the disgust that he felt toward a specific expression, which he considered to be perverse. Clearly, he was not the least amused by the commercial trick designed to attract attention. While many would consider this slogan as a sinister wink to help mark Kidum in the minds of listeners, Cheshin was dismayed by the low level of sales promotion and thought it appropriate for the Broadcasting Authority to determine the boundaries of esthetics. Blocking his nose to avoid the bad smell brought Cheshin to block the petitioner's mouth. Many liberals would disagree, thinking that it is better to block the nose while leaving the mouth free. Indeed, the use of such slogans as "the tyranny of free expression" may be unnecessary and damaging. Considering the case at hand, this was a misplaced and exaggerated statement by a Supreme Court justice, who is often called to secure free expression in the absence of a specific law that protects this essential right.

Justice Gabriel Bach, who testified that he enjoyed reading the opinions of his two colleagues, wrote the deciding opinion. Agreeing with Cheshin, he argued that the Free Speech Principle does cover commercial speech, but at the same time commercial expressions should not be accorded the same level of protection as political, moral, social, and scientific expressions (paragraph 2, p. 37). Bach departed from Cheshin in his assessment of the importance of the case. Unlike Cheshin, he did not think that the issue was minor and trivial and therefore not worthy of consideration by the High Court of Justice. On the contrary, democratic principles are maintained by giving attention to "small" daily decisions concerning ordinary citizens and not necessarily by attending only to the "big" decisions concerning grand issues of importance (paragraph 5, p. 39).

Justice Bach opined that the correct test to apply was not the probability test of public offense, but rather a quantity test: a commercial advertisement can be prohibited if its content or manner of presentation offends good taste in a meaningful and substantial way (paragraph 6). He suggested four criteria that must be taken into account:

1   The extent to which the advertisement offends good taste. This is a question that must be observed from the viewpoint of modern, enlightened and liberal society.
2   Whether the advertisement offends the public or segments of the public. To this end, we should consider "the sensibilities of a significant minority, which does not represent a faction that is characterized by extreme opinions" (paragraph 9, p. 41). Justice Bach had reservations regarding Justice Dorner's claim that good taste, which is a com-

peting value with freedom of expression, reflects the broad acceptable consensus in society and therefore "we should not consider minorities' sensibilities". Bach rightly thought that this claim was too broad and sweeping (paragraph 7, p. 40). It can be assumed that Justice Bach would also have had reservations regarding Justice Etzioni's opinion in *Keinan*.

3   The extent of harm to the publisher as a result of refusing to air its advertisement. In this case, the expression "Go Excel" had become the symbol of Kidum and had been advertised in all of its promotional material. Hence, prohibiting its use might cause the petitioner significant damage.

4   Certain side effects, such as the presence of this same offensive expression in other or previous advertisements. The logic of proportionality leads us to conclude that if the public were regularly exposed to the same advertisement in newspapers and on television, without a public outcry or severe reaction from viewers and readers, then there would hardly be a reason to object to airing it on the radio. This consideration is related to the assessment of the offense to good taste. If the offense had been serious and shocking, then all other considerations would have been minor in comparison, but this was not the case here. According to Justice Bach, the use of "Go Excel" was nothing but a publicity gimmick that would only elicit a light smile among listeners. As such, the expression should not be disallowed (p. 42).

In suggesting these criteria, Justice Bach took the first step toward formulating the Offense to Sensibilities Argument, concealed in this case in the consideration of offending good taste, separately from public order considerations. Bach explicitly argued that when we take actions to prevent danger to state security, to public safety or to foreign relations, the probability test assessing whether the danger might materialize is an appropriate one. However, this test cannot be applied when the concern is offense to good taste caused by a certain broadcast: "The decision-maker must determine whether or not offense to good taste exists, and it is difficult to agree with the conclusion that in this case there is 'probability of offending good taste'!" (paragraph 6, p. 40, exclamation mark in the opinion).

Another criterion should be taken into consideration, namely the ability of those who might be offended by a particular slogan to avoid being exposed to it. As more options are open to the sensitive public to avoid exposure to the offensive broadcast, the easier it should be for us to approve its airing. In a reality of mass communication, with abundant radio and TV channels, cable, satellite, Internet, etc., all that people need to do is switch to another means of communication in order to avoid offensive commercials and maintain peace of mind.

Pornography that offends public sensibilities and social morals

It should be pointed out from the start that the importance of this case lies in the debate between President Barak and Justice Cheshin about the scope of judicial discretion and the appropriate extent of separation of powers. In another place I referred to this as a debate between the formalistic approach and the creative approach.[42] The issue of offense to sensibilities is secondary in this verdict.

The petition concerned a Japanese–French film called *Empire of the Senses*. The Censorship Council of Films conditioned its screening on cutting out several pornographic segments likely to cause severe offense to the public sensibilities and social morals, including the final scene.[43] The distributors of the film could not accept such a "compromise". They responded that censoring the film would undermine its overall artistic–social value within which the questionable segments should be understood. Furthermore, the Council decided and the distributors of the film agreed that *Empire of the Senses* would be limited to an adult audience only. The audience would not be captive, the public standards are geared to openness and permissiveness, and in any event, people have access to materials that include sex scenes similar to those included in the movie. The petitioners also noted that the film had been screened on cable television and no proven offense had resulted (paragraph 4 in President Barak's opinion).

The petitioners maintained that the state should refrain from interfering in the decisions of adults to view films; that the Council's decision was undemocratically paternalistic and inappropriate; that they were discriminated against by the Council, which had approved the screening of other films with hard-core sexual scenes, such as *Clockwork Orange*; and that the Council did not give enough weight to freedom of expression, especially in light of Basic Law: Human Dignity and Freedom (1992), which is said to protect free expression. The aim of the law is to protect human dignity and freedom in order to anchor the values of Israel as a Jewish democratic state.[44]

The respondents claimed in response that the film included several scenes that abased and offended human dignity, including close-up shots of the amputation of a man's penis, the severing of women's genitals, and sexual abuse of minors and elderly people. The Council opined that those scenes lacked any artistic value, and even if their artistic value was to be proven, still this value should be overridden by the profound offense to public sensibilities and social morals that might result from showing the film in its uncensored format (paragraph 5).

42 See Cohen-Almagor, *Boundaries of Liberty and Tolerance*, esp. Chapter 10.
43 H.C. 4804/94 *Station Film Company* v. *Censorship Council of Films* (decision granted on 9 January 1997).
44 Book of Statutes 1391 (25 March 1992).

In his judgment, President Barak avoided analyzing the offense argument and instead chose to speak yet again about public order. To his mind, pornographic expression could be restricted if probability exists that it might severely, seriously, and gravely harm public order (paragraph 11). Barak maintained that free expression (I believe it was more appropriate to speak specifically of artistic freedom, RCA) could be restricted if it extended beyond the standards of social tolerance and rocked the foundations of reciprocal tolerance. According to President Barak (paragraph 11):

> Such an offense can justify restricting pornographic expression when the expression might humiliate the woman and portray her as a 'sexual slave'. Such a portrayal undermines – directly and indirectly – the equal status of women in our society and encourages violence in general and violence against women in particular.

Yet Barak avoided developing a discussion about this complex issue. Instead he chose to deal with the question of whether the film was pornographic and thus lacked artistic value and sat outside the scope of tolerance, or alternatively was not pornographic and possessed artistic value. In addressing this question, Barak thought that we must consider the film as a whole. It might be that one or another part of the film would not be entitled for protection under the Free Speech Principle in one context, but would receive protection when viewed in the context of the integral artistic product: "Parts that might in and of themselves and when viewed separately be perceived as pornographic, lose this character when they are enveloped and integrated in the artistic piece or in a piece that has a different social value" (paragraph 14). This rationale was adopted from the American court cases.[45]

Barak's remaining arguments are a bit confusing. On the one hand, he wrote that the Censorship Council must decide "whether the film as a whole has an artistic value, and whether the alleged pornographic parts are necessary for the development of the plot and the message". On the other hand, Barak contended that "the Council should not become an artistic critic. It should not grade a film in determination of whether it is

---

45 In *Miller* v. *California* 413 U.S. 15 (1973), the American Supreme Court formulated its obscenity test. Three factors should be examined: whether the average person, applying "contemporary community standards", would find that the work in question, taken as a whole, appeals to prurient interest; whether the work depicts or describes, in a patently offensive way, sexual conduct specifically defined by the applicable state law; and whether the work, taken as a whole, lacks serious literary, artistic, political, or scientific value. If the answer to all three questions is positive, then the speech is considered obscene and is not protected under the First Amendment. See also *Roth* v. *U.S.* 354 U.S. 476 (1957).

of high or low artistic standard" (paragraph 15). I am sorry to say that I do not fully understand how both statements could be reconciled – that is, how the Council can decide whether a film has artistic value without becoming an artistic critic. To my mind, such a decision entails a critique. Possibly what President Barak meant to say is that despite the negative criticism of the film, the Council should still be open to other critiques contradictory to theirs and try to apply neutral criteria without letting their own tastes dictate the ultimate decision. This could be inferred from his treatment of the court's role, which – like the Council itself – is not that of an artistic critic. Barak suggested that the court should ask itself whether, based on the presented facts, the production has an artistic value even if the evaluation of value is controversial (paragraph 16).

Moving from the general to the particular, and bearing in mind that *Empire of the Senses* received many artistic rewards and the attention of some of the world's most important newspapers, it seems that the film does possess a serious artistic value negating its classification as a pornographic film. Barak contended, "where there is a reliable and serious foundation for the artistic nature of the film, it is enough to consider it as having artistic value, even if there are contrasting opinions on this matter, and even if the contrasting opinion is that of the Council members themselves" (paragraph 19).

President Barak concluded that there was no escape from overruling the Council's decision and permitting the screening of the film without the requested censorship (except for the censorship of two segments involving minors, to which the petitioners agreed), while restricting the film to adults only (paragraph 21). Indeed, restricting the age of viewers is the appropriate compromise and solution. Restriction of the film to adults above a certain age prevents its exposure to minors and gives the privilege of viewing the film to those who willingly buy a ticket. Those who might be offended by the film's pornographic and violent parts can simply remain outside the cinema.

Justice Eliyahu Matza joined the opinion of his colleague Barak in a laconic statement ("I agree"), and this is where we arrive at another intriguing opinion of Justice Cheshin. He commenced by addressing the appropriate framework for the discussion, namely a conflict between two interests: freedom of expression versus another interest that varies from one case to another and is imprecisely named "public order", "public good", "public sensitivity", and other names and nicknames that involve the public good (paragraph 2 in Cheshin's opinion). For a moment, readers may hope that Justice Cheshin would continue from where Justice Bach left us in the *Kidum* case and attend to the distinction between "public order" and "public sensibilities", but this hope is disappointed. Justice Cheshin did relate to *Kidum*, but only to emphasize his own words in that verdict by repeating Voltaire's immortal statement and explaining that what he had said about the slogan "Go Excel" applies also to *Empire of the Senses.* That is, if we were to ask Voltaire whether he would defend till death the film distributors' rights to screen it, then he would have asked us to repeat the question: so far this was from Voltaire's intention. According to Cheshin, "the imposition of meta-expressions that concern free speech on a film that some consider as pornographic – and in any case, a film that involves much sex – diminishes the importance of free expression and makes those meta-expressions worn tokens" (paragraph 4).

I think that Voltaire, while considering the cultural context in which we now live, would have defended this problematic artistic expression despite the fact that it is filled with pornography. Furthermore, this defense would not minimize the importance of free expression. Quite the opposite: the Free Speech Principle does not apply only to non-problematic expressions. Indeed, its strength stems from protecting questionable, costly, and gross expressions (see Introduction). The Principle does not cover only those expressions that are "qualitative" and "important". "Quality" and "importance" are subjective and controversial terms, and it is not the role of a judge or of any other person to evaluate them. The role of a judge in a democracy is limited here to the examination of two questions: first, whether the court has authority to interfere in the considerations of a constitutional body that was appointed to critique films, bearing in mind that by such interference the court would – for all practical matters – take the place of that body; and second, whether there are heavy enough considerations to prevent the controversial expression.

Justice Cheshin dedicated a considerable part of his discussion to the first question, and his decision was contrary to Barak's. President Barak does not flinch from juristic legislation and believes that it is within the court's authority to intervene in the considerations of constitutional bodies whenever it seems that the body in question is not operating appropriately[46] (as he did in *Laor, Universal,* and *Indor*). Justice Cheshin, on the other hand, is much more reluctant to interfere and prefers that the legislature decides the appropriate remedies. Accordingly, it is up to the legislature to determine whether the Censorship Council is an obsolete body that should be dissolved. The court should not take the Council's role into its own hands and make a laughing stock of the Council's decisions.

Justice Cheshin avoids clarifying exactly what role the Council should assume. On the one hand, he says that because of the tolerant atmosphere toward sex boutiques and massage parlors, the Council today seems to be "a last Victorian island in the sea surrounding it". Cheshin asks rhetorically (paragraph 9):

> Is the Council these days more of an anachronistic institution, a
> clumsy dinosaur walking amongst us, a creature that belongs in a

---

46 See A. Barak, *Interpretation in Law* (Jerusalem: Nevo, 1994), three volumes (Hebrew), esp. Vol. 3 concerning constitutional commentary.

different time and era? What is the value of closing the front door to the uninvited guest if that guest can enter the house easily through the back door (which is also no longer much of a back door?).

On the other hand, Cheshin does not deny social paternalism with regard to film critique. The opposite is true: "We shall remember and know that the term social paternalism does not always connote negation and is not necessarily a term of disgrace – and the question is only how far shall we go" (paragraph 10).

Cheshin is much clearer about the court's boundaries of interference. In his opinion, the Council is composed of public representatives and their opinion is what counts (paragraph 15). Cheshin admits that were he a member of the Council, then he would have approved the film without any cuts. But this is not the question: "The authority is granted to the Council by the legislature – to the Council and not to the court ... The principle of separation of powers requires us, in my opinion, not to interfere in the Council's decision" (paragraph 18).

According to Cheshin, "the work load share" between the Council and the court should be respected, and the Council's decision should not be ignored as if it did not exist. Cheshin expresses his concern that President Barak's approach might annul the Council (paragraph 29) and might be the Council's requiem (paragraph 48). Cheshin adds that the very existence of the Council is a question for the legislature to ponder, as the legislature is supposed to represent the public will. Until a change takes place in the existing law, judges should not impose on the Council norms that it does not accept (paragraph 46).

Furthermore, Cheshin objects to the test that Barak employed, examining the artistic piece "as a whole". Whereas Barak avoids judging the segments that the Council wished to cut, Cheshin does not see how one cannot examine them if one contemplates interference in the Council's decision. Cheshin doubts the application of the *Roth* test to Israeli cases.[47] This is not only due to the differences between Israeli and American reality, or because of the different status assigned to free expression in the two countries, but also because the test was created for use in the area of punitive law. Therefore, its applicability to the examination of Censorship Council considerations is questionable (paragraphs 26, 34). Accordingly, Cheshin thinks that it is possible to judge certain segments of a film and demand their removal. As evidence, Cheshin rightly contends, the film distributors themselves agreed to cut two parts that involved minors (paragraph 40). Furthermore, the Council enjoys the explicit authority to censor parts of films; therefore, the legislature anticipated the possibility that segments of films might require trimming (paragraph 30).

47 *Roth* v. *U.S.* 354 U.S. 476 (1957).

Justice Cheshin expresses surprise as to the lack of focus in Barak's opinion, and I join his astonishment. Although the issue is presented as a conflict between free expression and the offense to public sensibilities and morals, most of the discussion steers clear of the possible offense to sensibilities and morals. The test is not artistic, whether we are discussing a piece that is worthy of protection or "just" pornography, but rather a consequential test regarding the film's influence on those viewing it. Cheshin refers to "public order" and "public morals" as if they are one and the same (I believe that these two topics are different in essence, as is evident from the debate between Professor Hart and Lord Devlin regarding the place of homosexuality in society[48]), and he avoids analyzing the offense argument. His conclusion is that it is not the film's artistic value that should determine its offensiveness, but rather the outcome effects on its viewers. When we address the question of a certain film's influence on public sensibilities and morals, the artistic value is considered marginal. Adequate attention should thus be given to unfold the question of offense.

In sum, although Barak values the opinions of experts about the film's artistic merit, Cheshin does not see much importance in their opinion. He assumes that art experts and Council members have completely different considerations. Art experts are interested in art for art's sake and in general esthetic values, whereas Council members and the court are interested in the film's effects on viewers, human dignity and respect, and social morals (paragraph 37). If we were to adhere only to artistic considerations, then we would allow the inclusion of segments showing children in sexual activities because in judging the film as a whole, these segments might have artistic-esthetic merit. Furthermore, the authority to consider films has been assigned *only* to the Censorship Council by legal command. Thus, the Council should operate independently and should not delegate authority to others (paragraph 37).

The principled debate between President Barak and Justice Cheshin, who hold polar opinions about the scope of judicial intervention, reveals that Barak does not flinch from judicial intervention when it seems necessary to protect such democratic values as free speech, even if this means taking upon himself legislative roles. This is the broad judicial approach ("everything can be judged") that Barak preaches in many of his writings.[49] Cheshin, in contrast, wishes that legislative-like decisions be left for the legislature.

---

48 H. L. A. Hart, *Law, Liberty and Morality* (London: Oxford University Press, 1963); P. Devlin, *The Enforcement of Morals* (Oxford: Oxford University Press, 1965).

49 See, for example, A. Barak, *Interpretation in Law*, Vol. 1 (Jerusalem: Nevo, 1992) and "The role of the Supreme Court in democratic society", in R. Cohen-Almagor (ed.), *Basic Issues in Israeli Democracy* (Tel Aviv: Sifriat Poalim, 1999), pp. 129–141 (both in Hebrew).

When the court enters the territory of other governmental bodies, then it de-legitimizes those bodies and undermines the separation of powers, a notion that Cheshin considers crucial for the maintenance of democracy.

Now, it would be quite unwise categorically to state that one school is better than the other. Judges of the formalistic school of restrictive inter-pretation can be liberal judges if they safeguard liberal principles by their reluctance to make illiberal changes, whereas creative judges can intro-duce illiberal changes if they think that the changes supply better answers to specific problems or coincide with illiberal public demands for change. Both approaches have rationales and criticisms. On matters of free speech, however, it would be wise to recommend a middle ground.

On the one hand, too much intervention on the part of the court into legislative decisions might arouse alienation and distrust between the legislative and the judiciary branches of government. The legislature might justly feel that the court has taken upon itself excessive power, and might seek to weaken the people's trust in the judiciary. Such alienation and resentment between the legislature and the judiciary can be detri-mental to the workings of democracy. On the other hand, for partisan political considerations, the legislature might avoid addressing pressing social issues and might prefer to leave the "hot potatoes" for the judiciary. In this situation, the courts are pressed to enter into contentious realms that are better handled by public representatives.

The golden path that lies between the two approaches may be called the *creative interpretation* approach. It does not advocate that the courts take legislative roles, which might undermine separation of powers, and at the same time it allows room for creativity. Judges in states like Israel, which lack specific laws to guarantee freedom of expression, may be required to resort to creative judgments in order to protect this right. The creative approach allows room for judges to express their opinions when it seems that free expression is not receiving due protection. At the same time, there are no values that stand above the law, and no judge stands above the legislature. Judges must make fresh judgments about the rights of parties who come before them. This does not mean that judges create rights, but rather that they acknowledge them. They are authors as well as critics. They are asked to assume, insofar as possible, that the law is struc-tured by a coherent set of principles about justice, fairness, and pro-cedural due process, and then to enforce these principles anew in each case that comes before them. In this way, each case can be treated fairly and justly according to the same standards.[50]

50 I follow the law-as-integrity theory, as developed by Ronald Dworkin in his various writings and especially in *Law's Empire* (Cambridge: Harvard University Press, 1986). See also R. Dworkin, "The model of rules", *University of Chicago Law Review*, 35 (1967): 14–46; "Hard cases", *Harvard Law Review*, 88 (1975): 1057–1109; "No right answer?", *New York University Law Review*, 35 (1978): 1–32; "Natural law revisited", *University of Florida Law Review*, 35 (1982): 165–188;

Conclusion

The offense argument must be treated with caution. In all the cases reviewed here, the upholding of this argument was very problematic. In all cases where it was rejected, it was rightly rejected. Yet, as we have seen, the rejection of the argument was grounded on consequential reasoning about insufficient offense to public safety or public order. Because no probability of such offense could have been proved, freedom of expression won. The court avoided undertaking a thorough analysis of the argument's validity independent of public order considerations.

Liberal democracy puts the individual, not public order, at the center of attention. It is clear that the maintenance of public order is meant to protect the individual. Yet, we encounter a leap of logic over the individual to focus on the consequences that individuals who consider themselves offended might bring upon society. What happens to the individuals themselves? Are they not in need of protection?

My line of reasoning places the individual at the center, examining whether she or he needs protection from certain expressions because they might offend that person's emotional and spiritual system. The Offense to Sensibilities Argument in and of itself can serve as grounds for restricting freedom of expression in extreme cases when the offense is severe and the target group (individual or individuals) cannot avoid being exposed to the offense.

It is emphasized that we are dealing with an especially offensive expression that might damage the sensibilities of the individuals whom the speaker wishes to offend. In order to determine how offensive the expression is, we must examine its content and manner of expression, and the speaker's intention. As for the circumstances, these must be such that the target group cannot avoid being exposed to the expression. Following Joel Feinberg, this consideration is called "the reasonable avoidability standard".[51] The argument advanced is:

> Under the Offense to Sensibilities Argument, when the content or manner of expression is designed to cause severe psychological offense against a target group, and the objective circumstances make that group inescapably exposed to that offense, then the expression in question has to be restricted.

The example I use in Chapter 5 illustrates the Argument and applies the above criteria. It concerns the attempts of Member of Parliament Meir Kahane to visit Arab villages in Israel.

"Law's ambitions for itself", *Virginia Law Review*, 71 (1985): 173–187; see also R. Cohen-Almagor, *The Boundaries of Liberty and Tolerance*, Chapters 10–13.
51 J. Feinberg, *Offense to Others* (New York: Oxford University Press, 1985), pp. 1–26.

5   Offense to sensibilities: part II

> I want them out, out, out!!
> Meir Kahane

Introduction

In the last chapter I reiterated that offensive speech may be restricted only if the target group finds itself in an impossible no-win situation. That is to say, if the target group were to confront the offending group, on the one hand, it would be exposed to the particularly offensive expression. On the other hand, if the target group were to choose to avoid the exposure, then this would mean a victory for the opponent – viewed as an equally noxious offense by the target group. I wish to examine this argument in the context of Jewish political extremism and hatred against Arabs in Israel.

Application: Kahane's visits to Arab villages

Meir Kahane was the most extreme right-wing politician ever to be elected to Israeli parliament. His hatred and contempt for the Arabs was manifest and blunt. He openly called them "dogs", and wrote that the Arabs were "a time-bomb", "a malignant disease", and that they "multiply like fleas". Kahane urged people to induce the Arabs to leave Israel, by persuasion if possible, by coercion if necessary. According to his perspective, the non-Jew had no share in the Land of Israel. This Land belonged to the people of Israel; it was they who controlled and defined it. It was their vessel, their territory in which to create the society of Israel, the Torah society of God. The answer to Israel's political problems was to remove the Arabs of Eretz Israel from the land, to have the courage to be Jewish and sane, which meant to throw away the "needless and false burden of guilt", and to be free from the constraints of morality.[1] Kahane explained that the expulsion of the Arabs through the process of transfer would result in the moral

---

1 M. Kahane, *They Must Go* (New York: Grosset & Dunlap, 1981), p. 225; *Listen World, Listen Jew* (New York: The Institute of the Jewish Idea, 1983), p. 139.

regeneration of Israeli society and would prepare the way for acceptance of the Laws of the Torah, the halacha, as the Law of the state.[2]

Immediately after his election to the Knesset in 1984, Kahane began a series of visits to Arab villages in order to preach his Orwellian message about "emigration for peace", which he claimed would bring about a just and efficient solution to the national split in Israel. Kahane sent letters to Arab residents in order to promote the message, but did not stop at this and asked to deliver the message personally to the villages. The first visit was on 30 August 1984, to the village of Umm El Fahm. Kahane arrived with a group of people dressed in yellow shirts on which the Jewish Magen (Star of) David was drawn together with a clenched fist. The group was stopped by the police three kilometers outside the village. Kahane turned to the court to overrule the police action. However, Kahane himself cancelled the appeal on 4 July 1985, on the grounds that the issue was no longer relevant because of measures taken by the Knesset to stop the visits. In December 1984, the Knesset House Committee voted in a twelve-to-eight decision to restrict Kahane's parliamentary immunity, namely the legal provision that secures members of the Knesset free access to any public place. The restriction was intended to enable the police to prevent Kahane from entering Arab communities in which his presence might provoke a breach of the peace.[3]

The decision to restrict Kahane's immunity in order to prevent him from entering Arab villages was correct not only on grounds of disturbing the peace, but also on grounds of the Offense to Sensibilities Argument.[4] The main consideration here should be the offense that such a visit could

2 Cf. R. Cohen-Almagor, "Vigilant Jewish fundamentalism: from the JDL to Kach (or 'Shalom Jews, Shalom Dogs')", *Terrorism & Political Violence*, 4(1) (1992): 44–66. See also http://www.masada2000.org/kahane.html.

3 Cf. R. Cohen-Almagor, *The Boundaries of Liberty and Tolerance* (Gainesville: The University Press of Florida, 1994), Chapter 12.

4 There are those who would claim that these visits should be restricted because of other reasons associated with the racial character of the message that Kahane wished to deliver. As stated in Chapter 1, David Kretzmer and Justice Eliyahu Matza hold the opinion that racial expression constitutes special expression that does not deserve democracy's defense. See Eliyahu Matza's words in H.C. 2831/95 *Rabbi Ido Elba* v. *State of Israel* (24 September 1996) and H.C. 6696/96 *Benjamin Kahane* v. *State of Israel*, especially paragraph 18 of his opinion. Also, D. Kretzmer, "Freedom of speech and racism", *Cardozo Law Review*, 8 (1987): 445–513. In the United States, critical race theorists wish to ban racist hate speech on the grounds that it has a direct psychic impact on the members of targeted minority groups, and because it reinforces racist ideas in the minds of the majority, which further entrenches racism and leads to discriminatory acts. See M. J. Matsuda *et al.*, *Words that Wound: Critical Race Theory, Assaultive Speech, and the First Amendment* (Boulder: Westview Press, 1993); S. D. Gerber, "The politics of free speech", *Social Philosophy and Policy*, 21(2) (2004): 28–31; D. Jacobson, "The academic betrayal of free speech", *Social Philosophy and Policy*, 21(2) (2004): 49.

have caused to the Arabs in the village, not public order considerations, although such a danger certainly existed. The Arabs' likely hostile response should not serve as a critical consideration in this case. Expressions should not be prohibited merely because of a hostile audience.[5] It is further emphasized that here we are dealing with offense to sensibilities, not with physical offense to the Arabs, as was the case in John Stuart Mill's example of the corn dealer (see Chapter 6).[6] The Arabs were not in danger of immediate physical harm as a result of the demonstration, the goal of which was allegedly to explain to the Arabs the main points of Kahane's "emigration for peace" plan.

A close examination of the case shows that the content of Kahane's expression was extremely problematic and offensive. Kahane wished to explain to the Arabs that their place was outside of Israel, and that they had better leave now when they still could, rather than later when Kahane would "take care of them" with more drastic actions. In this context, it does not matter whether the content of the expression was true or false. The possible implications of the offensive expression that could have resulted from delivering the Kahanist message to the target group were extremely harmful.

It was not just the content of the expression that was problematic and offensive. The manner in which it was intended to be delivered also contributed to the stimulation and excitation of emotions. In his loud speeches, in his violent actions against Arabs, in his arrogant manner, and in his offensive outfits, Kahane delivered a message of threat and hatred. To a great extent, the yellow shirt with the clenched fist transmitted to the Arabs a message that resembled what the swastika conveys to Jews. Both messages communicate deep-seated hatred between the conflicting sides that cannot be overcome through the democratic means of debate and discussion, mutual tolerance, and compromise. These require reciprocity, and cannot exist or be promoted when they are accepted by only one of the sides. What compromise would be acceptable to a Nazi? Babbi Yar instead of Auschwitz? And what compromise would be acceptable to a Kahanist – transfer to Jordan instead of Lebanon as a first step? Those statements are intolerable as far the target groups are concerned. They cannot be expected to consider whether to leave or to be eliminated.

As for the speaker's intention, it is difficult to imagine that the message Kahane wished to deliver was truly intended to convince the Arab citizens of the righteousness of his ideology. Kahane did not really expect the Arabs to become convinced of the truthfulness of his messages and con-

---

5 See H.C. 153/1983 *Levy* v. *Commander of the Southern District of Israeli Police*, P.D. 38 (2), 393, 404.
6 J. S. Mill, *Utilitarianism, Liberty, and Representative Government* (London: J. M. Dent & Sons, 1948), p. 114.

sequently adopt them. Only a complete cynic could claim that Kahane was hoping that the Arabs would greet him by saying, "Ahalan and Sahalan, tomorrow we will leave our homes" – homes in which they had lived for generations, since long before Kahane's arrival in Israel in 1971. To a certain extent, the situation that Kahane wished to stage may be compared to a discussion between Nazis and Jews about the advisability of the Nazi doctrine. The Arabs could not realistically hold a debate with a person who preached to banish them or kill them. This was exactly the solution that the Nazis espoused at the beginning of the Madagascar plan, later to be replaced by the "final solution".

Kahane preached his opinions all over the country, and publicized them in a series of books and in numerous pamphlets and articles.[7] The message about the appropriate place for the Arabs was delivered via hundreds of communication channels. The visits were conducted for no other reason than to offend the public that was exposed to them directly, in a way that they could not ignore. As the Nazis who wished to strut in Skokie did not wish to create a "good environment", so Meir Kahane did not wish to create such an environment in Umm El Fahm to promote and shape the opinions of the Arab citizens.[8]

Another factor that must be examined is the circumstances. The analysis of the court cases in the previous chapter emphasized that free expression should not be restricted if the audience who might be offended by the expression can *avoid* the exposure to it. In the case at hand, Kahane's intended visits to Arab villages created a problematic and highly tense situation. The audience that was targeted by Kahane, the residents of Umm El Fahm, could not have avoided the offense. They would have found themselves in a situation where either way they would suffer: were they to choose to confront Kahane so as to say that Kahanism would not be accepted in their vicinity, then they would expose themselves to hatred, to offensive expressions, to yellow shirts and clenched fists. Alternatively, were they to choose to ignore the Kahanists coming into their village, then this might imply that they were allowing Kahanism to exist, even in an Arab village. With the latter alternative, they would have played into Kahane's hands, leaving him the stage for victory. This was an impossible

---

7 See, for instance, M. Kahane, *Listen World, Listen Jew, Uncomfortable Questions for Comfortable Jews* (Secaucus: Lyle Stuart, 1987); *The Challenge – The Chosen Land* (Jerusalem: Center for Jewish Consciousness, 1973, in Hebrew); *Forty Years* (Jerusalem, 1978, in Hebrew).

8 T. M. Scanlon, "A theory of freedom of expression", in R. Dworkin (ed.), *The Philosophy of Law* (Oxford: Oxford University Press, 1977), pp. 153–171; *idem.*, *The Difficulty of Tolerance* (Cambridge: Cambridge University Press, 2003); R. Cohen-Almagor, "Harm principle, offense principle, and hate speech", in *Speech, Media and Ethics: The Limits of Free Expression* (Houndmills and New York: Palgrave-Macmillan, 2005), pp. 3–23.

no-win situation for the residents of Umm El Fahm or any other Arab village.[9]

This form of expression could not be permitted because the extent of the possible offense was very high and because the Arabs lacked the ability to avoid the offense. The criteria of the content of the expression, its manner, the speaker's intent, and the circumstances together supplied valid grounds to restrict free expression under the Offense to Sensibilities Argument. It is emphasized that one should not conclude from this rationale that Kahane's visits to Jewish cities also should have been prohibited. One cannot compare a visit to an Arab village, which is in a sense the backyard (or front yard) of the target group, to a visit to any city in Israel. Furthermore, the scope of tolerance would entertain Kahane's public meetings in mixed cities where Arabs and Jews reside, such as Lod and Jaffe (but not in front of mosques in those cities), or in campuses and halls of universities, such as Jerusalem and Haifa. Only in Arab cities and villages, the Offense of Sensibilities Argument may serve as a trump card (in the words of Ronald Dworkin[10]) that is superior to the Free Speech Principle.

Liberals might advance a number of arguments against the Offense to Sensibilities Argument. They might say that it was most logical for Kahane to transmit his message in Umm El Fahm of all places because this was, from his point of view, the optimal stage. It was logical for him to choose a place where he could receive the public resonance that he was seeking. I agree that, indeed, this would be logical on his part, but then – while acknowledging the "democratic catch" – a question arises: does this consideration justify a grave offense to the sensibilities of the target audience? Democracy is not required to provide those who preach hatred with the optimal stage to transmit their hateful messages. Rather, it should protect weak groups who cannot avoid exposure to such messages.

A second argument would ponder whether the prohibition of the Kahanist parade in Umm El Fahm might serve as grounds for prohibiting a civil rights parade in the Kahanist Jewish settlement of Kfar Tapuach, thus drawing the scope of tolerance too narrowly. People might argue that were we to prohibit Kahanist parades in Arab villages, then by the same token we should also prohibit liberal demonstrations in the Kahanist fort. They would maintain that it is better to permit both demonstrations than to prohibit

---

9 The point about not being able to avoid the offensive speech is made by a US Supreme Court case, which allows the state to ban picketing around private residences. Cf. *Frisby* v. *Schultz*, 487 U.S. 474 (1988). 108 S. Ct. 2495 (1988). For discussion of this case, see R. Cohen-Almagor, "The right to demonstrate *v.* the right to privacy: picketing private homes of public officials", in *Speech, Media and Ethics*, pp. 24–41.

10 R. Dworkin, "Liberalism", in *A Matter of Principle* (Oxford: Clarendon Press, 1985), pp. 181–204.

both; consequently, they would side with the right of the hate-mongers to march and demonstrate in any place, including in Arab villages.

However, this argument leads to moral relativism, as if people are unable to distinguish between good and evil, between respect and concern for people on the one side and hate and discrimination on the other. Democracy is based on two basic rights: respect for others and not harming others. Those who reject these principles find themselves in a dilemma and pose a problem for society. It is contradictory to expect democracy to assist those who work against it and who wish to undermine its basic rights.

The analogy between Kahane's group and the Civil Rights Movement is flawed because the rules that guide each group are essentially different and thus impair the supposedly equal treatment each deserves. Kahane and his followers in Kfar Tapuach base their ideology on hating non-Jews and on disrespecting and harming them. This ideology stands in stark contrast to the principles of democracy. At the same time, activists of the Civil Rights Movement seek to protect democracy and to promote the principles of not harming others and of respecting others in every place, including in Kfar Tapuach.

Even if we assume that the people of Kfar Tapuach are indeed greatly offended by the "hurtful" message evinced by civil rights marchers and that the intensity of the offense does not fall short of that which the Arabs might feel upon encountering the Kahanist message, we must still concede that democracy does not operate within a moral lacuna. It does not operate in a relativist, confused space, where good is bad and bad is good. Democracy operates under certain cherished values. The people of Kfar Tapuach do not have a problem with the Civil Rights Movement alone, but rather with democracy itself. If we truly wish to protect them from liberal values, then we must annul democracy completely and accept their "values", which would be too high a price to pay in the eyes of most liberals.

A third argument that liberals might raise is the "slippery slope" argument. According to Lackland H. Bloom, who examines how American courts have addressed offensive speech appeals, there are so many different types of offensive speech claims pressed on society and the courts by aggrieved groups and individuals that it would be legally and politically difficult to resist the granting of exceptions for all once relief has been accorded to some.[11] How can we frame the Offense to Sensibilities Argument in a way that will not open the door to prohibiting any speech that some might consider offensive? In response, let me first say that the slippery slope argument does not really address the Offense to Sensibilities Argument and does not question its core rationale. All it does is warn

---

11 L. H. Bloom, "Fighting back: offensive speech and cultural conflict", *Southern Methodist University Law Review*, 46 (1992): 145, at 160.

against employing it carelessly.[12] Indeed, we must be strict with the formulation of this argument and narrowly define it so as to prevent its cynical misuse in prohibiting freedom of expression. Prescribing boundaries to freedom of expression requires a painstaking effort, involving careful consideration and lucid articulation, so as to avoid sliding down the slope and allowing room for illiberal interpretations that would broaden it unnecessarily.

Thus, it is reiterated that the Offense to Sensibilities Argument is applicable only when it concerns speech that might cause profound psychological offense to the unwilling target group, resulting in dejection and shock. The concern here is not with just any offense. Society is full of "sensitive" people, such as racists who are offended by the mere sight of a Jewish woman and an Arab man holding hands. However, the Offense to Sensibilities Argument is not meant to assist those "sensitive" people, or to equip them with instruments to fight against democracy. It is also clear that we are not talking about mere annoyance or feelings of discomfort. Life is full of expressions that make us uncomfortable, but only fascists would seriously demand their censorship. Here we are dealing with expressions that might cause an unwilling target group severe emotional trauma that is morally on a par with physical harm. Deep emotional distress that undermines one's psychological system may be no less harmful than bodily injuries.

How can we identify a serious offense as distinguished from a relatively minor offense? It would appear that certain expressions stand out under specific circumstances, and that it is possible logically to deduce that they should not be tolerated. This is the case when Kahanists wish to "pay a visit" to Arab villages, or when pornography lovers attempt to advertise their merchandise in religious neighborhoods. In less striking situations, judges are advised to consult psychologists and other experts for advice in order to assess the seriousness of the harm in pertinent cases. This is not to say that psychologists should replace judges. All I say is that we should encourage judges to seek psychologists' advice before reaching conclusions. Just as the courts seek the advice of art critics and professionals in assessing the artistic quality of questionable productions, so the courts are advised to consult professionals in assessing psychological damage.

Those who oppose my suggestion might do so on two grounds: first, it is not democratic for psychologists to decide the law; second, at issue here are values, so why should we accept the opinions of psychologists? As for the first claim, I reiterate that the last word will be that of the judges. All I suggest is that expert opinion be sought. As for the second claim, I do not agree that we are dealing only with values; we also need to assess the potential offense to people's psychological systems. I do not suggest a test

12 Cf. F. Schauer, "Slippery slopes", *Harvard Law Review*, 99 (1985): 361; E. Volokh, "The mechanisms of the slippery slope", *Harvard Law Review*, 116 (2003): 1026.

for moral determination, but assistance in assessing possible damage to the target group in question.

Granted, psychology, like most (if not all) sciences, is not precise. Psychologists, however, are better equipped than members of any other profession to examine and weigh offenses to the soul. As is the case with medicine, here too it is advisable to ask for a second opinion. When the two opinions are in agreement, then judges will have another central criterion to consider before writing their judgment. If there is a conflict between the two opinions, then the judges will decide which one is more appealing, or they may disregard both opinions or ask for a third opinion. In any case, it would be unwise to discard this procedure from the outset.

Thus far, most liberals (Joel Feinberg stands out as a notable exception) have avoided addressing this complex issue because of the difficulty in assessing emotional offenses. Finding themselves unable to reach an appropriate solution, they chose instead to throw away the baby with the bathwater – that is, not to deal with the issue at all. This is not a solution. As soon as we are convinced of the authenticity of the problem and of the seriousness of the issue, there is little wisdom in ignoring it simply because of the difficulties involved in assessing offenses. On the contrary, these difficulties should press us to dedicate more thought to the issues rather than to disregard them.

Lastly, some might claim that the combination of factors mentioned above under the Offense to Sensibilities Argument presents such a high standard to fulfill that it would be almost impossible to use it at all. If this is indeed the feeling, then the goal set in this study is achieved. This chapter is intended to present a narrow argument that would justify prohibiting free expression only in exceptional cases. While reviewing the court cases in Chapter 4, I argued that it was right to reject the offense argument when it had been rejected, and I expressed my dissatisfaction with the cases in which it had been accepted. There are noteworthy and weighty differences between the use of the offense argument in the above cases and the example of Kahane's visits to Arab villages.

Having said this, the situation of Kahane's visits to Arab villages was special, but not unique. We can imagine other similar cases in which the Offense to Sensibilities Argument would provide grounds for limiting free expression. The Skokie case was mentioned as a situation in which it would have been appropriate to make use of the Offense to Sensibilities Argument to restrict free expression to the neo-Nazis. There was testimony by psychologists on the possible injuries many Jews would suffer as a result of the march. They argued that this speech act might be regarded as the equivalent of a physical assault.[13] Dr William G. Niederland, a clinical

13 L. Bollinger, *The Tolerant Society* (Oxford: Clarendon Press, 1986), pp. 197–200. See also D. A. Downs, *Nazis in Skokie* (Notre Dame: University of Notre Dame Press, 1985), Chapters 1, 8; and the statement of Sol Goldstein, a concentration camp survivor whose mother was killed by the Nazis, in A. Neier, *Defending My Enemy* (New York: Dutton, 1979), p. 46.

professor emeritus of psychiatry, warned of the intense adverse physical and emotional reactions to the sight of such symbols of persecution and murder as Nazi parades, swastikas, and Nazi-like uniforms.[14] Similarly, the scope of tolerance should not include hate speech of an anti-homosexual preacher in a gay neighborhood in San Francisco, or the burning of a cross by the Ku Klux Klan outside the home of an Afro-American family in Harlem.[15] In contrast, the preacher, the neo-Nazis, and the KKK still enjoy the right to express their homophobic and racist opinions in other places, where the target groups will not feel compelled to stand against and suffer the offense.[16]

Likewise, it is one thing to allow the publication of *The Satanic Verses*[17] and quite another to grant Salman Rushdie permission to promote his book in a religious Pakistani neighborhood in Bradford, northern England, should he wish to do so.[18] This fictitious book contains scurrilous and derisive comments regarding Islam and its prophets. It remarks on the sex life and other habits of Muhammad. It calls him an impostor and "a smart bastard" who treated religion as a kind of business, and who slept with so many women that his beard turned half-white in a year. Furthermore, Rushdie's offense goes beyond mocking the prophet. The book scornfully reduced the Koran to a book of spouting rules about how to

14 Dr William G. Niederland's letter to the Editor, *New York Times* (7 February 1978), p. 22.
15 In his comments on the first draft of this chapter, Jack Pole wrote: *"Only* in Harlem? I cannot see a case for permitting it anywhere since it is a notorious incitement to hatred and violence." Many American lawyers and scholars would disagree, believing that the First Amendment should protect such political speech, despite its offensive character. After all, pleasant speech does not need protection. It is the harmful speech that requires exercising tolerance. As Fred Schauer puts it, the values underlying the right to free speech are values not themselves derived from the fact of speech's harmfulness and are not therefore undercut by the fact of speech's harmfulness on particular occasions. Cf. F. Schauer, "The cost of communicative tolerance", in R. Cohen-Almagor (ed.), *Liberal Democracy and the Limits of Tolerance* (Ann Arbor: University of Michigan Press, 2000), p. 29.
16 Cf. *R.A.V.* v. *City of St. Paul* 112 S.Ct. 2538 (1992). For further deliberation, see E. J. Eberle, "Hate speech, offensive speech, and public discourse in America", *Wake Forest Law Review*, 29 (1994), 1135.
17 S. Rushdie, *The Satanic Verses* (New York: Viking, 1988).
18 On 14 January 1989, the book was burned by a Muslim crowd in Bradford. For discussion of the Rushdie affair, see D. E. Arzt, "Religious human rights in the world today", *Emory International Law Review*, 10 (1996): 139–161; A. Chase, "Legal guardians: Islamic law, international law, human rights law, and the Salman Rushdie affair", *American University Journal of International Law & Policy*, 11 (1996): 375–435; http://www.subir.com/rushdie.html; http://www.nytimes.com/books/99/04/18/specials/rushdie.html#news1. For further discussion, see A. A. An-Na'im, "The contingent universality of human rights: the case of freedom of expression in African and Islamic contexts", *Emory International Law Review*, 11 (1997): 29–66.

fart, to fuck, and to clean one's behind.[19] The story implies that the entire Koran is derived not from God but from Muhammad and thus it is a human artifact and the Islamic faith is built on a deceit.[20] Some people believe that the book's title implies that the Koran is the work of the Devil.[21] *The Satanic Verses* is considered blasphemy, an act of deep offense to religious beliefs, an insult to sacred Islam. Rushdie claims the book is fictitious, and I certainly do not call for it to be banned, but the point of going to Muslim neighborhoods to promote it could only be to assault the psyche of the Pakistani population. Even if Mr Rushdie himself and/or his publishers were willing to take the risk and bear the consequences of such a questionable book promotion – given Ayatollah Ruhollah Khomeini's apostasy *fatwa* (religious decree) of 14 February 1989 against him and his publishers,[22] speaking of the duty of every Muslim to kill Rushdie – the offense to the relevant neighborhood involved in such an act remains too great to be overridden by his right to free speech.[23]

19 B. Parekh, "The Rushdie affair and the British press", in D. Cohn-Sherbok (ed.) *The Salman Rushdie Controversy in Interreligious Perspective* (Lewiston: Edwin Mellen Press, 1990), p. 75.
20 D. Pipes, *The Rushdie Affair: The Novel, the Ayatollah, and the West* (New York: Carol Publishing Group, 1990), p. 61.
21 Pipes, *ibid.*, pp. 116–117.
22 The fatwa ordered the death not only of Rushdie but also of his publishers, calling on all zealous Muslims to execute them quickly, wherever they may be found, as penalty for blaspheming against the Muslim sanctities. Indeed, the Japanese translator of *The Satanic Verses* was stabbed to death in 1991. Shortly afterwards, the Italian translator was also stabbed. Luckily he survived. In 1993, the Norwegian publisher of the book was injured in a gun attack. See D. Pipes, *The Rushdie Affair: The Novel, the Ayatollah, and the West, op. cit.*, p. 27. See also T. M. Franck, "Is personal freedom a Western value?", *American Journal of International Law*, V91 (1997): 593–627, at 602–603; http://www.crf-usa.org/bria/bria15_1.html.
23 Other examples might be advertising abomination to a captive audience that would be offended because of its religious or conscientious beliefs (for example, advertisement of pornographic material to a captive feminist audience). For useful discussions on feminism and pornography, see A. Dworkin, *Pornography: Men Possessing Women* (New York: Perigee, 1979); S. Griffin, *Pornography and Silence* (New York: Harper & Row, 1981); M. M. Killoran, "Sticks and stones can break my bones and images can hurt me: feminist and pornography debate", *International Journal of Women Studies*, 16 (1983): 443–456; D. Turley, "The feminist debate on pornography: an unorthodox interpretation", *Socialist Review*, 16 (1986): 81–96; R. Baird et al. (eds), *Pornography: Private Right or Public Menace* (New York: Prometheus, 1991); C. A. MacKinnon and A. Dworkin (eds), *In Harm's Way: The Pornography Civil Rights Hearings* (Cambridge: Harvard University Press, 1997).

Conclusion

The Offense to Sensibilities Argument provides valid grounds to limit expression when the content and/or manner of expression (symbolic speech) causes severe psychological offense to a certain target group, and the objective circumstances are such that the target group cannot avoid subjection to the offense. In December 1996, the Association of Widows and Orphans of the Israeli Defense Forces petitioned against the decision of the Cable Broadcasting Authority to screen a movie entitled *Sex, Lies and Dinner*, claiming that the movie greatly offended feelings of IDF widows. Justices Shlomo Levin, Yitzhak Zamir, and Tova Strasberg-Cohen, in a laconic decision, denied the petition.[24] The Justices said that while acknowledging the debt each and every citizen owes to the soldiers who sacrificed their lives – a debt that entails respect and appreciation to the widows and orphans of these soldiers – this debt was not enough to decide the principled issue presented before the court. Although the court is usually reluctant to interfere in the decisions of bodies authorized by law, the Justices recognized that sometimes exceptions can be made – however, this was not the case here.

The Offense to Sensibilities Argument does not stand in such cases, even if the offense is serious and severe, because the reasonable avoidability standard is not satisfied. Those who might be offended by the film's content could easily avoid it by clicking the remote control. My position would be different were we to talk about the state-controlled public channel (Channel 1), which is expected to show a higher level of sensitivity regarding such problematic messages that concern soldiers. However, there is certainly no room to restrict the screening of cable films just because a certain sector of the public might be offended. Israeli television viewers have more than enough channels from which to choose, and they are not obligated to view a film that offends their sensibilities. Note that it is not suggested that the Offense to Sensibilities Argument be applied differently to public or state broadcasting than it is to private commercial radio or television. What is suggested is more responsibility and respect on the part of public broadcasting, showing more consideration to society's various sections. Not all people are connected to cables and satellite. Some people in Israel have access only to the two public channels, 1 and 2. Public broadcasting, I feel, should be more cautious about what is aired.

In his comments on a draft of this chapter, Jack Pole wrote that he is uneasy about the view that a person who does not want to listen or see a certain program can simply switch it off. In cases where the program is gravely offensive or damaging, the knowledge that it is influencing other people, possibly one's neighbors, can itself lead to fear and suspicion.[25]

24 H.C. 9447/96 *Association of Widows and Orphans of IDF Soldiers* v. *Cable Broadcasting Authority and Others* (26 December 1996).
25 Professor Pole's personal communication.

I do not find this line of argument very convincing, because then the line-drawing of the scope of tolerance would become an impossible task. It gives too much room for speculation and suspicion. How can one know what is influencing one's neighbors? It might entail inquiring into the character of our neighbors, what might influence and what not – this in an age when many people do not even know their neighbors (or, at least, many of them). And even if you know that a certain program might offend some people, it is still not a sufficient argument to prohibit speech. If this were to serve as a rationale for limiting free speech, then we might end with no speech at all. It would be a prescription for disastrous policy.

Another pertinent matter concerned the screening of a film originally entitled *Good Holocaust.* This film documents the activities of a Holocaust survivor who visits different places, where he talks about his experiences during that dark period in Europe. The controversy was not related to the film's content, but rather to its oxymoron title *Good Holocaust* – a tasteless, offensive title to which Holocaust survivors objected. Eventually, the court was not required to decide the case because the petitioners withdrew their appeal. For my part, I do not know what the possible effects of this title might have been on Holocaust survivors exposed to it through newspapers and public billboards. It can be assumed that they would find it difficult to avoid the advertisements. In this and similar cases, it is advisable that the courts consult psychologists about whether the Offense to Sensibilities Argument may serve as possible grounds for restricting free expression.[26]

The sensitivity of Holocaust survivors was at the center of another controversy regarding the question of whether to play the music of anti-Semitic composers. For many years various symphonies in Israel have wished to play the music of Richard Wagner, and every time faced the criticisms and objections of Holocaust survivors, who claimed that Wagner – whose works accompanied the suffering of the Jewish people during the Holocaust – should not be played. Wagner (1813–1883), the official composer of the Third Reich, was often played in Nazi assemblies, in the concentration camps, and on the way to the mass killings. He also wrote anti-Semitic tracts from which Hitler drew inspiration.[27] For their part, speaking of the need to distinguish between an anti-Semitic person and his appreciated works of art, the various symphony orchestras claim that any self-respecting orchestra includes in its repertoire some of Wagner's works.

In one case, two Holocaust survivors filed a petition against the Rishon LeZion Symphony in the Tel Aviv District Court, arguing that playing the music of Richard Wagner and Richard Strauss (who was appointed by

26 See R. C. Carson, J. N. Butcher and S. Mineka (eds), *Abnormal Psychology and Modern Life*, 10th edn (New York: HarperCollins, 1996).
27 http://www.tau.ac.il/taunews/98fall/wagner.html; http://w3.rz-berlin.mpg.de/cmp/wagner.html.

Hitler in 1933 to be President of the "Reichsmusikkammer" and composed the *Olympic Hymn* for the 1936 games in Berlin)[28] profoundly offended the feelings of Holocaust survivors, and would do damage to the image of the state of Israel. The Symphony claimed that free speech had precedence over the possible offense to the sensibilities of some people, and that the courts should avoid interfering in artistic freedom as they do in decisions of academic institutions.[29]

Judge Yehuda Zafet wondered why the petitioners appealed to the court only nine days before the scheduled concert in October 2000, when the symphony had presented its controversial program for the concert season in March 2000. Judge Zafet spoke of the importance of free expression as a basic right that should be restricted only sparingly, maintaining that the controversy over playing the music was fundamentally ethical and not a matter for the courts. Zafet was not convinced that playing the controversial music would seriously offend the petitioners, and hence denied relief. The petitioners then appealed to the High Court of Justice. In a laconic decision, Justice Yaacov Tirkel did not find enough justification to overturn the District Court's decision. He expressed regret that no solution was found "to this painful controversy by way of agreement", and that the court was asked to intervene.[30]

In 2001, this issue was again put on the public agenda when the former Israeli conductor, Daniel Barenboim, announced his wish to play Wagner in the annual Israel Festival. Holocaust survivors protested against Barenboim's intention, saying that playing Wagner during the most important public music festival would greatly offend their sensibilities. Barenboim, director and chief conductor of the Berliner Staatsoper (State Opera of Berlin), explained that he has the greatest understanding and compassion for all Holocaust survivors and the terrible associations of Wagner's music. He said that he also understands that some people cannot forget these strong associations, and that they should never be forced to listen to Wagner's music in a concert. Therefore, Wagner's works should not be played during concerts for regular season ticket-holders, when faithful subscribers would be confronted with music that raises painful memories. However, the question must be asked whether any person has the right to deprive any other person who does not have these same associations of the possibility of hearing Wagner's music. This, argues Barenboim, would indirectly serve the misuse of Wagner's music by the Nazis. Moreover, Israel must act as a totally democratic state, which entails not preventing

28 http://www.richard-strauss.com/biography.html.
29 File 001442/00, 27228/00 *Podlovski and Others* v. *Rishon-LeZion Symphonic Orchestra and Others*, Tel Aviv District Court (24 October 2000). Also see D. Gabai, "The court decided: it is allowed to play Wagner", *Maariv* (Israeli daily) (25 October 2000).
30 Civil Appeal 7700/00 *Podlovski and Others* v. *Rishon LeZion Symphonic Orchestra and Others* (26 October 2000).

people who are free of these associations from listening to Wagner's music.[31]

Barenboim's viewpoint was not accepted. After pondering the issue for some months, on 30 May 2001 the management of the Israel Festival decided that the time was not yet ripe to play Wagner. Barenboim agreed to perform instead musical pieces of other composers. This decision was reached after receiving many appeals from Holocaust survivors and other concerned citizens, among them State President Moshe Katzav, Minister of Science, Culture and Sports Matan Vilnai, and Mayor of Jerusalem Ehud Ulmert.[32]

Based on the above criteria, the petition of the Holocaust survivors would only be appropriate if they, as orchestra subscribers, were required to listen to Wagner. However, this was not the case. The festival repertoire is broad and varied. It includes more than enough concerts in which Wagner is not played. Accordingly, all that Holocaust survivors would have to do is remain outside the concert hall. The mere knowledge of the Wagner concert is not weighty enough to cause profound offense to sensibilities. At the same time, this rationale has one single exception: the Israeli Philharmonic Symphony. Because of its importance and rank in Israel as first among equals, and its representative status as the State orchestra, it is appropriate for the Israeli Philharmonic to avoid playing Wagner as long as Holocaust survivors are still amongst us. State bodies, sponsored by the public, are expected to exhibit more restraint and sensitivity than other bodies.

The same rationale of restraint and sensitivity is also true for other such state-sponsored bodies. For instance, the public TV channel should not screen the film *The Last Temptation of Christ* so as not to offend the Christian public. The film may be broadcast on cable channels or on channels sponsored by commercials, but broadcasting this film on the state channel transmits a symbolic uncaring message to the public.

In 1998, when Israel celebrated fifty years of independence, many resources were invested in staging a central art event called "Jubilee Bells". A leading ballet group, "Bat Sheva", chose to perform a production called *One Who Knows*, involving indecent exposure of their bodies. Because this was the main event of the 1998 Independence Day and because it was broadcast live by the two main channels – the public channel (Channel 1) as well as the commercial channel (Channel 2) – religious people asked that the performance be censored on the grounds that it offended their feelings.

I believe that it could have been possible to prevent the "cultural war"

---

31 D. Barenboim, "A rationale for performing Wagner", *Los Angeles Times* (22 May 2001).

32 I. Shachar and Y. Avidan, "Finally: Wagner will not be played in the Israel Festival", *Maariv* (31 May 2001), p. 19.

that ensued if thought had preceded action. "Bat Sheva" is a prominent ballet group with a rich and varied repertoire, and it could have easily chosen a beautiful performance that would not have offended any public sector. After all, the performance was meant to be for the enjoyment of *all* sectors and not only for the secular. Unfortunately, the planning of the fiftieth anniversary celebration was not characterized by much thought. Hasty thinking caused a heated atmosphere that could have been prevented.

From this viewpoint, it seems that the religious outcry was justified, because the choice of performance did offend people's sensibilities. Those who object to my conclusion might say that the offense was not severe enough to rock the sensibilities of religious people. Yet here the special historical circumstances of the occasion and the magnitude of the event – the main celebration of the fiftieth year of independence – required special and sensitive consideration of all public sectors.[33] The avoidability standard in this case was not reasonable, because we could not expect religious people (some 20 percent of the Israeli population) to avoid the major event of this important holiday and to shut themselves off from the two major television channels that broadcast the special live performance.

In the end, a compromise was reached: "Bat Sheva" performed the production it wanted, but the dancers were clothed. It was shown on both prominent TV channels, and people from all sectors watched it live.

---

33 An essentially different line of reasoning was expressed by Ohad Naharin, the creator of *One Who Knows*. See A. Bernheimer, "I did not come to demonstrate, I came only to work", an interview with Naharin in the 7 Days supplement of *Yedioth Ahronoth* (Israeli daily) (8 May 1998), pp. 22–30, 81.

6   On incitement

My Captain does not answer, his lips are pale and still;
My father does not feel my arm, he has no pulse or will;
The ship is anchor'd safe and sound, its voyage closed and done;
From fearful trip the victor ship comes in with object won:

Exult, O shores, and ring, O bells!
But I with mournful tread,
Walk the deck my Captain lies,
Fallen cold and dead.

Walt Whitman O Captain! My Captain! (1865)

Introduction

On 4 November 1995, Prime Minister Yitzhak Rabin was assassinated in the main square of Tel Aviv. Cynically, it was at the close of a large demonstration that had called for peace and protested against violence. Following the assassination, people felt the need to ponder their own activities and statements before the assassination. Questions were raised about whether the leadership, the media and others were responsible for the atmosphere which might had been conducive to the rise of people like the assassin Yigal Amir. People who had a say in public forums utilized the media to ask themselves whether they had a share in creating a violent atmosphere that nourished murderous thoughts. Voices were raised declaring that there was "too much freedom in Israel", too much freedom of expression, too much freedom on the part of the media. Other people warned against silencing expression.

As part of this soul-searching, not long after Rabin's assassination I was invited to a head-to-head debate with an esteemed philosopher on the topic "Free speech and its limitations". I was stunned when the co-panelist claimed that we should protect incitement on the premise that it is better to allow such expressions than to provide latitude for government to dictate boundaries to freedom of expression. Before coming to the debate I thought that it was commonly agreed that incitement lies squarely outside the scope of tolerance (see Chapter 1). After the debate, I decided to dedicate time and thinking to this issue. That heated debate prompted the writing of this chapter.

In this chapter I discuss the issue of incitatory speech, focusing attention on four examples of incitement prior to Prime Minister Rabin's assassination that required intervention, but insufficient measures were taken to forestall them or to punish the individuals involved. These cases occurred after the signing of the Oslo Accords in September 1993, which increased the rift between "left" and "right" in Israel. The first two are examples of stark political extremism; the other two are examples of incitement under religious disguise. I argue that the scope of tolerance should not be extended to include instigative speech. Indeed, the more recent Supreme Court decision, *Rabbi Ido Elba* v. *State of Israel*, explicitly condemned racist incitement and held that such incitement should not be treated mercifully. This clear and loud voice is understood within the context and atmosphere generated by Prime Minister Rabin's assassination.

I open the discussion by devoting attention to one of the proposals that was voiced immediately after the tragic assassination. The Attorney General, Michael Ben-Yair (his official title is Legal Advisor to the Israeli Government), called on the media not to broadcast incitement. I object to this proposal because of its sweeping language, arguing that media editors should apply self-restraint in deciding what should be broadcast and what should not. There is a stark difference between a legitimate invitation for voluntary compliance, and legal regulation. I would not like government officials to use their authority to tell the media what to say. Free journalism is one of the foundations of democracy, and should be safeguarded and strengthened. At the same time it should have some guidelines on news coverage prescribed by the media.

Boundaries to freedom of communication

On 8 November 1995, four days after Prime Minister Rabin's assassination, Attorney General Michael Ben-Yair warned the media that they must not hold interviews with inciters, and must refrain from quoting incitements and curses, whether in writing or in speech. Ben-Yair wanted to prevent direct reportage of inciters who condoned the murder, since the report might justify further murders.[1] Later, Ben-Yair explained that we must differentiate between *indirect* reporting of incitement brought to the knowledge of the public, and live interviews constituting *direct* report of

1 A letter by Attorney Amir Zolti, Senior Assistant to the Attorney General, to the newspaper editors concerning non-publication of praise of the murder of the Prime Minister and Defense Minister (8 November 1995, in Hebrew). See O. Galili, "Democracy should defend itself", *Haaretz* (Israeli daily) (8 November 1995), p. B.

incitement.[2] The National Union of Israeli Journalists rejected the Attorney General's motion, stating that a sweeping, *a priori* prohibition on any mention of incitement in the media would not conform to the common procedure, which requires that each case be examined separately, giving precedence to freedom of speech and the public right to know. Moreover, carrying out the Attorney General's suggestion would not achieve the intended purpose but rather its opposite, since the media are the watchdog of democracy, and it is their role to reveal and report eccentric phenomena, wrongs or illegalities. If asked to refrain from reporting, extremist elements would remain uncovered and public safety would be jeopardized. Attorney Ilan Bombach, who represented the National Union of Journalists, wrote bluntly to Attorney General Ben-Yair: "Your directive is characteristic of totalitarian governments and reminds us of dark periods which we all wish to forget ... The role of the attorney general is not to terrorize the public nor to be the 'hound' that hunts the 'watch dog'."[3] A few days later, the Journalists Union petitioned the Supreme Court to order Attorney General Ben-Yair to clarify why he would not cancel his directives.[4]

On 14 December 1995 Attorney Uzi Fogelman of the Attorney General's office published an announcement on behalf of Michael Ben-Yair, stating that there was no intention to prevent reports of the variety of views and opinions prevalent in the public, including those of a radical or outrageous nature. Fogelman made clear that it was not the Attorney General's intention to give instructions or to use the authority given to him by law; rather, he wanted to clarify his own position regarding incitement, given the special circumstances following Prime Minister Rabin's assassination. Therefore there was no basis for the claim that he overstepped his authority, since this was not at all a case of using authority.[5]

In a private conversation, Ben-Yair repeatedly clarified that he did not intend to direct the media how to behave but rather to make an open call expressing his concerns, an appeal, a request to be more careful in covering hate speeches.[6] However, the reading of the letter of 8 November 1995 easily reveals why it was not understood to be a request. The letter said

2 Personal discussion with A. G. Ben-Yair. See also D. Meiri and T. Zimuki, "There exists a danger of another political murder", *Yedioth Ahronoth* (Israeli daily) (12 November 1995), p. 7.
3 A letter by Attorney Ilan Bombach to Attorney General Ben-Yair on "The legality of your directives to the press on publication of incitement" (9 November 1995).
4 H.C. (High Court of Justice) 7094/95 *The National Union of Journalists* v. *Attorney General Ben-Yair*.
5 U. Fogelman, "An announcement from the plaintiff", H.C. 7094/95 *The National Union of Journalists* v. *Attorney General Ben-Yair* (14 December 1995).
6 Ben-Yair also clarified his position in a TV interview given to *Tik Tikshoret*, Channel 2 (11 November 1995).

that the Attorney General regarded very severely the interviews that expressed happiness and satisfaction at Prime Minister Rabin's assassination, and called for further murders. In his mind, the reporting of statements apparently violated Article 134 of the Penal Law (1977), which prohibits circulating seditious publications, and Section 4(A) of the Prevention of Terrorism Ordinance (1948), which instructs that a person publishing praise, sympathy or encouragement for acts of violence calculated to cause death or injury, and a person assisting the organization in its activities, is subject to criminal proceedings and a maximum penalty of three years' imprisonment. Moreover, it stated that "on this matter it shall be clarified that publication as mentioned lays criminal responsibility not only on those uttering the words but also on those publishing them", and that "freedom of speech is not a complete virtue: when its actualization could endanger lives or the public order with near certainty, forceful measures shall be taken against those using it for this purpose".[7] Therefore, it should be no surprise that the National Union of Journalists quickly protested against the Attorney General's initiative and warned of its consequences and implications for the free press.

Although I disagree with the way Attorney General Ben-Yair chose to raise an important issue, and the wording he used, I do agree with the rationale guiding his thought.[8] Journalists should think of the consequences of their acts. The media should not serve as a stage for inciters calling for violence and murder, especially given the state of affairs in Israel at that particular time, when there was reason to suspect that the assassin was not a "stray weed", but that more were in our midst. Those people intended to nip the Oslo Accords in the bud by violently eliminating the leaders whose policies were regarded as treacherous and dangerous before the Accords were fully actualized. It is possible to report about those people, their intentions and deeds, in the name of the public right to know, without playing into the hands of inciters and serving as their loudspeaker. Responsible media are moral media. The setting of limits on the public right to know should be left in the hands of journalists, but it is important to stress that inciting messages should not be protected under the Free Speech Principle, nor by the inclusive right of the public to be informed. It is possible to report stormy demonstrations, curses and hatred without, say, printing photos of Israeli leaders dressed in black Nazi uniforms. Moreover, such occurrences should be reported along with an unequivocal and clear condemnation by media editors and reporters

7 A letter from Attorney Amir Zolti to the newspaper editors regarding non-publication of praise of the murder of the Prime Minister and Defense Minister (8 November 1995).
8 For further discussion, see Michael Ben-Yair's speech, "Critique of press criticism", a lawyers convention in Zichron Ya'akov (10 September 1996, in Hebrew).

acting as responsible citizens in a democracy. The media should not confer any legitimacy on instigators (see Chapter 1).

There are limits to free expression and to free journalism. Prime Minister Rabin's assassination brought about an increased sense of urgency, greater sensitivity to words, symbols and phrases, and growing awareness regarding the power of the word in creating an atmosphere and in shaping reality. It is not only actions that shape reality; words and speech acts (like symbolic speech) also have a significant role. Language constructs and deconstructs images, ideologies, cultures, and societies. Prime Minister Rabin's assassination sparked a debate as to what constitutes incitement and what forms of speech should be excluded from the protection of the Free Speech Principle.

Exception to the Free Speech Principle: the case of incitement

As stated in Chapter 1, in his celebrated work, *On Liberty*, John Stuart Mill wrote that opinions lose their immunity when the circumstances under which they are expressed constitute by their expression a positive incitement to some mischievous act. Thus, the opinion that corn-dealers are starvers of the poor may be prevented from being delivered orally to "an excited mob assembled before the house of a corn-dealer, or when handed about among the same mob in the form of a placard".[9]

Mill considered as incitement a speech that the speaker intended to lead to some mischievous action, made under circumstances conducive to the taking of that action. Mill implied that the intention to lead people to take a harmful action – in circumstances likely immediately to mobilize people to take that action – constituted incitement. In a footnote, Mill pointed out that instigation to assassinate a tyrant may be a proper subject of punishment, but only if an overt act had followed and at least a probable connection could be established between the act and the instigation.[10]

The essential distinction between "incitement" and "advocacy" or "teaching" is that those to whom the incitement is addressed are being urged to perform some mischievous act now or in the immediate future, rather than merely being urged to believe in something, and the circumstances are such that might transform the speech into harmful action. Incitement is a speech act, an expression that is closely linked to action.[11] In *Brandenburg* v. *Ohio*, the United States Supreme Court declared that speech could not be proscribed except where the advocacy is directed to

---

9 J. S. Mill, *Utilitarianism, Liberty, and Representative Government* (London: J. M. Dent, 1948), Everyman's Edition, p. 114.
10 *Ibid.*, p. 78.
11 R. Cohen-Almagor, *The Boundaries of Liberty and Tolerance* (Gainesville: University Press of Florida, 1994), Chapter 7.

inciting or producing imminent lawless action and is likely to incite or produce such action.[12] Emphasis is put on the circumstances. Constitutionally protected "political hyperboles" during peaceful times are not tolerable during times of tense circumstances when the speech in question might incite violence.[13]

Thus, the peculiarity of cases of incitement is that the likelihood of immediate danger is high, and we have little or no opportunity to conduct a discussion in the open and to bring conflicting considerations into play, which may in turn reduce the effect of the speech. Justice Holmes agreed that in some circumstances, when speech was closely related to action and might induce harmful consequences, it should be curtailed. In a way similar to the Millian corn-dealer example, Holmes asserted in a renowned opinion that we cannot allow false shouting of *"Fire!"* in a crowded theater.[14] Here, too, a restriction on speech is justified on the grounds that the content of the speech (that is, its effect, not its intrinsic value), the manner of the speech, and the intentions of the agent are aimed to bring about harm, while the audience dwells under conditions that diminish its ability to deliberate in a rational manner. Therefore, such a shout might lead the audience to act in a harmful manner (harmful to themselves as well as to others). Hence, to the extent that speech entails an immediate effect, the arguments that assign special status to freedom of speech are less compelling. Boundaries have to be introduced in accordance with the context of the speech, otherwise the results could be too risky. As Zechariah Chafee stated: "Smoking is all right, but not in a powder magazine."[15]

Mill's theory was essentially consequentialist in nature.[16] Mill believed that we need to pay careful consideration to circumstances and to ponder the likely results of a given behavior in accordance with the given factors of each case. There are two interrelated issues ignored by Mill which are of relevance to the ensuing discussion and crucial to the understanding of incitement as I perceive this term today. One is the role played by the media in airing incitement. Mill did not consider this issue for obvious reasons. In his time, only selected circles of society, i.e. the elite, read newspapers, and there were no airwaves to transmit opinions. The second

12 *Brandenburg* v. *Ohio* 395 U.S. 444, 447, 89 S. Ct. 1827, 1830 (1969).
13 Cf. *Miller* v. *State of Delaware* 374 A.2d 271 (12 April 1977) concerning an inflammatory speech delivered after a young black girl was shot and seriously wounded by a white adult male.
14 *Schenck* v. *U.S.* 249 U.S. 47 (1919).
15 Z. Chafee, *Free Speech in the United States* (Cambridge: Harvard University Press, 1946), p. 397.
16 For further deliberation, see L. W. Sumner, "Should hate speech be free speech? John Stuart Mill and the limits of tolerance", in R. Cohen-Almagor (ed.), *Liberal Democracy and the Limits of Tolerance* (Ann Arbor: University of Michigan Press, 2000), pp. 133–150.

issue is strongly connected to the influence of the popular media, and it has to do with generating an *atmosphere* of incitement. The corn-dealer example speaks of a single incident where an immediate connection could be inferred from the harmful speech to the violent action. When one examines the events of the period from September 1993 to November 1995, from the signing of the Oslo Accords until Prime Minister Rabin's assassination, one cannot ignore the turbulent atmosphere that was generated by dozens of incidents which were orchestrated by the opposition to the Accords to undermine the government, to hinder the peace process and, more specifically, to portray Yitzhak Rabin as a traitor who was giving away the Land of Israel to an archterrorist (Yasser Arafat) – by this ignoring the Bible and the faithful Jews who believe in the Bible, sacrificing the State's security, and betraying the people of Israel. These incidents were magnified by the media.[17]

For instance, Rabbi Korf was quoted as saying that Rabin was an enemy and that he would not be sorry if Rabin were to be assassinated.[18] Rabbi Abraham B. Hecht was quoted as saying that Rabin deserved death. Everyone who delivers Jewish land or other Jewish assets to foreigners is a sinner, and a person who kills the sinner is doing a good deed.[19] *Hashavua*, an ultra-orthodox weekly, published incitements against Rabin and his government on a regular basis, calling for Rabin to be put on trial and executed, denouncing Rabin as a traitor, liar, Kapu, insane, evil, and murderer. *Hashavua* initiated a debate on the question of whether Rabin should be killed and, if so, how.[20] Benjamin Kahane, head of the Kahane Chai (Kahane Is Alive) movement, proclaimed that "many people think that the solution is to kill Rabin and Peres".[21] In a public gathering, Rabin was greeted by "Go to Gaza" and "Here, the dog arrives".[22] Rabbi Nachum Rabinowitz compared the Rabin government to those who helped the Nazis in Europe, saying that Rabin endangered the Jewish people and therefore he put himself in jeopardy. Moshe Feiglin of the Zu Artzenu (This Is Our Country) movement drew an analogy between Rabin and

17 For depiction of the heated atmosphere at that time, see Michael Karpin's film, *The Road to Rabin Square* (in English and Hebrew).
18 A. Eldar, "Leader of Habad in Florida: I would not be disappointed if Rabin will be killed", *Haaretz* (15 October 1995), p. A4. See also A. Barzilai, "Yigal Amir's sources of hatred", *Haaretz* (9 November 1995), p. B2.
19 S. Shamir and R. Saar, "Rabbi Hecht who determined that Rabin deserves death was ousted from chairmanship of his synagogue in New York", *Haaretz* (November 9, 1995), p. A6.
20 S. Ilan, "Hashavua: Rabin and Peres – evils of Israel, Judenrat and Kapus", *Haaretz* (10 November 1995), p. A5; M. Karpin and A. Friedman, *Murder in the Name of God* (Tel Aviv: Zmora, Bitan, 1999), p. 121 (in Hebrew).
21 M. Nesher, "Here the dog arrives", *Haaretz* (6 November 1995), p. B4.
22 A. Arazi, "A planned setup: demonstrator from the right jumped from the crowd and tried to assault Rabin", *Haaretz* (11 October 1995), p. A2.

Hitler, who came to power in democratic elections and later put Jews "on the trains".[23] Placards declaring "Rabin is the Engineer", relating to Yahya Ayyash, the Hamas engineer who prepared the explosives for the suicide murderers who launched many attacks on Israel, were distributed. (Ayyash was later assassinated by the Israeli security forces.)[24] Other placards showed Rabin dressed in an Arab kafiya, blood on his hands, and called him a traitor like the French Vichy government under Nazi occupation.[25]

Speaking of an "atmosphere" of incitement might evoke fear that too wide a scope is being opened for limiting free expression. It might be argued that while earlier I insisted that the speech in question must be directly connected to specific harmful actions for it to be considered as incitement, the notion of "atmosphere" introduced here fails that criterion. It loses temporality. Robert Post noted in his comments on this chapter that once you bring in atmosphere, you might as well not speak about incitement at all, but merely about bad tendency. He maintained that in America this concept of atmosphere has always justified the worst kinds of oppression.[26]

Indeed, in some countries the attempt to safeguard values, such as the security of the state, or to resist revolutions has brought about illegitimate suppression of free speech. Hence I object to any free speech limitations based on bad tendency. This is too far-fetched a consideration to be taken seriously. My discussion has two purposes, jurisprudential and ethical. I argue that legal authorities should not ignore incitement to murder; individuals who call for murder should be prosecuted and receive deterrent punishments. Furthermore, the discussion is intended to raise ethical awareness of the role played by the media when they transmit messages of hate. This is not a legal test. The argument is that we should not ignore the impact of the media in airing violent messages and hatred that reduce the time span between the harmful speech and the encouraged harmful conduct. The media help in planting the seeds of violence and hatred, but one does not know for sure when the ensuing harmful action might occur. Obviously, we can only assess the danger, but we are unable to

23 M. Karpin and A. Friedman, *Murder in the Name of God, op. cit.*, pp. 126, 158, 160.
24 http://www.jewishvirtuallibrary.org/jsource/biography/ayyash.html.
25 See S. Yerushalmi, "Frightening smell of gun powder", *Maariv* (1 September 1995), pp. 8–9, 18; E. Sprinzak, "The dynamics of incitement prior Rabin's assassination", in M. Konfino (ed.), *Power of the Words and Weakness of Mind* (Tel Aviv: Yitzhak Rabin Center/Am Oved, 2002), p. 278 (in Hebrew). On the establishment of the Vichy Government, see http://www.us-israel.org/jsource/Holocaust/vichy.html.
26 According to the bad tendency test, which was popular in the United States during the 1920s, a publication could be suspended if it revealed any tendency – however slight or remote – toward breaching the peace. Cf. *Gitlow* v. *N.Y.* 268 U.S. 652, 45 S. Ct. (1925).

know for sure when the harmful action might occur. I should clarify that I am not calling upon the legislature to take preventive action. I urge media professionals and agencies to take this consideration seriously. I definitely do not think that the media in democracies should simply ignore this consideration of incitatory atmosphere. The cost might be too high, as the events in Israel well illustrate.

In the following sections I discuss four cases of incitement prior to the assassination that required rigorous intervention, but insufficient measures were taken to prevent them or to punish the individuals involved. It is beyond the scope of this chapter to provide a detailed account of all relevant cases.[27] The four cases are illustrative rather than exhaustive. They illustrate a trend, an approach common within the Israeli courts. All are cases of incitement – that is, all of them intended to produce violence against a given target, and there was temporal proximity between the speech and the desired act of violence. All contributed to generating an atmosphere of de-legitimation and uproar against the government, and particularly against Prime Minister Rabin. They occurred after the signing of the peace accords. The first two cases are examples of stark political extremism, while the remainder are examples of incitement under religious disguise. I continue by shedding light on the more recent Supreme Court *Ido Elba* decision whose tone and substance seems to indicate a change in the Supreme Court's treatment of incitement.

Incitement: Examples from the recent Israeli experience

Stickers carrying the slogan "Rabin Should Be Killed"

On 30 October 1993, stickers were circulated in a small town called Or Akiva during a visit of the then Minister of Labor, Ora Namir. The stickers conveyed the following statement: "Rabin Should Be Killed". This statement constituted pure incitement that should not be protected under the Free Speech Principle. A target was mapped, and a clear statement conveyed as to what the target's fate should be. It was an explicit call for murder. Moreover, the social setting was such that it increased the likelihood of harmful action. The stickers were distributed during a visit of a

---

27 See also Criminal File 553/94, 554/94, 555/94, *State of Israel* v. *Shmuel Ben-Yishai, Aryeh Ben-Yoseph, and Amnon Tadmor* (Magistrate's Court, Jerusalem). Decision rendered on 22 January 1995; verdict on 2 March 1995. Judge Zilbertal convicted the three for praising the vicious massacre of Baruch Goldstein at the Cave of Machpellah on 25 February 1994. The verdict was a four-month sentence conditional for a period of two years, and a fine of NIS 1,000 (roughly $350). Criminal Appeal 243/93, *State of Israel* v. *Benjamin Kahane* (District Court of Jerusalem, decision from 14 December 1995). The appeal was concerned with seditious pamphlets of the Kahane Chai (Kahane Is Alive) movement distributed prior to the elections to the thirteenth Knesset.

minister in Rabin's government, and there was a possibility that one or more of the people in the public, many of whom objected to the Oslo Accords and the policies of Rabin's government, might take measures to kill Rabin's representative.[28]

The two who circulated the stickers, Ahuva Vaanunu and Gil Sharon, stood trial for conducting seditious actions (under Section 133 of the Penal Law, 1977) and for circulating seditious publications (under Sections 134a, 26, and 499 of the Penal Law, 1977). They received very lenient sentences. Judge Amiram Sharon sentenced them to three months' imprisonment, six months' conditional imprisonment, and a fine of NIS 1,500 each (approximately US$500).[29] This sentence could not be regarded as a proper deterrent against those who incited the murder of Prime Minister Rabin. Instead of giving a powerful indication that the courts would not tolerate explicit calls for murder, the court dismissed the issue as a mistake made by the two defendants, ignoring the context in which the stickers were circulated and the heated atmosphere that required law-and-order intervention to calm it down.

Rabin in black SS uniform

In October 1995, during a large demonstration held in Zion Square, Jerusalem, by the Israeli political right in protest against the Oslo Accords, some Kach activists waved photomontages of Rabin dressed in a black SS uniform. The Prime Minister's face was placed over the body of the notorious Nazi leader Heinrich Himmler.[30] The legal authorities took no steps to curtail those incitements or to prosecute those who waved the alarming pictures. In the Israeli culture, it is clear what the fate of a Nazi should be. Nazis are the most vehement enemies of the Jews, and therefore have no place within Israeli society. They should be eliminated. In this context I emphasize the difference between calling a group "Nazis", and targeting one individual by this revolting title and dressing him in a black SS uniform. The legal authorities ignored this clear incitement.

In his comments on this chapter, Robert Post wrote:

> I can't fathom how the picture of Rabin in Nazi clothes could be categorized as an incitement. In America we would view that as satire –

---

28 Robert Post notes in his comments that certainly this case would fail any American test for incitement: no temporal connection; no connection to any specific action likely to happen. Post remains unconvinced that this explicit call for murder, in the heated circumstances of hatred and resentment, might have been translated into a violent action against a minister who was very close to Rabin at that time.

29 Criminal file 152/94. *State of Israel* v. *Gil Sharon and Ahuva Vaanunu*, Hadera Magistrate's Court.

30 See *Maariv* (8 October 1995).

The issue would be offense, outrage, or perhaps intentional infliction of emotion distress, but no issue of incitement at all would arise. Nothing is being even advocated.[31]

Post is oblivious to the stark cultural differences between the United States and Israel. He fails to see that in Israel when one portrays a leader as a Nazi one does not merely advocate something: one is calling for removal of the danger before it fulfills the desired end of destroying the Jewish people. Post ignores context: the violent and hateful atmosphere in Israel at that time in general, and the especially heated atmosphere in Zion Square in particular.

Post, like many of his American colleagues, is convinced that what is suitable for the United States is suitable for other democracies. However, not all countries take this tolerant stance with regard to such speech. Germany bans the display of Nazi uniforms.[32] In Austria, the Insignia Act of 1960 prohibits the wearing or display of Nazi medals and symbols.[33] France has outlawed the wearing or public display of any uniform, insignia, or emblem of organizations and people responsible for crimes against humanity. The French Penal Code classifies this offense as a severe

31 Post's personal communication.
32 The German Criminal Code, *Bundesgesetzblatt Teil* I (p. 945) holds:

> Sect. 86 (1)(4): Anybody who disseminates within Germany, imports or exports means of propaganda which are designed to continue the efforts of a former national-socialist organization can be punished by imprisonment of up to three years or with a fine. The same is true if the person produces such means within Germany or abroad with the intention of disseminating them within Germany.

> sect. 86a (1) Any person who in Germany disseminates or publicly, in a meeting ... displays signs of one of the parties or associations specified in sect. 86 (1) is punishable with up to 3 years imprisonment or fine.

> (2) Signs in the sense of paragraph 1 are in particular flags, stickers, parts of uniforms, paroles and greeting forms. The same applies to signs that can be confused with the signs in the sense of the preceding sentence.

> I am grateful to Georg Nolte for translating the relevant paragraphs from German.

33 *Abzeichengesetz* 1960 (5 April 1960) in Bundesgesetzblatt, No. 84 (1960). This law was later amended by the Federal Law of 5 March 1980 in Bundesgesetzblatt, No. 117 (1980). The Act holds: "Insignia of an organization prohibited in Austria must not be worn publicly, displayed, depicted or disseminated. Insignia include emblems, symbols and signs." See also http://www.nizkor.org/ftp.cgi/orgs/austrian/austrian-resistance-archives/lachout-document.

crime against the people, the state and public safety.[34] In Britain, the wearing of Nazi uniforms at a public meeting might come in principle within the ban on wearing uniforms in the 1936 Public Order Act. Such a speech would be regarded as offensive, and possibly defamatory sufficiently to give rise to an action for libel or slander.[35] The way in which this discretion is exercised is influenced by the Human Rights Act 1998. The police, the Crown Prosecution Service and, ultimately, the courts must decide whether there is a pressing social need to prevent the Prime Minister being represented as a Nazi, and if so, whether stopping the display of the placard or prosecuting the person displaying it would interfere with freedom of expression more than necessary for that purpose. It is clear that political expression carries a high value, and so interference with it requires particularly strong justification if it is to be regarded as proportionate. On the other hand, racist expression (even if political) carries a relatively low value. Geoffrey Marshall commented that the authorities might resort to legal action if the circumstances in which the Nazi symbol is used give rise to a public order offense or can be interpreted as incitement to racial hatred. David Feldman has enlightened me in this context that the Anti-terrorism, Crime and Security Act (2001), Part 5, imposes a higher maximum sentence for a range of offenses if they are found, in an individual case, to have been motivated by religious hatred. Section 39 of the Act amends the Crime and Disorder Act 1998 and the Powers of Criminal Courts (Sentencing) Act 2000 to allow heavier sentences to be imposed for "religiously aggravated offenses" of assault, criminal damage, harassment, and offenses against public order. In addition, section 39

34 Pen. Art R-645-1. Furthermore, this Article also prohibits exhibition of Nazi propaganda and artifacts for sale. It was used by the High Court of Paris to order Yahoo! to eliminate French citizens' access to any material on the Yahoo.com auction site that offers for sale any Nazi objects, relics, insignia, emblems, and flags. See Interim Court Order No. 00/05308, 00/05309 (22 May 2000). The United States holds a different position: *Yahoo!* v. *La Ligue Contre Le Racisme Et l'Antisemitisme* et al., 169 F. Supp. 2d 1181; 2001 U.S. Dist. LEXIS 18378; 30 Media L. Rep. 1001 (decided on 7 November 2001).

35 It is an offense under the Public Order Act 1986, Section 4A, to display any writing, sign or other visible representation which is threatening, abusive or insulting with intent to cause another person harassment, alarm or distress. Under Section 5 of the Act, it is an offense to display any writing, sign or other visible representation which is threatening, abusive or insulting, within the hearing or sight of a person likely to be caused harassment, alarm or distress thereby. Under Section 18, it is an offense to display written material with the intent to stir up racial hatred or in circumstances where it is likely to stir up racial hatred. A constable may arrest a person without warrant on reasonable suspicion that he or she is committing an offense contrary to Section 4A or section 18, and may arrest a person after a warning for an offense under Section 5. It is a matter for the constable to decide whether it is appropriate to make an arrest. A person may be prosecuted for the offense, at the discretion of the Crown Prosecution Service.

amends the Police and Criminal Evidence Act 1984 to make religiously aggravated offenses arrestable without warrant on reasonable suspicion.[36]

In Israel, only after Prime Minister Rabin's assassination were measures taken to track down the inciters and investigate them. The two activists stood trial for brandishing the photomontage. Defendant 2 was also accused of writing the slogans "Rabin A Victim of Peace, Peres Is Next", and "Peres Continues the Way of Nazi Hitler".[37] Judge Ben-Dor noted that the two defendants had no previous criminal records and that their behavior stemmed from their ideological convictions. In his opinion, the balancing formula required withdrawal of freedom of expression when the harm to public order was severe and serious, as was the case here. The defendants' offense severely damaged public order. The photograph of Prime Minister Rabin dressed in SS uniform evoked outrage in every Jew. People who conceived the prime minister as a traitor, as a person whose policies might lead to the destruction of Israel as the Nazis brought about the destruction of the Jewish people, were urged by this photomontage to harm Prime Minister Rabin. Graffiti such as "Rabin A Victim of Peace, Peres Is Next" evoked similar feelings in like-minded people. Both defendants were accordingly convicted. Defendant 1 was sentenced to three months' conditional imprisonment for one year and 152 hours of communal work. Defendant 2 had just opened a new business and needed to devote his time and energy to this enterprise, so the considerate judge sentenced him to three months' conditional imprisonment for one year and a fine of NIS 950 (roughly US$300).

With all due respect, I think that these are ludicrous sentences. Incitement must be excluded from the scope of tolerance. It should be regarded as a criminal offense carrying severe punishment. This and similar events show the need for sharper legislation to elucidate the distinction between incitement and advocacy. The Penal Law should enable the trial of anyone who incites the murder of another or encourages

36 Feldman's personal communication. See the full text of the Act at http://www.legislation.hmso.gov.uk/acts/acts2001/20010024.htm. A private Member's Bill (the Religious Offences Bill) was later introduced in the House of Lords by Lord Avebury. It would have made the offense of incitement to religious hatred part of the law, and would also have abolished the common law offense of blasphemous libel. However, it ran into opposition on account of fears that it would unjustifiably interfere with freedom of expression (ECHR Article 10), and would be used particularly and discriminatorily against Muslims, violating the right to be free of discrimination in the protection of other Convention rights (ECHR Article 14). Lord Avebury's Bill was committed to a specially constituted Select Committee of the House of Lords that issued a report with no real conclusion as to the desirability of the proposed legislation. Consequently, the Bill made no further progress. However, Lord Avebury is quite likely to reintroduce it at a later date.
37 Criminal file 673/95 of 17 March 1996, judgment delivered by Judge Uri Ben-Dor, Magistrate's Court, Jerusalem.

violence and murder. People (including myself) called after Rabin's assassination for the addition of an article concerning enticement to kill a certain person or people, to determine a severe punishment by law for such a transgression, and to ensure its proper and serious implementation.

I also support the amendment of the Penal Law to the effect of prohibiting the use of Nazi symbols in Israeli political culture. It seems that in Israel legislators did not previously consider passing such a law, assuming that Jews would refrain from using Nazi symbols for political purposes. The last few months of 1995 proved them wrong. Legislation must say clearly that there is no room for Nazi symbols in the Israeli social arena.[38]

I should add that apparently not all the facts of this affair were revealed to the public. There is room to suspect that the lenient sentences may have been handed down because of the involvement of the Israeli Internal Security Service (SHABAC) in the circumstances. It appears that the ideological zealots were acting under the directive of a SHABAC agent named Avishai Raviv. The SHABAC actually helped to found a terrorist organization named Eyal that was headed by Raviv. I repeat: it was not a case of installing an agent into an existing terrorist organization in order to disclose its activities and warn against violent actions; rather, it was a case of founding a *new* terrorist organization that was extremely instrumental in generating an atmosphere of hatred and incitement against Prime Minister Rabin.

Raviv was one of the leading figures in the radical camp that had fought against any compromises for peace and for the unity of *Eretz Israel* since the mid-1980s. His activities included not only hate speech, but also violent attacks on Arabs. I confess that the logic of assisting such a person, making him a leader against the foundations of Israeli democracy, and the financing of a terrorist organization by a prominent government agency is beyond my understanding.[39] Note that the SHABAC is funded by the Prime Minister's Office; that is, Rabin's office had funded a terrorist organization that promoted his murder. I do not suggest there was some sort of conspiracy. I rather opt for a more simple explanation: this conduct was the result of careless thinking and shortsightedness, to use an understatement.

Raviv was later put on trial for failing to prevent Rabin's assassination.

38 Robert Post writes: "All Nazi symbols are not incitements, yet here you would ban them all. I think this shows that this case belongs in your chapter on offense, not incitement." Again, Post fails to see that the American political and social cultures are very different from those of Germany and Israel. These two countries, for obvious reasons, are far more sensitive to Nazism and its symbols than are other countries in the world, and rightly so. No European democracy has adopted the complacent American view about Nazism.
39 See E. Adato, "Raviv knew about Amir's intention to murder Rabin", *Yedioth Ahronoth* (2 August 2002), p. 7.

The head of the investigation team assigned by the SHABAC agent named "Yoni", testified that two days after the assassination Raviv admitted that he had heard Yigal Amir saying that he would kill Rabin. "Yoni" added that this statement contradicted Raviv's earlier testimony from the night of the assassination, when he said that "he had never heard Amir saying that he intended to harm the prime minister".[40] The SHABAC suspected that Raviv was hiding some information. Another agent named "Ronny" said that Raviv had indeed heard Amir saying that Rabin should be killed, but that he "did not take this seriously".[41]

On 31 March 2003, after a two-year trial, Raviv was exonerated of the charge against him of failing to prevent Rabin's assassination. The assassin's testimony played a crucial role. Amir testified that he was not Raviv's friend, did not respect him, and regarded him as one who sought publicity and did not know how to keep a secret. He was fully aware of the speculation floating in his circles that Raviv was a SHABAC agent, and thus did not trust him.[42] Raviv's lifestyle was too lavish. The verdict contained implicit criticisms of the SHABAC for recruiting to its ranks an immature person who lacked self-control, one with an inferior, weak, dependent personality; a person who sought to please others, who was incapable of differentiating between what was essential and what was redundant, and who had a narcissist disorder.[43]

A further note has to be made with regard to the role of the media in the Rabin/Himmler affair. In the Israeli culture and social context, the printing of photographs showing Prime Minister Rabin in Nazi uniform is unethical. This assertion relates to Attorney General Ben-Yair's distinction between direct and indirect reporting of incitement. It is one thing to report that during a demonstration pictures of Rabin dressed in a Nazi uniform were waved, and quite another actually to print the pictures in the newspapers and by this serve the interests of the inciters. The media should not serve as a platform for spreading hatred and violence. Indeed, Moshe Vardi, Editor of the major Israeli newspaper, *Yedioth Ahronoth*, applied self-censorship and refrained from printing these pictures. So did Hanoch Marmari, the Editor of *Haaretz*. This is an example of applying ethical codes without the need for governmental or legal interference. *Maariv*, I am sorry to say, published the hateful photomontage.

40 *Ibid.*
41 *Ibid.*
42 Criminal File 2070/99 *State of Israel* v. *Avishai Raviv*, Jerusalem Magistrate Court (31 March 2003), para. 86.
43 *Ibid.*, paras. 66–67. See also A. Ben-David, "Innocent", *Maariv* (1 April 2003), p. 10.

Rabbi Ginsberg's seditious pamphlet

In September 1994, Rabbi Yitzhak Ginsberg published a pamphlet entitled "Baruch the Man: Five General Commandments (*Mitzvot*, commands from the torah) that are Intrinsic Perspectives in the Act of Saint Rabbi Baruch Goldstein", in which he set forth *Halachic* (derived from Jewish law) and ideological justifications for the murder in the Cave of Machpellah (the burial place of the Patriarchs and their wives in Hebron). To recall, on 25 February 1994 Dr Baruch Goldstein entered the Cave of Machpellah and massacred, in cold blood, some twenty-nine Palestinians praying in the mosque inside the Cave. It should be noted that Ginsberg is regarded by many orthodox circles as a religious authority, and his words are closely and carefully observed.[44]

The five *mitzvot* which were the impetus for Dr Goldstein's act, according to Rabbi Ginsberg, were revenge, removal of evil, *Kiddush Ha'shem* (sanctification of the Holy Name), deliverance of souls, and war. Such a pronouncement calls into question whether Judaism is compatible with humanism. It was for Attorney General Ben-Yair to examine whether this praise constituted sedition according to the Penal Law.

The Penal Law defines "sedition", *inter alia*, as arousing discontent or resentment amongst inhabitants of Israel or promoting feelings of ill-will and enmity among different sections of the population.[45] I am not too happy with the language of this law, which provides great latitude to limit essential freedoms. I think the law should be reformulated in more restrictive terms. Nevertheless, I argue that on some occasions involving incitement it is better to apply the law as it is than to convey an indulgent message to inciters that their malicious declarations may be voiced and nothing will be done to curb them.[46] In my view Rabbi Ginsberg's pamphlet aroused discontent and resentment amongst Palestinians and Israelis and it prompted feelings of ill-will and enmity among different sections of the population. There was room to try him for sedition.

Moreover, I think that Rabbi Ginsberg should have stood trial for violation of two other laws. He should have been prosecuted for violation of Section 4 of the Prevention of Terrorism Ordinance (1948). Alternatively, or additionally, Rabbi Ginsberg should have been charged with "incitement to racism" under Sections 144 (A-E) of the Penal Law. In August 1986, in its battle against the Kach movement established by Meir Kahane (see Chapter 5), the Knesset passed a law that specifies "incitement to

44 See M. Gorali, "Will Rabbi Ginsberg escape trial again?", *Haaretz* (25 December 2001), pp. B3–B4.
45 Chapter Eight, Article One, Section 136 (3) (4) of the Penal Law. *Laws of the State of Israel, Special Volume: Penal Law*, pp. 5737–1977.
46 For further discussion, see R. Cohen-Almagor, "Combating right-wing political extremism is Israel: critical appraisal", *Terrorism & Political Violence*, 9(1) (1997): 82–105.

racism" as a criminal offense. Anyone who publishes anything with the purpose of inciting to racism is liable to five years' imprisonment (144B), and anyone who has racist publications in his or her possession for distribution is liable to imprisonment for one year (144D). The term "racism" is defined as "persecution, humiliation, degradation, manifestation of enmity, hostility or violence, or causing strife toward a group of people or segments of the population – because of color or affiliation with a race or a national-ethnic origin" (144A).[47] The reading of Justice Matza's recent judgment in *Rabbi Ido Elba* v. *State of Israel*[48] leads me to infer that today, after Prime Minister Rabin's assassination, Rabbi Ginsberg might have been charged for inciting to racism.

However, at that time Rabbi Ginsberg did not stand trial either for incitement to racism or for sedition, or for contravention of the Prevention of Terrorism Ordinance. Only after the abominable assassination did the authorities take action against him. On 10 March 1996, Rabbi Ginsberg was put under administrative detention, one of the most antidemocratic measures in the legal framework of Israel, for a period of two months. The grounds for his detention order were classes in which Rabbi Ginsberg told his students that there was a *halachic* duty to take revenge against Arabs for the massacres conducted by the Hamas and the Islamic Jihad in Jerusalem, Ashkelon, and Tel-Aviv.

Rabbi Ginsberg appealed to the Supreme Court against the detention decision.[49] His main contention was that nothing in what he had said could serve as basis for the assumption that a probable connection existed between his statements and harm inflicted upon Arabs by his students. Rabbi Ginsberg maintained that his views were not one-sided. In support, he brought evidence showing that in one of his publications he said: "... it is forbidden to harm a non-Jew who is not at war with us".[50] The state representative argued in response that Rabbi Ginsberg exercised strong influence on his followers, and that his preaching to take revenge on Arabs established grounds to suspect that the students might act upon their Rabbi's instructions.

Justice Dalia Dorner accepted Rabbi Ginsberg's appeal. She explained that there was scope for administrative detention when standard measures were deemed insufficient to secure public peace. Thus, when it was impossible to issue an indictment because the evidence, though reliable, was inadmissible, and a near probability existed that forbearance from detention might bring about substantial harm to public and state security,

---

47 For critical discussion of this law, see R. Cohen-Almagor, *The Boundaries of Liberty and Tolerance*, Chapter 13.
48 Criminal Appeal 2831/95. *Rabbi Ido Elba* v. *State of Israel* (24 September 1996).
49 A.A.D. (Appeal Against Administrative Detention) 4/96. *Rabbi Yitzhak Ginsberg* v. *Prime Minister and Minister of Defense* (28 March 1996).
50 *Ibid.*, para. 3.

then detention was justified. In the present matter, it was not claimed that Rabbi Ginsberg might do things that would endanger public security. Rather, Rabbi Ginsberg was arrested out of fear that his pronunciations might prompt his students to harmful conduct. Moreover, Rabbi Ginsberg lectured frequently to hundreds of people, and published his views on paper. Justice Dorner mentioned that in one of his publications Rabbi Ginsberg regarded Baruch Goldstein's massacre at the Cave of Machpellah as *Kiddush Ha'shem*. Unfortunately, she refrained from voicing an opinion as to whether this writing contravened Israeli law.[51] It was nevertheless obvious that Rabbi Ginsberg's lectures and publications exhibited no lack of clear evidence and material, so there was no need to resort to the exceptional measure of administrative detention.

I agree with Justice Dorner that there was no reason to place Rabbi Ginsberg under administrative detention. I have strong reservations with regard to the employment of this measure in democratic societies. In another article, I wrote that the procedure of administrative detention is manifestly unjust because it lacks proper hearing and due process of law. It is contrary to the democratic spirit and to liberal reason that proscribes arbitrary arrests. This procedure is commonplace in authoritarian regimes. It is the kind of instrument despots use to suppress opposition. They see no obligation to insist on rules of evidence and to disclose information to individuals under arrest. In contrast, democracies require that all legal procedures be exhausted before putting individuals behind bars. In a court of law, the prosecution has to prove that criminal offenses have been committed which justify penalties. Defendants have the right to be represented by lawyers, to summon witnesses, and to cross-examine them. The administrative detention procedure eschews this, and therefore is contrary to the notion of ensuring justice. Thus, my contention is the following: let the prosecution prosecute, the defendants defend themselves, and the court of justice mete out justice in accordance with material evidence. And if there is not sufficient evidence to prosecute, or if the prosecution is unable to produce relevant material, the defendants should retain their freedom. No procedure should exist to override the administration of justice.[52]

While agreeing that detention should not be considered just another preventive measure to be selected from the arsenal of preventive measures, and that it should not serve as a tranquilizer or as a substitute for criminal proceedings, I nevertheless think that there was reason to file

---

51 In a private conversation, Justice Dorner explained that this task was beyond the case at hand. The role of the Court was limited to the review of the detention decision.

52 R. Cohen-Almagor, "Administrative detention in Israel and its employment as a means of combating political extremism", *New York International Law Review*, 9(2) (1996): 1–25.

criminal charges against Rabbi Ginsberg for his inciting statements. I reiterate that he should have stood trial for inciting to racism, for provoking acts of terror, and for sedition.[53]

In a lecture delivered in February 1998, Talya Sasson, the Director of Special Assignments Division in the State Attorney Office, said that Rabbi Ginsberg had not been put to trial as a result of an error, and that he had been warned that he would stand trial if he continued his hateful incitement.[54]

In January 2001, Rabbi Ginsberg granted an interview in which he said, *inter alia*, that the Arab nation was the most primitive of all nations, lowest in the Third World ranking, with an animal nature that urges the killing of Jews; "Yishmael is people of slaves, and the character of a slave is uncontrollable and wicked".[55] In another publication, Ginsberg urged people to expel the Arabs from Israel, not to buy from them, and not to employ them. God erected covenant with Israel, and no foreigner should interfere and contaminate the atmosphere. Ginsberg mentioned some religious authorities who recommended the killing of Arabs, and only if this was impossible, their expulsion. Reflecting on this suggestion, the "moderate" Ginsberg commented that the first need was "to expel the *goyim* but if there is no way to do this, we ought then to kill them".[56] Ginsberg further recommended that the IDF kill a hundred Arabs for every Jew they kill, and to avenge by razing the nearest Arab village "to the ground".[57]

Pulsa Denurah

The last example of incitement concerns a religious curse called *Pulsa Denurah*. The year of 1995 was a bloody year in Israel's history. The country suffered a series of atrocious terrorist attacks against innocent civilians. Dozens of people lost their lives in those massacres. The public was polarized *vis-à-vis* the question of whether the implementation of the Oslo Accords should be continued. In October, on the eve of the most sacred day in the Jewish calendar, Yom Kippur, a person named Avigdor

53 At that period of time I wrote to the President of Israel, asking him to raise his powerful voice to condemn instigators of the extreme right who, day in and day out, preached hatred against the government. I thought that Ezer Weizman would be the right person to calm the atmosphere, due to his charisma and popularity in both political camps. President Weizman promised me that he would find the right opportunity to raise this issue and to condemn instigators. As far as I recall, he did not find such an opportunity.
54 T. Sasson, "The prosecution's policy on incitement and sedition", lecture delivered on 17 February 1998 at The Israeli Democracy Institute, Jerusalem (in Hebrew), p. 10.
55 Cf. M. Gorali, "Will Rabbi Ginsberg avoid prosecution again?" *Haaretz* (25 December 2001), pp. B3–B4.
56 *Ibid.*
57 *Ibid.*

Eskin, together with some other people, distributed this curse which was composed by three Cabbalists (*Mekubalim*) against Prime Minister Rabin. Eskin was photographed during the recitation of the *Pulsa Denurah* prayer outside the Prime Minister's official residence in Jerusalem. The prayer called on Rabin to cease his wrongful deeds in this world; it was recited in the presence of media reporters who were invited to the scene to publicize the ceremony and to deliver an inciting message to the public.[58] The message was that Prime Minister Rabin could not escape the curse that was placed upon him because of his evil policies. In effect, Rabin's blood was allowed – this was a provocative measure calling for his death.

The legal authorities took no action against Eskin. The Attorney General office adopted a strong liberal stand favoring free speech, and exhibiting manifest tolerance (see Chapter 1) regarding those who repeatedly called for murder of their political opponents. There was no sense of urgency to beat down such calls, believing that Israeli democracy could cope with such assertions, and that there was lack of proximity between the hateful and harmful speech and consequential harmful action. Only after the assassination, when Eskin appeared on television and declared that "our prayer was fulfilled in full", did the authorities begin to look for him. Liberals may dismiss the entire story as ridiculous, saying "Pulsa Shmulsa". But liberals are not prone to believing in such curses. They will not be moved to help God in executing such wishes. This prayer constituted an incitement that – with the help of the curious media – fell on eager ears and helped to generate an atmosphere that was conducive to triggering Yigal Amir and encouraging him to carry out his heinous act.

In early March 1996, Palestinian terrorists launched a series of vicious attacks which caused the death of tens of civilians. Following those massacres, on 6 March, Eskin approached the media and announced that it was his intention to perform the *Pulsa Denurah* ceremony once again, this time against Prime Minister Shimon Peres. After all, the curse had proved very effective the first time, so why not give it a second shot? Once again, the media served as a good mobilizer of his intentions. On 7 March 1996, the two popular daily newspapers, *Yedioth Ahronoth* and *Maariv*, published Eskin's contentions in full. In doing so, they provided an unfettered platform for incitement. They should have informed the public of the occasion, with explicit condemnation, not to provide unfettered platform for Eskin's incitement.

Eskin stood trial for (1) performing the *Pulsa Denurah* ceremony and for noting the connection between the ceremony and the death of Prime Minister Rabin the day after he was assassinated; and (2) for declaring that he intended to perform a similar ceremony calling for the death of Rabin's successor, Shimon Peres. The court found Eskin guilty on both

58 S. Zesna, "Zealots of the right prayed for Rabin's death", *Maariv* (3 October 1995), p. 2.

accounts of violating Section 4 of the Prevention of Terrorism Ordinance (1948). His verdict was imprisonment for a period of four months, and an additional one-year sentence conditional for a period of three years.[59]

Yedioth Ahronoth started that a survey conducted among Russian immigrants revealed that Eskin was regarded by this large sector (about 18 percent of the Israeli population) as the fourth most prominent political personality in Israel in 1997. There was speculation that Eskin also had some connections with the SHABAC.[60]

The *Pulsa Denurah* episode was neither the first nor the last in Eskin's rich political extremist career. In 1979 Eskin has been convicted for assault, damaging the property of two Arab families in Hebron, and trespassing. Eskin, with two other men, entered the two houses, and while claiming they belonged to Jews had beaten their residents and broken their furniture. The Supreme Court concluded that those were brutal acts of violence legitimized by extreme ideological views. However, the verdict then was also very lenient, and was not enough to deter Eskin: 100 days in prison, then fifteen months' probation for three years, and reporting to a probation officer for a similar period of time.[61]

Indeed, Eskin continued to contemplate further provocation. In 1997, he was indicted for three separate issues. The first charged that Eskin had conspired with Haim Pakovitch to put a pig's head in the old Muslim cemetery, where it is believed Az A din Al Kassam (a terrorist who fought the British and Jews before the establishment of the State of Israel) is buried. On 4 September 1997, Pakovitch bought the head and put it on the grave in the Nesher cemetery. On 10 September 1997, Eskin and Pakovitch took part in illegal demonstration outside the cemetery.[62] Pakovitch was convicted and received a penalty of three and a half years' imprisonment.

The second indictment was concerned with setting the Jerusalem branch of Dor Shalem Doresh Shalom (Whole Generation Demands Peace, a popular movement calling for peace) on fire on 29 October 1997. This was in retaliation for arson at the house of Yigal Amir's parents. It was argued that Pakovitch was incited by Eskin to carry out this conduct.[63]

The third indictment concerned a conspiracy between Eskin,

59 Criminal file 827/96. *State of Israel* v. *Avigdor Eskin* (Jerusalem Magistrate's Court).
60 S. Mulah, "Why does nobody stop that person?", *Yedioth Ahronoth* (7 November 1997), pp. 12–15, 71 ('7 Days' supplement). See also http://eskinweb.tripod.com/index2.html.
61 Criminal Appeal 522/79 *Eskin* v. *State of Israel*, P.D. (Piskei Din, i.e. Court Judgments) 34 (1), 113, at 114.
62 Criminal File 108/98 *State of Israel* v. *Eskin*, Jerusalem Magistrate Court (decision rendered on 5 October 1999).
63 Criminal File 108/98 *State of Israel* v. *Eskin*.

Pakovitch, and a third person named Herschtik to throw a pig's head, holding a Koran in its mouth, into the *Haram esh-Sharif*, the Noble Sanctuary (or Temple Mount) area where al-Aksa Mosque, one of the holiest mosques in the world, is situated, during Friday prayers in the month of Ramadan.[64] Thankfully the plan did not materialize, as a fourth person named Polack leaked it to the authorities. One can only try to imagine what could have happened had the conspiracy materialized. Such an act, based upon crude religious provocation, in a place holy to millions of Muslims, and which is at the heart of a difficult, bitter religious and nationalistic dispute, concurrent with a Muslim religious holiday when many worshippers were expected to be at the site, was likely to enrage people at the mosque and to bring about severe harm to public order to the point of undermining the proper functioning of government.[65]

Judge Yehudith Zur convicted Eskin for the first two charges. Not enough evidence was found to connect Eskin to third charge. This time Eskin received a serious sentence: two-and-half years' imprisonment followed by a year-and-half probation for a three-year period.[66]

State of Israel *v.* Ido Elba

In April 1995, Rabbi Ido Elba was charged and convicted by the Jerusalem District Court on five different counts: first, the publication of a pamphlet entitled "An Examination of Religious Directives (*Halachot*) Concerning the Killing of Gentiles"; second, attempts to produce weapons; third, trying to persuade an officer of the Israel Defense Forces (IDF) to steal weapons and explosives for him, and fourth – alternatively – to persuade an officer to disclose the location of IDF bases which he could penetrate and from which he could steal ammunition. Finally, Rabbi Elba was charged for trying to obstruct and disrupt legal proceedings. Rabbi Elba was sentenced to two years' imprisonment and to conditional imprisonment of two additional years for a period of three years.[67]

---

64 Ramadan is the ninth month of the Muslim calendar. The month of Ramadan is also when it is believed the Holy Koran "was sent down from heaven, guidance unto men, a declaration of direction, and a means of Salvation". Muslims fast during this month. It is a time of worship and contemplation, when Muslims concentrate on their faith and spend less time on the concerns of their everyday lives. See http://www.holidays.net/ramadan/story.htm.

65 Cf. M. Gur-Arye, "Can freedom of expression survive social trauma? The Israeli experience", *Duke Journal of Comparative & International Law*, 13 (2003): 155, at 171. For good depiction of the intricacy of the site, and the heightened emotions involved, see the film *Eye of the Storm: Jerusalem Temple Mount* (Princeton, N.J.: Films for the Humanities & Sciences, 2004). For a different interpretation of this affair, see http://www.makorrishon.net/article.php?id=3998.

66 Criminal File 108/98 *State of Israel* v. *Eskin*.

67 Criminal File 251/94. *State of Israel* v. *Ido Elba* (Jerusalem District Court), verdict rendered on 13 April 1995.

Rabbi Elba appealed to the Supreme Court, which affirmed the conviction in a five to two decision. The two dissenting Justices, Zvi Tal and Yaakov Tirkel, accepted the conviction for four of the charges but objected to the conviction on the first charge – the subject of our discussion – that the publication constituted incitement. Speaking for the majority of the Court, Justice Matza argued that the pamphlet incited racism under Section 144B of the Penal Law, and that it also encouraged violence against Arabs in violation of Section 4 of the Prevention of Terrorism Ordinance.[68]

Justice Matza elaborated on the content of Rabbi Elba's writing. In the center of the publication were *halachic* justifications for the killing of non-Jews. It explicitly stated that the prohibition on murder did not include instances where a Jew kills a non-Jew. Rabbi Elba's pamphlet further postulated that it was a *mitzvah* to kill gentiles who believed in other religions that denied the basic beliefs of Israel and the eternity of the Torah; that during periods of war "it is a *mitzvah* to kill every gentile rival, even women and children"; that it was permissible to launch an attack against gentiles in order to kill them if suspicion existed that these gentiles might attack Jews in the future; and that it was obligatory to attack gentiles whose aim was to make Jews abandon their settlements (para. 6 in Justice Matza's opinion).

Justice Matza explained that a publication would be considered a racist incitement "if the publisher was aware of the nature of the publication, the given circumstances, and the probability of causing racist incitement", and if his intention was to incite to racism or at least if he foresaw the probability that the publication would incite to racism (para. 21). In Justice Matza's opinion, the publication delivered an unequivocal message of racist incitement and it embodied a considerable risk to public peace and security. Rabbi Elba intended to convey to his readers an actual and political message of a racist nature, and to encourage them to violent attacks against non-Jews. Although Rabbi Elba argued and wrote that his discussion was academic and theoretical, ample evidence was provided to sustain that his real intention was to mobilize people to violent action. The so-called "academic" and "theoretical" framework was only a facade (para. 30). We cannot ignore the fact that Rabbi Elba chose to circulate his publication among the yeshiva students of the Cave of Machpellah two months after Baruch Goldstein's massacre at that same place. In addition, the other charges against Rabbi Elba, which included attempts at manufacturing and stealing ammunition and weapons, proved that his intentions were more than purely theoretical.

In sustaining Rabbi Elba's conviction under Section 4 of the Prevention of Terrorism Ordinance, Justice Matza explained that a publisher would

---

68 Criminal Appeal 2831/95. *Rabbi Ido Elba* v. *State of Israel* (24 September 1996), paras. 5, 23, 28, 30, 31, 42, 46.

be found guilty of violation of the Ordinance if his publication might lead to provocation to violence. In other words, it was not necessary to prove that the words of praise, sympathy or encouragement for acts or threats of violence might *actually* bring about the killing or maiming of another person. Justice Matza argued that "suffice it to show that the acts of violence which the publication praised, supported or encouraged were of the kind which might lead to one of these harmful results". Justice Matza further made clear that the Ordinance prohibited such publications even if behind it stood one person, or members of a group, who did not identify themselves as members of a terrorist organization. The prohibition on such publications was derivative from the terrorist nature of the violent conduct, and not from the publisher's affiliation to a terrorist organization (para. 44).

It is interesting that Justice Matza conclusively argued that of the five serious charges against Rabbi Elba, the first – racist incitement – was the most severe (para. 61). It was more serious than plotting to manufacture and to steal weapons. It was more serious than the obstruction of justice. Justice Matza explained that Rabbi Elba's publication offended basic values: the equality of a person and that person's right to defend his or her life, body and dignity. Racist incitement damaged the character of the State of Israel as a Jewish democratic state. Justice Matza maintained that the State of Israel was founded upon general as well as Jewish moral values, and that "it could not afford, nor could it permit, for the sake of its integrity and future, to treat the foul phenomenon of racist incitement mercifully" (para. 61).[69]

This loud and clear voice against incitement should have been raised by the Supreme Court as well as the lower courts prior to Prime Minister Rabin's assassination, with the effect of punishing more severely inciters like Ahuva Vaanunu, Gil Sharon, Rabbi Ginsberg, and Avigdor Eskin. Justice Matza and his fellow Justices Barak, Bach, Goldberg, and Dorner have delivered the notion that the lenient attitude adopted by the courts in the past needs to be replaced by a more stringent policy toward inciters.

Let me focus on one contention by Justice Matza that is often raised when speaking of racism. Justice Matza argued (para. 24) that the Free Speech Principle does not include racist expressions. I beg to differ. Like Justices Barak (para. 4 in Barak J.'s judgment), Bach (para. 5 in Bach J.'s judgment), Goldberg (para. 2 in Goldberg J.'s judgment), Dorner (para. 2 in Dorner J.'s judgment), and Tirkel (para. 9 in Tirkel J.'s judgment), I think that the Free Speech Principle covers racist expressions as well. I do not see why verbal utterances on race, color, religion, etc. should be regarded as a unique type of speech which does not deserve protection. As

---

69 For further discussion, see M. Kremnitzer, "The Elba case – the law of incitement to racism", *Mishpatim*, 30 (1999): 105 (in Hebrew).

I said in Chapter 1, I find it difficult to see why racist expressions should be thought different from verbal attacks on our most fundamental ethical and moral convictions – as, for instance, in the debates on abortion, on the right to die with dignity and assisted suicide, and on pornography. While acknowledging that one cannot be held responsible for one's race in the way that one is responsible for one's ethical convictions, I still do not see why dignity or equal respect and concern are more at stake in the one case than in the other. Sometimes (but not at all times) racist expressions should be excluded from the protection of the Free Speech Principle (as explained in Chapter 5), but we should not outlaw racist provocation merely because of its content without regard to the speakers' intentions and the given circumstances.

An important more recent decision came in *State of Israel* v. *Benjamin Kahane*.[70] In 1992, the Kahane Chai movement attempted to participate in the elections for the Knesset. The party was disqualified because its purposes included "incitement to racism", contrary to Sections 7A (2) and (3) of Basic Law: The Knesset.[71] Before its disqualification, the party's leader Benjamin Kahane (Meir Kahane's son) distributed a pamphlet that called:

> Bomb Umm El Fahm!... Why is it that every time a Jew is killed we shell Lebanon and not the hostile Arab villages within the State of Israel? For every attack in Israel – shell an Arab village – a nest of murderers in the State of Israel! Only Kahane has the courage to tell the truth! Give Kahane the power and he will take care of them.[72]

Kahane was charged with sedition under Section 133 of the Penal Law and possession of seditious publications under Section 134(c) of the Penal Law. It was argued that distributing the pamphlet was likely to promote feelings of ill-will and enmity among the Jewish and Arab populations under the definition of sedition in Section 136(4) of the Penal Law. After a lengthy legal struggle, the Supreme Court in a further hearing decided

---

70 Cr.F.H. 1789/98, *The State of Israel* v. *Benjamin Kahane*, P.D. 54(5), 145.
71 Section 7A reads:

> A list of candidates shall not participate in Knesset elections if any of the following is expressed or implied in its purposes or deeds:.
>
> 1. Denial of the existence of the State of Israel as the State of the Jewish people;
> 2. Denial of the democratic character of the State;
> 3. Incitement to racism.

> For further discussion, see R. Cohen-Almagor, "Disqualification of Lists in 1988 and 1992: a comparative analysis", in M. Troper and M. M. Karlsson (eds), *Law, Justice and the State* (Stuttgart: Franz Steiner Verlag, 1995), pp. 88–103.

72 *Ibid.*, para. 3 in Orr J.'s judgment; Cr.A. 6696/96, *Kahane* v. *The State of Israel*, P.D. 52(1), 535.

in a five-to-two majority to convict Kahane. The majority (Justice Orr joined by Levin, D. P., Kedmi, Dorner and Matza J. J.) ruled that such expression lies outside the scope of tolerance. The offense of sedition is intended to protect the ability of various segments of the population to live together in peace and security. Justice Orr called this value "social cohesiveness".[73] This value is of particular importance in a multicultural, pluralistic society with a delicate societal mosaic, such as in Israel, in which minorities and members of different religious sects live side by side, and in which the differences between the various population groups are quite significant.[74] Thus the purpose of allowing for the continued existence of Israel, with all its varied groups, properly justifies limiting explicit calls for violence. That purpose requires, quite rightly, that the offense of sedition be applied to Kahane's hateful and malicious pamphlet. The Court further explained that the said pamphlet was not a one-off expression, but part of an orchestrated campaign intended to plant hatred between the Jewish and Arab populations and to bring about acts of violence.[75] The Court refused to dismiss the pamphlet as merely an infantile expression that did not require legal intervention.[76] Against the backdrop of hostilities and violence between Arabs and Jews, this was the correct decision.

Further thoughts

Prime Minister Rabin's assassination forced us to think harder than before about the limits of liberty and tolerance in our democracy. The legal authorities were mistaken in their lenient attitude to inciters. The security forces did not give ample consideration to existing threats which mentioned the likelihood of assassination.[77] Israel is a young democracy. It is in process of development and undoubtedly it will face further challenges and tests. I hope these tests will not be of the nature and scope of the tragic murder of 4 November 1995. On the whole, I think Israeli democracy coped quite well

73 Para. 21 in Orr J.'s judgment.
74 Para. 22 in Orr J.'s judgment.
75 Para. 35 in Orr J.'s judgment.
76 Para. 35 in Orr J.'s judgment. For further discussion and critique of this case, as well as of the *Jabrin* decision (Cr.F.H. 8613/96, *Jabrin* v. *The State of Israel*, P.D. 54(5), 193) that was concurrently decided, see M. Gur-Arye, "Can freedom of expression survive social trauma? The Israeli experience", *op. cit.*, esp. pp. 166–186.
77 See Y. Valter, "Someone might rise to kill 40 leftists", *Maariv* (8 October 1995), pp. 6–9 (Sukkut supplement); Y. Levi, "Former SHABAC agent: there is a valid danger that Rabin might be assassinated", *Maariv* (12 October 1995), pp. 2–3; A. Kaspi, "Who is on target?" *Haaretz* (20 October 1995), pp. 10–11 (supplement); M. Negbi, "The judges' guilt", *Maariv* (10 November 1995), p. 23; B. Meeri and S. Mitelman, "Ben-Yair: two weeks before the murder I warned against such a possibility", *Maariv* (13 November 1995), p. 19.

with the challenge imposed by Prime Minister Rabin's assassination. Immediately after the assassination, I feared that we might lose our brakes and that illiberal measures would be introduced that might hinder the Israeli nation-building tradition as a democratic state. I am happy to say that those fears were too pessimistic. Nevertheless, we must acknowledge that the assassination opened up new frontiers of political radicalism, and that safeguards should be installed to protect our vulnerable reality. We live in an era of political violence and extremism, and we need to find answers to the radical forces that seem to go from strength to strength, and to overcome them. We need to acknowledge the "catch of democracy" and that free speech might be very costly. Incitement is and should remain well outside the boundaries of tolerance. We need not hesitate to prosecute people who call for murderous attacks on others.

After Rabin's assassination the government established an Inquiry Committee, headed by the former President of the Supreme Court, Meir Shamgar, to investigate the terrible deed. The Committee decided to refrain from investigating the incitement campaign prior to the assassination. Shamgar explained that the Committee was not nominated to probe the factors that yielded the particular cultural and political environment which manifested itself by the murder. Its mandate was not to search for the reasons that brought about the assassination. Shamgar thought this was an assignment that an inquiry committee should not take upon itself.[78]

For my part, I am sorry that the government did not decide to establish some public body to investigate the events leading to the assassination. On the one hand, the proximity in time might have constituted an obstacle for lucid probing of all the relevant findings. On the other hand, at that time all the institutions and organizations in Israel would have cooperated fully with such an investigation, being afraid to lose face if they did not. It was a golden opportunity to bring to light thoughts that were circulating in inner rooms, and to clean the stables. That golden opportunity was lost.

One more observation regarding the Penal Law is in order. After Prime Minister Rabin's assassination, the Minister of Justice David Libai and Attorney General Ben-Yair recommended that the Penal Law dealing with seditious conduct be refined and defined more clearly. After much deliberation, an offense of incitement to violence or terror was added to the Penal Law. The Amendment (No. 66) repeals the offense of publishing praise for acts of violence, as defined in Section 4(A) of the Prevention of Terrorism Ordinance, and adds to the Penal Law an offense of incitement to violence and terror. The offense provides:[79]

78 *Inquiry Committee for Prime Minister Rabin's Murder: Report* (Jerusalem: Government Printing, 1996), p. 203 (in Hebrew).
79 *Penal Law (Incitement to Violence)* (Amendment No. 66), 2002, passed in the Knesset on 15 May 2002.

a   Any person who publishes either a call to commit a violent act or terror, or a praise, support or encouragement of violent acts or terror (for the purpose of this section – "an inciting publication"), and according to its content and the circumstances in which it was pub-lished there is a valid possibility that it will lead to a violent act or terror, shall be liable to imprisonment for five years.

b   For the purpose of this section "a violent act or terror" – offense that harms or endangers human life or bodily integrity.

c   Publishing a fair and accurate report of a publication unlawful under the provisions of subsections (a) and (b), does not constitute an offense under this section.

As opposed to the offense of praising acts of violence under section 4(A) of the Prevention of Terrorism Ordinance, the offense of incitement to violence or terror does not prohibit speech that contributes to creating a climate of violence, unless there is a real possibility that it will lead to a violent act or terror.[80]

Unfortunately, nowadays we hear constant threats against high-ranking officials whose conduct runs counter to certain beliefs of extremists. It seems that within the radical spheres, all boundaries are broken. The assassination of Prime Minister Rabin legitimized a new mode of conduct. The terms "political assassination" and "liquidation lists" became part of this. I do not recall having heard these expressions prior to Prime Minis-ter Rabin's assassination with the frequency and intensity that I have heard them since. Even in the heyday of the quasi-fascist Meir Kahane, during the mid-1980s, people were much more careful in expressing themselves. Thus, for instance, in Purim (the most joyful Jewish holiday) in 2003, some 100 people of the extreme right, headed by Kach activists, held a memorial for the death of Baruch Goldstein, noting nine years since his "brave act" in the Cave of Machpella. During the ceremony, some people called for the murder of Prime Minister Ariel Sharon. Those people masqueraded as soldiers and staged a show in which they killed Sharon by guns and knives. People shouted: "Sharon, your day will come".[81]

In July 2004, a poll conducted among the Israeli Jewish population

80 For further discussion, see M. Gur-Arye, "Can freedom of expression survive social trauma? The Israeli experience", *op. cit.*, pp. 198–202; M. Kremnitzer, "What is forbidden incitement?", in M. Konfino (ed.), *Power of the Words and Weakness of Mind, op. cit.*, pp. 100–111. Compare this law to the Austrian *Verhet-zung*, Section 283 of the Criminal Code – incitement to hostile action, and to Sections 281, 282. (English translation available at European Monitoring Centre on Racism and Xenophobia, *EUMC Study on Anti-Discrimination Legisla-tion in EU Member States, Austria* (Vienna, 2002), p. 12; http://eumc.eu.int/).

81 U. Yavloncka, "Youth called for Sharon's murder during Goldstein's memor-ial", *Maariv* (18 March 2003), p. 19.

revealed that 11 percent of people who identified themselves with the right agreed with the statement: "When national disaster is on the threshold and all protest measures exhausted, inflicting physical harm on politicians might be forgiven."[82] The same month, Prime Minister Ariel Sharon called upon the Justice Ministry to act vigorously to uproot dangerous incitement from the far right-wing. "It saddens me that one who has spent his whole life defending Jews in Israel's wars now needs to be protected from Jews out of fear that they will harm him", Sharon said.[83] Minister of Internal Security, Tzachi Hanegbi, said: "I have no doubt that there are people who have already decided that they will 'save the people of Israel' and will assassinate a minister, the prime minister, an army officer or a police officer" – in imitation of Rabin assassin Yigal Amir.[84] The SHABAC Director, Avi Dichter, has warned against growing extremism among militant opponents of Prime Minister Ariel Sharon's disengagement plan to withdraw from the Gaza Strip (the so-called "Gaza First Plan").[85] Spurred on by Dichter's comments, Attorney General Menachem Mazuz plans to convene the SHABAC Chief, the IDF Judge Advocate General, and senior police and Justice Ministry officials to discuss policies regarding bringing suspects to trial over incitement to violence.[86]

My book, *The Boundaries of Liberty and Tolerance*, ends with voicing alarm that the radical right might assassinate an Israeli political leader. A year after the book's publication, Yitzhak Rabin was assassinated. I raise the same cautionary alarm today. There are enough people in Israel who conceive of Yigal Amir as a hero, and who think that his terrible deed helped to avert the "disastrous" Oslo Accords. Some may try the same method to forestall Sharon's "catastrophic" disengagement plan. After all, if murder was successful once, why not commit another? The Israeli authorities are not complacent regarding the instigating calls for murder, and rightly so. Incitement to murder is not protected speech.

Furthermore, we need to defeat all forms of terrorism, whether directed against Jews or against Arabs. Terrorism and democracy cannot live together. One must make way and advance at the expense of the other (see Chapters 8 and 9). It is in our common interest to work for the victory of democracy.[87] We also need to build bridges and promote understanding between different factions of the population, especially between

82 D. Rattner, "11% of the right: inflicting physical harm on politicians is forgiven", *Haaretz* (8 July 2004).
83 A. Barkat *et al.*, "PM: Justice Ministry must uproot right-wing incitement", *Haaretz* (5 July 2004).
84 B. Burston, "Background/A bullet with Sharon's name on it", *Haaretz* (7 July 2004).
85 See R. Cohen-Almagor, "The best first step", *The Baltimore Sun* (18 December 2003).
86 B. Burston, "Settler as Israel's victim: the right cries abuse", *Haaretz* (5 July 2004).
87 See A. Pedhazur, *The Israeli Response to Jewish Extremism and Violence* (Manchester and New York: Manchester University Press, 2002).

the secular and the religious factions. Terminology such as "we are enlightened liberals while they constitute the forces of darkness", which is often utilized by Israeli civil libertarians, will not help the forces of democracy. There are enlightened individuals within the religious circles, just as there are intolerant individuals within the secular circles. Israel, as a religious and democratic state, needs to work out ways to bring about the good of both traditions, and to enrich the citizens' understanding of both great forces that made Israel the state it now is.

At the time this book was being proof-read, a group of zealots had gathered together to recite the *Pulsa Denurah* curse against Prime Minister Sharon, calling on the Angels of Destruction to come to their aid and kill the person who wishes to give up lands of Eretz Israel. Same or similar people. Same voices. Same ideas. Only the target is different. Then Rabin. Now Sharon. Did we learn something, or not?

The two tabloids did not learn much. It is one thing to report about the small gathering of the extremists who call for the death of Prime Minister Sharon, and quite another to actually print the pictures in the newspapers and by this serve the interests of the inciters. The media should not serve as a platform for spreading hatred and violence. *Maariv*, I am sorry to say, had published the hateful recitation of the curse on its first page along with words of the editor, Amnon Dunkner, dismissing the ceremony as "nonsense".[88] *Yedioth Ahronoth* printed the ceremonial photo on its third page with a reminder that the same took place regarding Prime Minister Rabin.[89] On the other hand, David Landau, editor of *Haaretz* quality newspaper, applied self-censorship and refrained from printing these pictures.[90] This is an example of applying ethical codes without the need for governmental or legal interference.

88 Amnon Dunkner, "Pulsa the nonsense", *Maariv* (27 July 2005), p. 1.
89 Anat Tal-Shir and Guy May-Tal, "Curse of death", *Yedioth Ahronoth* (27 July 2005), p. 2.
90 Amiram Barkat, "Extremists put pulsa denura death curse on PM Ariel Sharon", *Haaretz* (27 July 2005).

7 Hate speech in Canada

> In 50 or 100 years, when the Holocaust Myth has met its proper demise, what Revisionists believe today will be standard historical canon from which only cranks and religious zealots will dissent.
>
> Bruce Hagen, The Zundelsite

Preliminaries

Hate speech can be defined as "any form of expression directed at objects of prejudice that perpetrators use to wound and denigrate its recipient". Hate speech presents itself in many different forms, including direct talk, symbols contained in parades and cross burnings, and, more recently, Internet websites. It is speech that conveys a message of inferiority, is directed against members of a historically oppressed group, and is persecutory, hateful, and degrading.[1]

Important international conventions prohibit the dissemination of ideas hostile to racial groups. Article 4 of the International Convention on the Elimination of All Forms of Racial Discrimination (CERD), which Canada ratified in 1970, requires state parties to declare as criminal offenses "all dissemination of ideas based on racial superiority or hatred, incitement to racial discrimination" and participation in organizations which promote and incite racial discrimination. Article 20 of the International Covenant on Civil and Political Rights (CCPR), of which Canada is a signatory, declares that "any advocacy of national, racial or religious hatred that constitutes incitement to discrimination, hostility or violence shall be prohibited by law". Irwin Cotler, Canada's Minister of Justice, said in an interview I conducted with him in 2002 that International treaties are important because they state that hate speech does not enjoy the protection of free speech;

---

1 Dr Frances Henry's Expert Report for the Canadian Human Rights Commission, on the complaint of Richard Warman against the Canadian Ethnic Cleansing Team, Kulbashian, Richardson, and the Tri-City Skins (24 April 2004).

that hate speech is outside the ambit of protected speech.[2] A Supreme Court Justice, who preferred to remain anonymous, said that international treaties are very important. They are interpretory aids in looking at the content of rights and in justifying certain decisions.[3]

This chapter is founded on the following specific premises, additional to the premises that underlie the book. The first relates to the harms of hate speech and the cost society is required to pay when it tolerates such speech. Hate speech causes immediate mental and emotional distress to its targets. It might also inflict psychological harm on them. The Canadian Supreme Court acknowledged this by using a harm-based rationale to justify criminalizing hate speech in *Keegstra*, arguing that hate propaganda can harm society as a whole.[4] South Africa holds that the racial insult "harms souls". In the United Kingdom, a statutory offense (Public Order Act 1986, section 18, restricts such speech in part to avoid harm to the public order.[5] Furthermore, French and German statutory documents affirm a corollary proposition about the effect of hateful speech on the community at large. In France, a national report recognized that, in addition to psychological and moral harm, hate speech damages the individual and collective reputations of its victims. The preamble to a statute on group libel declares that such "aggression is directed against the whole body politic and its social and moral fabric".[6] Germans view a racial or ethnic attack as an affront to a person's core identity. Article 131 of the German Criminal Code seeks to protect the "social harmony" endangered by incitement to racial hatred.

Therefore, the second premise is that, with due appreciation for our liberal innate inclination to provide wide latitude to freedom of expression, we must also acknowledge the need for setting limits. The media should develop sensitive and responsible mechanisms in their coverage of hate speech. By providing unfettered loudspeakers to hate-mongers, the media play to their hands and help in spreading their hatred and harmful messages. As early as 1965, the Special Committee on Hate Propaganda noted its concern that Canada "has become a major source of supply of hate propaganda that finds its way to Europe and specifically to West Germany".[7] Canada remains a major exporter of hate literature in the world, and it is of interest to examine to what extent the media cooperate with hate-mongers by giving them a platform for disseminating their ideas.[8]

2 Interview with Irwin Cotler MP in Montreal on 24 July 2002.
3 Interview at the Canadian Supreme Court, Ottawa (19 July 2002).
4 *R.* v. *Keegstra* [1990] S.C.J. No. 131; 3 S.C.R. 697.
5 See R. Delgado and J. Stefancic, *Must We Defend Nazis?* (New York: New York University Press, 1997), esp. p. 128.
6 *Ibid.*, p. 128. For further discussion, see E. Bleich, *Race Politics in Britain and France* (Cambridge: Cambridge University Press, 2003), esp. Chapters 6–9.
7 M. Cohen, *Report to the Minister of Justice of the Special Committee on Hate Propaganda* (Ottawa: Queen's Printer, 1966), p. 69.

To reiterate: it is *not* argued that the media should not cover incidents of racist manifestations and hate propaganda. The public should be aware of these phenomena, know about the individuals and groups who preach hate, their drives and means. At the same time, it is possible to report about political extremists, their intentions and deeds, in the name of the public's right to know, without playing into the hands of inciters and serving as their loudspeaker. Responsible media are moral media. The setting of limits on the public's right to know should be left in the hands of journalists, but it is important to stress that explicit inciting messages should not be protected under the Free Speech Principle.[9] Furthermore,

8 For further deliberation, see W. Kinsella, "Challenges to Canadian liberal democracy", in R. Cohen-Almagor (ed.), *Challenges to Democracy: Essays In Honour and Memory of Professor Sir Isaiah Berlin* (London: Ashgate, 2000), pp. 119–135. See also *Jersild* v. *Denmark* (15890/89) [1994] ECHR 33 (23 September 1994) where the European Court of Human Rights, in a majority opinion, allowed a broadcasting journalist freedom to interview racist people, providing them with a platform to air derogatory and hateful remarks against minorities. The Court held that the punishment of a journalist for assisting in the dissemination of statements made by another person in an interview would seriously hamper the contribution of the press to discussion of matters of public interest, and should not be envisaged unless there are particularly strong reasons for doing so. The dissenting judges insisted, quite rightly, that while broadcasters can interview racists, it is absolutely necessary to add at least a clear statement of disapproval. They thought the statements made and willingly reproduced in the relevant broadcast on Danish television, without any significant reaction on the part of the commentator, "did indeed amount to incitement to contempt not only of foreigners in general but more particularly of black people, described as belonging to an inferior, subhuman race". They maintained: "A journalist's good intentions are not enough in such a situation, especially in a case in which he has himself provoked the racist statements." The dissenting minority concluded that the protection of racial minorities cannot have less weight than the right to impart information. http://www. mediator.online.bg/eng/jersild1.htm.
9 Racist views are not necessarily explicit inciting messages. David Ahenakew, a Saskatchewan native leader, expressed offensively anti-Semitic views in December 2002. He called Jews a "disease", praised the slaughter of Jews in Europe by explaining that "The Jews damn near owned all of Germany prior to the war", and that Hitler was only trying to clean Europe. "That's how Hitler came in. He was going to make damn sure that the Jews didn't take over Germany or Europe. That's why he fried six million of those guys. . . . Jews would have owned the goddamned world." Subsequently Ahenakew was charged under Section 319(2) of the Criminal Code. The incident was widely reported in the media, and rightly so. I would suggest the reportage should have been accompanied by explicit condemnation of his contemptible and vile statements in the editorial columns. Cf. R. Mofina, "Hitler right to 'fry' Jews, chief claims", *Ottawa Citizen* (15 December 2002), p. A4; "RCMP to probe native leader's racist remarks: Jewish leaders want ex-chief stripped of Order of Canada", *Ottawa Citizen* (17 December 2002), p. A1; M. Blanchfield and M. Brooks, "Hitler praise called vile", *The Gazette* (16 December 2002), p. A14; T. MacCharles, "RCMP to probe pro-Nazi tirade", *Toronto Star* (17 December 2002), p. A1. See also http://www.cbc.ca/story/ canada/national/2005/07/08/ahenakew050708.html.

it is possible to report demonstrations and protests, without printing hateful messages (such as photos of Israeli leaders dressed in a Nazi black uniform: see Chapter 6). Media editors and reporters acting as responsible citizens in a democracy should report such occurrences along with an unequivocal and clear condemnation. I shall reiterate this point later on.

The third contention of this chapter is that the media are not under an obligation to remain impartial or neutral with regard to all concepts: some concepts may co-exist with the principles of democracy while others contradict them completely.[10] It is for the media to take a firm stance to defend democracy whenever it is threatened.[11] On this issue, my view differs significantly from the view of some commentators and media codes of conduct that speak of neutral and partial reporting.[12] It is one thing to ask the media to be neutral in their coverage of news, but there is no obligation on the part of the media to adhere to neutrality in editorials and opinion columns. Indeed, often columnists provoke partial views, strongly criticize decision-makers, and offer remedies and alternative policies. Professional and ethical reporting means, in a nutshell, caring for the consequences of reporting. Such caring prescribes partiality rather than neutrality when hate speech and Holocaust denial are concerned. Otherwise, impartial reporting might confer legitimacy on racist diatribes and blatant lies.

10 In his comments, Eric Barendt wrote that broadcasters in the UK are not required to be impartial between democratic governments and terrorists or fascists. This was spelt out in the Broadcasting Act 1990, section 6, as a qualification from the general due impartiality requirement. The provision is not repeated in the Communications Act 2003, but Barendt is sure the principle is still valid.

11 See, for example, the struggle of the *Times-Picayune* in New Orleans against a bigot named David Duke, who wished to become the governor of the state of Louisiana (20 October–17 November 1991 issues). See D. E. Boeyink, "Reporting of political extremists in the United States: the Unabomber, the Ku Klux Klan, and the militias", in R. Cohen-Almagor (ed.), *Liberal Democracy and the Limits of Tolerance* (Ann Arbor: Michigan University Press, 2000), pp. 215–231. For discussion on the concept of neutrality, see R. Cohen-Almagor, "Between neutrality and perfectionism", *Canadian Journal of Law & Jurisprudence*, VII(2) (1994): 217–236.

12 For instance, the Radio/Television News Directors Association code begins by saying: "The responsibility of radio and television journalists is to gather and report information of importance and interest to the public accurately, honestly, and impartially." For further discussion, see G. Gauthier, "In a defence of a supposedly outdated notion: the range of application of journalistic objectivity", *Canadian Journal of Communication*, 18(4) (1993): 497–505; R. A. Hackett, "An exaggerated death: prefatory comments on 'objectivity' in journalism", in V. Alia, B. Brennan and B. Hoffmaster (eds), *Deadlines and Diversity* (Halifax: Fernwood, 1996), pp. 40–43; J. McManus, "Who's responsible for journalism?", *Journal of Mass Media Ethics*, 12(1) (1997): 5–17.

Hate speech in Canada

The core of racist hateful activity has been Ontario and, more specifically, Toronto. Metropolitan Toronto has a sordid history of open fascist activity dating from the late 1920s. Groups such as the Caboto Committee, the National Unity Party, and, from early 1930s, various Swastika Clubs sprung up across Ontario, their members openly sporting swastikas and other fascist symbols in an attempt to keep parts of Toronto free of Jews and other "undesirables". On 16 August 1933 this culminated in the Christie Pits Riots involving racists and Jews.[13]

During the late 1930s, a good deal of hate material was distributed across Canada. Most of the propaganda was anti-Semitic in nature, stressing such themes as "Communism is Jewish". Much of the activity centered on two people, Adrien Arcand and John Ross Taylor. Arcand was the founder of the National Unity Party in Quebec, and Taylor was active in Toronto. Both were interned during World War II. Both resumed their hate operations after the war.[14]

In the mid-1960s, anti-Jewish and anti-black hate propaganda was widespread in Canada, especially in Ontario and Quebec. Simultaneously, neo-Nazi and white supremacist groups, based largely in the United States, became active in Canada.[15] The Canadian Nazi Party made its first appearance in Toronto in 1965 under the leadership of William John Beattie. The party provoked much fear and anger, especially among Jews in Toronto. This prompted, in the same year, the establishment of the Special Committee on Hate Propaganda in Canada (the Cohen Committee). In its conclusions, the Committee said that although the hate situation in Canada was not alarming, clearly it was serious enough to require action: "The Canadian community has a duty, not merely the right, to protect itself from the corrosive effects of propaganda that tends to undermine the confidence that various groups in a multicultural society must have in each other."[16] The Committee therefore recommended that the government take action against hate propaganda.

---

13 B. M. Farber, *From Marches to Modems: A Report on Organized Hate in Metro Toronto* (Ontario: Peel Community Information Database, January 1997), Record: BRA0727.

14 M. Cohen, *Report to the Minister of Justice of the Special Committee on Hate Propaganda* (Ottawa: Queen's Printer, 1966). See also "Hate propaganda in Canada", in B. D. Singer (ed.), *Communications in Canadian Society* (Toronto: Copp Clark Publishers, 1975), p. 343.

15 P. Rosen, *Hate Propaganda* (Ottawa: Law and Government Division, Research Branch of the Library of Parliament, 1989), p. 1.

16 *Ibid.*, p. 361. See also W. Kaplan, "Maxwell Cohen and the Report of the Special Committee on Hate Propaganda", in W. Kaplan and D. McRae (eds), *Law, Policy and International Justice* (Montreal: McGill-Queen's University Press, 1993), pp. 243–274.

The mid-1970s saw another wave of racist group activity due to the efforts of the Edmund Burke Society, the Nationalist Party of Canada, and the Western Guard Party. The Ku Klux Klan was revived in Ontario and British Columbia. Hate propaganda was anti-Jewish, anti-black, anti-East Indian, anti-Catholic, anti-French,[17] and anti-Native people. It was transmitted in the form of leaflets and pamphlets as well as by telephone, video recordings and computers.[18]

In 1982, the Charter of Rights and Freedoms came into force. Section 2(b) of the Charter is of special importance for hate-mongers, as it guarantees freedom of expression: "Everyone has the following fundamental freedoms: b) freedom of thought, belief, opinion and expression, including freedom of the press and other media of communication."[19]

In 1990, The Supreme Court of Canada issued its judgment in *R.* v. *Keegstra*[20] and *R.* v. *Andrews.*[21] James Keegstra was a high-school teacher. He patently graded his students according to their willingness to espouse and reiterate his vile and hateful anti-Semitic views. If they did not, they were marked down.[22] This manipulation certainly curtailed his students' independent thinking and their sense of voluntariness. Keegstra was convicted for describing Jews in his classes as "treacherous", "money-loving", "child-killers", and "sadistic". He was convicted under Section 319(2) of the Canadian Criminal Code, which outlaws public communications that willfully promote hatred against any identifiable group. In turn, Donald Andrews and his collaborator, Robert Smith, in Ontario were members of the white supremacist Nationalist Party of Canada, and were responsible for publishing and distributing the *Nationalist Reporter*. A legal search of their home revealed hateful materials for distribution, including mailing lists, racist stickers, publications with anti-Semitic and white supremacist themes, and diatribes about racial mixing and Holocaust denial. Keegstra, and Smith and Andrews, were charged and convicted under the hate propaganda laws. They were sentenced to seven-month and one-year jail terms respectively, but the provincial courts of appeal reached opposing conclusions on the constitutionality of Section 319 (2) on the willful promotion of hatred. Ultimately, the Supreme Court upheld the constitutionality of the law, albeit by the narrowest majority.[23]

17 See *R.* v. *Buzzanga* [1977] O.J. No 134 (judgment rendered on 23 December 1977); *R.* v. *Buzzanga and Durocher* [1979] 25 O.R. (2d) 705, 101 D.L.R. (3d) 488 (17 September 1979).
18 P. Rosen, *Hate Propaganda*, p. 2.
19 http://laws.justice.gc.ca/en/charter/.
20 *R.* v. *Keegstra* [1990] 3 S.C.R. 697.
21 *R.* v. *Andrews and Smith* [1990] 3 S.C.R. 870.
22 D. Matas, *Bloody Words* (Winnipeg: Bain & Cox, 2000), p. 50.
23 K. Mock, *Countering Anti-Semitism and Hate in Canada Today*, on http://www.nizkor.org/hweb/people/m/mock-karen/countering-hate.html.

Zündel

The emergence of Ernst Zündel during the 1980s evoked a lot of attention in the political, legal, and media circles. Quite surprisingly, the most notorious figure in Canada for his hateful campaign against Jews was never charged with the willful promotion of hate. On 18 November 1983, Sabina Citron of the Canadian Holocaust Remembrance Association brought charges against Zündel for his publication *Did Six Million Really Die?* under the "false news" Section (number 181, formerly Section 177) of the Criminal Code. This section provides that "Every one who wilfully publishes a statement, tale or news that he knows is false and that causes or is likely to cause injury or mischief to a public interest is guilty of an indictable offence and liable to imprisonment..."[24] Personally, I think that books should not be censored or banned only because their content is false or even malicious. Many books contain false ideas. They should be discussed in the open, probed, analyzed, exposed – not silenced. People learn from the confrontation of ideas. In my first volume on free speech, *The Boundaries of Liberty and Tolerance*, I advanced the Millian Truth Principle to argue for toleration of vile and racist publications.[25] While considering the publications of people like J. Philippe Rushton, the Canadian psychologist who conducted research on the brain configuration of black people and brought forward evidence to prove that they are intellectually inferior to whites, I asked whether we should allow this scientific, or quasi-scientific, publication.[26] I answered this question in the positive, holding that we may allow this publication not because its findings contain some truth or because its potential contribution to science, but instead because through this research we might learn more about white–black relationships, the prejudices and feelings against blacks that pervade the white population of North America, and maybe elsewhere. This knowledge could assist us in bridging the gap between races and in fighting prejudice. We may allow the publication not because consideration of the scientist and his followers is foremost in our eyes, but because consideration of the blacks and the whites who resent these findings, as well as those who remain undecided, is what really counts. The Truth Principle is still in place, but not the truth that the research explores. Instead, it is the truth with regard to race relations, the truth as it emerges from the discussion of these findings.[27] Only in special circumstances, when concrete

---

24 http://laws.justice.gc.ca/en/C-46/text.html.
25 R. Cohen-Almagor, *The Boundaries of Liberty and Tolerance* (Gainesville: University Press of Florida, 1994), Chapter 6.
26 See, for instance, J. P. Rushton, *Race, Evolution and Behavior* (New Brunswick: Transaction Publishers, 1999). See also "Rushton book held at the border", *Canadian Press Newswire* (3 January 1996); http://www.ssc.uwo.ca/psychology/faculty/rushton_bio.htm.
27 For contrasting view, see D. Matas, *Bloody Words, op. cit.*, pp. 99–100.

harm may result from incitement statements, should books be removed from the protection of the Free Speech Principle (see Conclusion). In most cases, including this one, the way to deal with derogatory and discriminatory ideas is by education and by contrasting them with vigorous counter-arguments, exposing their falsehood and the evil intentions of the authors. Here, the media may play a vital role.

The media fully covered Zündel's trial for distributing hate literature, making the trial a media event.[28] The main personality, the defendant, did what he could to capture media attention. His hard hat, his short controversial quotations, and his staged appearances were a recipe for camera exposure. He was a master manipulator of the media. *Media Tactics I* and *Media Tactics II* were the titles of instructional audio tapes produced by the defendant and available for purchase during the course of the proceedings. Commentators and experts discussed at length how the media coverage would affect the Canadian public's beliefs about Nazism, the Holocaust, the justice system, and Jews. The trial received an exceptional amount of media attention.[29] Indeed, Zündel understands very well the "democratic catch" and, like many hate-mongers, promotes himself as champion of free expression, as a person who dedicates his life to the furthering of truth and knowledge in the world, and to letting each and every individual speak as he or she pleases without any restrictions.

On the Zundelsite, in a file titled "Zündel-Haus – Ernst Zündel: His Struggle, His Life", which is Zündel's biography (most probably autobiography), the author writes that in the early 1980s the media took "a vigorous and often favorable interest" in Zündel's court case. "The media had a field day, with the entire booklet *Did Six Million Really Die?* prominently splashed on the nation's TV screens." Time and again, Canada saw nationwide headlines and broadcasts on the topic of "Freedom of Speech" and "the Zündel Holocaust Trial".[30] Each of Zündel's court appearances was accompanied by massive media turnouts. Newscasts about his case on nightly TV were commonplace. Everywhere there was talk of Zündel's "media spectacles" – carefully planned and carried out for maximum media benefit, since Zündel realized clearly that the information war had to be won in the media.

In the second half of 1984, the press concentrated heavily on the trial. The level of media interest was astounding, exclaims Zündel on his website.[31] After a lengthy trial commencing on 7 January 1985, Zündel was convicted on 28 February by a jury on the charge concerning *Did Six Million Really Die?* and sentenced on 25 March to fifteen months' impris-

---

28 On the concept of media events, see D. Dayan and E. Katz, *Media Events* (Cambridge: Harvard University Press, 1992).
29 G. Weimann and C. Winn, *Hate on Trial* (Oakville: Mosaic Press, 1986), p. 83.
30 http://www.Zundelsite.org/english/ezchron/zhausa.html.
31 *Ibid.*

onment plus probation for three years. This trial, lasting 39 court days, was a worldwide media sensation. All of Canada's television stations and most of the radio stations reported through well-known reporters or columnists almost every day, prominently and in detail, about the events in court. Zündel explained that he was "now engaged in 'public education' on a grand scale, via Canada's media, far above and beyond the courtroom scene – in the country's living rooms, offices and universities".[32] He maintained that headlines proclaiming "Gassings disputed: Nazi Confessions false, Prof. claims", "Disease killed Nazi's prisoners, MD says", "Survivor never saw actual gassing deaths", "Holocaust scholar quoted madman, publishing trial told", and "Scientific evidence of Holocaust missing", shocked a complacent and ignorant public.[33]

Marvin Kurz, National legal counsel for B'nai Brith League for Human Rights, Irwin Cotler MP, Harvey Goldberg of the Canadian Human Rights Commission, and David Lepofsky of the Ministry of the Attorney General in Ontario, have similar recollections of the first Zündel trial. Kurz explained that in 1985, the press was taken for a ride by Zündel. The press did not know how to deal with him. It was the first time they had dealt with Holocaust denial, and they simply did not know how to cover it. They saw Zündel as a harmless eccentric who had bizarre views. Holocaust denial was consequently reported as if it was sensational news. Newspapers had headlines that blared statements like: "Auschwitz was like a country club, expert said". The media, in their efforts to cover the trial neutrally, spoke of an "alleged crematorium" in Auschwitz, publishing headlines like "Women Dined and Danced in Auschwitz, said an Expert Witness". The court admitted those testimonials, and when the courts accepted certain individuals as "experts" the media followed suit. In his relentless appetite for media coverage, Zündel staged events and the press reported them. Thus, for instance, Zündel was pictured carrying a cross to court, fighting religiously for his exceptional views.[34]

The *Globe and Mail* carried a large picture of a swimming pool with the caption "This is the swimming pool that Zündel's defense claims visitors to former Auschwitz Camp are not allowed to see". There was no mention that Ditlieb Felderer, the photographer, was a Nazi photo-refinisher. At no time during the trial were actual photographs of the horrors of Auschwitz published.[35] In another headline, the Nazi extermination was called "a theory".[36]

32 *Ibid.*
33 *Ibid.*
34 Interviews with M. Kurz in Toronto on 15 July 2002, Irwin Cotler in Montreal on 24 July 2002; Harvey Goldberg, Deputy Director, Policy and Liaison Branch, Canadian Human Rights Commission, Ottawa on 17 July 2002; and David Lepofsky, Ministry of the Attorney General, Toronto, on 13 July 2002.
35 D. Matas, *Bloody Words, op. cit.*, p. 75.
36 *Ibid.*, p. 76.

In his critique of the first Zündel trial, Irwin Cotler argued that the public might have believed what those "experts" were saying when the Holocaust was presented in such a neutral fashion, and some might have taken them seriously. The court should have established that the Holocaust did exist as a fact, and refused to allow those "expert witnesses" to enter its gates. Under Zündel's mastery, it was not Zündel who stood trial; rather, the Holocaust was on trial. The prosecution should have asked the court to take a judicial notice that the Holocaust existed, but neither the prosecution nor the courts had any experience in dealing with Holocaust denial, and they did not think carefully about the matter at hand.[37] Later, in the second Zündel trial, the court did take a judicial notice that the Holocaust did take place.

The media are reluctant to comment on the substance of a given case while the trial is in motion. This is partly due to the contempt of court law. Most jury trials are not isolated. The jury goes home at night. Therefore the media are restricted in publishing opinions about trials while they are in progress, and many reporters confine themselves to reporting merely what is happening in the trial.[38] Furthermore, the media are reluctant to take sides. There are many opinions, and the media do not wish to reflect mainly or only the government's opinion. Having said that, if a person during a trial does not tell the truth, it is the role of the reporter to ask difficult questions and to expose the falsehood behind the statements. Reporters should investigate the facts carefully. Experts may be invited to rebut dubious statements. Journalists can ask: isn't it a travesty that an expert says there were swimming pools in Auschwitz? They can and should speak about revisionist history, anti-Semitism, and the dangers of tolerance.[39] They can point out the links between Holocaust deniers and neo-Nazi organizations. They are not breaching their journalistic mores when they report that deniers have no credence among professional historians.

Zündel appealed against his conviction, to the Ontario Court of Appeal, and on 23 January 1987, the court allowed the appeal, quashed the convic-

---

37 Interview with Irwin Cotler MP on 24 July 2002.
38 Professor Roderick A. Macdonald, former President of the Law Commission of Canada, explained that the media can report what the witnesses say; but if the media express an opinion about the judge or what the judge said with regard to a given testimony, then the reporter can be held in contempt. Interview on 25 July 2002.
39 On anti-Semitism in Canada, see R. Menkis, "Antisemitism in the evolving nation: from new France to 1950", and J. Bauer, "Between prejudice and acceptance: a post-war case study", both in R. Klein and F. Dimant (eds), *From Immigration to Integration* (Toronto: Institute for International Affairs, B'nai Brith, 2001). See also M. Richter, *Oh Canada! Oh Quebec! Requiem for a Divided Nation* (New York: Knopf, 1992); M. Shain, *Antisemitism* (London: Bowerdean, 1998), pp. 60–83; B'nai Brith Canada, League for Human Rights. Annual Audit of Anti-Semitic Incidents in Canada. 1987 – present. [1996–1998 available at www.bnaibrith.ca].

tion, and ordered a new trial.[40] On 18 January 1988, the second trial commenced. It lasted sixty-one days. Zündel was again convicted by a jury on 11 May 1988, and this time was sentenced to nine months' imprisonment. Zündel obtained leave to appeal to the Supreme Court of Canada on 15 November 1990, on the issue of whether or not the "false news" law was a violation of the constitutional guarantee to freedom of expression contained in the Canadian Charter of Rights and Freedoms. On 27 August 1992, the Supreme Court of Canada acquitted Zündel and struck down the "false news" law as a violation of the guarantee to free speech contained in the Canadian Charter, adopting Zündel's viewpoint on freedom of speech.[41] Section 181 of the Criminal Code was declared unconstitutional.

The "false news" law dates from the Statute of Westminster of 1275. It created penalties for publishing "false" news or other statements that could create discord between the ruler and his subjects. The language was broad and unrestrained. It provided "that from henceforth none be so hardy to tell or publish any false News or Tales, whereby discord, or occasion of discord or slander may grow between the King and his People, or the Great Men of the Realm".[42]

Although the offense of spreading false news was abolished in England in 1887, and did not survive in the United States, it was enacted in Canada as part of the 1892 Criminal Code. Section 181 had been judicially considered only three times in Canada, excluding this case; the jurisprudence on it is virtually non-existent. This is of little wonder. It was a very problematic piece of legislation indeed. People spread falsehood all the time, intentionally or unintentionally. I don't think anyone should be prosecuted just for spreading falsehood, no matter how false his or her "truth" might be. This does not mean that people should be allowed falsely to shout "Fire!" in a crowded theater,[43] or to libel each other,[44] but generally speaking falsehood should be exposed through the contrast with other "truths" offered. Therefore I think the result was correct.

---

40 *Regina* v. *Ernst Zündel*, 58 O.R. (2d) 129 (23 January 1987), Ontario Court of Appeal. The court ordered a new trial because of fundamental errors of the trial judge, particularly those relating to the selection of the jury and the misdirection on the essential elements of the offense. The judge erred in instructing the jury that one of the two basic issues was whether the evidence showed that the appellant published the pamphlet with no honest belief in its truth. Unfortunately, this was the final instruction to the jury and thus enhanced the importance of the misdirection. Instead, the issue was not whether the appellant published the pamphlet with no honest belief in its truth, but whether the Crown had proved beyond reasonable doubt that Zündel knew it was false when he published it.

41 *Ernst Zündel* v. *Her Majesty The Queen*, [1992] S.C.J. No. 70.

42 Justice MacLachlin in *Zündel* v. *Her Majesty The Queen*, at 501. See also http://www.lrwc.org/news/news_rules4.php.

43 See Justice Oliver W. Holmes in *Schenck* v. *U.S.* 249 U.S. 47 (1919).

Mark Freiman, Deputy Attorney General and Deputy Minister responsible for Native Affairs for the Province of Ontario, explained that Zündel was tried for disseminating falsehood because there were doubts as to whether it would have been possible to convict Zündel for hate propaganda. It has to be proved that the incitement would be likely to lead to a breach of peace, and there were doubts as to whether it would be possible to get a conviction for hate speech. The criminal hate speech provision is very specific, and stringent demands must be met to obtain a conviction.[45] It was probably thought that there would be a better chance of getting a conviction for spreading falsehoods.

David Matas thinks it would have been more appropriate to prosecute Zündel for dissemination of hate. Then the issue would have been not whether Zündel's Holocaust denial was false, or whether he knew it to be false, but whether by his Holocaust denial he was willfully promoting hatred against Jews.[46] This, indeed, was the focus of the court in *R.* v. *Keegstra.* Section 319(2) of the Criminal Code holds:

> Every one who, by communicating statements, other than in private conversation, wilfully promotes hatred against any identifiable group is guilty of (a) an indictable offence and is liable to imprisonment for a term not exceeding two years.[47]

The Attorney General, however, felt it did not have a strong case to bring charges against Zündel under this provision. We should bear in mind that the concern at that time was the *Did Six Million Really Die?* thirty-two-page pamphlet, nothing else. The Zundelsite and Zündel's dozens of other hateful publications were not of concern then. The Zundelsite was not yet in existence.

Is Holocaust denial a form of hate speech?

A question arises as to whether Holocaust denial constitutes hate under the definition provided *supra.* If you ask a person on the street what he or she knows about the Holocaust, and that person admits to having no knowledge of it, this is not Holocaust denial. Denying reality is not a form of hate. Even if the person seems to know, this is not necessarily a form of hate. The component of hate depends on the content of the speech and the intention of the speaker.

Disputing certain historical facts is also not a form of hate, and I doubt

44 *Gertz* v. *Robert Welch, Inc.,* 418 U.S. 323, 94 S.Ct. 2997, 41 L.Ed.2d 789 (1974).
45 Interview with Mark J. Freiman, Toronto (11 July 2002).
46 D. Matas, *Bloody Words, op. cit.,* p. 72.
47 http://laws.justice.gc.ca/en/C-46/text.html.

whether it can be considered as Holocaust denial. If one argues that five million, not six million, were murdered during the period 1938 to 1945, based on a study of sorts done on Jewish demography in Europe, this is an issue that can and should be discussed in the open in order to discover a possible new facet of the truth. If one brings evidence showing that an alleged massacre did not happen, or that it happened on a different date, or that more people were killed in it than we thought, or that an alleged war criminal was not in an alleged place at a particular time, these are all issues that should be probed and discussed. None of this constitutes Holocaust denial, or a form of hate.

Furthermore, people in liberal democracies are entitled to hold and express vilifying and outrageous views, to voice their dislike of other people, to use deregatory words and discriminatory adjectives against others. They may also praise the killing of another group of people for reasons other than self-defense. We don't enjoy it, we feel this is wrong, we feel outraged confronting such statements. Still, liberals believe that such speech is protected under the Free Speech Principle and is sheltered in the shade of tolerance. The way to fight such discriminating and damaging opinions is by more speech, not by silencing and censoring speech. This, indeed, is the essence of tolerance, as explained in Chapter 1.

Having said that, Holocaust denial constitutes a special and problematic category of speech. It is far from being innocent. Holocaust denial is a form of hate speech because it willfully promotes enmity against an identifiable group based on race and religion. It is designed to underestimate and justify murder, genocide, xenophobia, and evil. Holocaust denial lends a form of legitimacy to racism in its most evil manifestation to date, under the guise of the pursuit of "truth". It speaks of an international Jewish conspiracy to blackmail nations, and to exploit others to create Israel. It depicts a scenario in which Jews convened to create a hoax, the greatest fabrication of all times. Holocaust denial indicates that Adolf Hitler did not plan genocide for the Jews but instead to move them out of Europe; no gas chambers ever existed. Deniers state that the Holocaust is an invention of the Jews to dramatize the mere "fact" that in every war there are casualties; World War II was no different – and yes, Jews were killed during the war, as were lots of people from many other nations and religions. They say that the Holocaust is the product of partisan Jewish interests, serving Jewish greed and hunger for power, that some Jews disguised themselves as survivors, carved numbers on their arms and spread atrocious false stories about gas chambers and extermination machinery. They believe that it was not Germany that acted in a criminal way; instead, the greatest criminals are the Jews. The Jews were so evil that they invented this horrific story to gain support world-wide and to extort money from Germany. For their extortion and fabrication, for creating the greatest conspiracy of all times, they deserve punishment, possibly even death. In effect, argues Marvin Kurz, the ultimate purpose of

Holocaust denial is to legitimize another Holocaust against the demonic and crooked Jews.[48]

Marcel Danis and Dennis J. Murphy of Concordia University also think that Holocaust denial constitutes hate. Those who deny the Holocaust are anti-Jewish. It is demeaning to deny the Holocaust; it is to deny history, reality, suffering.[49] Stephen Scheinberg and Frank Chalk, also of Concordia, expressed concern that Holocaust denial might create a climate of xenophobia that is detrimental to democracy. The package of lies is so sophisticated and the resources the public has to scrutinize those lies so poor that one should not trust the public capacity to do this. The public might be swayed by those lies to carry out violent acts. This is especially true during a crisis. At such times, simple explanations for the crisis might be appealing and take hold. We should learn the lessons of Nazi Germany.[50]

This line of reasoning will not convince everybody. Some might conceive it as illiberal and paternalistic. Liberals would prefer, on the whole, to trust the people rather than the government on free speech questions. In his comments on this chapter, Wayne Sumner wrote: "Why should we not trust the public's capacity to judge the truth on this matter? The vast majority of Canadians seem to have had no difficulty reaching the conclusion that Holocaust deniers are a bunch of crackpots." Many other Canadian people and organizations (like B'nai Brith and the Canadian Race Relations Foundation) think, however, that some forms of speech are so dangerous that they deserve prosecution under the provisions of the Criminal Code. Prosecution of hate speech shows that hate is wrong. It reassures threatened, vulnerable minorities that the state is here to protect them, that they are not neglected nor victimized. This is of special importance in multicultural societies as in Canada, as the Charter well recognizes. Authorities at the Department of Justice, Ottawa, explained that prosecution of such cases serves a certain purpose in consolidating pluralism and in drawing the boundaries of tolerance.[51] Section 7 of the Charter holds: "Everyone has the right to life, liberty and security of the person and the right not to be deprived thereof except in accordance with the principles of fundamental justice", while Section 15(1) dictates:

48 Interview with Marvin Kurz, National Legal Counsel for B'nai Brith League for Human Rights, Toronto (15 July 2002).
49 Interview with Professor Marcel Danis, Vice Rector, and Professor Dennis J. Murphy, Executive Director of Communications, Concordia University, Montreal (24 July 2002).
50 Interview with Professor Stephen Scheinberg, Department of History, and Professor Frank Chalk, Co-Director, Montreal Institute for Genocide and Human Rights Studies, both from Concordia University, Montreal (23 July 2002).
51 Interview in Ottawa on 17 July 2002.

Every individual is equal before and under the law and has the right to the equal protection and equal benefit of the law without discrimination and, in particular, without discrimination based on race, national or ethnic origin, colour, religion, sex, age or mental or physical disability.[52]

Here the reader should note that, as in the previous chapter, we have at least two layers of discussion that do not necessarily coincide. One concerns the law and its application, while the other concerns ethics and communication aspects. Weighty but different considerations are involved in both. Free expression is one of the foundations of democracy; democracy cannot survive without it. At the same time, we need to be cautious of the democratic "catch". Previously I said that racist publications should be included within the scope of tolerance. Consequently, books that deny the Holocaust should not be prohibited for the same reasons outlined for not banning Rushton's scholarship. However, what alarms me is the volume of the hateful denial. Volume can make a difference, especially when the denial is carried out on a massive scale, involving all possible channels of communications, including books, flyers, letters, notes, newspaper articles, TV and radio programs, phone messages, and the Internet. It is one thing to allow the publication of books. It is quite another thing to allow *carte blanche* for all communications. The cumulative effect of the hateful denial cannot be ignored. This mass-scale vicious manipulation and blatant lie creates, in Scanlon's terms, "bad environment"[53] and a real challenge for democracies. It also offends the sensibilities of Jews, especially of Holocaust survivors. Each society should debate the issue and the confines of tolerance regarding hate speech. The scope of tolerance may vary from one country to another.[54] All people who are concerned with the implications of hate should take part: law professionals, academics, media professionals, religious authorities, politicians, and non-government organizations (NGOs) involved in advancing human and civil rights.

Media coverage of hate

To understand why so much latitude was given to Zündel's "media spectacles" by many of the columnists who covered Zündel's Holocaust denial, let me quote from the words of Barbara Amiel-Black, a political columnist who wrote for *Maclean's* magazine and Conrad Black's sixty Canadian dailies:

52 Cf. http://laws.justice.gc.ca/en/charter/.
53 T. M. Scanlon, "Freedom of expression and categories of expression", *University of Pittsburgh Law Review*, 40(3) (1979): 519–550. Reprinted in *The Difficulty of Tolerance* (Cambridge: Cambridge University Press, 2003).
54 See R. Delgado and J. Stefancic, "Ten arguments against hate-speech regulation: how valid?", *Northern Kentucky University Law Review*, 23 (1996): 475.

It is a popular assumption that the prosecution of Zündel and the upcoming prosecution of Alberta teacher James Keegstra on similar charges are necessary in order to prevent the development of a climate that could lead to a new Third Reich . . . Hitler was right, alas. You either have free speech for everyone or you do not have free speech. You cannot have a little free speech or free speech "except for".[55]

Amiel-Black maintained: "What all the people who support the prosecutions of the Zündels and Keegstras don't understand is that limiting free speech creates the conditions for the rise of Hitler or his equivalent. The problem with freedom is that it is indivisible."[56]

This liberal point of view is extremely sweeping and, at the same time, naïve and false. As said at the outset, freedom of speech – and indeed any freedom – is not indivisible. Freedom of speech can inflict a lot of harm. It is not an absolute value that should be protected no matter what. Amiel-Black's reasoning puts emphasis on the positive consequences of fighting speech with more speech, and very little – if any – attention is paid to the harmful consequences of such speech. Hate speech calls for discrimination against certain people, denying their right to equal protection and treatment as citizens in a democracy. As premised earlier, it inflicts on its target emotional and psychological suffering, humiliation, and distress; sometimes it also evokes intimidation and fear.[57] Hate speech might also generate a certain discriminatory atmosphere against the target group and instigate violence against its members. As stated, I am not arguing that all societies should necessarily resort to law in order to ban hate speech. Some societies might feel that law is an inappropriate instrument to curtail speech, even hateful speech. Thus each society should decide for itself how to combat hate; but each society should combat hate. None should remain oblivious to hate. All should devise appropriate ways to defend themselves against the possible negative effects of hate.

Amiel-Black does not share this view. She thinks that we simply need to grant unqualified protection to freedom of speech. By pursuing this reasoning, she and like-minded journalists gave publicity and even credence to the views of Holocaust deniers and hate-mongers. A York University his-

55 M. Barlow and J. Winter, *The Big Black Book* (Toronto: Stoddart, 1997), p. 110.
56 *Ibid.*
57 Further harms include feelings of isolation and self-hatred. See R. Delgado, "Words that wound: a tort action for racial insults, epithets, and name-calling", *Harvard Civil Rights-Civil Liberty Law Review*, 17 (1982), p. 137. See also R. Post, "Racist speech, democracy, and the First Amendment", *William and Mary Law Review*, 32(2) (Winter 1991): esp. pp. 272–277; K. Greenawalt, *Fighting Words: Individuals, Communities, and Liberties of Speech* (Princeton: Princeton University Press, 1995), pp. 47–70.

torian, Ramsay Cook, was quoted as saying: "Those people who denied the Holocaust were given the same objective treatment as the others so it sometimes appeared in the newspapers that this was really a matter that was open to question."[58] The media should, of course, cover Zündel – the trials and the phenomenon – but at the same time they should also condemn the man and his views in editorials and opinion columns, try to analyze the framework within which Zündel operates, and press hard the question of whether the liberty to hate is a liberty that should be safeguarded under the Free Speech Principle. At any rate, denying the Holocaust is not simply offering "another truth" in the free marketplace of ideas;[59] instead, it is a method of provoking hatred against Jews. Hatemongers should be looked at as the enemies of democracy, and not merely as people who offer a credible interpretation of history.

Furthermore, not all people are "reasonable people". Not all people accept the Holocaust as an indisputable historical fact. Zündel is preaching his views especially to young people whose minds are still being shaped. He urges them not to accept without question the common, accepted views, appealing to their rebellious nature. When the media cover Zündel's views without qualification, presenting him as a legitimate thinker who is offering his truth in the free market of ideas, they provide him with a convenient platform to mislead and to rewrite history, and confer his views with undeserved legitimacy.

Weimann and Winn spoke of the positive outcomes of the coverage, arguing that the first Zündel trial gave the general public a greater awareness of – and sensitivity to – Holocaust denial. They maintained that the media balanced their apparently neutral reporting of Holocaust denial with significant exposure for Holocaust survivors testifying at the trial, and with very extensive reporting on the Holocaust outside the context of the trial. Media users had good opportunities to learn the facts of the Holocaust outside the context of the trial itself. Viewers of television and readers of the press could decide for themselves whether the Holocaust had ever taken place.[60]

It is interesting to note that the big hate trials in Canada were covered unevenly in the different provinces. *Keegstra* and *Zündel* were significant stories in Ontario and Alberta, but attracted far less interest in the other

---

58 Professor Cook was quoted by M. Polanyi, "Holocaust fact, historians state", *Globe & Mail* (30 May 1985), p. 11. Also in N. Russell, *Morals and the Media*, p. 26. Interviews with Ramsay Cook, General Editor, Dictionary of Canadian Biography, University of Toronto (1 October 1998; 12 July 2002).

59 For a critique of the "free marketplace of ideas" concept, see J. Pole, "Freedom of speech: from privilege to right", in R. Cohen-Almagor (ed.), *Challenges to Democracy: Essays In Honour and Memory of Professor Sir Isaiah Berlin, op. cit.*, pp. 11–54; S. Ingber, "The marketplace of ideas: a legitimizing myth", *Duke Law Journal*, 1 (1984): 1.

60 G. Weimann and C. Winn, *Hate on Trial*, p. 105.

provinces. Marcel Pepin, former Ombudsman of Radio Canada, said that nobody knew Zündel in Quebec.[61] His successor, Renaud Gilbert, told me that he was not aware of any complaints regarding hate speech during the twenty-five years that he was in office in the French services of CBC.[62] These views coincide with the study of Weimann and Winn, who found differences in the coverage of the trial by the English and French media. They argued that the differences in the coverage paralleled the differences in the attitudes of English and French Canadians towards Jews.[63] The English press and television provided much more coverage of the trial and of the Holocaust outside the context of the trial. The English media (except for Newfoundland) granted extensive coverage of non-violent Jewish events, while the French media essentially provided no such coverage. Jews in French news were portrayed almost exclusively in the context of victimization.[64]

In his study of how the Canadian media cover hate propaganda, Warren Kinsella argued that in the *Keegstra* case the Alberta and national news media generally provided good coverage of the issues and personalities involved in the prosecution of the former high-school teacher. In the Zündel trials a less satisfactory approach was taken, with the media providing the pro-Nazi with what he called "one million dollars' worth" of free publicity.[65] Kinsella contended that in their coverage of the first Zündel trial, the willingness of reporters and editors to provide an uncritical platform for a parade of Holocaust-denying witnesses was shameful. In the process, the media gave a far wider circulation to the Holocaust-denying propaganda than Zündel had been able to achieve on his own. After a period of self-analysis and debate, the news media in Canada pursued a different approach regarding Zündel's second trial, with some of them electing to give it very little, if any, prominence.[66]

Indeed, the attitude of the media to hate speech during the 1990s had changed.[67] Conrad Winn argued that the 1980s were the heyday of media

---

61 Interview with Marcel Pepin (22 September 1998).
62 Interview with Renaud Gilbert on 24 July 2002.
63 In his comments on this chapter, Richard Warman contested this view, explaining that the differences in coverage should be attributed to Zündel's residence in Toronto, the fact that he does not speak French, did not distribute material in Quebec, and did not make numerous appearances there.
64 G. Weimann and C. Winn, *Hate on Trial, op. cit.*, p. 164. See also p. 105.
65 W. Kinsella, *Web of Hate: Inside Canada's Far Right Network* (Toronto: Harper-Collins, 1995), p. 422. Interview with J. Warren Kinsella (2 October 1998).
66 W. Kinsella, "Challenges to Canadian liberal democracy", *op. cit.*
67 Rod Macdonald noted in his comments on a draft of this chapter that one of the most notorious hate speech cases took place in 1977, when people in Windsor, Ontario woke up to see pamphlets and leaflets entitled "Wake Up Canadians Your Future Is At Stake" put under their cars' windshields. These pamphlets accused French-Canadians of being dirty traitors, subversives, and of other crimes and sins. It turned out that the pamphlets were written by fran-

coverage of hate speech. He maintained that the media were neutral in their coverage, and that Zündel made people become anti-German because he claimed to be speaking in the name of the German civilization.[68] Similarly, David Lepofsky and Marvin Kurz argued that there was less coverage of hate speech trials and literature during the 1990s than in the 1980s because of the outcry and criticism regarding the extensive coverage during the 1980s. Unlike their behavior during the preceding decade, in the 1990s the media refrained from quoting Zündel's "expert witnesses" who said that there was no Holocaust.[69] Mel Sufrin, Executive Secretary of the Ontario Press Council, said that in 1992 the major Toronto-based newspaper, the *Toronto Star*, was tired of covering the "ridiculous stories of Zündel".[70] Authorities at the Ministry of the Attorney General in Ontario explained that the media have matured in their coverage of such cases. They are not giving hate-mongers the soapbox that was provided during the 1980s. The media are now fulfilling educational purposes, speaking of cases in context and perspective, with less emphasis on sensationalism.[71]

The Canadian Broadcasting Corporation (CBC) has been far more hesitant about covering Zündel over the past few years. David Bazay, Ombudsman of the English CBC, asserted that Zündel was not news any more. He maintained that the CBC had broadcast Zündel enough, paying far too much attention to someone who did not deserve it. Bazay testified: "We provided him with too much publicity and at some point we said enough is enough. The issue was exhausted."[72]

Balancing

James Littleton, a producer who works for the CBC, supported these contentions. He said that, in principle, Zündel is not invited onto CBC programs. Littleton testified that Zündel was interviewed by telephone once in 1987, and that "it was a mistake". The incident took place after Zündel's first trial, when Zündel was ready to appeal against the court decision. The

cophones who wanted to stir up the "decent" population into denouncing racism against francophones and to gain support for their campaign to create a French-language high school in the city. Unfortunately, wrote Macdonald, the media played it up as a kind of new FLQ crisis. So far from dissipating resentment against French-Canadians in Windsor, it exacerbated it.

68 Interview with Professor Conrad Winn, Chairman, "Compas", and Department of Political Science, Carleton University (28 September 1998).
69 Interviews with M. David Lepofsky (13 July 2002), and Marvin Kurz, Toronto (15 July 2002).
70 Interview with Mel Sufrin, Toronto (6 October 1998).
71 Interview in Toronto on 15 July 2002.
72 Interview with David Bazay, Ombudsman, Canadian Broadcasting Corporation, Toronto (6 October 1998).

CBC decided to do a radio show, hosted by David Shatsky, in which people could phone in regarding the topic: Does Mr Zündel deserve a new trial? Sabina Citron, of the Holocaust survivors organization, was invited to speak from the studio and to answer questions. She agreed to do so after receiving assurance that she would be spared the need to confront Zündel. He would not be invited.

The CBC held promotions for the program, announcing its subject matter, and soon enough Zündel heard and called. He argued that the program was about him and that he deserved equal time to pronounce his views. Michael Hughes, Legal Counsel for the CBC, said that "Zündel had put us in an odd situation", and this was just shortly before the program. "We were in a quandary."[73] Hughes further explained:

> Zündel said, more or less, that the Canadian Charter of Rights and Freedoms guaranteed his right of free speech, and that under the circumstances CBC, a federal Crown Corporation, was obliged to allow him to exercise that freedom. At that time, the CRTC [Canadian Radio-television and Telecommunications Commission], which is somewhat similar to the US FCC, effectively recognized the US "fairness doctrine" of equal time, and it was out of consideration of these various factors that it was decided, with considerable reluctance, to allow Zündel to speak on the program.[74]

The CBC called Citron to inform her about this new development, "but it was too late".[75] She was already on her way to the studio. Citron was unpleasantly surprised shortly before the show. Zündel was allowed to voice his views, to say that the Holocaust was a hoax.[76] The host of the program, David Shatsky, interviewed Citron for approximately the same length of time (six minutes) as he had first interviewed Zündel. The interview with Citron followed immediately after his interview with Zündel. After her interview ended, Shatsky took over and fielded the calls from

---

73 Discussion with Michael Hughes, Legal Council for the CBC, on 4 February 2004.
74 Personal communication of Michael Hughes (28 July 2004).
75 *Ibid.*
76 In his Zundelsite, there are quotes of what Zündel said on the radio show:
   Germans are innocent of the charge of genocide against the Jews ... Sabina Citron's friends, and Sabina Citron herself, had every opportunity during that seven and a half week trial, Mr. Shatsky, to bring us the orders for the extermination of the Jews. They cannot because there is none. And Sabina Citron, I want to add right here, is only one person ... to bring that lady on is to open up old wounds, to agitate the Jewish community, to create community discontent, to create community unrest. She is an agitator. She was even too uncomfortable for the generally wise leadership of the Jewish community who did not want to have this trial.

listeners. Citron's original understanding was that she would go on to field callers' questions after her interview, but Hughes explains that in view of the fact that "phone-in" radio programs can become incendiary very quickly, it had been decided by CBC's radio management that, in order to avoid the possibility of unfortunate exchanges which could present possible legal problems, Shatsky should handle the callers' questions himself.[77] Citron wanted to respond to callers, but the producers turned her microphone off. Citron was very upset and left the studio.

Zündel exploited the CBC's commitment to balance. The producers decided to extend the scope of tolerance to include this prominent Holocaust denier and by this to put the Holocaust survivor in an impossible situation: to confront a person who says she is lying and is exploiting others by inventing "Jewish conniving propaganda". Littleton reiterated that this mistake was never repeated.[78] He acknowledged that the invitation to "counterbalance" a Holocaust survivor conferred unjustified legitimacy upon Zündel and portrayed him as one whose "truth" should be heard, on an equal footing with Holocaust survivors. The natural liberal tendency to balance without much thought is a real concern. After all, the CBC could have allowed Zündel to speak the following day; there was no urgency to hear him when Ms Citron was at the studio. Zündel gave his usual propaganda diatribe, calling Citron and other Holocaust survivors liars, and she had to sit there and listen. At least Citron was allowed to respond, and she did so vehemently.

Citron called her lawyers to issue a complaint and to start legal proceedings against the CBC. She asked for a complete apology for betraying their word regarding Zündel's participation, and for turning her microphone off. To my complete surprise, the case was never resolved. It is still outstanding, because apparently both sides to the dispute lost interest in bringing it to a conclusion.[79]

Today when one searches the Internet using the term "Holocaust", one will get information on the Holocaust and also on Holocaust denial. I did a search for "Auschwitz lie", looking for material on the German law that explicitly prohibits denying or belittling the Holocaust, and found a significant number of sites claiming that Auschwitz was a big lie. Young people might be confused between the two "truths" offered to them, not knowing which "truth" they should believe. As skeptical thinkers they might grow to believe that, like in most cases, the "truth" lies somewhere between the two proposed "truths"; that there is some "truth" in the one

---

77 Personal communication of Michael Hughes (28 July 2004).
78 Interview with James Littleton, CBC, Toronto (4 October 1998).
79 I discussed the details of this affair with Ms Citron in two lengthy conversations in March 2004. She, however, refused to be quoted. I should note that her version of the affair is somewhat different to CBC's version described *supra*.

view and some "truth" in the other. This trend is especially worrisome in light of the following considerations: (1) within a few years there will not be any Holocaust survivors among us; (2) the sites launched by hate-mongers are numerous and graphically compelling, attracting the youth who excel in surfing the Internet and enjoy the exploration of its marvels (see Conclusion); and (3) the media's inclination to balance between views. This unqualified inclination in the name of objective reporting might lead to balancing between a historian who probes the horrors of the Nazi racist constitution and the subsequent mass murders, and a revisionist historian who denies that any of the harsh consequences of racist hatred actually took place. If such a mistake could have taken place by the CBC before the turn of the twenty-first century, when Holocaust survivors are required to hear that they are imagining and lying in order to exploit Germany and other countries, what will happen in another fifty years when the horrors of World War II will have become yet another historical phenomenon remote from the living generations?

Thus it is reiterated that the media should not treat hate-mongers in a neutral fashion. The media are oriented to public questions. Media organizations are expected to safeguard democracy and to have a sense of social responsibility.[80] Their prime roles are to inform and report. Some organs of the media take an active part in politics. All of them should be committed not to the partisan interests of this or that government, but to the inherent values of democracy.

The media need not stay neutral when values and institutions of democracy are threatened and attacked. Journalists are also citizens. Theodore Glasser[81] notes that one of the unfortunate consequences of the view of objective reporting is that it denies journalists their citizenship: as disinterested observers, as impartial reporters, journalists are expected to be morally disengaged and politically inactive.[82] This consequence is, indeed, unfortunate. Ethical journalism, in the sense of caring for individuals as human beings, caring for democracy, and showing responsibility with regard to what one writes, is more important than the notion of moral neutrality that is embedded in the technique of objective reporting.

80 The 1947 Report of the Commission on Freedom of the Press, headed by Robert M. Hutchins and entitled "A Free and Responsible Press", is the chief source of the idea that has dominated discussion of journalism ethics for the past fifty and more years – the concept of social responsibility of the press. For further discussion, see E. B. Lambeth, *Committed Journalism* (Bloomington: Indiana University Press, 1992); C. G. Christians, J. P. Ferré and P. M. Fackler, *Good News* (New York: Oxford University Press, 1993).
81 T. L. Glasser, "Objectivity precludes responsibility", *The Quill* (February 1984), p. 15.
82 Glasser cites Walter Cronkite, who said: "I don't think it is any of our business what the moral, political, social, or economic effect of our reporting is. I say let's go with the job of reporting – and let the chips fall where they may." *Ibid.*, p. 16.

However, two criticisms could be made about this line of argument. First, as Eugene Volokh claimed in his remarks on a draft of this chapter, some members of the public will only begin to sympathize with hate groups, because they may stop trusting the media's criticisms. Second, some reporters believe that all they need to do is to report the story, and let the public, who are able to differentiate between right and wrong, use their judgment. What is required from them is to report the facts in a so-called objective manner. Let me say something about these criticisms.[83] Hate speech is not like any other matter that should be covered in an objective tone. It is not like any other piece of news: road accidents; the weather; elections; abortion; death of the Pope; flooding the rice fields; or raising taxes. I think all humane people conceive hatred of other groups – whether these are religious, cultural, national or racial minorities – as immoral, wrong, malicious, and odious. People who care about the underlying values of democracy, respecting others and not harming others, may feel that the media's condemnation of hate speech is redundant, expressing the obvious, but they will not grow in sympathy to hate-mongers only because the media condemned hatred. Nor do I think that these citizens will mistrust the media on the sole ground that the media see it as their obligation to fight hatred against people. People on the whole would accept the media's expressed and explained rationale as to why they are duty-bound to denounce hate speech.

Furthermore, people who believe in the values that underlie democracy also think that the media's views on hate speech are true, i.e. in this case people might be sufficiently confident to say that they know they are true, and that people who disagree are making a bad mistake. People think, moreover, that their opinions are not just subjective reactions to the ideas of disrespect, discrimination, and hate against others, but also reflections of their own moral character. Following Ronald Dworkin, I would say that people think that it is an objective matter – a matter of how things really are – that hate speech is wrong and wicked. This claim that hate speech is objectively wrong is equivalent to the claim that hate speech would still be wrong even if no one thought it was.[84]

---

83 I am paraphrasing statements made in another essay, "Objective reporting in the media: phantom rather than panacea", in *Speech, Media and Ethics, op. cit.*, pp. 69–86.

84 R. Dworkin, "Objectivity and truth: you'd better believe it", *Philosophy & Public Affairs* (1996): 87–139, at 92–98. Notwithstanding, Dworkin is strongly opposed to proscription of hate speech. See his "A new map of censorship", *Index on Censorship* (1994): 14; "Pornography and hate" and "MacKinnon's words", in *Freedom's Law* (Cambridge: Harvard University Press, 1996); "Forked tongues, faked doctrines", *Index on Censorship* (March 1997).

Doug Collins

Doug Collins, a columnist with the *North Shore News*, which was circulated freely in Vancouver, penned anti-Semitic diatribes on a regular basis. One of his articles was called "Hollywood propaganda", referring to the movie *Schindler's List* as "Swindler's List". The Canadian Jewish Congress brought a complaint against him and his publisher to the British Columbia Human Rights Commission under the British Columbia Human Rights Code. Section 7 of the Code states as follows:

> 7. (1) A person must not publish, issue or display, or cause to be published, issued or displayed, any statement, publication, notice, sign, symbol, emblem or other representation that...
> b. is likely to expose a person or a group of persons to hatred or contempt because of the race, colour, ancestry, place of origin, religion, marital status, family status, physical or mental disability, sex, sexual orientation or age of that person or group of persons.

The Jewish Congress lost the case. The BC Human Rights Tribunal considered two issues. The first was whether the communication itself expressed hatred or contempt of a person or group, and would a reasonable person understand this message as expressing hatred or contempt in the context of the expression? Second, assessed in its context, was the likely effect of the communication to make it more acceptable for others to manifest hatred or contempt against the person or group concerned? Would a reasonable person consider it likely to increase the risk of exposure of target group members to hatred or contempt? The Tribunal concluded that although the publication was likely to make it more acceptable for others to express hatred or contempt against Jewish people because of their race, religion or ancestry, it did not itself express hatred or contempt. Therefore the complaint was not justified and, pursuant to Section 7(1) of the Code, the complaints against the Respondents Doug Collins and the *North Shore News* were dismissed.[85]

Harry Abrams, an active member of the Jewish community in Victoria, then decided to launch another complaint. The case was identical in many respects to the previous one, with the significant difference that this case related not only to the "Swindler's List" article but to additional articles as well. Abrams said that an anti-Semitic pattern could be discerned. Because the Tribunal had previously upheld the constitutionality of the Code after a lengthy hearing in the Jewish Congress case, it pondered

---

85 *Canadian Jewish Congress* v. *North Shore Free Press Ltd. and Doug Collins*, British Columbia Human Rights Tribunal, Reasons for decision (May–June 1997), part VII, available at http://mpd.selkirk.bc.ca/webdev/arcom/viewcontent.asp?ID=71.

whether Collins had violated the Code by publishing statements that were likely to expose Jews to hatred or contempt. The Tribunal concluded that Collins had breached the Code. It found that four of his articles displayed a pattern of anti-Semitism. They were found to "contain themes that reinforce some of the most virulent forms of anti-Semitism".[86]

They conveyed notions that:

> Jews, individually and collectively, are selfish, greedy and manipulative; that they have conspired to control government institutions and the media; and that they use that control to perpetuate inflated figures concerning the victimization of Jews during the Holocaust and to persecute anyone who speaks out against them.[87]

The Tribunal concluded that the publication of these messages in a community newspaper that was delivered to almost every home in the community was likely to increase the risk to Jewish people of being exposed to hatred or contempt because of their race, religion or ancestry:

> Mr. Collins expresses hatred or contempt indirectly and subtly. He does not overtly incite hateful or contemptuous expressions. However, he reinforces negative stereotypes of the Jews that have been promulgated for centuries. Further, publication of these ideas in a credible newspaper increases the likelihood that others will manifest hateful and contemptuous views in a more directly harmful manner.[88]

Collins and his publisher were ordered to cease publishing statements that would be likely to expose Jewish persons to hatred and contempt, and to refrain from committing the same or a similar contravention; and to make a payment of $2,000 to Harry Abrams as compensation for "the injury they have caused to his dignity and self respect". The *North Shore News* was ordered to publish a summary of the Tribunal's decision.[89]

It was the first time that any Canadian government agency or court had dictated editorial content to a newspaper and ordered that it be published. The British Columbia Council raised its voice against the decision,[90] and I tend to agree with its resolution that the Tribunal

---

86 *Harry Abrams* v. *North Shore Free Press Ltd. and Doug Collins*, British Columbia Human Rights Tribunal, Reasons for decision (July 1998), para. 69.
87 *Ibid.*, para. 84.
88 *Ibid.*, para. 99.
89 *Ibid.*, para. 85.
90 S. Pearlstein, "In Canada, free speech has its restrictions", *Washington Post* (12 December 1999), p. A41; D. Moore, "Columnist guilty of promoting hatred", *The Calgary Herald* (4 February 1999). See also P. Wilcocks, "B.C. tribunal rules against paper, controversial columnist", *Globe & Mail* (4 February 1999).

exceeded its powers in the case. From reading the contested articles one can see that Collins trivialized the Holocaust, but he did not deny its happening. Collins was not a Nazi sympathizer. Collins was born in Britain, fought in World War II in Dunkirk, was captured by the Germans, and served as a prisoner of war for five years. Influenced by revisionist teachings, Collins thought that the figure of six million Jews killed during the Holocaust was "exaggerated" and "nonsense". He thought too much notice was taken of the Holocaust, while other human tragedies (such as in Armenia and Indonesia) were ignored. But unlike Zündel, Collins was not engaged in a world campaign of hatred against Jews, nor was he a teacher in a classroom like Keegstra, where students were subjected to his manipulations. Collins had denied he was anti-Semitic. He contended that the articles were not meant to deny the Holocaust, but to complain that Jewish influence on the media and on Hollywood led to an exaggeration of the number of people who died.[91]

Reading Collins' columns, it is quite evident that he had biased ideas against Jews and perpetuated common hostile stereotypes (Jews control the American media; Jews run Hollywood; they are motivated by greed and money). In one of his articles he quoted another person who said that the Zionist lobby "is malicious, implacable, mendacious and dangerous".[92] Still, I think the Free Speech Principle should protect such statements. Obviously they are not pleasant. They are untrue and quite cruel, but the essence of tolerance is to protect such objectionable views. The way to fight Collins' columns is by more speech, not by silencing him. Newspapers do not and should not publish what is only politically correct. The BC Press Council was therefore right in arguing that the government has no business setting up special tribunals to tell newspapers what to print.[93] Unsurprisingly, the British Columbia Civil Liberties Association strongly denounced the decision and expressed its concern for the future of free expression.[94] Newspapers should be allowed to voice unpopular opinions, to contest and to challenge common truths.

For many years Collins was a columnist in several newspapers, including the *Vancouver Sun*, *The Province* and the *Calgary Herald*. For the last fourteen years of his newspaper career he wrote at least one column a month for the *North Shore News*, in engaging and controversial prose. Collins reflected on many issues which he thought might provoke some interest and generate debates. He was not afraid to tackle many "hot potatoes" that others were reluctant to handle (for instance, since the mid-1980s he

---

91 A. Dowd, "Canadian columnist fined for anti-Semitic articles", *Reuters* (3 February 1999).
92 D. Collins, "Some value freedom of the press, some don't", *North Shore News* (26 June 1994).
93 B.C. Press Council Press Release of 3 February 1999.
94 Cf. http://www.bccla.org/index.html.

protested against multiculturalism). Speaking of Collins, D. Schreck said in parliament that "Mr Collins is a talented writer who from time to time drifts to extremes".[95] Evidently, like many people, Collins enjoyed being an *enfant terrible*. He was certainly not unique among columnists in his attempts to be outrageous and controversial. Newspapers actually relish such columns, which help them to sell. Controversy, so it is thought, is good for the business. People are not forced to read newspapers; certainly they are not obliged to read certain columns published in newspapers. The *North Shore News* published many columns, not only those of Doug Collins. People are free to choose what to read, and their sense of voluntariness in reading or adhering to one opinion or another was not undermined in any sense by his columns. They are still able to exercise their autonomy. In many newspapers you find ideological columnists, with unsavory biases and strong opinions that raise discontent and resentment. They gain a certain reputation by writing the way they do, and they often generate controversy. Newspapers usually welcome *contra* responses, and sometimes publish strong responses. This is the way free journalism flourishes, and the public right to know is benefitted. This is the essence of liberal democracy.[96]

Furthermore, if one does not believe in fighting columns with letters and contra-columns, still there is plenty that can be done before petitioning the courts. One can protest to the publisher, complain to the BC Press Council, ask not to get the free paper, rally others to protest and/or stop getting the paper, and ask advertisers to cease publishing their ads in the given newspaper. Publishers wish to sell, and if they come to realize that the price for free speech is becoming too high, they may reconsider the publication of the controversial columns. Harry Abrams was right in fighting against the distortion and intolerance that Collins was peddling. He was certainly not the first to protest against Collins' offensive and inflammatory remarks.[97] Abrams chose, however, the wrong way to pursue this. If we petition the courts against every opinion we do not like, and the courts respond in the way the Tribunal responded here, democracy would erode and we might eventually lose our freedoms.

Having said that, newspapers have the right and responsibility to scrutinize what is published in their pages. They can set restrictions on free speech when they feel that a certain columnist has overstepped the boundaries of tolerance and abused the right to free journalism. For instance, calling for criminal activities like incitement to murder, child molestation, and terrorism should not be published. Now, I have not read

---

95 See *Hansard*, Volume 4, No. 14 (Victoria, 12 June 1992).
96 Many would disagree with my analysis, including Richard Warman, who commented "You are way off here ... Collins was a whacko hater". See also http://www.warrenkinsella.com/words_extremism_fh.htm.
97 See J. Dalton's speech in *Hansard*, Volume 4, No. 14 (Victoria, 12 June 1992).

all the dozens of articles that Collins wrote. I did read the four articles under review. Personally, were I the editor of the *North Shore News*, I would probably have allowed the publication of all four debatable articles. At the same time I would have seen that counter-arguments were published so as to offer readers contrasting perspectives.

In September 2001, during the debate on the constitutionality of the case, Collins died. Consequently, the British Columbia government and B'nai Brith have argued that the case was moot. Collins' lawyer, Doug Christie, said that Collins' widow, who inherited Collins' estate, had the right to appeal. The case was considered by the British Columbia Court of Appeals. Chief Justice Finch, Lambert J. and Hollinrake J. dismissed the appeal, arguing that the case became moot upon the death of Collins, and that Mrs Collins did not stand in the place of her husband for the purposes of this litigation.[98]

Conclusion

It has been argued that hateful messages desensitize members of the public to the harmful consequences of bigotry. They build a sense of possible acceptability of hate and resentment of the other which might be more costly than the cost of curtailing speech. Hate speech, in its various forms, is harmful not only because it offends, but also because it might silence the members of target groups and exclude members individually as well as a group from communicative interaction and from integration into society.[99] It has been argued that hate speech undermines their right to equal respect and treatment, their self-esteem and standing in the community.[100]

On the other hand, I think that hate speech provokes different reactions: it might silence the targeted group, but it might also provoke loud protests, recruitment, and orchestrated conscious efforts to rebuke hate. Hateful remarks might reduce the target group member to speechlessness or might stir its members to activity. In Canada, Jewish individuals and organizations rose to fight against Zündel, Keegstra, Collins, and their ilk. The notion of silencing and inequality suggests great injury, emotional

---

98 I thank Richard Warman for providing this piece of information (personal exchange on 25 May 2004).

99 F. Kubler, "How much freedom for racist speech? Transnational aspects of a conflict of human rights", *Hofstra Law Review*, 27 (1998), p. 367; J. Weinstein, *Hate Speech, Pornography, and the Radical Attack on Free Speech Doctrine* (Boulder: Westview, 1999), pp. 127–135. For further discussion, see A. Tsesis, *Destructive Messages* (New York and London: New York University Press, 2002), and M. Matsuda, "Public response to racist speech: considering the victim's story", *Michigan Law Review*, 87 (1989): 2320.

100 See R. Moon, *The Constitutional Protection of Freedom of Expression* (Toronto: University of Toronto Press, 2000), p. 127.

upset, fear and insecurity that target group members might experience. But, as argued in Chapters 4 and 5, emotional upset or discomfort is not enough to curtail speech. Only profound offense might constitute grounds for excluding speech from the scope of tolerance. As said, the Offense to Sensibilities Argument is applicable only when it concerns speech that might cause profound psychological offense to the unwilling target group, resulting in dejection and shock. Furthermore, such speech might be excluded from the protection of the Free Speech Principle when it might incite to physical harm.

The historical and cultural context is obviously of great significance. Propagating Holocaust denial in Canada is quite different from propagating this idea in Israel. We can assume that Jews will hardly be persuaded by such propaganda. Indeed, Israel considers Holocaust denial as highly offensive, especially to Holocaust survivors. The Prohibition on Holocaust Denial Law of 1986 holds that anyone who publishes verbally or in writing statements that either deny the crimes committed against Jews or humanity during the Nazi regime, or aim to belittle them in order to protect those criminals or to express sympathy or identify with them, is liable to five years' imprisonment. Germany prohibits Holocaust denial due to its sensitivity to the horrors of the Nazi era. In 1994, it passed a law making Holocaust revisionism in and of itself a criminal offense. The German Constitutional Court ruled that freedom of speech was not a defense available to groups propagating the "Auschwitz lie".[101] In 1995, a Berlin state court convicted a leader of Germany's neo-Nazi movement for spreading racial hatred and denigrating the state by telling people visiting the Auschwitz concentration camp that the Holocaust was a fiction.[102] In Austria, §3h of the Verbotsgesetz (Prohibition Law) provides for the punishment of anyone reviving National Socialist organizations, campaigning for such organizations, approving of National Socialist measures or trivializing National Socialist crimes against humanity. The Austrian courts have always taken a clear stand against the neo-Nazi propaganda lies that there were never gas-chamber mass murders in the National Socialist concentration camps.[103] France, another country that is highly sensitive to World War II, passed the Gayssot Law (named after French MP J. C. Gayssot) in 1990. The law punishes, by heavy fines or imprisonment, any "public expression of denial of the Genocide perpetrated on the Jews by the Nazis during WWII". This law was used in 1991 to condemn the infamous

---

101 Holocaust Denial Case 90 BVerfGE 241 (1994). See also http://globalfire.tv/nj/04en/persecution/bz_130_en.htm. For general overview, see D. P. Kommers, *Constitutional Jurisprudence of the Federal Republic of Germany* (Durham: Duke University Press, 1997).

102 A. Tsesis, *Destructive Messages, op. cit.*, p. 188.

103 StF: StGBl. Nr. 13/1945 idF BGBl Nr 148/1992. See also http://www.nizkor.org/hweb/orgs/austrian/austrian-resistance-archives/ld-14.html.

revisionist academic, Robert Faurisson,[104] as well as some of his followers, notably the philosopher Roger Garaudy, in 1999.[105]

In a perfect world, the remedy for hate speech is education, developing in the population a sophisticated capacity to understand the past, understand politics, and understand history; being wary and sensitive to the prosecution of groups of people. But, as Rod Macdonald noted, we do not live in the best of all possible worlds. We do not have the perfect structure.[106] Thus each society needs to develop its own appropriate mechanisms to combat and denounce Holocaust denial. We need to characterize it as hate speech and fight against Holocaust denial as such. History shows that when bigotry and discrimination are allowed to develop over time, they can lead to crimes against humanity. Hate speech has been inspired and translated to hate crimes.[107] The Hon. Shirley Maheu said in a recent speech in Parliament that "anti-Semitism is clearly a serious problem in Canada today".[108] The B'nai Brith audit, published in March 2004, noted that the number of anti-Semitic incidents in Canada reached nearly 600 in 2003. The number has doubled since 2001.[109] "Bashing" people, including gay people, is a growing concern.

During the 1990s the world witnessed the horrendous effect of hate propaganda in Rwanda, where Radio Television Libre de Mille Collines (RTLM) became the most widely reported symbol of "hate radio" throughout the world. Its broadcasts, disseminating hate propaganda and inciting murder of Tutsis and opponents to the regime, began on 8 July 1993, and greatly contributed to the 1994 genocide of hundreds of

104 See D. Goldberg, "Protecting wider purposes: hate speech, communication, and the international community", in R. Cohen-Almagor (ed.), *Liberal Democracy and the Limits of Tolerance, op. cit.*, pp. 257–260; D. Matas, *Bloody Words, op. cit.*, p. 64.
105 Text of the law may be found in French in www.jura.uni-sb.de/france/Law-France/I90-615.htm; http://www.phdn.org/negation/gayssot/. For a useful discussion on French historical revisionism, see P. Vidal-Naquet, *A Paper Eichmann (1980) – Anatomy of a Lie*, available at http://www.anti-rev.org/textes/VidalNaquet92a/ (in English). See also E. Bleich, *Race Politics in Britain and France, op. cit.*, Chapter 7.
106 Interview with Professor Rod Macdonald, McGill University School of Law, Montreal (25 July 2002).
107 C. Wolf, "Needed: diagnostic tools to gauge the full effect of online anti-Semitism and hate", and "Regulating hate speech *qua* speech is not the solution to the epidemic of hate on the Internet", OSCE Meeting on the Relationship Between Racist, Xenophobic and Anti-Semitic Propaganda on the Internet and Hate Crimes (Paris, 16–17 June 2004); B. Marcus, speech at the Session on the Nature and Extent of the Relationship between Racist, Xenophobic and Anti-Semitic Propaganda on the Internet and Hate Crime, OSCE Meeting (16 June 2004).
108 Senators' Statements, Human Rights Committee Study on 2002 Berlin Resolution (21 April 2004); http://www.cicweb.ca/parliament/parl_042104.cfm.
109 http://www.bnaibrith.ca/publications/audit2003/audit2003-02.html.

thousands of people. RTLM, aided by the staff and facilities of Radio Rwanda, the government-owned station, called on the Hutu majority to destroy the Tutsi minority. The programmes were relayed to all parts of the country via a network of transmitters owned and operated by Radio Rwanda.[110]

There are obvious differences between liberal democracies like Canada and authoritarian countries like Rwanda. As Steve Newman commented,[111] in Canada religious groups are not at one another's throats looking for an excuse to kill, and Jewish groups are not weak and powerless; nor is the government feckless. Still, hate speech potentially warrants horrendous crimes if allowed freely without scrutiny. As said, I don't necessarily suggest invoking a law in every society. There are various ways to fight against hate, but one thing is assured: we should not remain complacent. Democratic institutions, including the education system, should be mobilized to fight against hate. The media may and should play an instrumental role in exacerbating tensions and divisions, or in calming them down. The key factor is awareness: reporters should be aware of their role and of the consequences of their reporting. The media are not excused from acting in a responsible and professional manner. Indeed, all professions, without exception, should have concepts of responsibility and ethics. Being objective does not require that one refrains from commenting on the credibility of one's interview subject. On the contrary, objectivity requires that one be able to assess credibility. Journalists are required to check and tell their audience that what a speaker says is untrue or biased. It is wrong to report that someone believes something to be true when one knows it is patently false. Reporting it without evaluative comment might incline some people in one's audience to believe that it is true. It is wrong to serve the interests of hate-mongers without exercising some measure of scrutiny. It is wrong for any citizen in a democracy, indeed for any human being, to act without thinking about the consequences of his or her action.

The remainder of the book grapples with these issues and with the concept of responsible reporting, reflecting on the media's relationships with terrorists who, like hate-mongers, fully recognize the "democratic catch", using the principles that underlie democracy to undermine it and bring about its destruction.

110 J. Silverman, "Rwanda's 'hate media' on trial", *BBC News* (29 June 2002), http://news.bbc.co.uk/2/hi/africa/2075183.stm. See also http://www. rnw.nl/realradio/dossiers/html/rwanda-h.html, and C. Edwin Baker, "Genocide, press freedom, and the case of Hassan Ngeze", University of Pennsylvania Law School, *Public Law Working Paper No. 46* (17 June 2004).
111 Private communication on 15 June 2004.

8 The terrorists' best ally: media coverage of terror

> The job of the press is not to worry about the consequences of its coverage, but to tell the truth ... As much as those of us in the press would like to be popular and loved, it is more important that we are accurate and fair ... and let the chips fall where they may.
>
> Larry Grossmann, President, NBC News[1]

Introduction

In the nineteenth century, a terrorist attack in Washington DC would have become known to the people in Jerusalem only after a few days. The evolution of mass communication has dramatically changed the scene of terrorism and the way in which terrorists conduct their affairs. Today's terrorists are well aware of the power of the media, and manipulate them to their own advantage and need. By giving unusual events extensive coverage, the mass media have evoked the notion that "you cannot be revolutionary without a color TV: it's as necessary as a gun".[2] The German terrorist, Michael (Bommi) Baumann wrote, in *How It All Began*: "We took a great interest in the press. We always immediately looked how the newspapers, especially in Berlin, reacted to our actions, and how they explained them, and thereupon we defined our strategy."[3] Baumann explained why the media are so important for the terrorists' success by saying:

1 Quoted in J. Tusa, "The problems of freedom and responsibility in broadcasting", *Terrorism & Political Violence*, 2(4) (1990): 550.
2 D. C. Rapoport, "The international world as some terrorists have seen it: a look at a century of memoirs", in D. C. Rapoport (ed.), *Inside Terrorist Organizations* (New York: Columbia University Press, 1988), p. 33. See also G. Weimann and C. Winn, *The Theater of Terror* (New York: Longman, 1994), pp. 58–64; B. Cordes, "When terrorists do the talking: reflections on terrorist literature", in D. C. Rapoport (ed.), *Inside Terrorist Organizations*, pp. 150–171.
3 R. P. J. M. Gerrits, "Terrorists' perspectives: memoirs", in D. L. Paletz and A. P. Schmid (eds), *Terrorism and the Media* (Newbury Park: Sage, 1992), p. 48.

At that time, we were already very much on that media trip ... It was always great when those actions were planned. You could have a good laugh. They were really well put together, so that the symbolism would appear. And when all went well, you had great fun. We would go home and watch it all on the telly. That was great.[4]

Some studies have delved into discussion of the distinction between terrorists and freedom fighters.[5] This distinction serves the interests of terrorists who wish to blur issues and to gain legitimacy and public support. Senator Henry Jackson rebutted the notion that one man's terrorist is another's freedom fighter by saying:

> The idea that one person's "terrorist" is another's "freedom fighter" cannot be sanctioned. Freedom fighters or revolutionaries don't blow up buses containing non-combatants; terrorist murderers do. Freedom fighters don't set out to capture and slaughter schoolchildren; terrorist murderers do. Freedom fighters don't assassinate innocent businessmen, or hijack and hold hostage innocent men, women, and children; terrorist murders do. It is a disgrace that democracies would allow the treasured word "freedom" to be associated with acts of terrorists.[6]

This chapter restricts its assumptions to terrorism in liberal democracies, where people are free and able to promote their rights and freedoms by legal means. As for authoritarian regimes, people rightly resist oppression. No one wishes to be denied basic liberties and rights. Thus, fighting repressive regimes by violent means is justified. Utilizing violence against democracies, on the other hand, is not justified. It is a misplaced euphemism to describe violence against innocent civilians as "freedom fighting". The more difficult cases involve democracies where part of the territory is occupied and martial rule is enforced upon certain people. Those people are justified in resisting oppression and occupation. We are born free, and we like to remain free.

4 *Ibid.*, p. 57.
5 G. Weimann, "Terrorists or freedom fighters? Labeling terrorism in the Israeli press", *Political Communication & Persuasion*, 2 (1985): 433–445; M. Stohl, "Demystifying terrorism: the myths and realities of contemporary political terrorism", in M. Stohl (ed.), *The Politics of Terrorism* (New York and Basel: Marcel Dekker, 1988), pp. 1–28; G. Jackson, "Terrorism and the news media", *Terrorism & Political Violence*, 2(4) (1990): 521–528; B. K. Simmons, "U.S. newsmagazines' labeling of terrorists", in A. O. Alali et al. (eds), *Media Coverage of Terrorism* (Newbury Park: Sage, 1991), pp. 23–39.
6 Quoted in G. Shultz, "The Challenge to the democracies", in B. Netanyahu (ed.), *Terrorism: How The West Can Win* (New York: Farrar, Straus, Giroux, 1986), pp. 18–19.

Terrorism is defined here as the threat or employment of violence against citizens for political, religious or ideological purposes by individuals or groups who are willing to justify all means to achieve their goals. Terrorism needs to be distinguished from guerilla warfare, defined as the deliberate use of violence against military and security personnel. Under this definition, the militant attacks against military targets would not be called terrorism. While guerilla warfare may be considered legitimate (for instance, when carried out in occupied territories against the occupying forces), terrorism designed to maim civilians is morally reprehensible.

The underlying assumption is that a zero sum game exists between terrorism and democracy, i.e. a win for the one constitutes a loss for the other. Democracy needs to provide ample alternatives for citizens to voice their satisfaction as well as their grievances with regard to social policies. Political groups and associations have legal avenues to explore in order to achieve their aims. Terrorism is conceived as inhuman, insensitive to human life, cruel, and arbitrary. To remain morally neutral and objective toward terrorism and to sympathize with terrorist acts is to betray ethics and morality.[7] Terrorists should be explicitly condemned for their deeds by all who care about the underlying values of democracy: not harming others, and granting respect to others. Terrorism, by definition, runs counter to these underlying values. Acts of terror are newsworthy, but when the media report on terrorists, journalists do not have to view themselves as detached observers; they should not only transmit a truthful account of "what's out there".[8] Instead, they may feel free to make moral judgments. Here, I reiterate about terrorism what I previously stated about hate speech (see Chapter 7): it is an objective matter that terrorism in democracies is wrong. That is another way of emphasizing that terrorism is plainly wicked, not wicked only because people think it is.[9]

There is a delicate relationship between terrorists and the media. Free speech and free media – the basic instruments (many would say values) of every democracy – provide terrorists with the publicity they need to inform the public about their operations and goals. Indeed, democracy is the best arena for those who wish to reach their ends by violent means. Violent movements and individuals recognize the "democratic catch" and exploit the available liberal instruments to find "golden paths" (from their point of view) to further their ends without holding themselves to the

---

7 See R. Cohen-Almagor, "Objective reporting in the media: phantom rather than panacea", in R. Cohen-Almagor, *Speech, Media, and Ethics: The Limits of Free Expression* (Houndmills and New York: Palgrave-Macmillan, 2005), Chapter 4.

8 S. D. Reese, "The news paradigm and the ideology of objectivity: a socialist at the Wall Street Journal", *Critical Studies in Mass Communication*, 7 (1990): 390–409, at 394.

9 See R. Dworkin, "Objectivity and truth: you'd better believe it", *Philosophy & Public Affairs*, 25 (1996): 87–139, at 92–98.

rules of law and order. Those movements and individuals would be crushed immediately were they to employ similar tactics in autocratic systems.[10]

The media have been accused of being the terrorists' best friend. Walter Laqueur explains that if terrorism is propaganda by deed, the success of a terrorist campaign depends decisively on the amount of publicity it receives. A terrorist's act by itself is nothing; publicity is all.[11] Dowling goes as far as arguing that terrorists owe their existence to the media in liberal societies.[12] The media are helping terrorists to orchestrate a horrifying drama in which the terrorists and their victims are the main actors, creating a spectacle of tension and agony. As this chapter will show, the media sometimes do not merely report the horror of terror; they become part of it, adding to the drama.

Some scholars speak of the "theatre of terror". At the heart of the theatre metaphor is the audience. The media personnel are a bit like drama critics who convey information to the public. Furthermore, like good drama critics, the media also interpret the event. The slant they give by deciding what to report and how to report it can create a climate of public support, apathy or anger.[13] By their theatrics, the insurgent terrorists serve the audience-attracting needs of the mass media, and since the media care primarily about holding the attention audience, this symbiosis is beneficial for both.[14] However, terrorism is *not* a theater. Terrorism concerns real people, with concrete fears, who wish to go on with their lives without being coerced into becoming victims.

Terrorists, news people, and media experts share the view that those whose names make the headlines have power. Getting one's name on the front page and being included in prime-time electronic news constitutes a major political achievement. Modern terrorists seek access to the media by committing acts that closely fit news agencies' definitions of news: being timely and unique, involving adventure or having entertainment value,

10 For further deliberation, see R. Cohen-Almagor, "Ethical boundaries to media coverage", *Australian Journal of Communication*, 26(2) (1999): 11–34.
11 W. Laqueur, *The Age of Terrorism* (Boston: Little, Brown & Co., 1987), p. 121; *idem, Terrorism* (London: Weidenfeld and Nicholson, 1977); *idem*, "The futility of terrorism", *Harper's* (March 1976). See also A. P. Schmid, "Editors' perspectives", in D. L. Paletz and A. P. Schmid (eds), *Terrorism and the Media* (Newbury Park: Sage, 1992), pp. 122–123.
12 R. E. Dowling, "Terrorism and the media: a rhetorical genre", *Journal of Communication*, 36(1) (1986): 22.
13 J. Z. Rubin and N. Friedland, "Theater of terror", *Psychology Today* (March 1986): 24. See also W. R. Catton Jr, "Militants and the media: partners in terrorism", *Indiana Law Journal*, 53 (1978): 703–715.
14 B. Jenkins, *International Terrorism* (Los Angeles: Crescent Publications, 1975); A. P. Schmid and J. de Graaf, *Violence as Communication* (London and Beverly Hills: Sage Publications, 1982), p. 72.

and affecting the lives of those being informed.[15] Gerbner and Gross argued that representation in the media gives an idea, a cause, and a sense of public identity, importance, and relevance. No movement can get going without some visibility.[16] This is especially true when the movement is weak. Then media access might be its major, sometimes sole, significant asset.

During the past forty years there have been many instances in which media coverage of terrorist events has been problematic and irresponsible, evoking public criticism and antagonizing the authorities. Let me shed light on a number of irresponsible actions of some organs of the media in crisis situations. The tone of the discussion is obviously critical, but I do not argue that the media always behaved irresponsibly in their coverage of terrorist incidents. On the other hand, unfortunately the sampling *infra* is not exhaustive.

Troubling episodes

A Rand Corporation review of sixty-three terrorist incidents between 1968 and 1974 showed that terrorists achieved 100 percent probability of gaining major publicity.[17] Media coverage of some of these episodes was ethically problematic, helping terrorism or contributing to the prolongation of the violent episodes. Laqueur mentions two incidents in this regard: the Bogota siege of 1977, which lasted sixty days, and the 444 days' detention of the American diplomats in Tehran two years later. Only after the captors had squeezed the last drop of publicity out were the hostages released.[18] A question arises as to whether members of the media understood the difficult position they put President Carter in when they repeatedly dwelled on the suffering of the hostages and their families, or when they pressed the president for action. Hermann and Hermann argue that

---

15 R. E. Dowling, "Terrorism and the media: a rhetorical genre", *op. cit.*, p. 14.
16 G. Gerbner and L. Gross, "Living with television: the violence profile", in H. Newcomb (ed.), *Television: The Critical View* (New York: Oxford University Press, 1979), p. 368.
17 J. B. Bell, "Terrorist scripts and live-action spectaculars", *Columbia Journalism Review* (May–June 1978), p. 49.
18 W. Laqueur, *The Age of Terrorism, op. cit.*, p. 124. See also P. Schlesinger, "Terrorism, the media, and the liberal-democratic state: a critique of orthodoxy", *Social Research*, 48 (1981): 74–99; M. D. Meeske and M. Hamid Javaheri, "Network television coverage of the Iranian hostage crisis", *Journalism Quarterly*, 59 (1982): 641–645; R. A. Friedlander, "Iran: the hostage seizure, the media, and international law", in A. H. Miller (ed.), *Terrorism, the Media and the Law* (Dobbs Ferry: Transnational, 1982), Chapter 2; D. L. Altheide, "Impact of format and ideology on TV news coverage of Iran", *Journalism Quarterly*, 62(1–2) (1985): 346–351; *idem*, "Three-in-one news: network coverage of Iran", *Journalism Quarterly*, 59 (1982): 482–486; J. F. Larson, "Television and U.S. foreign policy: the case of the Iran hostage crisis", *Journal of Communication*, 36(4) (1986): 108–127.

the media need to continue their considerations of what responsibilities of a free press are in covering hostage episodes, including the distinction between reporting new developments and rekindling a story that for the moment has not changed. Some guidelines might heighten their sensitivity to the role they can play in enhancing such stress.[19]

Endangering life

On 4 February 1974, Patty Hearst, daughter of the media tycoon Randolph Hearst, was kidnapped by terrorists associated with the Symbionese Liberation Army (SLA). Later she was coerced to join that violent revolutionary group. Marilyn Baker, a reporter for KQED television station, became obsessed with the story. She and her aides played "cops and criminals" with the SLA, took upon themselves police work, stalked suspects, chased cars, endangered lives. With her news director, Joe Russin, she tuned in to FBI channels and broke their code to enable them to listen to the FBI's communications. One night Baker and two friends thought they saw Emily Harris, an SLA member, shopping. The girl was with her boyfriend. The couple drove away in their car, and the reporter began a wild chase that endangered the couple's lives, their own lives, and well as lives of bystanders. The dangerous chase ended when the couple stopped at a police station, screaming for help. The fanatical reporter had mistaken their identity: the girl was not a suspected SLA member, nor was her boyfriend. The couple thought the trio in the chasing car were a group of murderers who sought to kill them.[20] They nearly did. The astonishing thing is that Marilyn Baker brags about this, feels no shame, being completely unaware of her irresponsible, unprofessional, and unethical behavior. Baker rushed to publish a book about her direct involvement in the Hearst affair, which was on the shelves a few months after the Hearst kidnapping, even before Hearst was arrested (in September 1975), so eager she was to publish her story. Unsurprisingly, her book is filled with misinformation, misconceptions, fundamental mistakes (like, for instance, the identity of the SLA leader, and the reasons that drove Hearst to join the SLA) as well as simple mistakes. Even the revolutionary names of some of the SLA are misspelled.[21]

19 M. G. Hermann and C. F. Hermann, "Hostage taking, the presidency, and stress", in W. Reich (ed.), *Origins of Terrorism* (Washington, DC: Woodrow Wilson Center Press, 1998), p. 226. For further discussion, see J. Scanlon, "The politics of hostage rescue: is violence a route to political success?", *Journal of Contingencies & Crisis Management*, 9(2) (2001): 88–97.

20 M. Baker with S. Brompton, *Exclusive! The Inside Story of Patricia Hearst and the SLA* (New York: Macmillan, 1974), pp. 132–134.

21 Compare Baker's version of the SLA story to Hearst's version in P. Campbell Hearst with Alvin Moscow, *Patty Hearst: Her Own Story* (New York: Avon, 1982).

There have been cases in which hostages were endangered or killed because of the urge for journalistic scoops. During the forty-five days of the kidnapping of Hanns Martin Schleyer in 1977, the German media refused, on the whole, to cooperate with the terrorists, and instead abided by the authorities' directives. They went to the undesired extreme of not reporting *any* developments in this tragic affair. At the same time, there were some breaches of this news blackout. *Der Stern* magazine, in its 19 September 1977 edition, reported that the government remained firm in its decision not to succumb to the terrorists' demands, and that it was said to be entering into mock negotiations to play for time. This report could have endangered the life of Schleyer. When the kidnappers saw that the government was unwilling to negotiate, they approached Schleyer's son, who was ready to pay $15 million for the release of his father. The German news agency DPA revealed this, and also mentioned the time and place of the transaction. Hundreds of journalists flooded the Hotel Intercontinental in Frankfurt. The terrorists, of course, could not carry out the deal. Four days later, Schleyer's body was found.[22]

There have been other episodes in which victims were killed – for instance, the slaying of a German businessman in November 1974 in a British Airways plane on its way from Dubai to Libya, and the murder of Jurgen Schumann, the captain of a Lufthansa jet, in Mogadishu in October 1977. In both cases, the hijackers had learned from the media that their demands had not been fulfilled and the authorities were just playing for time to prepare a rescue mission. In the case of the German captain, killed on 16 October 1977, he had passed on information via the plane's radio. The media broadcast the information he had transmitted, the terrorists heard the broadcast and their leader, Zohair Youssef Akache, executed him.[23]

The Israeli television coverage of the hijacked Lufthansa aeroplane in Mogadishu was also problematic. A special German anti-terrorist unit, established after the massacre of eleven Israeli athletes at the 1972 Munich Olympic games, freed the passengers from the plane in a daring military act on the night of 18 October 1977. The ethical problem arose when Michael Gordus, the Kol Israel's radio expert, managed to locate the German attack force's frequency while they were preparing to take over the plane. In the evening edition of the news on the national TV, the Channel 1 anchorman, Haim Yavin, decided to broadcast the item, disregarding Gordus' pleas to wait until after the take-over of the plane. The item was reported about five hours before the manoeuvre, at 9pm, when

22 H. J. Horchern, "Terrorism in Germany: 1985", in P. Wilkinson and A. M. Stewart (eds), *Contemporary Research on Terrorism* (Aberdeen: Aberdeen University Press, 1987), pp. 159–160.
23 W. Laqueur, *The Age of Terrorism, op. cit.*, p. 126; A. P. Schmid and J. de Graaf, *Violence as Communication, op. cit.*, pp. 102–103.

the action was scheduled for 2 am. Mr Yavin insisted that the broadcast take place. It seems that he did not consider the potentially dangerous consequences of his action: the possibility that the hijackers would discover the rescue plan before the rescuers could make their move, further jeopardizing the hostages and causing difficulties for the German force.[24]

Another hijacking incident took place on 22 November 1974, when four terrorists took over a British Airways airplane, demanding the release of thirteen imprisoned terrorists in Egypt and two in the Netherlands. The Egyptian authorities claimed that they were freeing the requested terrorists and sending them to the hijackers. At this point, a reporter revealed that there were no freed prisoners on board the Egyptian aircraft and that the terrorists were being deceived. The hijackers apparently heard the report and executed one of the hostages, a German banker.[25]

Immature and irresponsible behaviour on the part of the media was manifested during the Turkish embassy siege in Ottawa in 1985, when a reporter asked the Armenians occupying the embassy if they had any demands other than the vague ones announced to the media.[26] This half-witted question could have pushed the hijackers to more violent acts and increased the drama in this highly tense crisis.[27]

A better known siege started on 30 April 1980, when six terrorists, members of an Arabistan anti-Khomeini movement called The Mahealdin Al-Naser Martyr Group, took over the Iranian Embassy in London.[28] They held twenty-six people as hostages, demanding the release of ninety-one

---

24 The details of this episode were confirmed in separate private conversations I had with Miki Gordus and Haim Yavin in June 1996. Yavin explained that he was a young and dedicated editor at that time, in pursuit of news without thinking too much of consequences. He further said that he was sure that if he would not broadcast, others would and he would lose the scoop. Some time after the interview, when Yavin appeared on Yair Lapid's talk show in February 1998 (Channel 3, Israel Cable TV), he publicly confessed that this was the most serious error of judgment he had ever made in thirty years of broadcasting. This event did not prevent Haim Yavin – Israel's "Mr Television" – from winning the Israel Prize for Journalism, the highest prize Israel awards its leaders in their respective fields.

25 A. P. Schmid and J. de Graaf, *Violence as Communication, op. cit.*, p. 102.

26 See R. D. Crelinsten, "Victims' perspectives", in D. L. Paletz and A. P. Schmid (eds), *Terrorism and the Media* (Newbury Park: Sage, 1992), p. 233.

27 For further deliberation and examples of irresponsible behavior by the media, see J. E. Magnet, "Freedom of the press and terrorism", in R. Cohen-Almagor (ed.), *Liberal Democracy and the Limits of Tolerance* (Ann Arbor: University of Michigan Press, 2000), pp. 200–214; also J. Tusa, "The problems of freedom and responsibility in broadcasting", *Terrorism & Political Violence*, 2(4) (1990): 544–553.

28 The movement was active in the predominantly ethnically Arab area of Iran called "Khuzistan" by the Iranian government and "Arabistan" by the autonomists. See "Rescue 'made us proud to be British'", *The Associated Press* (7 May 1980).

ethnic Arab militants being held in Iran, and a plane to fly themselves and their hostages to an unspecified destination outside Britain. They threatened to blow up the embassy and kill the hostages if their demands were not met in twenty-four hours.[29] During the negotiations the authorities pressurized the terrorists to release some hostages, and indeed they agreed. They were about to release more hostages when they heard on the radio that the police had changed their mind regarding the number of gunmen inside the embassy. Earlier reports had said there were three gunmen, and now they said there were six. "See what happens when I release hostages", said the leader of the group to one of the remaining hostages.[30] The released hostage had been promised that nothing from his statement would be released.[31] Still, vital information found its way to the media. That leak and report could have endangered the prospects of the release of more hostages and possibly pushed the angered terrorists to harm the hostages.

On 10 March 1977, a group of Hanafi Muslims took over three buildings (B'nai Brith national quarters, the city Islamic Center, and the District Building) at the heart of Washington DC. The location was perfect from the terrorists' perspective and the hostage-taking immediately became a major media event.[32] Reporters from all over the country gathered in Washington. TV and radio stations interrupted their programs to provide their audiences with some live drama during the thirty-nine-hour siege. The Hanafi leader, Hamaas Abdul Khaalis, was asked by Robert A. Dobkin of *The Associated Press* if he had set a deadline, when none had been stated earlier.[33] The security experts thought that the absence of a deadline was an encouraging sign; luckily Khaalis was too engrossed in his own rhetoric to pay adequate attention to this thoughtless question. One radio reporter prompted Khaalis to mark ten hostages for execution after suggesting to the Hanafi leader that the police were trying to trick him. To calm him down, the police withdrew sharpshooters from nearby build-

29 "Six days of waiting, then executions and an assault", *The Associated Press* (6 May 1980); E. Blanche, "Iraqi named as mastermind of Iranian Embassy takeover", *The Associated Press* (14 May 1980).
30 C. Cramer and S. Harris, *Hostage* (London: John Clare Books, 1982), p. 96.
31 *Ibid.*, p. 104.
32 Israel's Prime Minister Yitzhak Rabin visited the capital during the Hanafi takeover, and President Carter gave "a most remarkable press conference" in which he proposed many programs on the home front and suggested many compromises and innovations abroad. Both Rabin's visit and Carter's press conference received only little attention. Cf. J. Reston, "Terrorists and the press", *New York Times* (11 March 1997) p. 17. See also C. B. Seib, "The Hanafi episode: a media event", *Washington Post* (18 March 1977), p. A27. Seib has a very positive view of the media's conduct during the Hanafi takeover. See also B. L. Nacos, *Mass-Mediated Terrorism, op. cit.*, Chapter 3.
33 "Excerpts from Khaalis interviews", *New York Times* (11 March 1977), p. 12; see also J. Weisman, "When hostages' lives are at stake ... should a TV reporter push or pull back?", *TV Guide* (26 August 1978), p. 5.

ings. Hostage Alan Grip recalled a broadcast reporting that a fire ladder was being erected outside the District Building, and police were going up the ladder. The reporter implied that they were about to break into the room where the hostages were kept. "One of the gunmen just went crazy. He screamed, 'You tell those police to take the ladder away or we're gonna start blowing people away.'"[34] Evidently the journalists decided to increase the tension for their audience, as if the tension for those under duress was not enough.

Among the terrorists' demands was stopping the screening of a film called *Mohammad, Messenger of God*, which the Hanafis regarded as blasphemous. The film opened on 9 March 1977 in New York cinemas, but was stopped quickly in mid-screening when the police relayed a request to the United Artists distributor.[35] The Washington TV station WTTG showed a forty-second segment of the film, which might have satisfied the curiosity of the audience but could have been dangerous to the hostages. Many viewers, more cognizant of the danger than the stations' directors, called the studio and voiced concern that the clip might endanger the hostages' lives.[36] Furthermore, when the police negotiators tried to build their credibility with the terrorists, one talk-show journalist asked the Hanafis: "How can you believe the police?"[37] It was as if an alliance was formed between the terrorists and the media against the police.

As opposed to those troubling episodes, I wish to commend the *Washington Post* and the *New York Times* for their conduct in the Unabomber case. Between May 1978 and April 1995, Theodore J. Kaczynski, nicknamed the Unabomber by the FBI because the targets he picked for his attacks – mainly university and airlines professionals – had killed three people and injured twenty-three others in a series of sixteen attacks. In June 1995, the Unabomber demanded that the *New York Times* and the *Washington Post* publish a 35,000-word manifesto calling for an industrial and technological revolution. If the two newspapers complied, the Unabomber promised to refrain from any further bombings. Publication of three additional annual statements was also demanded. Federal authorities, including Attorney General Janet Reno, pleaded with the newspapers to accede to the request for publication. After weighing the question for nearly three months, the *Washington Post* and *New York Times* agreed to publish the lengthy manuscript. Donald E. Graham, the *Post*'s publisher,

---

34 J. Weisman, "When hostages' lives are at stake . . . should a TV reporter push or pull back?", *ibid.*

35 "Hanafi Muslim bands seize hostages at 3 sites", *Washington Post* (10 March 1977), p. A1.

36 T. Shales and J. Carmody, "A media race to the air with a life and death story", *Washington Post* (10 March 1997) p. B15; A. P. Schmid and J. de Graaf, *Violence as Communication, op. cit.*, p. 78.

37 "Crisis cop raps media", Lt Frank Bolz interview with Robert Friedman, *More* magazine, 7 (June 1977), p. 19.

and Arthur O. Sulzberger Jr, publisher of the *New York Times*, said they jointly decided to publish the document "for public safety reasons".[38]

Kaczynski was a crude terrorist. The FBI was after him for many years, unable to track him down. During those bloody years he did not even establish contact to explain his deadly venom. Suddenly he did, and the FBI thought that readers might recognize the distinct style and ideology of the Unabomber and provide leads to capture him.[39] The record of the serial killer established his willingness and ability to kill. His threats were credible and to be taken most seriously. Human lives were at stake. Thus, after consultation with the authorities, both papers decided to take the right professional and ethical decision and publish the manifesto. Indeed, one reader, David Kaczynski, the Unabomber's brother, recognized the marked ideas and style of the killer and led the FBI to Kaczynski's isolated cabin in Montana, where he lived close to nature, averse to technology and to human beings.[40] After eighteen years of investigations, the man most sought by the FBI was captured. Many people, especially in the American academic and aviation circles, were finally relieved.

People in media circles voiced concerns at that time that now that the two leading American papers had succumbed to terrorist extortion in sponsoring this expensive personal advertisement for the Unabomber, the road to further extortion was opened.[41] However, the slippery slope argument has not materialized. Prior to this incident the last high-profile

38 The papers agreed to split the cost of an eight-page insert, which appeared only in *The Post* because it had the mechanical ability to distribute such a section in all copies of its daily paper. See H. Kurtz, "Unabomber manuscript is published", *Washington Post* (19 September 1995), p. A1. For a very good filmed depiction of the case, see *Hunt for the Unabomber*, American Justice, New Video Group, 126 Fifth Avenue NY, NY 10011, Cat. No. AAE-16180. Another valuable resource is ABC News production, *The Unibomber*, 20/20 (4 May 1998), T980504-01.
39 You may find the entire 35,000 words manifesto on http://www.panix.com/~clays/Una/.
40 B. Duffy et al., "The mad bomber?", *US News & World Report* (15 April 1996), p. 28; R. D. McFadden, "From a child of promise to the Unabom suspect", *The New York Times* (26 May 1996), p. 1. For further discussion, see S. F. Kovaleski and P. Thomas, "Had substantial evidence before arresting Kaczynski", *Washington Post* (14 June 1996), p. A2; M. Lavelle, "Defending the Unabomber", *US News & World Report* (17 November 1997), p. 18; D. E. Boeyink, "Reporting on political extremists in the United States: The Ku Klux Klan, the Unabomber, and the militias", in R. Cohen-Almagor (ed.), *Liberal Democracy and the Limits of Tolerance, op. cit.*, pp. 218–222. For a general discussion, see A. Chase, *Harvard and the Unabomber: The Education of an American Terrorist* (New York: Norton, 2003).
41 The manuscript appeared as the Unabomber submitted it, with his subheads and paragraph breaks. The text ran five columns per page with a black border around the edges. There were 232 numbered paragraphs, some of them several inches long, and nearly a full page of "notes". The only graphic was a Unabomber diagram at the end of the text showing "symptoms resulting from

publication in the face of threatened violence occurred in 1976, when *The Washington Post, New York Times, Chicago Tribune* and *Los Angeles Times* published a statement by Croatian nationalists who had hijacked a Chicago-bound airplane and threatened to kill its ninety-two passengers. The hijackers later surrendered in Paris after receiving an ultimatum from authorities. To date, the papers have not succumbed to further terrorist extortion to publish their ideas.

Hindering government activities

During the Patty Hearst kidnapping, John Bryan, publisher of a small newspaper called *The Phoenix*, printed a long, rambling letter he claimed was written by the SLA as an answer to his request to contact him. This was a hoax. Bryan himself wrote that communiqué. Apparently he was far more concerned with his selfish journalistic gains than with Patty Hearst's life. He should have stood trial for harming police investigation.[42] The SLA appreciated the recognition and publicity generated by the hoax, and later on they returned Bryan's favor by sending their next communiqué to him.[43]

NBC played a pernicious role in the Tehran crisis when it reported, in the early days of the hostage-taking, that two US emissaries were being dispatched to Iran. The report was broadcast despite government objections, and shortly thereafter Ayatollah Khomeini announced that the emissaries would not be received in Tehran.[44] NBC had failed to understand the delicacy of the situation and the need to cooperate with the government in such sensitive matters, concerning human lives. Instead of cooperating with the American authorities, the media network had competed with them, proving their "independence".

The media also failed adequately to consider the consequences of their reporting in an incident that took place in 1974, when terrorists took over part of the courthouse in the District of Columbia. The hostages were kept in a room separated by a two-way mirror from another room, which allowed the police to watch them closely. This advantage was removed when the media disclosed the fact, whereupon the terrorists ordered the hostages to tape over the mirror with newspapers.[45]

disruption of the power process". The cost of publication was between $30,000 and $40,000. Cf. D. Gersh Hernandez, "Entire Unabomber manifesto published by New York Times, Washington Post", *Editor & Publisher Magazine* (23 September 1995), p. 10. http://www.editorandpublisher.com.

42 M. Baker with S. Brompton, *Exclusive! The Inside Story of Patricia Hearst and the SLA, op. cit.*, pp. 141–153.

43 P. Campbell Hearst with A. Moscow, *Patty Hearst: Her Own Story, op. cit.*, p. 126.

44 G. Sick, "Taking vows: the domestication of policy-making in hostage incidents", in Walter Reich (ed.), *Origins of Terrorism*, p. 242.

45 A. P. Schmid and J. de Graaf, *Violence as Communication, op. cit.*, p. 102.

Another problematic episode concerned the extensive media coverage of the hijacking of flight TWA 847 to Beirut, 14–30 June 1985. The United States turned to the International Committee of the Red Cross (ICRC) in the initial twenty-four hours after the hijacking to arrange a swap for the passengers and the prisoners. However, because of published and broadcast reports that the US army had dispatched its Delta force anti-terrorist squad to the Middle East, the terrorists fled Algeria and soon landed in Beirut, where it was far more difficult for the Americans to carry out a rescue operation.[46] Especially noteworthy was the inappropriately detailed account of *The Times* in London:

> The US has reportedly sent a commando unit to the Mediterranean ready to storm the hijacked plane if necessary ... The unit is said to be part of a crack anti-terrorist squad of several hundred men ... The commandos, known as the Delta Unit, may have been sent to the aircraft carrier Enterprise which is currently in the western Mediterranean.[47]

American newspapers also published reckless, unprofessional, and unethical speculation about military movements and the possible use of military force. For instance, the *New York Times* published the following: "The United States has reportedly sent a commando unit to the Mediterranean to be ready to storm the hijacked Trans World Airlines plane if deemed necessary",[48] and "There have been reports that elements of a United States commando unit called Delta Force left their base at Fort Bragg, N.C., Saturday for a destination in the Mediterranean area."[49] In turn, the *Los Angeles Times* wrote: "The Army's Delta Force, an anti-terrorist unit, is understood to have been dispatched to the Mediterranean, probably to a base on Cyprus."[50] It is believed that those and other reports might have prompted hijackers to decide to fly between Beirut and Algiers several times in addition to taking hostages off the plane due to fears of military intervention.[51] Departing from the normal practice of confirming general locations for some military units, the Pentagon decided to ban reports on US deployments in response to the much-publicized reports on

46 D. B. Ottaway, "Early swap of hostages went awry", *Washington Post* (20 June 1985), p. A1.
47 M. Binyon "Crack commando squad in position for action", *The Times* (17 June 1985), p. 4.
48 B. Gwertzman, "U.S. said to send commando squad", *New York Times* (16 June 1985), p. 1.
49 J. Berger, "Gunmen negotiate as hostages urge caution from U.S.", *New York Times* (17 June 1985), p. 1.
50 N. Kempster and D. Irwin, "Reagan warning: Hijackers, beware", *Los Angeles Times* (15 June 1985).
51 "Pentagon bars reports on U.S. deployments", *New York Times* (18 June 1985).

the movements of the Delta Force. In reference to the publication of those reports, Michael I. Burch, a Pentagon spokesman, said: "There seems to be more respect for the next fall's scripts for 'Dynasty' and 'Dallas' than there is for US contingency plans ... A number of news agencies are doing their darnedest to report US contingency plans in advance and thereby are defeating them."[52] In hindsight, we know that the hostages as well as the hijackers had extensive access to the media. Journalists must be aware of the consequences of their reporting, especially at times when the lives of innocent victims are at stake.

One of the Hanafi leader Hamaas Abdul Khaalis's demands was that the convicted murderers of his family and their accomplices be delivered to him. The negotiator stalled by pleading ignorance of the accomplices' location, but a reporter unwittingly leaked that one of these people was in Washington at that time. This information not only enhanced Khaalis's position in the negotiation process; it also undermined the relationship the negotiator was trying to build.[53]

After the hostages' release, one of them said about the media: "They are poison. They don't care about us. They would be happier if we were dead because that would make a much bigger story." Another said: "The press is after blood, gore and mayhem. The press revels in sickness and perversion."[54] The *Washington Post* reported: "One hostage's husband punched a photographer in the face while the wife, in tears, shouted, 'Animals! Animals!' at the journalists."[55]

Glorifying terrorists

As stated above, Patricia Hearst was kidnapped by a small terrorist organization called the Symbionese Liberation Army. The SLA demanded that the media carry its messages in full, and the media agreed; they magnified the case out of proportion and provided sensational mass entertainment that served the publicity needs of the ephemeral organization. Yonah Alexander argued that the most disturbing aspect of this case was that the media gave a small group of criminal misfits a Robin Hood image, and

52 "Pentagon Bars Reports On U.S. Deployments", *ibid.*
53 A. P. Schmid and J. de Graaf, *Violence as Communication, op. cit.*, pp. 41–42, 76–78, 101, 105, 115; Y. Alexander, "The media and terrorism", in D. Carlton and C. Schaerf (eds), *Contemporary Terror* (London and Basingstoke: Macmillan, 1981), pp. 56–57; L. N. Deitch, "Breaking news: proposing a pooling requirement for media coverage of live hostage situations", *UCLA Law Review*, 47 (1999): 249–253. See also J. Herbers, "Carter says coverage of sieges is a problem for the news media", *New York Times* (15 March 1977), p. 16.
54 A. P. Schmid and J. de Graaf, *Violence as Communication, op. cit.*, p. 78.
55 T. Shales and K. Ringle, "Weighing the media's coverage at the close of the crisis", *Washington Post* (12 March 1977) p. B1.

transformed it into an internationally known movement possessing power and posing an insurmountable problem to the authorities.[56]

During the hijacking of flight TWA 847 to Beirut in June 1985, some of the hostages bitterly resented the activities of the American media networks, referring to ABC as the "Amal Broadcasting Corporation" and NBC as the "Nabih Berri Corporation". Each morning, ABC anchormen called Berri from New York to negotiate the day's news story, requesting to talk to the hostages and, if the request was denied, interviewing Berri himself. There was no good reason to invite Berri to appear regularly on network television, communicating his demands. Berri undoubtedly understood that public opinion would create pressure to strike a deal to save the hostages, even if the price was high. However, it was quite unnecessary to do so.[57] One American hostage stated, "Maybe ABC had us hijacked to improve their ratings."[58] The CBS Evening News devoted nearly two-thirds of its air time to the hijacking.[59]

Sensational coverage

Since the early 1990s Israel has been subjected to many atrocious and bloody suicide attacks. The phenomenon of suicide murderers started on 16 April 1993, at a restaurant near Mechola in the Jordan Valley. Between April 1993 and February 2004 there were 152 suicide attacks. They resulted in 631 people being killed and 4,107 people injured.[60]

The media, in their craving to cover each and every aspect of those events, served as a platform and loudspeaker for the terrorists, magnifying the impact of their horrifying brutality. The most popular newspaper in Israel is *Yedioth Ahronoth*, a tabloid that has the largest circulation in the country: 390,000 daily and 660,000 on Fridays. Given the size of the Israeli

56 Y. Alexander, "The media and terrorism", *op. cit.*, p. 53.
57 S. Klaidman, "TV's collusive role", *New York Times* (27 June 1985), p. A23.
58 W. J. Brown, "The persuasive appeal of mediated terrorism: the case of the TWA flight 847 hijacking", *Western Journal of Speech Communication*, 54 (1990): 228; W. Laqueur, *The Age of Terrorism, op. cit.*, p. 125. See also G. Weimann, "Media events: the case of international terrorism", *Journal of Broadcasting & Electronic Media*, 31(1) (Winter 1987): 21–39; A. P. Schmid, "Terrorism and the media: the ethics of publicity", *Terrorism & Political Violence*, 1(4) (October 1989): 539–565; T. Atwater, "Network evening news coverage of the TWA hostage crisis", in A. Odasuo Alali *et al.* (eds), *Media Coverage of Terrorism* (Newbury Park: Sage, 1991), pp. 63–72; G. Weimann and C. Winn, *The Theater of Terror, op. cit.*, pp. 1–4, 95–103.
59 D. C. Martin and J. Walcott, *Best Laid Plans: The Inside Story of America's War against Terrorism* (New York: Harper and Row, 1988), p. 188. For an excellent depiction of the crisis, see MPI Home Video, *Great TV News Stories: The Hijack of TWA 847*, ISBN 1-55607-634-7.
60 Cf. http://www.ict.org.il/. I thank Arie Perliger for the updated information (personal communication on 16 March 2004).

population (some 6.5 million people) there are not many newspapers in the world that surpass *Yedioth's* achievement. *Yedioth* has circulation of more than 40 percent of the press market on weekdays and 70 percent of the press circulation on weekends. This circulation exceeds the circulation of all the Hebrew dailies combined, and is more than double the circulation of its main competitor *Maariv*. This is an impressive achievement that makes *Yedioth* a monopoly in its field.[61] Neither *Yedioth* nor *Maariv* had much experience in covering suicide bombings and they played into the terrorists' hands, in effect putting their pages at the service of Israel's enemies. After each and every terror attack, the pages were full of hair-raising stories that frequently violated the victims' privacy, and with horrifying pictures taken immediately after the attacks. The headlines screamed: "Nation in Fear", "Nation in Shock", with running headers of young women screaming. It seems that no senior editor stopped to ponder for a minute, asking what purpose the paper serves when it dedicates the vast majority of its pages, sometimes *all* of its news pages, to a brutal attack in such a sensational, graphic way, that does not calm the public, quite the opposite, and has little or no respect for the victims. I am not saying that the media should not report such events. Of course they should, but not in such an exaggerated, possessed manner, with little reflection and thinking. Standards of magnitude, decency, and good taste should be upheld by editors who make the decisions.

To illustrate: on 19 October 1994, a suicide bomber exploded inside a bus on Dizengoff Street, at the heart of Tel Aviv, killing twenty-five people and injuring many others. *Yedioth Ahronoth*'s main headline on the following day was: "A State in Shock and Outrage".[62] Beneath it was a large photo of the "deadly bus" shortly after the suicide attack. All the news pages, twenty-eight in number, were dedicated to the bloody event, with a running header "Blood Bath in Dizengoff". There were colored photos of injured people, covered in blood, clearly in a state of shock, of a person picking up body parts, of the destroyed bus, of security officers crying in the face of the horror. There were headlines like "Horror at the Heart of Tel Aviv",[63] and "For Hours Body Parts, Ashes and Dust Were Collected".[64] Other headlines asked: "Where is Mom?",[65] "My Daughter Was There, Where Is She?"[66] In later terrorist attacks the papers refrained from showing close-ups of bodies inside blasted buses, at bus stops, and in restaurants, and the volume of coverage was somewhat reduced. Still, when events cost many casualties, most of the news pages were devoted to them, with colorful front-page pictures.

61 D. Caspi, *Mass Media and Politics* (Tel Aviv: The Open University, 1997), p. 20 (in Hebrew).
62 *Yedioth Ahronoth* (20 October 1994), p. 1.
63 *Ibid.*, pp. 4–5.
64 *Ibid.*, p. 7.
65 *Ibid.*
66 *Ibid.*, pp. 12–13.

Sensationalism is at its best when television broadcasts grisly scenes. After each and every suicide attack, Channels 1 and 2 (and, later, also the newly established Channel 10) of Israeli television dedicated long hours to bringing into citizens' homes pictures from the killing scenes without appropriately considering the effects of needless repetition on viewers. Is it really prudent to broadcast live pictures, when reporters can only rehash what they said some minutes earlier and perhaps, in desperation, relay the latest unchecked rumor? Are those photos considerate of the victims' families? Granted, the public will wish to know the situation and may like to see pictures. Censorship is not an issue; instead, balance and consideration are. Respect for the victims and their families should be a significant interest. Sometimes it seems that editors and reporters confused quantity with quality, thinking that more pictures will compensate for the lack of quality information and of new insights.

Immediately after the 11 September 2001 terrorist attacks, the broadcast media played and replayed the recorded exchanges between victims in the World Trade Center and emergency police dispatchers. They exploited the suffering of the people who were trapped and subsequently died inside the struck towers, playing again and again the emotional mayhem of people who were trying to cope amidst overwhelming horror, disbelief, fear, and terror. Those sensational broadcasters showed very little sensitivity to the victims, or their families, in pursuit of better ratings.[67]

During the Hanafi Muslim take-over in 1977, the *New York Post* ran the headline "Capital Horror ... Special Coverage ... Siege of Death" on four pages. Beneath it one headline screamed: "Beheadings Threatened". Photos of four men were printed, with the caption "These men are marked for death".[68] On 11 March the *Washington Post* reported that a "killing room" will be set up at B'nei Brith "and heads will be thrown out of windows".[69] Neither report considered the hostages' families who awaited peaceful resolution.

As Lt Bolz of the New York City police said, this was in a very poor taste. Furthermore, Bolz noted that the anxiety that the hostages and the perpetrators feel is also felt by the police, and might damage the course of negotiations. The negotiators act under severe pressure. Moreover, that kind of journalism tends to inflame, and may lead terrorists to entertain such bloody ideas.[70]

67 B. L. Nacos, *Mass-Mediated Terrorism* (Oxford: Rowman and Littlefield, 2002), p. 53.

68 J. S. Lang *et al.*, "Beheadings threatened", *New York Post* (10 March 1977), p. 2.

69 D. B. Feaver, "Church bells peal as over 100 hostages leave headquarters", *Washington Post* (11 March 1977) p. A23; E. Meyer and E. Becker, "Hanafis' house: an armed camp", *Washington Post* (10 March 1977) p. A1.

70 "Crisis cop raps media", Lt Frank Bolz interview with Robert Friedman, *More* magazine, Vol. 7 (June 1977), p. 21. More responsible journalists asked: "Have

Irresponsible terminology

The media amplify and personalize crises, but journalists should strive to resort to responsible terminology that does not help the terrorists in their attempt to undermine the democratic order. In February 1974, when I heard of the Patty Hearst kidnapping by the SLA, the first picture that came to my mind was of an army storming an American city. I was a teenager at that time, and the highly-publicized army's symbol, the seven-headed cobra, made great impression on me. I was also impressed by their demand for distribution of food to the poor. The media did not advise that the so-called "army" included only a dozen people. They portrayed the group as "soldiers" in some sort of heroic image, as a group caring for the weaker segments of society, providing a wide platform for their obscure agenda of fighting the establishment and protecting the rights of "the people". Organs of the media elaborated on the group's strange name, their agenda and their "operations". Of course, nineteen-year-old Hearst, the granddaughter of the legendary newspaper publisher, William Randolph Hearst, who joined the SLA and two months after her abduction participated in a bank robbery, attracted a lot of attention.

The media are expected not simply report whatever the terrorists are saying. It is the media's duty to exercise some judgment and scrutinize the terrorists' messages. The media need not play into the hands of terrorism, serving their interests and their political agenda.

Journalists are morally required to be conscious of the terminology they employ in their reports.[71] An ephemeral terrorist organization is not "an army". People who kidnap and murder randomly are not "students" or "saints" or "soldiers" or "freedom fighters". The killing of innocent civilians traveling on a bus or a train should not be described in terms of a "military operation". A difference exists between covering news and providing terrorists with a platform to declare their agenda. To remain objective in the sense of moral neutrality with regard to terrorism is to betray ethics and morality. Terrorists deserve no prize for their brutality. Here I take issue with the CBC Ombudsman, David Bazay, who in comments about the use

the mass media allowed themselves too to be held hostage by terrorists – and do they in the process contribute to the plague rather than the cure?" Cf. P. Goldman et al., "The delicate art of handling terrorists", *Newsweek* (21 March 1977), p. 25. For further critique of the American media in this affair, see J. G. Yuste, "La negociacion puso fin al drama de Washington", *El Pais* (12 March 1977), p. 5.

71 American critiques may hold that under the First Amendment there is no such requirement, and that journalists should be left free to express themselves as they see fit. I am not arguing for government interference or for government education; I am arguing for awareness regarding the issues at hand and acting in a moral and responsible way when covering terrorist events.

of the word "terrorist" wrote that "There is nothing in the CBC's journalism policy that prevents the public broadcaster's journalists from calling a spade a spade or a terror attack a terror attack".[72] However, at the same time, he instructed the CBC to be careful with the use of language. While quoting his colleague Jeffrey Dvorkin, Ombudsman for the American National Public Radio, Bazay explained that while the use of "the 't' word" may be accurate, it also has a political and "extra-journalistic role of de-legitimizing one side and enthroning the views of the other".[73] In his view, this is not the role of responsible journalism, "which is and should be to describe with accuracy and fairness events that listeners may choose to endorse or deplore".[74] Indeed, this *is* the role of responsible journalism and therefore journalists should resort to the term "terrorism" when such acts are conducted. Bazay took pains to explain that sides to a given conflict use and abuse the word "terrorist" to frame issues to advance their political agenda, but it does not matter how one side or another characterizes the acts of violence. What *does* matter is whether the acts fall within the definition of terrorism. However, because the description of a given event as terrorist might be difficult and controversial, the CBC is opting, in general, for the simple solution of refraining from using the term.[75]

I asked David E. Hoffman, Foreign Editor of the *Washington Post*, about its policy on coverage of terrorism and the usage of words. He explained that one of their first principles is that "the language we use should be chosen for its ability to inform readers". Hoffman maintained, "We seek to rely first on specific facts, not characterizations. Our first obligation to readers is to tell them what happened, as precisely as possible." When the *Post* resorts to labels, "we strive to avoid being tendentious. We do not automatically apply a label to a group just because someone else has used it." Reporters believe "we should use our journalism to delve into the specifics about an organization rather than slap a label on it. We should give readers facts and quotes – even if from disputed parties – about how to characterize an organization." The *Post* prides itself on observation and discovery at first-hand, rather than relying on derivative or second-hand

---

72 D. Bazay, "The ombudsman's comments about the use of the word 'terrorist'", Office of the Ombuds, an *Annual Report 2001–2002* (23 July 2002), Appendix 1, p. 47.

73 *Ibid.*, p. 49.

74 *Ibid.*

75 Similarly, as a general rule, the BBC World Service refrains from using the term "terrorists", which is perceived to be too loaded, and prefers to resort to more neutral terms, even when the brutality involved in the violent crime against innocent civilians is obscene. I thank Mr Fraser Steel, BBC Head of Programme Complaints; Ms Margaret Hill, Senior Advisor, BBC Editorial Policy; and Mr David Levy, BBC Policy and Planning, for providing me with vast material about the BBC and its policies. For the most recent controversy relating to the 7 July 2005 attack on London, see http://www.bbc.co.uk/complaints/news/2005/07/13/20561.shtml.

information from others, whenever possible. The *Post* strives to tell the reader as much context as possible about the actions by both sides. Hoffman concluded that "In general, we seek to be careful and precise when describing the motivations of groups or individuals involved in violence and terrorism." He rightly noted that "A more full and specific description is better than a shorthand one."[76]

Cooperation with terrorists and payment for interviews

There have been rumors that reporters have paid terrorists for granting them interviews. The media reported much of the Shi'ite leader Nabih Berri's version of the TWA story, portraying the person who orchestrated the ordeal as a peacemaker. Berri made an appeal through the media, urging Americans to write to the president supporting the release of 700 Shi'ite prisoners in Israel. The news media helped Berri's attempt to equate the fate of the innocent American hostages with the fate of the Shi'ite terrorists imprisoned in Israel. ABC news, as well as the other media, broadcast pictures of the hostages of the TWA jet and the Shi'ite prisoners, equating in the minds of the public these two very different groups. *Good Morning America* featured the families of the imprisoned terrorists, drawing an analogy between them and the families of the hostages. During the crisis, ABC had obtained an interview with John Testrake, the captain of the hijacked aircraft, sitting in his cockpit while one of his captures waved a pistol above his head. Michael O'Neill, President of the American Society of Newspaper Editors later described this staging "an orgy of overkill that exploited the hostages, their families, and the American people".[77] ABC denied that it paid the terrorists for those interviews.[78]

Irresponsible mediation

A related episode in the TWA saga has to do with ABC's David Hartman, who took upon himself the role of a mediator when he concluded a live interview with the Amal militia's spokesman by asking: "Mr Berri, any final words to President Reagan this morning?",[79] as if the president of the United States and the terrorist spokesman were equal and legitimate

---

76 Personal communication on 11 May 2004.
77 D. C. Martin and J. Walcott, *Best Laid Plans: The Inside Story of America's War against Terrorism, op. cit.*, pp. 189–190.
78 A. P. Schmid, "Terrorism and the media: the ethics of publicity", *op. cit.*, p. 550.
79 *Good Morning America* (28 June 1985); T. Shales, "On the air", *Washington Post* (29 June 1985), p. G1; T. Shales, "TV's great hostage fest", *Washington Post* (29 June 1985), p. G1; Thomas Raynor, *Terrorism: Past, Present, Future* (New York: Franklin Watts, 1987), pp. 150–151; D. C. Martin and J. Walcott, *Best Laid Plans, op. cit.*, p. 190.

partners in a dialogue, and as if it were part of the media's role to serve as mediator. David Hartman is a capable broadcaster, but his qualifications as mediator in such a tenuous situation are questionable. This delicate role, involving human life, appropriately needs to be left to those who have the proper expertise. Dan Rather of CBS asked the hostages questions about what messages they had for Reagan, and "What would you like President Reagan to do?" The networks were interviewing the hostages as if they were official US emissaries perfectly free of coercion to speak their minds, serving the terrorists' interests in pressurizing the government.[80]

In the next chapter I will analyze in detail another example of irresponsible mediation during the FLQ crisis of October 1970.

Dangerous speculations

During the 1980s, the national sport of the militias in the no-man's-land called Lebanon was kidnapping of Westerners. When Father Jenco was released from captivity in July 1986, the other hostages who were held with him were forced to make videos that were delivered with Jenco. In one of them, David Jacobsen expressed condolences to William F. Buckley's wife and children. Buckley did not survive his kidnapping.[81] A television station reported that Buckley was in fact a bachelor and speculated that Jacobsen meant to convey a coded message. Jacobsen was threatened by his guards. A month later he was forced to write a letter, dictated by his guard, which included grammatical errors. When the media received the text, again there was speculation about encoding messages, and Jacobsen's captors were led to believe he made the mistakes deliberately. Jacobsen was harshly beaten and placed in solitary confinement in a small room.[82] Careless behavior on the part of the media can be very costly and painful.

Lack of homework, and live interviews during crisis

As if all the misconduct that took place in the Hanafi event were not enough, Khaalis was outraged when a misinformed reporter, Jim Bohannon of WTOP radio, referred him as "Black Muslim", not knowing that the Hanafis were bitter rivals of the Black Muslim sect, and that members of Khaalis' family were murdered by Black Muslims. Khaalis threatened to kill one of the hostages and "throw him out of the window" if Bohannon

---

80 T. Shales, "On the air", *Washington Post* (29 June 1985), p. G1. See also J. Corry, "The intrusion of television in the hostage crisis", *New York Times* (26 June 1985).
81 For information about Buckley, see http://www.arlingtoncemetery.net/ wbuckley.htm.
82 D. C. Martin and J. Walcott, *Best Laid Plans, op. cit.*, p. 353.

did not apologize publicly. Only after the newscaster had issued an apology on radio and television did Khaalis back down from his threat.[83]

The *Washington Post* attacked Max Robinson of WTOP radio "all-news" station for conducting the first interview with Khaalis.[84] However, the *Post* had published excerpts from Robinson's interview just two days before.[85] In fact, the paper went on to print the entire transcript of a commentary Robinson had delivered from the Hanafi compound.[86] It seems hypocritical that the newspapers attacked certain tactics that they themselves were utilizing. The *Washington Post* also published a very sympathetic interview with Khaalis' wife on 11 March 1977 in which Joseph D. Whitaker, the reporter, sounded very understanding, if not sympathetic, to the motives that brought Khaalis to take hostages.[87]

During the TWA 847 crisis, the White House had let it be known that it was considering asking the networks to refrain from broadcasting hostage interviews because they were proving "terribly harmful" to negotiations.

83 T. Shales and J. Carmody, "A media race to the air with a life and death story", *Washington Post* (10 March 1997) p. B1; L. N. Deitch, "Breaking news: proposing a pooling requirement for media coverage of live hostage situations", p. 253. See also "Excerpts from Khaalis interviews", *New York Times* (11 March 1977), p. 12. After their surrender, Khaalis and his men complained that the media attention they received interfered with their right to fair trial. See *Khaalis* v. *United States*, 408 A.2d 313 (D.C. 1979).

84 T. Shales and K. Ringle, "Weighing the media's coverage at the close of the crisis", *Washington Post* (12 March 1977) p. B1.

85 "Tell them payday is here ... No more games", *Washington Post* (10 March 1977).

86 M. Robinson, "A compassion that was too long denied", *Washington Post* (12 March 1977), p. A 19.

87 Here are some excerpts: "Khaalis: OK. Would you like to come home and find your little girl in tub, foam on the mouth, drowned?.
Whitakers: No, I wouldn't.
Khaalis: A little violence would stir up in you wouldn't it?
Whitaker: Yes.
Khaalis: Okay. We're human beings. That's the way Hamaas came in and found four babies stacked up in the tub, foam coming from the mouth. He went upstairs and found my older son in the prayer room with his brains blown out. He was in the room, he found my other son with a coat tied around his head, shot in the head. He found my daughter coming down the stairs bleeding profusely. She was covered with blood. He went to the basement, he found BeeBee down there covered with blood. And he found the other baby, in the sink, shot, and then drowned. Drowned in front of her mother. And the little boy was beaten and she heard his screams when they took her upstairs. Heard the little boy screaming and the man beating him, before they drowned him, 'cause he was old enough to fight back. He was three. What would stir in you?.
Whitaker: It would certainly stir anger ... I certainly would want to do something about it."
See J. D. Whitaker, "Khaalis' wife: 'He's going to get murderers ... You would call it ... retribution", *Washington Post* (11 March 1977), p. A1.

The networks showed no indication that they would comply, even if asked directly.[88]

It is inappropriate for journalists to interview members of terrorist groups while acts of terror are underway. This type of interview has occurred many times during the course of prolonged acts of terror like hijacking, building sieges, and kidnapping.[89] Interviews under such conditions are a direct reward for the specific act of terrorism underway, and can interfere with efforts to resolve the crisis. In addition, such interviews all too often increase the spectacle of the event, spread fear, impede the negotiations between the terrorists and the authorities, and provide a contrived platform for the views of the groups involved.[90] Khaalis gave so many interviews that the lines were jammed and the authorities found it difficult to reach him.[91]

Live coverage

For the prime reason of not endangering lives, the media would be better refraining from live coverage of terrorists events. This is especially true when attempts are carried out to free hostages. Live media coverage showing special security forces preparing to enter the building where hostages are held may risk the entire operation and put the hostages in jeopardy. The terrorists might be attentive to media coverage and hear and even see the rescue operation while in progress. Their reaction might be deadly. Furthermore, hostages could hear about the plans, become alarmed and confused, and perhaps act in a way that would jeopardize the

88 T. Shales, "On the air", *Washington Post* (29 June 1985), p. G1. See also E. Randolph, "Coverage of hijacking raises question of who's exploiting whom", *Washington Post* (23 June 1985), p. A20; J. Corry, "The intrusion of television in the hostage crisis", *New York Times* (26 June 1985); T. Shales, "TV's great hostage fest", *Washington Post* (29 June 1985), p. G1.

89 For problematic episodes concerning Irish terrorism in Britain, see R. Clutterbuck, *The Media and Political Violence* (London: Macmillan, 1983), esp. pp. 109–123. For further disturbing episodes, see L. N. Deitch, "Breaking news: proposing a pooling requirement for media coverage of live hostage situations", *op. cit.*, esp. pp. 244–255.

90 R. G. Picard, "News coverage as the contagion of terrorism", in A. Odasuo Alali and K. Kelvin Eke (eds), *Media Coverage of Terrorism* (Newbury Park: Sage, 1991), p. 59.

91 Cf. P. Goldman, "The delicate art of handling terrorists", *Newsweek* (21 March 1977), p. 27; T. Shales, "The crisis and the media", *Washington Post* (11 March 1977), p. B1. The *Frankfurter Allgemeine Zeitung* criticized the American media by saying: "[Khaalis] gave interviews on television, which took so long, that the interviewers told him: 'We have to stop now and to switch, we will call you again.' The first crime was the crime of television." Cf. L. Wieland, "Washingtons Schwarze sind beschaemt und zornig", *Frankfurter Allgemeine Zeitung* (12 March 1977), p. 3.

operation. What is suggested is not complete shutting off of the media; instead, I am suggesting delayed coverage so as not to risk human lives.

During the 1972 Olympic Games, terrorists from the Black September organization took hostage Israeli athletes and officials, demanding the release of some 200 terrorists, most of them jailed in Israel. The Israeli government refused to negotiate the release of prisoners, and the talks with the German authorities quickly reached a deadlock. The terrorists introduced a deadline, threatening to execute the hostages. The German police prepared to storm the building when the deadline expired. East German television broadcast live everything that was happening, showing the policemen surrounding the building and preparing for the attack. Some years after the unfolding of the events that resulted in the murder of eleven Israelis in an isolated airport, a police officer gave the following testimony, which I quote word for word:

> Later we discovered that there was a TV in every athlete's room and the terrorists had been able to watch us preparing live on screen. Thank God we called it off. It surely would have been a suicide mission if we had attacked.[92]

Another sensitive aspect concerns the victims and their families. When the first suicide attacks took place in Israel, television teams were sent to the scenes and they broadcast unedited footage. As a result, families of the victims saw their loved ones sitting dead inside the exploded buses. Most notorious was the photograph of a dead man sitting inside the blasted No. 5 bus on Dizengoff Street in Tel Aviv (19 October 1994). Apparently no one in the paper considered the effect this photo could have on the victim's family. After this incident, TV crews were more careful in airing live pictures from such carnage zones. Decency and human respect prescribe that the authorities must first notify the families about their loss before citing victims' names on the airwaves, not to mention showing their pictures. A qualified senior editor, with experience in covering such bloody scenes, should review the material prior to its broadcast or publication.

The hostage-taking event at the Iranian Embassy in London by six members of the Mahealdin Al-Naser Martyr Group ended on 5 May 1980 when members of the elite Special Air Services regiment (SAS) stormed the building and killed five terrorists, captured the sixth, and rescued the hostages. Two of the hostages were killed before the commandos took

---

92 Testimony in *One Day in September*, produced by Arthur Cohn; directed by Kevin Macdonald. 1999 Academy Award Winner for best documentary feature.
93 L. Downie Jr, "Assault on London Embassy frees 19", *Washington Post* (6 May 1980), p. A1; E. Blanche, "Iranian Ara gunmen faces London hearing", *The Associated Press* (8 May 1980).

action.[93] During the siege, senior media editors received briefings on government policy and were made aware of the likely outcome of the siege. The two television stations, BBC and ITN, went live from the scene only after the SAS had stormed the building and rescued the hostages. Millions of people watched the rescue on television as bank holiday entertainment on all channels was interrupted to show the drama unfold. The moment of entry into the Embassy was videotaped by both stations. The ITN report began four and a half minutes later. The BBC report started eight minutes after the operation began. Both reports were delayed in order not to provide the terrorists with vital information that might have endangered the operation and risked the lives of both hostages and SAS members.[94]

Staging events

It is advisable that media do cooperate with the staging of events. A notorious case occurred at Carrickmore in 1979, when a BBC production team received an anonymous phone call saying that they would see something interesting in this small village. On reaching Carrickmore, the IRA staged an event especially for the camera, showing that they controlled the village. A few armed men in balaclavas stopped four or five cars, checking the drivers' licenses. The IRA stayed in control of Carrickmore for three hours, and pulled out of the village once the *Panorama* film crew said that they had enough footage. The BBC was subsequently accused of arranging for IRA gunmen to take over an Ulster village for a stunt and an afternoon of treasonable activity. The Opposition Leader, James Callaghan, said that "it is not the duty of the media to stage manage news, but to report it".[95] Finally, the BBC decided not to show the film.

A similar incident took place the same year, when the American Embassy in Tehran was taken by the Iranians. The Canadian Broadcasting Corporation filmed a mob demonstration. As soon as the cameras were on them, the demonstrators began shouting "Death to Carter" and burned American flags. After two minutes, the cameramen signaled the end of the "take". The same performance was then repeated for the French-speaking Canadian, with the crowd shouting "Mort a Carter".[96]

Gideon Ezra, former deputy head of the Israeli SHABAC (Internal Security Forces), said that during the Palestinian Intifada (Palestinian

---

94 P. Schlesinger, "Princes Gate, 1980: the media politics of siege management", *Screen Education* (Winter 1981), p. 30.

95 R. Clutterbuck, *The Media and Political Violence* (London: Macmillan, 1983), pp. 115–118. For background information, see A. Smith, "Television coverage of Northern Ireland", *Index on Censorship*, 1(2) (1972): 15–32.

96 A. P. Schmid, "Terrorism and the media: the ethics of publicity", *op. cit.*, p. 559.

popular uprising) of 1987–1993, foreign reporters offered Palestinians money to initiate violence against Israeli forces: the tariff was $50 for stone-throwing, $100 for Molotov cocktails.[97]

Conclusion

A study of victims' attitudes toward media coverage of terrorism lists pushiness and failure to respect families' privacy as prime examples of unprofessional conduct. Sensationalism, being more interested in tears and grief than in the substance of the story, and posing as family members to gain access to the home were other complaints. While local newspaper and radio reporters were singled out for being unprepared and not knowing the stories they were reporting, television reporters were singled out for their obtrusiveness.[98]

The above discussion demonstrates how the irresponsible behavior of journalists can fuel events. Journalists wished to introduce a fresh new dimension to their stories, as if they were not dramatic enough, and by this unnecessarily endangered human lives. What is required is accountability: thinking about the consequences of reporting.

When people are forced into alarming situations, the media should accept the instructions of the authorities. Experienced personnel can be an important factor. In sensitive circumstances it is better to have senior reporters on the scene than overly eager, less experienced reporters who may act without adequate judgment – as, for example, in the Hanafi crisis, where young, highly-motivated and ambitious reporters were involved and risked the hostages' lives.

In this context, it is worth mentioning Article 10 of The Radio and Television News Directors Association (RTNDA) of Canada's Code of Ethics that holds:

> Reporting of criminal activities, such as hostage taking, will be done in a fashion that does not knowingly endanger lives, hamper attempts by authorities to conclude the event, offer comfort and support or provide information to the perpetrator(s). RTNDA members will not contact either the victim(s) or the perpetrator(s) of a criminal activity during the course of the event, with the purpose of conducting an interview for broadcast.

97 Gideon Ezra's talk in Forum on Terror and the Media, Department of Communication, University of Haifa (30 April 1996). Photographer Ed Keating was accused of staging a photo of a boy with a toy gun which was published by the *New York Times*. See D. Shaw, "A year of media missteps in rewind", *The Baltimore Sun* (23 December 2003), p. C1.
98 R. D. Crelinsten, "Victims' perspectives", in D. L. Paletz and A. P. Schmid (eds), *Terrorism and the Media, op. cit.*, p. 218.

The Code maintains that "Broadcast journalists will always display respect for the dignity, privacy and well-being of everyone with whom they deal."[99]

In turn, Section IV (A) 9.2 of the CBC *Journalistic Standards and Practices* (1993) says:

> CBC journalists must ensure that any action they take will not further endanger the lives of the hostages or interfere with efforts of authorities to secure the hostages' release. They must guard against being used or manipulated by the terrorists/hostage takers.[100]

The next chapter offers close analysis of the *Front de libération de Quebec* (FLQ) crisis in October 1970, arguably the most problematic event of all. Here, some organs of the French media (most notably two radio stations and some newspapers) cooperated with the terrorists because they felt sympathy with the *raison d'être* of the FLQ and did not really perceive its members as terrorists. It is emphasized that here it was not a case of "kidnapping" or coercing the media. The crisis escalated rapidly to the extent that Canada declared a state of national emergency and brought troops to the streets of Quebec.

The reckless behavior of some organs of the French media not only endangered the life of the two hostages but also contributed, to a certain extent, to the killing of one of them. The two French radio stations, CKLM and CKAC, played a significant role, because at that time Canadians tended to prefer radio in an emergency news crisis.[101] They felt that a radio broadcast was more easily cut into with a news flash than a TV program. One of the findings of the Special Senate Committee on Mass Media was that radio "is generally 'background' in most homes, it is more likely that a bulletin on radio would be received than if it were televised".[102]

---

99 The Radio Television News Directors Association of Canada Code of Ethics, revised in 1986. N. Russell, *Morals and the Media* (Vancouver: UBC Press, 1995), p. 200; http://www.crtc.gc.ca, http://www.screen.com/mnet/eng/issues/violence/LEGISLAT/code1.htm and http://www.cbsc.ca.

100 CBC *Journalistic Standards and Practices* (1993) p. 62. See http://www.crtc.gc.ca and http://www.cbsc.ca. For further discussion on codes of ethics around the world, see http://www.presscouncils.org/html/frameset.php?page=library2.

101 According to the Davey Report, over eight in ten Canadians fifteen years of age and over claim to look at and/or listen to TV, radio, and newspapers each day; 89 percent listen to the radio, and 88 percent read newspapers. Of Quebec French, 81 percent receive at least one newspaper daily. Report of the Special Senate Committee on Mass Media, *Good, Bad or Simply Inevitable?* (Ottawa, 1970), Vol. III, pp. 11, 12.

102 Report of the Special Senate Committee on Mass Media, *Good, Bad or Simply Inevitable?* (Ottawa, 1970), Vol. III, p. 43. See also W. B. Stewart, "The Canadian social system and the Canadian broadcasting audience", in B. D. Singer (ed.), *Communications in Canadian Society* (Toronto: Copp Clark Publishers, 1975), esp. pp. 56–64, 66–70.

Furthermore, the Quebec French media did not adequately reflect the views of the Ottawa government, but presented the terrorists' views in a sympathetic, cooperative manner. While the English-language newspapers perceived Canadian unity as a major objective in evaluating the developments during the crisis, some organs of the French media helped the FLQ terrorists by supporting their separatist inclinations. Moreover, the French newspapers on the whole were concerned in the main with the impact of the crisis on Quebec, without giving much consideration to the ethical aspects involved in dealing with a terrorist incident.

9 The terrorists' best ally: the FLQ crisis

Terrorist attacks are often carefully choreographed to attract the attention of the electronic media and the international press. Taking and holding hostages increases the drama. If certain demands are not satisfied, the hostages may be killed. The hostages themselves often mean nothing to the terrorists. Terrorism is aimed at the people watching, not at the actual victims. Terrorism is theater.

Brian Jenkins

Introduction

Philip Schlesinger has noted that the media generally reflect their government's perspectives when covering terrorism, and that perspectives which conflict with the government's views are rarely carried.[1] Robert Picard argues that journalists also amplify the rhetoric of government officials and leaders of other institutions targeted in or responding to political violence.[2] However, the FLQ crisis exhibits a totally different pattern of behavior on the part of the media. Unlike other occasions when the media reported acts of terror, some organs of the Quebec French media did not aim to reinforce the existing order in the face of the FLQ challenge. Instead of amplifying the government's argumentation, they served the interests of the terrorists. Their activities outraged the Canadian government, and did not help to mitigate the tension. On the contrary: the behavior of some organs of the French media exacerbated the crisis and forced the government to contemplate possible procedures for monitoring the media. There was a genuine feeling that large segments of the Quebec French media helped to mobilize public support for the terrorists' ends. Indeed, it could be argued that their conduct in this affair was arguably a model for teaching us how the media should *not* behave during a time of crisis.

1 Quoted in R. G. Picard, "News coverage as the contagion of terrorism", in A. Odasuo Alali and K. Kelvin Eke (eds), *Media Coverage of Terrorism* (Newbury Park: Sage, 1991), p. 60.
2 R. G. Picard, "The journalist's role in coverage of terrorist events", in A. Odasuo Alali and K. Kelvin Eke (eds), *Media Coverage of Terrorism*, p. 43.

To better understand the behavior of the media, some introductory contextualization of the crisis is useful. French Canadians (Quebecois) constituted 28 percent of Canada's population, but 80 percent of Quebec's. The Quebecois have had a provincial government, roughly comparable to a state government in the US, since 1867. They have the classical characteristics of a nation: sharing a common language, common culture, common history, and a geographical entity that is their home-land. The Quebecois consider themselves a nation, and have a well-developed national consciousness.[3]

The national struggle in Quebec has a very long history. Nationalist sentiment has constituted the core ideology of French Canadians for at least two centuries.[4] Since the late 1950s, Canada, like the rest of North America, had been in the throes of a serious economic recession, and Quebec was particularly hard hit by its effects. Unemployment at that period affected as many as 50 percent of households in some small communities in the rural areas, compared to 18 percent in the metropoli-tan areas. The time was propitious for the appearance of a protest move-ment.[5] In the 1960s, there was a growing nationalist struggle that was combined with tendencies towards socialism on the one hand, and sepa-ratism on the other. During that period, independent organizations of the Quebecois working class were developing. In their own province, French Canadians as a group occupied the lower rungs of the economic ladder. Their average incomes were lower, and unemployment remained a serious problem, with a much higher rate than that among the Anglo-Canadians, who controlled approximately 80 percent of Quebec industry. There were very few French-speaking people heading large corporations. The Quebecois tended to blame their economic and social ills on the

3 A. Young, *Quebec Nationalism: Its Roots and Meaning* (New York: Pathfinder Press, 1971), p. 4.
4 H. F. Quinn, *The Union Nationale: A Study in Quebec Nationalism* (Toronto: Uni-versity of Toronto Press, 1963), esp. pp. 3–47; R. Levesque, "Quebec independ-ence", and P. A. Gourevitch, "Quebec separatism in comparative perspective", both in E. J. Feldman and N. Nevitte (eds), *The Future of North America: Canada, the United States, and Quebec Nationalism* (Cambridge and Montreal: Center for International Affairs, Harvard University, and Institute for Research on Public Policy, Montreal, 1979), pp. 61–70, 237–251; D. Clift, *Quebec Nationalism in Crisis* (Kingston: McGill-Queen's University Press, 1982), pp. 51–68; R. Cook, *Canada, Quebec, and the Uses of Nationalism* (Toronto: McClelland & Stewart, 1986), pp. 48–59; A. A. Barreto, *Language, Elites, and the State* (Westport: Praeger, 1998), pp. 97–101. See also M. Reid, *The Shouting Signpainters: A Literary and Political Account of Quebec Revolutionary Nationalism* (New York: Malcolm Reid, 1972).
5 M. Pinard, *The Rise of a Third Party: A Study in Crisis Politics* (Englewood Cliffs: Prentice-Hall, 1971), pp. 5, 102.

Anglo-Canadians, and many saw separation from English-speaking Canada and independence for Quebec as the solution to their problems.[6]

Many Quebecois saw the language policy in their province during the 1960s as a profound form of discrimination and oppression. All offices functioned in English. Citizens had to speak English in order to be served in many of the stores. The federal government conducted all its meetings and functions in English only. Even to be a policeman in Quebec, one had to speak English. It was more advantageous in terms of economic opportunity to be a unilingual anglophone than to be a bilingual francophone, and many francophones could not use French in the ordinary course of their work.[7] Yet, in the same period, a quiet revolution was taking place in an attempt to change the norms and to shape history in a way that would better represent the French interests in Quebec. At the ideological level, this revolution constituted the long avoided reconciliation with social and economic development. Traditionalism was abandoned. Social and economic development were openly welcomed. The spirit of independence and enquiry that had been frozen for over a century reappeared, making the Quebecois realize that they possessed the power to change their society.[8] At a practical level, the government in Quebec had assumed many, if not most, of the powers associated with an independent state. While it lacked actual independence, the government had the capacity for it. For the first time a strong government had emerged, concentrating within itself the expectations of the French-speaking population and subsequently assuming the task of inspiring and promoting nationalist sentiment. This was a highly significant development.[9]

6 E. S. Wainstein, *The Cross and Laporte Kidnappings, Montreal, October 1970*, A report prepared for the Department of State and Defense Advanced Research Projects Agency (Santa Monica: Rand, February 1977), p. 1. See also M. Pinard, "The dramatic reemergence of the Quebec independence movement", *Journal of International Affairs*, 45(2) (1992): 471–497; R. Handler, *Nationalism and the Politics of Culture in Quebec* (Madison: University of Wisconsin Press, 1988), esp. pp. 30–51.

7 J. H. Carens, "Immigration, political community, and the transformation of identity: Quebec's immigration policies in critical perspective", in J. H. Carens (ed.), *Is Quebec Nationalism Just? Perspectives from Anglophone Canada* (Montreal: McGill-Queen's University Press, 1995), p. 44; A. Young, *Quebec Nationalism: Its Roots and Meaning, op. cit.*, p. 10.

8 K. McRoberts, *Quebec: Social Change and Political Crisis* (Toronto: McClelland and Stewart, 1988, 3rd edn), pp. 129–130.

9 D. Clift, *Quebec Nationalism in Crisis, op. cit.*, pp. 18–34, 88. For further reading on the Quiet Revolution, see A. A. Barreto, *Language, Elites, and the State, op. cit.*, pp. 101–105; D. R. Cameron, *Nationalism, Self-Determination and the Quebec Question* (Toronto: Macmillan, 1974), pp. 115–120, 132–141; M. D. Behiels, *Prelude to Quebec's Quiet Revolution: Liberalism versus Neo-nationalism, 1945–1960* (Kingston: McGill-Queen's University Press, 1985); K. McRoberts, *Quebec: Social Change and Political Crisis, op. cit.*, pp. 131–143, 209–211; R. Cook, *Canada, Quebec, and the Uses of Nationalism, op. cit.*, pp. 60–86.

Of all the attempts made to bring Quebec outside the mainstream of North America, the most problematic and violent was that of the *Front de liberation de Quebec* (FLQ). The FLQ was a small revolutionary organization that aimed to separate Quebec from Canada through violence and terror. Its members were influenced by the writings of Carlos Marighella, and in particular by his book, *Minimanual of the Urban Guerilla*.[10] Marighella recommended the formation of groups consisting of no more than four or five persons in order to reduce to a minimum the risks of penetration and betrayal. The FLQ organized its ranks accordingly.[11]

During the 1960s, the FLQ concentrated on bombings, hold-ups, and theft of arms, with few victims and little property damage. While public opinion was vocal in its condemnation of violence, it nevertheless rejoiced in the political effect it seemed to have on the use of the French language in business and industry, and on the sharing of power and responsibilities between Quebec and Ottawa.[12] However, the shape of events took a dramatic twist in October 1970. The FLQ crisis, known also as the Cross-Laporte affair, was the most serious terrorist crisis in the second half of the twentieth century in Canada.

The crisis

The crisis began on Monday, 5 October 1970, when James Cross, the British consul in Montreal, was kidnapped by a group of seven individuals who called themselves the Liberation Cell of the FLQ. Within a matter of a few hours, the kidnappers, in an anonymous call to the radio station CKAC in Montreal,[13] claimed credit for the abduction and subsequently issued a communiqué that enumerated seven specific demands and was accompanied by a political manifesto of several pages. The demands were:

10 C. Marighella, *Minimanual of the Urban Guerilla* (Havana: Tricontinental, 1970).
11 Special Committee of the Security Panel, RCMP submission re Police Strategy in Relation to the FLQ (20 November 1970), p. 3 (classified "Secret"). For further details about the FLQ, its founders, structure, history, objectives, and terrorist activities, see G. Morf, *Terror in Quebec* (Toronto: Clarke, Irwin & Co., 1970), pp. 1–151 and G. Pelletier, *The October Crisis* (Toronto: McClelland and Stewart, 1971), pp. 53–59, 197–247.
12 D. Clift, *Quebec Nationalism in Crisis, op. cit.*, p. 94.
13 CKAC, part of the Telemedia (Quebec) Ltd Group, has historically had a large French audience. It received a larger audience during the crisis. According to the Davey Report, its audience was more than 264,000 people. Report of the Special Senate Committee on Mass Media, *Words, Music and Dollars* (Ottawa, 1970), Vol. II, pp. 109, 512; Also personal correspondence with Professor Conrad Winn, Chairman, "Compas", and Department of Political Science, Carleton University (11 December 1999), and with Ronald Cohen, National Chair, Canadian Broadcast Standards Council (10 December 1999), as well as a telephone conversation with Michel Roy, President, Conseil de Press du Quebec (13 December 1999).

(1) the cessation of all police activities; (2) the publication of the FLQ manifesto in Quebec newspapers and its broadcast on national radio and television; (3) the liberation of twenty-three individuals described as "political prisoners"; (4) their transport to Cuba or Algeria; (5) the reintegration in the ranks of the Canadian Postal Service of the strikers; (6) a "voluntary" income tax of $500,000 to be paid to the prisoners; (7) the name and picture of the individual who had recently helped the police to apprehend members of another FLQ cell. A time limit of forty-eight hours was specified to meet these demands.[14]

Hostage-taking is one of the most spectacular terrorist phenomena. It has been called "smart" terrorism, because the terrorists involved maintain control over the situation, gain media attention for their cause over a sustained period of time, and force the government to recognize them in the course of negotiations to free the hostages. In effect, argue Margaret Hermann and Charles Hermann, the leadership of the terrorist group taking the hostages becomes the puppet master, pulling the strings of the concerned government. The aims of the terrorist organization are to gain maximum press and television coverage for their cause and themselves, and to increase their bargaining power for the next round.[15]

On 6 October, the Liberation Cell issued two further communiqués. A letter from James Cross to his wife was delivered through CKAC, calling upon the media to make all communiqués public and to break "the wall of silence that the fascist police have erected around the liberation operation".[16] Robert Lemieux, a Montreal lawyer who was sympathetic to the FLQ and who represented many of the FLQ members, complained to the press that the authorities were not allowing him to see some of his jailed clients who were on the list of twenty-three prisoners to be freed.[17]

The following day, the newspapers printed texts of the kidnappers' communiqués. This signaled a flood of communiqués containing specific

14 D. LaTouche, "Mass media and communication in a Canadian political crisis", in B. D. Singer (ed.), *Communications in Canadian Society* (Don Mills: Addison-Wesley Publishers, 1983), pp. 197–198. See also H. Winter, P. Waters and E. Collister, "UK envoy's life hangs on seven FLQ demands", *Montreal Gazette* (6 October 1970), by Maclean-Hunter Microfilm Service [Canadian press clipping service, microfilm series: FLQ]. See also the film *Action: The October Crisis of 1970*, Director: Robin Spry (Montreal: National Film Board of Canada, 1973).

15 M. G. Hermann and C. F. Hermann, "Hostage taking, the presidency, and stress", in W. Reich (ed.), *Origins of Terrorism, op. cit.*, p. 211.

16 J. Saywell, *Quebec 70* (Toronto: University of Toronto Press, 1971), p. 38; E. S. Wainstein, *The Cross and Laporte Kidnappings, Montreal, October 1970, op. cit.*, p. 9.

17 *Ibid.* See also "Lawyer polls clients, trial delayed again", *Montreal Gazette* (8 October 1970), by Maclean-Hunter Microfilm Service [Canadian press clipping service, microfilm series: FLQ].

demands, political objectives, and ideological propaganda. On the same day, CKAC broadcast the complete text of the manifesto live. Secretary of State Gérard Pelletier expressed the opinion in a closed Cabinet meeting that publication of the manifesto in itself would do little harm. The document was of an extreme nature, a fact that would be quite evident to listeners. However, there remained the question of the direction to be given to the CBC in this regard, as this was clearly a matter for government decision.[18] Prime Minister Pierre Elliott Trudeau said that the language of the manifesto was of a highly scurrilous nature, raising the question whether the government should stop its publication. He thought it was better to defer any decision on the matter until the situation could be assessed more fully.[19] Later in the afternoon, the Cabinet agreed that the government itself must be responsible for the decision on whether or not to broadcast the FLQ manifesto, and that the CBC should be informed that "the matter was an element of a situation which should be regarded as a national emergency", with the consequence that the CBC should take no action with regard to broadcasting the manifesto unless and until directed by the government to do so.

The FLQ manifesto stated that:

> The Front de Liberation du Quebec wants the total independence of Quebeckers, united in a free society, purged forever of the clique of voracious sharks, the patronizing "big bosses" and their henchmen who have made Quebec their hunting preserve for "cheap labor" and unscrupulous exploitation.

It maintained, "We are terrorized by the closed circles of science and culture which are the universities and by their monkey directors", calling upon "production workers, miners, foresters, teachers, students and unemployed workers" to "take what belongs to you: your jobs, your determination and your liberty".[20]

Some of the newspapers in Quebec saw no difficulty identifying with these goals. *Quebec-Presse* was a weekly, leftist paper, located in Montreal and supported by the major trades unions in the province of Quebec. It did not enjoy large circulation among the French Canadians, but was well read by students, intellectuals, and leftists. Michel Roy, President of Conseil de Press du Quebec, estimates that its circulation was around

---

18 Cabinet Minutes (7 October 1970), p. 3 (classified "Secret") (No. 58–70).
19 *Ibid.*
20 R. Haggart and A. E. Golden, *Rumours of War* (Toronto: James Lorimer, 1979), Appendix A, pp. 277–281. Alternatively, G. Pelletier, *The October Crisis, op. cit.,* pp. 59–67.

30,000–40,000 copies, maybe more, during the time of the crisis.[21] The *Quebec-Presse*'s declaration of principles holds the paper as being the people's response to "the domination of the press by cultural, political or economic dictatorship or by the private interests that support such a dicta-torship". It maintained that the paper is entirely independent of "the capitalist forces dominating society, and it intends to act in concert with the aspirations of the people and their organizations".[22]

Quebec-Presse published the manifesto of the FLQ several months before the outbreak of the October crisis, in June 1970. In October 1970, it gave editorial support to the FLQ's analysis, adding that *Quebec-Presse* saw itself as carrying out the same struggle – for the liberation of Quebec – but by other means, namely through information. In a special editorial, the *Quebec-Presse* wrote:

> The same authorities denounced by the FLQ took it upon themselves to speak for the majority and condemn this week's terrorist acts. That doesn't mean much in itself ... The only argument that counts is the one the people make. The FLQ knew how to speak to them as never before. The FLQ's actions have been a kind of crash course in politic-ization by total immersion ... The FLQ reached its main goal: to speak to the world in its own words. And to make the Quebecois aware of their own situation.[23]

The Montreal daily, *Le Devoir*, an elite newspaper for intellectuals that was described as "the best written newspaper in Canada",[24] soon became a key protagonist in the crisis, suggesting that the government negotiate "in good faith" with the FLQ to ensure the safe release of the hostages. It should be noted that although *Le Devoir* had a small circulation (Michel Roy estimates that its daily circulation was 38,000–42,000 copies, and that the circulation went up by a few thousand during the October crisis),[25] its

21 Telephone conversation with Michel Roy (13 December 1999). Professor Marc Raboy, Department de Communication, Universite de Montreal, estimated its circulation was about 30,000 (personal communication, 18 January 2000). Guy Caron, assistant-coordinator of the Réseau Éducation-Médias/Media Aware-ness Network, informed me that *Quebec-Presse* ceased in the second half of the 1970s (personal communication, 12 January 2000).
22 M. Raboy, *Movements and Messages* (Toronto: Between the Lines, 1984), p. 59.
23 M. Raboy, *Movements and Messages, ibid.*, p. 67.
24 W. H. Kesterton, *A History of Journalism in Canada* (Toronto: McLelland and Stewart, 1967), p. 94.
25 According to the Davey Report, *Le Devoir*'s circulation was 39,916. Report of the Special Senate Committee on Mass Media, *Words, Music and Dollars* (Ottawa, 1970), Vol. II, p. 511. See also J. Porter, "The ideological system: the mass media", in B. D. Singer (ed.), *Communications in Canadian Society, op. cit.*, pp. 167–168.

influence was always far greater than its numbers would indicate because political and media leaders always read it. The French intellectuals who supported the separatist movement primarily read this newspaper, and also contributed to it.[26] The Editor-in-chief and publisher of *Le Devoir*, Claude Ryan, organized and led a movement in support of a negotiated settlement.[27] Later, after he left the paper, Ryan became leader of the Quebec Liberal Party.

The members of the Liberation Cell were well aware of the power of the media and of the political views of the senior people who ran the affairs. They used the media, releasing communiqués once to CKAC, another time to the rival radio station, CKLM[28]; both were happy to receive the messages and to broadcast them. Both stations were eager to participate in this game and quite happy to provide the terrorists with open channels of communication. The fourth communiqué, issued on 7 October was addressed to CKLM reporter Pierre Pascau. The reporters were cooperative to the extent that when the terrorists released their later communiqués in which they set down their detailed demands, they also named two reporters, one working for CKLM, the other for CKAC, as observers to assure that everything would go smoothly.[29] The two radio stations had become active agents of the news. Not only were reporters not coerced to cooperate with the terrorists; they also willingly became the trustees of terrorists, taking part in the negotiation process.

Crelinsten argues that the Liberation Cell won the battle over the means of communication, in which the authorities blocked publication of the FLQ communiqués. by sending duplicates to the media. After two and

26 Correspondence with Ronald Cohen (10 December 1999); Professor Conrad Winn (11 December 1999); Professor Bob Rupert, Department of Communication, Carleton University (12 December 1999), as well as a telephone conversation with Michel Roy (13 December 1999).
27 D. LaTouche, "Mass media and communication in a Canadian political crisis", *op. cit.*, p. 201; B. Dagenais, "Media in crisis: observers, actors or scapegoats?", in M. Raboy and B. Dagenais (eds), *Media, Crisis and Democracy* (London: Sage, 1992), p. 126.
28 CKLM, like CKAC, was a Montreal-based private radio station, owned by the Quebec City media company Tele-Capitale, that appealed to the French audience. According to the Davey Report, its audience was more than 151,000 people (Report of the Special Senate Committee on Mass Media, *Words, Music and Dollars* (Ottawa, 1970), Vol. II, p. 512). Because it was well informed about the happenings, the station received a larger audience during the crisis. Correspondence with Professor Conrad Winn (11 December 1999) and Professor Mike Gasher, Dept of Journalism, Concordia University (18 January 2000), as well as a telephone conversation with Michel Roy (13 December 1999).
29 R. D. Crelinsten, "Power and meaning: terrorism as a struggle over access to the communication structure", in P. Wilkinson and A. M. Stewart (eds), *Contemporary Research on Terrorism* (Aberdeen: Aberdeen University Press, 1989), pp. 424–429.

a half days of futile attempts the government tried to stall, and instead of suppressing communiqués as they had done previously, officials tried to draw the kidnappers away from their use of the media and towards direct and secret negotiations. At the same time, federal officials tried to delay broadcast or publication of the manifesto for as long as possible, even to the point of telephoning newspaper publishers directly to request that they refrain from publishing the text. However, the redundancy created by the terrorists' provision of multiple copies to the media ultimately undermined these attempts.[30]

On Thursday, 8 October, the CBC decided to accept the FLQ's demand to broadcast its manifesto "for humanitarian reasons".[31] Even so, the CBC was careful to ensure that the broadcast was presented in an appropriate format, and issued instructions that the FLQ manifesto should be read as a "communication" rather than as a news item. It was to be read by an announcer rather than by a CBC reporter or commentator.[32] On Radio-Canada, announcer Gaetan Montreuil sat in front of a TV camera and for thirteen minutes read in a dull, flat, monotone voice the manifesto of the Front de liberation du Quebec. Because the broadcast was in French and few English-language newspapers carried the full text, it was argued that not many English-speaking Canadians appreciated the enormity of the government's concession.[33] Mitchell Sharp who, as external affairs minister was responsible for the safety of Cross, approved the CBC broadcast without requesting the permission of Prime Minister Trudeau, who was outraged, thinking that what the CBC did was giving way to blackmail.[34]

The public reaction to hearing the manifesto on Radio-Canada was remarkably sympathetic. Although most people condemned the kidnapping, more than 50 percent of callers to the radio stations talk shows were in favor of the spirit of the manifesto.[35]

30 R. D. Crelinsten, "The internal dynamics of the FLQ during the October crisis of 1970", in D. C. Rapoport (ed.), *Inside Terrorist Organizations* (New York: Columbia University Press, 1988), p. 79.
31 G. Morf, *Terror in Quebec, op. cit.*, p. 165.
32 "CBC, government made decision", *Montreal Gazette* (9 October 1970) p. 10, by Maclean-Hunter Microfilm Service [Canadian press clipping service, microfilm series: FLQ].
33 J. Saywell, *Quebec 70, op. cit.*, p. 46; R. Haggart and A. E. Golden, *Rumours of War, op. cit.*, p. 11.
34 Minutes of the Cabinet Committee on Security and Intelligence (9 October 1970), p. 1 (classified as "secret"). See also K. Nash, *The Microphone Wars* (Toronto: McClelland and Stewart, 1995), p. 397.
35 R. D. Crelinsten, "Power and meaning: terrorism as a struggle over access to the communication structure", *op. cit.*, p. 429. Indeed, the public expressed positive sentiments to the FLQ throughout the crisis. See also A. Charney, "Kidnappers won emotional support", *Toronto Star* (17 October 1970), p. 9, by Maclean-Hunter Microfilm Service [Canadian press clipping service, microfilm series: FLQ].

On 9 October, the FLQ manifesto was published in the newspapers. One paper devoted its entire front page to the text, and several papers introduced the text with warnings about its contents, either dissociating the paper from the message or justifying its publication as a humanitarian gesture aimed at saving the life of Cross. In addition, the practice of publishing the communiqués continued, and the full text of the fifth communiqué appeared in all the papers.[36] A *Le Devoir* editorial, signed by Claude Ryan, said that a number of jailed terrorists might be released to save Mr Cross' life.[37] Communiqué No. 6, addressed to Pierre Pascau of CKLM, went astray and was sent again at 6 pm, along with a later message (No. 7), accusing the authorities of trying to gain time by not releasing the earlier communiqué.[38]

The crisis escalated on 10 October, when Pierre Laporte, Quebec Minister of Labour and Immigration and Deputy Premier, was kidnapped by four people who identified themselves as members of the Chenier Cell, whose ends were very similar to those of the Liberation Cell.[39] The media were bombarded with communiqués issued by both Cells, and reported them. The role of the French media, which persisted in disseminating rumors, and which published the terrorists' communiqués before handing them over to the police,[40] troubled the government in Ottawa. Crelinsten reports that government officials were particularly angered over the role played by CKLM and CKAC in providing easy access and free publicity to the terrorists. The officials also felt that the French radio stations impeded the establishment of direct negotiations between the government and the kidnappers.[41] It seemed that the radio reporters were happy to take upon themselves a very subjective political role.

From its first communiqué, the FLQ specified that it wanted the media

---

36 R. D. Crelinsten, "Power and meaning: terrorism as a struggle over access to the communication structure", *op. cit.*, p. 428.

37 A. Siegel, *Canadian Newspaper Coverage of the F.L.Q. Crisis: A Study on the Impact of the Press on Politics*, Doctoral Thesis, McGill University (1974), p. 259.

38 J. Saywell, *Quebec 70, op. cit.*, p. 52; E. S. Wainstein, *The Cross and Laporte Kidnappings, Montreal, October 1970, op. cit.*, p. 12. See also P. Waters, "Cross reprieve to 6 P.M., letter proves he's alive", *Montreal Gazette* (10 October 1970), p. 1, by Maclean-Hunter Microfilm Service [Canadian press clipping service, microfilm series: FLQ].

39 Laporte was a French-Canadian, but apparently he was seen as a representative of the Francophone dominant class whose interests were perceived as significantly different from those of the French working-class people. See K. McRoberts, *Quebec: Social Change and Political Crisis, op. cit.*, p. 200.

40 The Symbionese Liberation Army sent a recorded tape with a long message to the KPFA radio station in Los Angeles. KPFA was delighted to receive the tape and broadcast it immediately without notifying the police or the FBI. See P. Campbell Hearst with A. Moscow, *Patty Hearst: Her Own Story* (New York: Avon, 1982), p. 281.

41 R. D. Crelinsten, "Power and meaning: terrorism as a struggle over access to the communication structure", *op. cit.*, p. 432.

to be associated with its action. Without the media, their act would become an isolated episode of an insignificant gang. They instructed that their political manifesto must appear in its entirety on the front page of all major Quebec newspapers. They also specified that upon their release from prison, the political prisoners be accompanied by at least two political columnists from two of Quebec's French-language dailies. They made the kidnapping a prolonged media event that lasted for weeks and months. Indeed, hostage situations are full of suspense because human life hangs in the balance, and the whole society, sometimes the world, is watching and praying for a peaceful resolution. The journalists were accused of manipulating information to further a cause that they approved.[42]

Early on Sunday 11 October, Daniel McGinnis of CKAC was informed of an envelope near a subway station. This was communiqué No. 1 from the Chenier Cell, accompanied by Laporte's National Assembly identification card, demanding that all seven demands of the Liberation Cell be met in full. Later in the afternoon, CKAC received communiqué No. 2, claiming to be its last, from the Chenier Cell. However, four hours later CKAC had another communiqué from the Chenier Cell containing Laporte's credit cards and a letter from Laporte to Premier Robert Bourassa. At 9.55 pm, five minutes before the deadline set by Laporte's abductors, Bourassa broadcast an appeal to the FLQ for negotiation mechanisms and for some assurance that the release of political prisoners would result in the release of the hostages. A few hours after the Premier's address, the kidnappers sent another note, this time to CKLM, reiterating their demands and suggesting Robert Lemieux as an intermediary between the two cells and the authorities.[43]

The same day, 11 October, *Quebec-Presse* published a pertinent editorial. Some of the striking paragraphs deserve to be quoted at length:

> To our way of thinking the shattering diagnosis attributed to the sickness in Quebec by the Front de liberation du Quebec (FLQ) is well-founded and correct ... Clandestine action is chosen for tactical reasons: when and in what circumstances is terrorist action justified? This much is certain, it is not up to those in power to pass judgment. The winners of the last election ... are not in a position to teach anyone any moral, political or social lessons. The fact that the spokes-

42 B. Dagenais, "Media in crisis: observers, actors or scapegoats?", *op. cit.*, p. 124. See also Y. Laplante, "Le rire d'Octobre: le discours des caricaturistes sur les evenements d'Octobre 1970", *Conflicts contemporains et medias* (Montreal, XYZ editeur, 1997), pp. 113–121; B. Dagenais, *La crise d'octobre et les medias: le miroir a dix faces* (Montreal: VLB editeur, 1990).

43 E. S. Wainstein, *The Cross and Laporte Kidnappings, Montreal, October 1970, op. cit.*, pp. 14–15.

men of an establishment, which has been denounced by the FLQ, take it upon themselves to speak on behalf of the majority and to condemn terrorist action this week proves nothing ... The only valid judgment possible can come from the people. In one week the FLQ has succeeded in talking to the people as never before. The FLQ's action has been a little like a course in political instruction by total immersion. A kind of political Berlitz. So the FLQ has achieved one main aim: namely, to speak in its own words to the world. And to keep the minds of the people of Quebec on their own situation. As far as we are concerned – agreeing as we do with the FLQ's aims without approving the methods – we reckon that the struggle for the liberation of Quebec is a basic requirement. This aim is incorporated in *Quebec-Presse*'s declaration of principles.[44]

On Monday, 12 October, the papers were full of FLQ communiqués. Communiqué No. 8 of the Cross kidnappers was received by CKLM. The Chenier Cell informed CKAC of a letter sent by Laporte. Later that afternoon, the Chenier Cell summarized the situation in a communiqué and sent it to Pierre Pascau of CKLM.[45] Two parliamentary correspondents reported that Ottawa was troubled by the lack of public outrage over both the kidnapping and the role played by the French media. While the people in Quebec spoke of the need for dialogue, the government in Ottawa distanced itself from the discussions and resorted to a display of military strength.[46]

On 13 October, all the papers focused their front-page coverage of the FLQ crisis on the beginning of negotiations between the Quebec government and the kidnappers' representative, Robert Lemieux. In Ottawa, Prime Minister Trudeau took advantage of Question Period in the House of Commons to attack the media for giving the FLQ the very publicity that it was seeking. He further argued that it was a mistake to encourage the use of the term "political prisoners" for men who were bandits.[47]

On 14 October, the two cells of the FLQ issued a joint communiqué through Pierre Pascau of CKLM.[48] In the Cabinet Committee on Security

44 Editorial, "Le FLQ et nous", *Quebec-Presse* (11 October 1970), quoted in J. Saywell, *Quebec 70, op. cit.*, pp. 61–62.
45 J. Saywell, *Quebec 70*, pp. 65–68.
46 R. D. Crelinsten, "The internal dynamics of the FLQ during the October crisis of 1970", in D. C. Rapoport (ed.), *Inside Terrorist Organizations, op. cit.*, p. 63; R. D. Crelinsten, "Power and meaning: terrorism as a struggle over access to the communication structure", *op. cit.*, pp. 432–433.
47 *Debates of the House of Commons*, 3rd Session, 28th Parliament (1970), Vol. I, p. 52; "PM urges press 'Show restraint' ", *Ottawa Journal* (13 October 1970), by Maclean-Hunter Microfilm Service [Canadian press clipping service, microfilm series: FLQ].
48 E. S. Wainstein, *The Cross and Laporte Kidnappings, Montreal, October 1970, op. cit.*, p. 17; J. Saywell, *Quebec 70, op. cit.*, p. 75.

and Intelligence convened that day, Prime Minister Trudeau expressed worries that the crisis might result in the creation of a separatist popular movement. To prevent such a development, he thought it would be necessary for the government to act quickly, and that such action "might have to include rigid control of the mass media and strong counter-propaganda action by the government".[49] Minister of Justice John Turner spoke of the need for voluntary cooperation of station owners to ensure that broadcasters would act in a more responsible manner than they had thus far. Turner maintained that if Quebec could demonstrate the need for unusual short-term police action, this cooperation would be forthcoming from the media, provided it stopped short of the suspension of fair comment. Turner said, "it was of the utmost importance that the government retain public support".[50] The Committee spoke of the need to secure the cooperation of press media in publicizing the Prime Minister's statements, and in ensuring responsible reporting of events.[51]

The police went public to deplore the attitude of the press in this affair, stating that, by publishing all sorts of rumors without verifying their authenticity and harassing headquarters with questions, the journalists were doing considerable harm to the police efforts.[52] The police called upon the press to show a greater concern for accuracy.

Besides broadcasting the messages before the police were even aware of them, and meddling with the hard-copy communiqués to the point of blurring all significant fingerprints, the reporters were accused of frequently broadcasting news that led only to confusion and sensational competition.[53] G. Constantineau, commentator for *Le Devoir*, wrote that the radio stations, particularly the "FLQ mailboxes" CKLM and CKAC, had become involuntary participants in the affair, and that journalism had become an active agent of the news instead of its passive purveyor.[54] I contest the usage of the adjective "involuntary".

In his editorial of 14 October 1970, Roger Bruneau of *L'Action*[55] wrote:

> In our opinion, many news items were communicated a little too rapidly on the weekend by radio and television throughout the

49 Minutes, Cabinet Committee on Security and Intelligence (14 October 1970, Morning Meeting), p. 3 (classified "secret").
50 *Ibid.*
51 *Ibid.*, p. 6.
52 *Le Devoir*, 14 October 1970.
53 *Le Journal de Montreal* (14 October 1970), quoted in B. Dagenais, "Media in crisis: observers, actors or scapegoats?", *op. cit.*, pp. 127–128.
54 *Le Devoir* (14 October 1970), p. 2, quoted in R. D. Crelinsten, "Power and meaning: terrorism as a struggle over access to the communication structure", *op. cit.*, p. 435.
55 A small Quebec paper with circulation of 30,000 copies. Report of the Special Senate Committee on Mass Media, *Words, Music and Dollars* (Ottawa, 1970), Vol. II, p. 513.

province. Several of these news items, some more sensational than others, were later proven to be either false, incomplete, or premature. The rapidity with which they were communicated, the context in which they were communicated ... created quite a troubling atmosphere under the circumstances and contributed to increasing the state of excitement into which the population felt it was plunged.[56]

That same day, the Editor-in-chief and publisher of *Le Devoir*, Claude Ryan, together with a group of respected Quebec citizens including the leader of the separatist Parti Quebecois Rene Levesque, signed a statement urging the government to comply with the demands of the FLQ.[57] The government in Ottawa met again on 14 October and discussed at length the media's role in the crisis. J. Davey, Program Secretary to the Prime Minister, reviewed a memorandum dealing with the role of communications. He said that communiqués from and speculation about the FLQ had dominated the media, and there was a need to ensure adequate provision of information from well-briefed ministers and from senior authorized personnel. Planning for communications was also aimed at obtaining from the media a degree of self-discipline in their reporting during the crisis.[58]

Marc Lalonde, Principal Secretary to the Prime Minister, noted that the press in Montreal appeared not to want to raise the pressure for further manifestations.[59] Prime Minister Trudeau said that the actions of the media generally had been "quite irresponsible", and had contributed significantly to an escalation of the crisis by giving the FLQ the status of a parallel government. It was therefore incumbent upon the government to consider what action might be taken to foster a more responsible attitude.[60] In turn, Minister of Justice Turner said that the government should avoid threatening the mass media in any way. If the government were to introduce restrictive legislation, it would be essential to have the support of the media as well as that of the public. He suggested trying to obtain the media's agreement to exercise voluntary restraint in their reporting of news relating to the crisis.[61]

56 Quoted in B. Dagenais, "Media in crisis: observers, actors or scapegoats?", *op. cit.*, pp. 128–129.
57 *Le Devoir* (15 October 1970), p. 1.
58 Minutes, Cabinet Committee on Security and Intelligence (14 October 1970, Evening Meeting), p. 8 (classified "Secret"). On media speculation see, for instance, R. Jackson, "'Nobody's informed me' – Trudeau. PM, Bourassa, Drapeau marked for assassination?", *Ottawa Journal* (7 October 1970), by Maclean-Hunter Microfilm Service [Canadian press clipping service, microfilm series: FLQ].
59 Minutes, Cabinet Committee on Security and Intelligence (14 October 1970, Evening Meeting), p. 8 (classified "Secret").
60 *Ibid.*
61 *Ibid.*

The terrorists did not exploit the media, but rather used them to gain public attention to their ends, and popular support in Quebec for separatism. The term "exploitation" is inappropriate to describe the behavior of media organs that willingly accepted the terrorists' terms and demands, and seemed quite happy to cooperate. The FLQ created a situation steeped in anxiety which was favorable for their strategic aims. The kidnapping demonstrated that the authorities were not in control, and exacerbated the ongoing social conflict, polarized the groups in tension, and probably also sought to encourage political militants across the threshold of using violence. This is a well-known strategy of terrorists around the world.[62] Some organs of the French media were happy to be used to the point that later they were accused of cooperating with the terrorists. The Editor of the popular (daily circulation of more than 200,000 copies)[63] Montreal weekly *Le Petit Journal* wrote: "I believe that the unrestrained freedom of the press led little by little to the death of a Quebec minister" (25 October 1970).[64] A great number of attacks were made on the press after the crisis, suggesting that the media were irresponsible in the way they amplified rumors during a time of severe threat.[65]

The French papers had about 40 percent more pictorial coverage than the English dailies, aiming to sensationalize the story. The French press editorial coverage was far more extensive in comparison to English press editorials, tending to put virtually all stories dealing with the FLQ negotiations on page one. In the editorial columns, negotiation was the most strongly pressed matter and the main thrust, especially of *Le Devoir*. Compared to the English press, the French press had more stories related to the FLQ's communiqués. This policy was designed to pressurize the government into a compromise approach to resolving the crisis.[66] The French media thought that their sympathetic viewpoint represented the view of large sectors of Quebec. An opinion was heard that "journalists agree that 50 percent of the people of Quebec sympathize with the aims of the FLQ".[67] Indeed, while the public condemned the kidnapping, many identified with their goals. As the crisis continued, public support for the

62 R. P. J. M. Gerrits, "Terrorists' perspectives: memoirs", in D. L. Paletz and A. P. Schmid (eds), *Terrorism and the Media, op. cit.*, p. 42.
63 Report of the Special Senate Committee on Mass Media, *Words, Music and Dollars* (Ottawa, 1970), Vol. II, p. 83; Report of the Special Senate Committee on Mass Media, *Good, Bad or Simply Inevitable?* (Ottawa, 1970), Vol. III, p. 240.
64 Quoted in B. Dagenais, "Media in crisis: observers, actors or scapegoats?", *op. cit.*, p. 129. *Le Petit Journal* no longer exists.
65 D. LaTouche, "Mass media and communication in a Canadian political crisis", in B. D. Singer (ed.), *Communications in Canadian Society, op. cit.*, p. 202.
66 A. Siegel, *Canadian Newspaper Coverage of the F.L.Q. Crisis: A Study on the Impact of the Press on Politics, op. cit.*, pp. 73–77, 84, 169.
67 R. Haggart and A. E. Golden, *Rumours of War, op. cit.*, p. 32.
68 *Black October* (CBC Home Video, 2000).

FLQ's cause continued to grow. Ottawa feared that things were getting out of control.[68]

On 15 October, the Cabinet gathered; it agreed that, in view of the existing situation, the government had no alternative but to declare an emergency, to give the abductors an ultimatum for the release of Cross and Laporte, to begin arresting FLQ members, and to invite the media privately to meet with the Secretary of State, who would order them to refrain from giving publicity to those advocating violence in Quebec.[69]

At 4 am on 16 October 1970, the government's tolerance ran out. Prime Minister Trudeau invoked the War Measures Act. Immediately afterwards, a massive arrest operation began. The following day, the Chenier Cell kidnappers executed Pierre Laporte by strangulation after he tried to escape and injured himself.[70]

Several members of the Quebec national assembly and government ministers criticized the media sharply. The Liberal Party whip, Louis-Philippe Lacroix, accused the journalists of being responsible for the death of Pierre Laporte; he labeled them the gravediggers of democracy. Legislative member Henri Coiteux called reporters "a gang of parasites, failures, pseudo-intellectuals".[71] Cultural Affairs Minister Francois Cloutier stated that there had clearly been abuse of freedom of the press. For him, the FLQ's use of the radio stations exceeded the normal rules of liberty in a democracy. Premier Bourassa said there was a need to examine, after the event, the limitless freedom of expression that Quebec enjoyed.[72]

The Cabinet Committee on Security and Intelligence met on the evening of 16 October. Secretary of State Pelletier said he had discussed the desirability of exercising voluntary restraint in reporting events related to the crisis with most of the owners of broadcast networks. They had been very cooperative, but unable to establish firm and consistent control within their own networks. Several owners of the media had expressed the fear that, without further legal sanctions, any restraints would result in a series of strikes by broadcast employees whose unions were Separatist-

69 Record of Cabinet decision, The F.L.Q. situation (Meeting of 15 October 1970, 2.30 pm) (classified "Confidential"); Cabinet Minutes of the meeting on 15 October 1970, p. 9 (classified "Secret") (No. 61–70).
70 *Black October* (CBC Home Video, 2000); Minutes of Cabinet Committee on Security and Intelligence (30 October 1970), p. 2 (classified "Secret"); E. S. Wainstein, *The Cross and Laporte Kidnappings, Montreal, October 1970, op. cit.*, p. 32. See also E. Cowan, "Quebec police find house where Laporte was held", *New York Times* (20 October 1970). The killing of Laporte was the second political murder in the history of Canada, the only one since a Fenian shot down Thomas D'Arcy McGee on the streets of Ottawa in the first year of Canadian nationhood, 102 years before.
71 *Ibid.*
72 B. Dagenais, "Media in crisis: observers, actors or scapegoats?", *op. cit.*, p. 128.

oriented. Pelletier said he had discussed ways of achieving restraint regulation with the Chairman of the Canadian Radio Television Commission (CRTC). However, both concluded that such action would lead to accusations of censorship and should not be attempted.[73]

Several ministers expressed concern at the apparent readiness of persons in authority in the networks to make their facilities available to Separatists and FLQ supporters. Some suggested that the Broadcast Act might be amended to give the government power of direction in cases where it believed the mass media were being used to promote the disintegration of Canada, and report its actions to Parliament. Prime Minister Trudeau suggested that the Cabinet Committee on Priorities and Planning might consider this in the context of the National Unity priority problem.[74]

After the invocation of the *War Measures Act* by the federal cabinet, the police arrested 456 Quebec citizens. All but a handful were released without any charges being made.[75] This suggests that the police reaction was panicky rather than carefully calculated. The media operations, as described above, had a considerable role in creating this panic. CBC news reporters in Ottawa received a directive that they were to broadcast only stories that could be attributed to an identifiable source. Although on the surface this could be defended as an attempt to keep rumors off the air, its effect was to confine CBC news to official reports from the government or to the restrained comments the opposition parties were willing to make. CBC reporters were reminded in another directive that they were not to allow their names to be identified with political statements.[76]

On Saturday, 17 October, the Liberation Cell sent out its tenth communiqué along with a letter from Cross to his wife. The Chenier Cell contacted CKAC to announce that Pierre Laporte had been executed, and directed the reporters to the location of his body.[77] The news of the murder wiped out all public sympathy for the FLQ. Only then did the media suddenly become very cautious, and the issue of censorship became

73 Minutes of the Cabinet Committee on Security and Intelligence (16 October 1970), p. 2 (classified "Secret").
74 *Ibid.* For further deliberation on laws and regulations governing broadcasting, see E. S. Hallman, *Broadcasting in Canada* (London: Routledge, 1977), pp. 35–39.
75 RCMP Strategy for Dealing with the FLQ and Similar Movements, Memorandum for the Cabinet Committee on Security and Intelligence (Ottawa: Privy Council Office, 16 December 1970), Appendix B (classified "Top Secret"). See also J. Starnes, *Closely Guarded: A Life in Canadian Security and Intelligence* (Toronto: University of Toronto Press, 1998), pp. 158–163, 220–235. The film, *Black October, op. cit.*, claims that 497 people were arrested.
76 R. Haggart and A. E. Golden, *Rumours of War, op. cit.*, p. 110.
77 E. S. Wainstein, *The Cross and Laporte Kidnappings, Montreal, October 1970, op. cit.*, pp. 21–22; J. Saywell, *Quebec 70, op. cit.*, p. 101.

a focus of intense debate in the ensuing weeks. Bernard Dagenais, a communications professor at Laval University and a specialist on the October crisis, said that the French media sided with the FLQ until Laporte's murder, whereas the English language media were less interested. Dagenais maintained that Laporte's murder was a "cold shower" for the media, and from that point they started to support the government. The media went from being a leader in the crisis to following the government line.[78]

The English-Canadian press gave cautious approval to the invocation of the War Measures Act. Most editorial writers were concerned about the suspension of civil liberties. The Toronto *Telegram* (16 October) saw it as "a drastic but necessary action". The *Winnipeg Free Press* (17 October) saw it as a "desperate cure", an unhappy choice "between anarchy and a period of repressive government". The popular newspaper in English in Quebec, read also by French Canadians, the Montreal *Gazette* (17 October), saw it as "the only course to take, however distasteful it may appear, if society is to be freed of the threat of continued terrorism".[79] The Ottawa *Citizen* (17 October) concluded that there was a need to "give the government full support . . . The cause is nothing less than making sure that the people we have elected by democratic process will run this country, and that a band of anonymous criminals will not". The *Globe and Mail* asserted (17 October):

> Only if we can believe that the Government has evidence that the FLQ is strong enough and sufficiently armed to escalate the violence that it has spawned for seven years now, only if we can believe that it is virulent enough to infect other areas of society, only then can the Government's assumption of incredible powers be tolerated.

And the *Vancouver Sun* (16 October) applauded the decision to "fight fire with fire and match ruthlessness with ruthlessness". All English-Canadian newspapers denounced the murder of Pierre Laporte.[80]

In French Canada, the two large and popular newspapers *La Presse* (based in Montreal) and *Le Soleil* (based in Quebec City) supported the

---

78 C. Cobb, "Looking back at the FLQ crisis", *Ottawa Citizen* (7 October 1995), p. B4.
79 The Montreal *Gazette* was, and still is, a conservative newspaper that has gained an enviable reputation as an excellent newspaper of record. Its daily circulation then exceeded 130,000 copies. See Report of the Special Senate Committee on Mass Media, *Words, Music and Dollars* (Ottawa, 1970), Vol. II, pp. 103, 511; W. H. Kesterton, *A History of Journalism in Canada, op. cit.*, p. 91. Current website: www.montrealgazette.com.
80 All quotations are taken from John Saywell, *Quebec 70, op. cit.*, pp. 94–95, 105–107. See also "250 held in drive on Quebec front", *New York Times* (17 October 1970), p. 12; W. Johnson, "New tenants occupy scenes of FLQ crisis", *Globe & Mail* (5 October 1971).

use of the act.[81] *Le Devoir* (17 October) did not, arguing that Quebec had been taken over by Ottawa.[82] The editors of *Quebec-Presse* (18 October) went as far as calling for passive resistance, saying, "we must resist the repression which is striking everywhere in Quebec", and calling upon popular movements, citizens committees, all associations, and the unions to organize resistance in a common, concerted effort. Most Quebec papers deplored Laporte's murder. *Quebec-Presse*, on the other hand, held a supportive view of the FLQ. One separatist writer said (25 October): "It is too easy to say that Pierre Laporte was killed by a handful of terrorists. A handful of terrorists with their finger on the trigger. But who put the gun into their hands?... I refuse to pass judgment."[83]

On 18 October, some radio and television stations broadcast erroneous news that the body of Mr Cross had also been found.[84] That same day the Cabinet contemplated posting policemen in radio and TV stations to prevent information coming from the FLQ or any other sources from being mishandled by the press. This measure would also have permitted the police to obtain such information instantly and to act on it. In the end it was decided that the Secretary of State should see that the public and private sectors of the media were to abide by the government decisions. Specifically, it was decided not to release any letters or other documents coming from Cross or his abductors.[85]

The following day, 19 October, the *Ottawa Journal* reported that the CBC had been served notice to refrain from editorial comment on the terrorist situation and that it was also hoped that the CTV network and all private stations would toe this policy line until the crisis was over. Sandy Gardiner voiced the opinion that the broadcasters should have been put in their place right from the outset, and that the two networks had to shoulder some of the blame for adding fuel to the fire. Gardiner added

81 *La Presse* of the Desmarais chain was Quebec's dominant mainstream French-language newspaper. Its circulation was more than 220,000 copies a day. *Le Soleil* was in Quebec City what *La Presse* was in Montreal: a popular newspaper with estimated daily circulation of 162,000 copies. Report of the Special Senate Committee on Mass Media, *Words, Music and Dollars* (Ottawa, 1970), Vol. II, pp. 83, 511, 513; Report of the Special Senate Committee on Mass Media, *Good, Bad or Simply Inevitable?* (Ottawa, 1970), Vol. III, p. 146. See also J. Porter, "The ideological system: the mass media", *op. cit.*, p. 167. Current website of *Le Soleil*: http://www.lesoleil.com/.

82 The 1970 Davey Report held that *La Presse* and *Le Devoir* "enjoy an influence and prestige within their community that perhaps no English-language newspaper can match". Report of the Special Senate Committee on Mass Media, *The Uncertain Mirror* (Ottawa, December 1970), Vol. I, p. 96.

83 J. Saywell, *Quebec 70*, *op. cit.*, pp. 96–99.

84 A. Siegel, *Canadian Newspaper Coverage of the F.L.Q. Crisis: A Study on the Impact of the Press on Politics*, *op. cit.*, p. 264.

85 Cabinet Minutes of a meeting held on 18 October 1970, pp. 3–4 (classified "Secret") (No. 62–70).

that viewers were entitled to the facts with analysis, if pertinent, but speculation should have been outlawed: "Speculation, especially at a time when lives are at stake, is irresponsible journalism."[86]

On 22 October 1970, the government met to discuss its strategy for dealing with the FLQ. Secretary of State Pelletier said the media heads needed reassuring: "They had got themselves into a difficult situation and had lost control."[87] Minister of Transport Donald Campbell Jamieson felt that the Prime Minister should meet with the heads of the media to explain to them what the problems were.[88] Two weeks later, Program Secretary to the Prime Minister, J. Davey, thought that the government should concentrate attention on four areas of interest, one of them the necessity for the Strategic Operations Centre to continue monitoring the media from week to week.[89]

On 6 November, police raided the Montreal apartment where the four Laporte kidnappers had been hiding since the murder; one of the suspects was captured, but the other three eluded the police. Later, they sent their last communiqué, describing their escape and mocking the police. The Liberation Cell sent their last communiqué on 21 November, to the *Quebec-Presse*, enclosing a letter from Cross. The communiqué complained of government torture, searches, arrests, and censorship, and called on the UN to mediate with the government to release the political prisoners.[90]

Conclusion

Previous research regarding the differences between the French-language and English-language dailies showed that English-speaking journalists saw their principal function as straight news reporting, while French-language journalists were much more inclined to perceive their journalistic function to include interpreting the news.[91] During the FLQ crisis, their

---

86 S. Gardiner, Between the Lines, "Give viewers facts without speculation", *Ottawa Journal* (19 October 1970), by Maclean-Hunter Microfilm Service [Canadian press clipping service, microfilm series: FLQ].
87 A Strategy for Dealing With the FLQ, The Government's Posture (22 October 1970), p. 4 (classified "Secret").
88 Cabinet Minutes of a meeting held on 22 October 1970, p. 4 (No. 63–70).
89 Minutes of the Cabinet Committee on Security and Intelligence (6 November 1970), p. 11 (classified "Secret").
90 E. S. Wainstein, *The Cross and Laporte Kidnappings, Montreal, October 1970, op. cit.*, p. 24.
91 See research reports of the Royal commission on Bilingualism and Biculturalism, F. Chartrand-McKenzie, "Les journalistes Anglo et Franco-Canadiens: leurs opinions et leurs comportements vis-à-vis de la coexistence des deux cultures"; H. Black, "French and English Canadian political journalists: a comparative study", both quoted in A. Siegel, *Politics and the Media in Canada* (Toronto: McGraw-Hill Ryerson, 1983), p. 209.

interpretation of events coincided with the terrorists' aims. Arthur Siegel, who conducted a multidimensional content analysis of Canadian newspaper coverage from the kidnapping of James Cross until the funeral of Pierre Laporte seventeen days later, found a tendency to homogeneity of content among the French dailies. The French-language papers stressed the search for a peaceful solution and the negotiation aspect of the situation; they were interested in the international reaction to the crisis, especially from Europe and *la Francophonie*. They also focused more on personalities and on civil rights issues. The English-language press, by contrast, focused attention on the manhunt for the terrorists, largely dealing with police activities connected with apprehending the kidnappers and freeing the hostages. They also reported on political institutions and on the economic cost of the crisis, and showed a greater interest in the national and American reaction to the crisis. The French papers were not nearly as interested as the English papers in raising the economic implications of the crisis, nor were they interested in the legalistic elements of the situation. Siegel explains this restrictive coverage of the crisis by saying that this was designed to lead to the emergence of a sharper, more easily defined picture.[92]

In addition, English-speaking editorials were more hostile to terrorism generally and the FLQ specifically. They expressed strong support for both the Ottawa and Quebec governments, enthusiastically endorsed the invocation of the War Measures Act, and stressed their support and concern for Canadian unity. The French-speaking editorials had a different perspective. Their editorial emphasis was on the implications of the crisis for Quebec society. Social and economic injustices, which were almost always associated with French Canadians, were often discussed. These editorials generally did not relate separatism to terrorism, tending to differentiate between legitimate separatism and "bad", terrorist separatism, and warning against the deterioration of civil rights. While the English dailies tended to stress the legislative branch of government, the Ottawa parliament that was asked to approve the War Measures Act, and emphasize the importance of Canadian unity, the French dailies emphasized the positions of the political executives, i.e. the federal and Quebec governments. Canadian unity ranked low in the French papers' editorials and so was the level of support for unity. On the whole, the picture that emerged from the French newspapers suggested far more popular opposition to the authorities than one would have envisaged from reading the English dailies.[93]

92 A. Siegel, *Canadian Newspaper Coverage of the F.L.Q. Crisis: A Study on the Impact of the Press on Politics, op. cit.*, p. 79.

93 A. Siegel, *Canadian Newspaper Coverage of the F.L.Q. Crisis: A Study on the Impact of the Press on Politics, op. cit.*, pp. 79, 84, 95–96, 163–164; A. Siegel, *Politics and the Media in Canada* (Toronto: McGraw-Hill Ryerson, 1996), 2nd edn, p. 225. For further discussion on the effects of the crisis on public opinion, see R. M. Sorrentino and N. Vidmar, "Impact of events: short vs. long-term effects of a crisis", *Public Opinion Quarterly*, 38 (1974): 271–279.

Throughout the roughly two weeks of peak crisis, some influential organs of the French media depicted the FLQ as an equal partner in a political dialogue with the government, as if speaking of symmetrically powerful rivals, with legitimate concerns and deeds (as discussed *supra*, this pattern was followed during the TWA crisis of 1985). Furthermore, in the rush for news under time constraints, some organs of the media were tempted to report first and make the proper inquiry and verification later. During the FLQ crisis a woman in Hull, Quebec, was allegedly tortured by the dissidents, who released her with a message that topped the Saturday *Vancouver Sun*: "New FLQ Warning: 'Women and children next' Hull Torture Message to PM".[94] It was a fearful development at a time of high tension. But it was a hoax. Several days later, a tiny story well inside the paper said the torture scars were apparently self-inflicted. No wonder Jean-Paul Desbiens, editorialist for *La Presse*, wrote on 24 October 1970 that "there would be a lot to say about the lack of intellectual rigour on the part of the written and spoken press".[95]

The French media took it upon themselves to play an active role as mediators. On Friday, 9 October, through Pierre Pascau of CKLM, Quebec Justice Minister Jerome Choquette asked the kidnappers to supply proof that Cross was still alive. In reply, through CKLM to Choquette, the kidnappers wrote back giving a fifth and final deadline for 6 pm Saturday 10 October.[96] In addition, Claude Ryan assumed the role of mediator. As said, such a delicate role of mediation should be left to professional negotiators who have the expertise to deal with kidnappers and potential murderers.

As in the Hanafi episode described in the previous chapter, some journalists during the FLQ crisis did not hesitate to make irresponsible speculation designed to introduce a fresh new dimension to the story, as if it were not dramatic enough. During the second week, Cross felt the hostility of his kidnappers increase as news speculation that he was sending coded messages appeared in the newspapers. In thus speculating, some journalists mentioned that Cross had previously worked for British military intelligence. His letters to his wife had been rewritten on the direction of his guards to prevent a code. When finally released on 4 December 1970, Cross reported that his treatment had deteriorated significantly during the second week, until he could convince his captors that the speculation was false: "There's been a lot of talk about journalistic

94 "Women and children next", *Vancouver Sun* (17 October 1970). See also N. Russell, *Morals and the Media, op. cit.*, p. 90; C. Lemieux, "FLQ carved on Hull woman's stomach", *Ottawa Journal* (19 October 1970), by Maclean-Hunter Microfilm Service [Canadian press clipping service, microfilm series: FLQ].
95 Quoted in B. Dagenais, "Media in crisis: observers, actors or scapegoats?", *op. cit.*, pp. 128–129.
96 R. Haggart and A. E. Golden, *Rumours of War, op. cit.*, pp. 231–232.

responsibility. But people have responsibility to the kidnapped, to the chap in there, he's the loneliest man in the world. And speculation about what he's trying to do may cost him his life."[97] Cross was further quoted as saying:

> The news media were either thoughtless, ruthless, or stupid … It should have been obvious that the speculation that [my] letters possibly carried a coded message, could create a dangerous situation for [me], or prevent [me] from sending any further messages.[98]

Ironically, it appears that Laporte did try to send hidden messages to the authorities, misdating a letter to his wife (the 12th instead of the 11th) and referring to "a dozen persons" in his family in a letter he sent to the Quebec premier. The double use of the number twelve was commented upon in one tabloid newspaper several days later. That same evening, Laporte tried to escape and was killed by his captors. It is unknown whether he attempted to escape after hearing of or reading the tabloid's story. Later it was discovered that a large number 12 was written on the roof of a nearby airplane hangar that was visible from where Laporte was held.[99]

Shortly after James Cross had been freed and his kidnappers had departed for Cuba, *Quebec-Presse* (13 December 1970) published the transcript of an audio tape recorded by the kidnappers prior to their capture. On this tape, the kidnappers confirmed having deliberately pitted two private radio stations against each other so as to have more coverage.[100] In fact, information was and remained uncontrolled until the imposition of the War Measures Act which set up an official state of censorship that was never applied, but was sustained by a real self-censorship and by the death of minister Laporte, which made any support for the assassins impossible.[101] On the tape, the kidnappers also observed smugly that the forced broadcast of their manifesto had elicited considerable sympathy: "For the

97 R. Haggart and A. E. Golden, *Rumours of War*, p. 234; R. D. Crelinsten, "Victims' perspectives", in D. L. Paletz and A. P. Schmid (eds), *Terrorism and the Media* (Newbury Park: Sage, 1992), p. 233.
98 *Globe and Mail* (15 December 1970), quoted in B. Dagenais, "Media in crisis: observers, actors or scapegoats?", *op. cit.*, p. 129.
99 R. D. Crelinsten, "Victims' perspectives", *op. cit.*, pp. 233–234.
100 The transcript of the tape was: "[We] deliberately pitted two private radio stations against each other so as to have more coverage by counting on the vice of this type of enterprise: competition and profit. We used the great capitalist press, we used radio stations to make our ideas known in order to reveal, to show, that we are in agreement with the demands of the Quebecois." C. Cobb, "Looking back at the FLQ crisis", *Ottawa Citizen* (7 October 1995), p. B4.
101 B. Dagenais, "Media in crisis: observers, actors or scapegoats?", *op. cit.*, pp. 124–125.

first time, patriots of the Front managed to express themselves by entering every home, through Radio Canada ... by making them read our manifesto."[102]

A month after the crisis, Premier Bourassa said in a Quebec National Assembly debate, "the government's leaders were treated like dogs by the newspapers", suggesting re-examination of the inherent dangers of verbal violence.[103] It is one thing to criticize the government for what might be conceived as inappropriate handling of a crisis, and quite another to serve the interests of terrorists, readily playing into their hands, assuming responsibilities that are outside the scope of journalism, and conducting their affairs in a way that might risk the lives of hostages.

May I conclude with some personal words: I have studied the relationships between terrorists and the media for many years and cannot think of a better example than this of irresponsible media behavior. Influential segments of the French media served the interests of the terrorists and ignored the interests of the victims, as well as the interests of Canada as a free, democratic society. Journalists broke almost every ethical norm that is accepted during hostage-taking episodes; they did not hesitate to sensationalize and to dramatize the event, stirring up emotions in a way that hindered governmental operations. Influential segments of the French media wanted to exert more pressure on the government by expressing concern for the fate of Cross and Laporte, thereby hoping to push the government to succumb to the terrorists' demands. They gladly offered their services as mediators and messengers for the terrorists, disregarding their obligation of accurate reporting, and broadcast the terrorists' communiqués without the consent of the authorities. Through their extensive sympathetic coverage, French journalists not only provided a grand platform for the terrorists, but also legitimized their demands and actions. Some of the editors also offered ways to resolve the situation – ways the government felt were damaging to the interests of Canada. With their sensational speculation about Cross's coded letters, the reporters endangered his life. They forgot that their story was Cross's real-life drama.

The FLQ crisis raises a loud and frightening alarm regarding the cost of irresponsible expression, signaling us to be aware of the media's lack of concern for human life if the terrorists' political ends are to the media's liking. The public's "right to know" then becomes a cover-up for the most

---

102　G. Weimann and C. Winn, *The Theater of Terror, op. cit.*, p. 114.
103　E. S. Wainstein, *The Cross and Laporte Kidnappings, Montreal, October 1970, op. cit.*, pp. 48–49. For further critical analysis of the role of the media in the crisis, see R. Nielsen, "The media: must we serve as tools for terrorists?", in B. D. Singer (ed.), *Communications in Canadian Society, op. cit.*, pp. 386–389; T. Moore, "Kidnap crisis has hidden dimensions", *Montreal Star* (19 December 1970), by Maclean-Hunter Microfilm Service [Canadian press clipping service, microfilm series: FLQ].

insensitive and irresponsible behavior. This type of media coverage, which does not consider the consequences of its actions, is unprofessional and immoral – and this is especially true during a time of crisis.

Suggested guidelines

The study of the FLQ crisis, as well as other troubling episodes described in Chapter 8, shows the need for developing a set of guidelines for the media when covering terrorism. The guidelines should include the following:

- The media need to be accountable for the consequences of their coverage.
- The media should not jeopardize human life.
- The media are advised to cooperate with the government when human lives are at stake in order to bring a peaceful end to the terrorist episode.[104]
- The media should not glorify acts of terror.
- The media should refrain from sensational and panic-inducing headlines, from inflammatory catchwords, and from needless repletion of photographs of bloody scenes.[105]
- Terrorism should be explicitly condemned for its brutality and violent, indiscriminate nature.
- The media must not pay or be paid for covering terrorist incidents.
- The media are advised not to take it upon themselves to mediate between the terrorists and the government; special qualifications are required before one assumes such a responsibility upon oneself. Journalists are there to cover the event, not to become part of it.
- The media are expected to refrain from dangerous speculation about the terrorists' plans, government response, hostages' messages and other matters. Speculation might hinder crisis management.
- Media professionals should have background information about the terrorists they cover, and do their homework prior to coverage.
- The media should not broadcast live terrorist incidents. This is not to say that the media should not cover such incidents; rather, there should be a delay of a few minutes during which an experienced

104 J. Warren, reporter for KPHO-TV, Phoenix, said: "The one basic guideline is that the media work closely with the authorities. No one tries to circumvent what the authorities want. We pretty much accede to what the authorities want." Cf. "Crisis cop raps media", Lt Frank Bolz interview with Robert Friedman, *More* magazine, Vol. 7 (June 1977), p. 21.

105 George Gerbner said: "Terror can only succeed if the act is conveyed to the audience whose behavior the terrorists are seeking to influence. The media, in conveying the terror, are cooperating. This makes them accomplices ... The press is directly responsible." Cf. "Crisis cop raps media", *ibid.*, p. 21.

editor can inspect the coverage and authorize what should be on air and what should not.

- The media should not interview terrorists while the incident is still in progress. Lines of communication between the authorities and the terrorists should be kept open. The media should not impede the negotiation process.[106]
- The media should not cooperate with terrorists who stage events.
- The media are required to show sensitivity to the victims and to their loved ones. This critical guideline should be observed during terrorist incidents and, no less importantly, after their conclusion.
- The media are expected not to report details that might harm victims' families.
- The area in which the terrorist incident takes place should not be open to anybody who testifies that he or she is a journalist; only senior and experienced reporters should be admitted. Junior and inexperienced reporters should undergo a learning process during which they fathom the complexities involved. Adequate training is a necessary precondition.

---

106 In the wake of the Hanafi incident, CBS News President Richard S. Salant issued guidelines on coverage of terrorism. A pertinent guideline instructs: "News personnel should be mindful of the probable need by the authorities who are dealing with the terrorist for communication by telephone and hence should endeavor to ascertain, wherever feasible, whether our own use of such lines would be likely to interfere with the authorities' communications." Cf. "Crisis cop raps media", *ibid.*

Conclusion

> The defence of democracy must consist in making anti democratic experiences too costly for those who try them; much more costly than a democratic compromise.
>
> Karl Popper *The Open Society and Its Enemies*

Introduction

This book tackles some of the most problematic free speech issues and attempts to elucidate boundaries to unlimited speech that might endanger democracy. Democracy has still a lot to learn with regard to the appropriate ways to counter people who exploit the foundations of democracy in order to destroy it. I hope this book will attract the attention of policymakers who undoubtedly will be required to find answers to the growing problems of extremism and political violence in the Western world.

The book's rationale is predicated on two foundations, and we have the obligation to ensure that they remain strong. The first prohibits harming others without justified reason. John Stuart Mill explained that "the only purpose for which power can be rightfully exercised over any member of a civilized community, against his will, is to prevent harm to others."[1] A similar idea was postulated by Rabbi Hillel: "What is hateful to you do not do unto your fellow people."[2]

The second foundation promotes respecting others. A person who wishes to deprive another of rights because the other is different from him or her is challenging the basic perceptions of democracy. Democracy does not encourage relativism, but rather neutrality in regard to different conceptions of good, so long as these conceptions accept the principles of not

---

1 J. S. Mill, *Utilitarianism, Liberty, and Representative Government* (London: J. M. Dent & Sons, 1948), p. 73.
2 Babylonian Talmud, Sabbath 31a.

harming others and of respecting others.[3] Democracy is not obligated to assist those who aim to harm others or to disrespect others. Democracy is not obligated to help racists, for instance, in enhancing racism, obviously at the expense of others. Quite the contrary: democracy should condemn the discriminating behavior and bring bigots to acknowledge that it is not the place of homosexuals, or Jews, or Arabs, or other minorities, or women, or blue-eyed people that they contest, but rather democracy itself. In democracies we should educate and promote tolerance although fundamentalists might not be happy with the liberal atmosphere that such education creates.[4] Education towards tolerance consists of the formation of a capacity to see beliefs and actions as parts of a coherent whole, constituting a moral character and being the consequence of a candid attempt to achieve meaning, justice, and truth. Education towards tolerance takes moral imagination, the ability to perceive others from their point of view, and it requires open-mindedness, healthy skepticism, deliberation, and the willingness to change one's mind upon confronting persuasive arguments.[5] The education system on the whole should aspire to be democratic, non-repressive, and non-discriminative. As Amy Gutmann argues, democratic education supplies the foundations upon which a democratic society can secure the civil and political freedoms of its citizens. Democracy thus depends on democratic education for its full moral strength.[6]

Indeed, citizenship education in Western democracies aims at inculcating simultaneously particularistic identities and values, such as patriotism and national pride, and universalistic and shared democratic codes such as tolerance and respect for a variety of civil liberties. Achieving a shared concept of citizenship that would bridge ethnic, national, and socioeconomic rifts is considered vital for the functioning of democracies because it "helps to tame the divisive passions of other identities".[7] It is generally agreed that pluralism must fit within certain kind of overarching unity,

3 See R. Dworkin, *A Matter of Principle* (Oxford: Clarendon Press, 1985); R. Cohen-Almagor, "Objective reporting in the media: phantom rather than panacea", in *Speech, Media and Ethics* (New York and Houndmills: Palgrave-Macmillan, 2005), Chapter 4, and "Between neutrality and perfectionism", *Canadian Journal of Law & Jurisprudence*, VII(2) (1994): 217–236.
4 See N. M. Stolzenberg, "'He drew a circle that shut me out': assimilation, indoctrination, and the paradox of a liberal education", *Harvard Law Review*, 106 (1993): 581–667.
5 D. Heyd, "Education to toleration: some philosophical obstacles and their resolution", in C. McKinnon and D. Castiglione (eds), *The Culture of Toleration in Diverse Societies* (Manchester and New York: Manchester University Press, 2003), pp. 203–204.
6 A. Gutmann, *Democratic Education* (Princeton: Princeton University Press, 1987), p. 289.
7 D. Heater, *Citizenship: The Civic Ideal in World History* (London: Longman, 1990), p. 184.

and certain ultimate values must be shared if the diversity in a democratic society is to be contained democratically.[8]

Unsurprisingly, among the greatest champions of free expression we find people who promote hatred and bigotry. It is the Free Speech Principle that allows them to spread their vile propaganda, and they blossom in its shade. Paul Fromm, the notorious hate propagandist, is the director of the Canadian Association for Free Expression (CAFE). Founded in 1981, the CAFE "believes free speech and discussion are essential to any functioning democracy. Freedom of speech and freedom to express one's beliefs are essential to human dignity."[9] The Association, through publishing, lectures, conferences, and lobbying tries "to protect these basic human rights and to promote to the maximum the *Charter* guaranteed rights of freedom of speech, freedom of belief, freedom of expression, and freedom of assembly".[10] Liberals would easily identify with the mission of CAFE. The official website of Meir Kahane calls to "Vote Now For Democracy In Israel".[11] In turn, Ernst Zündel is a vocal champion of free expression, and for a very good reason. His Zundelsite is filled with arguments for the importance of free expression in our democracies. Its banner calls people to support the Zundelsite, the most politically besieged website on the Net.[12] Zündel explains that

> [the] Zundelsite is dedicated to the sacred belief held by all independent people everywhere that a truly democratic society does not need to fear, suppress and persecute an alternate view of history, culture, race, religion or politics. If it does, it is no longer democratic. If it does, an alert citizenry will know and act accordingly to circumvent suppression.[13]

The Canadian authorities contest this argumentation. Zündel is presently in jail in Canada, as the Canadian authorities have declared that Zündel, who left for the United States in 2002 but was deported by the US authorities to Canada in February 2003, is inadmissible to Canada for security reasons. They wish to deport him to his home country, Germany, where he faces charges for his pro-Nazi activities, as well as for Holocaust

---

8 A. Etzioni, "On the place of virtues in pluralistic democracy", in G. Marks and L. Diamond (eds), *Reexamining Democracy* (Newbury Park: Sage, 1992), pp. 70–79; O. Ichilov, G. Salomon and D. Inbar, "Citizenship education in Israel – a Jewish-democratic state", in R. Cohen-Almagor (ed.), *Israeli Democracy at the Crossroads* (London: Routledge, 2005).

9 http://www.freedomsite.org.

10 http://www.freedomsite.org. Fromm is also active in CFAR – Canadians for Foreign Aid Reform, against immigration to Canada.

11 http://www.kahane.org/.

12 http://www.Zundelsite.org/index_old.html.

13 Cf. http://www.Zundelsite.org/english/misc/mission.html.

denial (discussed in Chapter 7).[14] It should be noted that Zündel holds German citizenship and that despite his forty-two years in Canada as a permanent resident, he has never obtained citizenship there.

The media

The media don't only tell us the news; they also create the news. The media don't just tell us about our lives; to some extent or another they shape our lives. In covering controversial issues, the media have the ethical responsibility to uphold basic percepts of journalism, such as balance, fairness, honesty, and accuracy, and must also make an effort to provide socially responsible coverage that fosters the common good in their communities and affirms constitutional freedom.[15] Thus, when covering issues such as hate speech, racism, and terrorism, the media should not adhere to neutrality. Condemnation of such phenomena is required.

The freedoms that the media enjoy in covering events are respected as long as they do not oppose the basic values that underlie the society in which they operate: not harming others, and respecting others. This issue becomes especially complicated when the media cover hate speech that, by definition, espouses the opposite principles: harming others and disrespecting others. It is not suggested that the media should ban hate speech. Whatever the reader might think about legal restrictions on bigoted speech, we should all agree that the media have a social responsibility far beyond the legal one to cover hate speech in a responsible and ethical manner. If the reader thinks the government may not stop people from spreading hateful messages and propaganda, it becomes *even more* important to urge powerful private institutions to adopt some ethical principles in their reporting of this troublesome phenomenon.[16] Freedom of speech is a fundamental right, an important anchor of democracy, but it should not be used in an uncontrolled manner. Unlimited liberty and

14 See *Ernst Zündel* v. *Her Majesty the Queen*, Ontario Superior Court of Appeal, File No. M74-03 (25 November 2003).
15 On the social responsibility theory, see D. Elliot (ed.), *Responsible Journalism* (Beverly Hills, CA.: Sage, 1986); K. Bunton, "Social responsibility in covering community: a narrative case analysis", *Journal of Mass Media Ethics*, 13(4) (1998): 232–246; M. Schudson, *The Power of the News* (Cambridge: Harvard University Press, 1995).
16 Geoffrey Marshall had made a general comment in a personal communication, saying that the phrases "hate speech" and "racial speech" ought to be made redundant since they blur all the necessary distinction between advocacy and incitement. The legislation in Israel and the United Kingdom rightly penalizes speech that incites to racial hatred, whilst much of the legislation in other countries blurs the issue by using language that on its face appears to make unlawful the public communication of views irrespective of the circumstances (or time and place or audience) that are significant when deciding on the imposition of legal penalties.

unqualified tolerance might deteriorate into anarchy and lawlessness, and in such an atmosphere democracy would find it difficult to function – and the media would be one of the first institutions to be undermined.

In their coverage of Holocaust denial, the assumption of the Canadian media was that viewers and readers were autonomous, rational, adult beings who were capable of making up their minds independently. Their drive was to moral neutrality by providing equal footing to Holocaust deniers and Holocaust survivors. The assumption was wrong, because not all people are rational people, and not all people are adults. Social responsibility requires the media to bear in mind that a substantial percentage of their consumers are young and have yet to crystallize their minds. The drive was wrong, because it lacked sensitivity to Holocaust survivors and provided credence and legitimacy to a lie whose aim was and still is to provoke hostility against Jews by alleging that they are blackmailing the world in spreading distorted stories about events that never happened.

Where terrorism is concerned, the media are required to cooperate with security authorities so as not to endanger lives and impede the authorities' attempts at reinstalling peace and order. In Chapters 8 and 9 I elaborated on this issue. The same rationale should guide the media when covering violent and illegal activities. A case in point is the Waco siege in Texas.

The media and Waco

In the United States, there are hundreds of militias and religious cults. The militia movement began in 1994, following the formation of the Militia of Montana and the Michigan Militia. It grew rapidly, and by 1996 there were 441 armed militias spread across all 50 states. I should emphasize that what had emerged was not a "movement" in the conventional sense. There were no national leaders or national headquarters. The movement consists of diverse, decentralized and, to a large extent, localized collection of groups and individuals with certain shared concerns.[17]

The bloody episode at Waco concerned one armed religious cult.[18] The

---

17 D. J. Mulloy, *American Extremism: History, Politics and the Militia Movement* (London: Routledge, 2004), p. 1.

18 People may question whether it is appropriate to call the Branch Davidian a militia. In his comments, Ken Karst argued that Koresh's group should not be called a "militia". That term has a more limited meaning in the US – a group that is, first and foremost, an armed defense against government. Koresh's group was just a religious cult that fell under his spell, under circumstances in which he had this Apocalyptic view of the group, and so stockpiled weapons, with disastrous results for all concerned. The Branch Davidian was an anti-government armed group, although I am uncertain whether that was its prime objective.

Branch Davidian cult was headed by David Koresh (formerly Vernon Howell). The Bureau of Alcohol, Tobacco and Firearms (ATF) suspected that Koresh was molesting children in his compound and violating laws concerning the possession and use of firearms. During the investigation, a local newspaper in Waco was also researching Koresh and his cult for a series entitled "The Sinful Messiah". After learning of the pending series, the ATF asked *The Waco Tribune-Herald* to delay its publication. The ATF was concerned that the publication might prompt Koresh to increase security at his compound. The newspaper declined the ATF's request because its editor felt that it had held the stories long enough.[19] The highly critical series started on 27 February 1993.[20]

The paper's refusal ultimately caused the ATF to change its plans regarding the timing of the raid on the compound. The Waco paper was not officially informed of the new date of the raid, but an unknown source leaked the information to the *Herald* and to other media organizations. Reporters were sent to cover the events outside the compound, while no instructions were provided to them regarding the need to maintain the secrecy of the operation. They drove around the back and front of the compound, and one cameraman, James Peeler, informed a mailman of the reason that brought him to the place, advising him to "better get out of here because . . . they're going to have a big shootout with the religious nuts".[21] The bystander was David Jones, Koresh's brother-in-law, who immediately informed his leader of the pending raid. On Sunday, 28 February 1993, when the raid took place, instead of surprising Koresh the ATF agents were themselves surprised. Four agents were killed and others were injured. At the end of a long siege, the Davidians set the compound on fire and most of them were killed.[22]

Following this, the ATF sued the media organizations, claiming that their misconduct had contributed to the fatal results. Plaintiffs asserted causes of action based upon negligence, breach of contract, intentional infliction of emotional distress, interference with and/or obstruction of a law enforcement officer in the performance of his official duties, and conspiracy. The court held that the First Amendment does not invest members of the press with absolute immunity from the consequences of

---

19 J. Holley, "The Waco watch", *Columbia Journalism Review* (May/June 1993). See also http://www.rickross.com/reference/waco/waco9.html.

20 M. England and D. McCormick, "The sinful Messiah", *Waco Tribune-Herald* (27 February 1993).

21 L. Hancock, "TV cameraman admits his words tipped off cult", *Dallas Morning News* (28 August 1993); "Six years later, Waco's horror is still hazy", *CNN.com* (25 September 1999), available at http://www.cnn.com/US/9909/25/wacos.dark.questions/.

22 *Risenhoover* v. *England*, 936 F. Supp. 392 (W.D.Tex 1996), at 403; L. N. Deitch, "Breaking news: proposing a pooling requirement for media coverage of live hostage situations", *UCLA Law Review*, 47 (1999): 244–245.

their acts.[23] Defendants are "no more free to cause harm to others while gathering the news than any other individual".[24] The court noted that the media vehicle was easily identifiable to the agents in the area as a news vehicle due to the number of antennae it possessed, just as it could have been identified by any other reasonable person, including the inhabitants of the Compound. The presence of vehicles on the road would certainly have been noticed, particularly when there was an unusual number of them driving aimlessly up and down the road. Common sense dictates that a reporter on the scene would have done everything possible to avoid detection when covering what was known to be a secret law enforcement operation, but instead "the media arrogantly descended on the Compound as if the First Amendment cloaked them with immunity from acting as reasonable individuals under the circumstances". Their actions were "particularly egregious" when considered in light of the fact that they knew how dangerous Koresh and his followers were. The newspaper knew of the weapons that were stockpiled, Koresh's hatred of the government, and the blind devotion of his followers. The newspaper further knew of the guards that were generally posted around the Compound and the likelihood that their presence would be detected.[25] Still it pursued its dangerous and irresponsible conduct in the name of the public's right to know.

The Defendants argued that the ATF's decision to proceed with the raid, despite knowing that the element of surprise had been compromised, was an intervening, superseding cause of the Plaintiffs' injuries that cut off any liability on the part of Defendants. The court concluded that the ATF was apparently unaware that the Davidians had been told definitely that a raid was imminent; its undercover agents could detect no unusual signs of increased activity in the Compound.[26] Accordingly, the court was unable to conclude as a matter of law that the actions of the Defendants were a proximate cause of the Plaintiffs' injuries.[27]

Boundaries to free expression

Whenever we come to consider whether free speech should be restricted, we should take into account four factors:

---

23 *Risenhoover* v. *England*, at 403.
24 *Ibid.*, at 404.
25 *Ibid.*, at 409.
26 An undercover agent was in the compound when Koresh learnt about the pending raid from his brother-in-law. Agent Rodriguez informed his superiors, but since there was no indication that the Davidians were preparing to repel an assault, it was decided to go ahead with the plan.
27 *Risenhoover* v. *England*, at 410. See also J. Smolows *et al.*, "February 28: Sent into a deathtrap?", *Time Magazine* (3 May 1993).

1   The content of the expression
2   The manner of expression
3   The intentions of the speaker
4   The circumstances.

The two most important factors are the first and the last: the content of the debatable speech, and the circumstances that must be such as to contribute to the transformation of the harmful speech into harmful action. Sometimes the manner of the expression integrates into the speech's content, as is the case with symbolic speech. Thus, when Kahanists parade at the heart of an Arab village wearing yellow shirts with Jewish Magen David and a clenched fist, they need not say anything (see Chapter 5). Similarly, when a KKK group burns a cross in front of the home of an African-American family, they need not say anything further. In both instances the message is loud and clear: no one can mistakenly interpret this message of hate as something positive.

Sometimes the manner of speech will not be that significant, as when a religious leader expresses death commands in the most calculated and peaceful voice. Khomeini's *fatwa* against Salman Rushdie might have been issued in the calmest possible tone. It does not subtract one bit from its gravity. And sometimes the speaker's intention will not be manifested clearly, yet the content might be so damaging and harmful that we can restrict the scope of tolerance even without proper evidence regarding the agent's intention. Thus, for instance, a man might publicly call for the help of God in ridding his country of the presence of his President, claiming that he did not mean to call for the President's murder; instead, all he wanted was to show that even the President is not omnipotent and should have respect for the highest authority. In some countries, under certain circumstances (see the Avigdor Eskin episode in Chapter 6), that person will be put to trial despite lack of evidence regarding the true intent of his calling.

We should be less tolerant toward offensive expressions when it can be proven that the speaker's intention is malicious and intended to hurt the target audience. This is the case when speakers announce beforehand that their aim is to hurt the sensibilities of their target group, as in the case of the Nazis who wished to demonstrate in Skokie.[28]

---

28 Cf. *Skokie* v. *NSPA*. 373 N.E. 2d, 21 (1978); *Village of Skokie* v. *NSPA*. 366 N.E. 2d 347 (1977); *Collin* v. *Smith* 578 F 2d. 1197 (7th Cir. 1978); R. Cohen-Almagor, *Speech, Media and Ethics*, Chapter 1; R. Delgado and J. Stefancic, *Must We Defend Nazis?* (New York: New York University Press, 1997); D. Goldberger, "Sources of judicial reluctance to use psychic harm as a basis for suppressing racist, sexist and ethnically offensive speech", *Brooklyn Law Review*, (1991): 1165, at 1168–1174. Goldberger shows that many state courts developed the tort of the intentional infliction of emotional harm and applied it to racist insults.

Lastly, as J. S. Mill explained in *On Liberty*, circumstances are of great importance in deciding the scope of tolerance (see Chapters 1 and 6). It is one thing to publish a pamphlet saying that blacks are lazy and thieves in the affluent neighborhood of Guilford, Baltimore, and quite another thing to publish the same pamphlet in August 1965 in Watts, Los Angeles, during the bloody riots.[29] The Free Speech Principle should not protect the publication of such pamphlets during heated circumstances.

In any event, we should ponder the four factors in each and every instance of considering the costs of free expression and whether we should proscribe the speech in question. Not tolerating the intolerant would be the least questionable when the content of a debatable speech is harmful, the manner it is expressed is derogative, the speaker's intentions are explicitly vile, and the circumstances are conducive to the operation of detrimental action.

Most liberals will not dispute Mill's corn-dealer argument and its application to prohibiting the distribution of malicious racist flyers during times of riot. Books, however, constitute a different category altogether. For many years I thought books should be immune to interference and should be published no matter how vile and contemptuous their content might be;[30] until I heard of *Hit Man: A Technical Manual for Independent Contractors*, published by Paladin Press.[31]

Aiding and abetting: *Hit Man*

Paladin publishes "action library", "burn and blow" books on self-defense and self-reliance, weapons and martial arts, bombs (including baby bottle and car bombs), improvised and plastic explosives, land mines, poisons, napalm, arson, and various ways of beating "the system".[32] One of their books, *Deadly Brew: Advanced Improvised Explosives*, was found in the possession of Timothy McVeigh, who detonated a truck bomb outside the federal building in Oklahoma City,[33] killing 168 people and injuring over 500. Paladin had engaged in a marketing strategy intended to attract and assist criminals and would-be criminals who desired information and instructions on how to commit crimes, including murder. In publishing, marketing, advertising and distributing *Hit Man*, Paladin knew that the publication would be used by criminals to plan and execute the crime of

29 http://www.brainyencyclopedia.com/encyclopedia/w/wa/watts_riot.html.
30 See the discussion in my *The Boundaries of Liberty and Tolerance* (Gainesville: University Press of Florida, 1994), Chapter 6.
31 http://www.paladin-press.com/.
32 *Rice* et al. v. *Paladin Enterprises*, United States Court of Appeals for the Fourth Circuit, Record No. 96–2412 (6 October 1996), Brief of Appellee. See also R. Smolla, *Deliberate intent* (New York: Crown, 1999), p. 241.
33 Rod Smolla, *Deliberate Intent*, p. 241.

murder for hire, in the manner set forth so meticulously in the book.[34] The purpose of the volume was to facilitate murder.

Hit Man was not designated by its author to be a manual. The author, who remains anonymous, originally proposed to Paladin that she should write a fictional account of a hit man's life. Paladin answered that she should change her plan, suggesting that she write an instructional how-to book.[35] The author complied, wanting to get a contract. The book opens with a dedication "To Those Who Think, To Those Who Dare, To Those Who Do, To Those Who Succeed". It is followed by a Preface which rationalizes contract murder. When "real justice" is unavailable because of America's dysfunctional legal system, "a man ... must take matters into his own hands".[36] Furthermore:

> Some people would argue that in taking the life of another after pre-meditation, you act as God – judging and issuing a death sentence. But it is the employer, the man who pays for the service, whatever his reason might be, who acts as judge. The hit man is merely the execu-tioner, an enforcer who carries out the sentence.[37]

The book talks about moving up the ladder of success by murdering people. After the first time, "you don't even need a reason to kill ... You realize what morons – *morons* – others are, because *you're superior.* You've taken charge of your life. You have killed once. Now you can kill repeat-edly" (emphases in text).[38] Furthermore, "You realize you don't even need a reason to kill", because "you're a *man* now" (emphasis in text).[39] Interest-ing statements, coming from a female author. The book concludes: "Then, some day, when you've done and seen it all; when there doesn't seem to be any challenge left or any new frontier left to conquer, you might just feel cocky enough to write a book about it."[40]

Most of the book describes in detail how to solicit a client, arrange and negotiate for a contract murder. It provides a broad array of methods of murder, including the selection and modification of firearms, poisons, knives ("The knife should have a double edged blade. This double edge, combined with the serrated section and six-inch length, will insure a deep,

34 *Vivian Rice* et al. v. *Paladin Enterprises,* 940 F. Supp. 836 (decided on 6 Septem-ber 1996), at 840; *Vivian Rice* et al. v. *Paladin Enterprises,* 128 F.3d 233; 1997 U.S. App. LEXIS 30889; 25 Media L. Rep. 2441 (decided on 10 November 1997), at 253.
35 R. Smolla, *Deliberate Intent,* p. 235.
36 *Rice* et al. v. *Paladin Enterprises,* United States Court of Appeals for the Fourth Circuit, Record No. 96–2412 (6 October 1996), Brief of Appellee.
37 http://ftp.die.net/mirror/hitman/preface.html.
38 R. Smolla, *Deliberate Intent, op. cit.,* p. 196.
39 *Ibid.,* p. 197.
40 http://ftp.die.net/mirror/hitman/9.html.

ragged tear, and the wound will be difficult, if not impossible, to close without prompt medical attention."), and other deadly means; the picking of locks and forging of documents; the actual murder ("Using your six-inch, serrated blade knife, stab deeply into the side of the victim's neck and push the knife forward in a forceful movement. This method will half decapitate the victim, cutting both his main arteries and wind pipe, ensuring immediate death."), including the precautionary measures that make a hit "successful", i.e. that the contractor will not be caught, and ways of disposing of the body ("If you have a really strong stomach, you can always cut the body into sections and pack it into an ice chest for transportation and disposal at various spots across the countryside.").[41] I will not quote further from this book. I think you've got the message.

It is hard to say how many murders have been committed under the influence and direction of *Hit Man*. Paladin estimated that 13,000 copies were sold. As the book's author states, if the directives of the book are followed to the letter, the independent contractor will be successful in committing the crime, getting the money, and spending it joyfully as a free person. Phil Coglin, an FBI agent, said that he had been involved in bank robbery and murder prosecutions in which the perpetrators used *Hit Man* and other Paladin books to commit crimes, including murder. *Hit Man* was used verbatim to kill a person and dispose of his body. This and other Paladin books were instrumental in training the murderers to commit the crimes. Coglin thought the murderers lacked the knowledge and expertise to commit the crimes without the books.[42]

In 1991, Lawrence Horn, former spouse of Mildred Horn and father of their eight-year-old quadriplegic son, Trevor, conspired with convicted felon James Perry to murder his family. Horn would then collect the $2 million that his son had received in settlement for injuries that had previously left him paralyzed for life. At the time of the murders, this money was held in trust for the benefit of Trevor, and, under the terms of the trust instrument, the trust money was to be distributed tax-free to Lawrence in the event of Mildred's and Trevor's deaths.[43]

In January 1992, Perry purchased *Hit Man* and another book titled *How to Make a Disposable Silencer, Vol. II* from Paladin. On 3 March 1993, Perry murdered Mildred and Trevor Horn, and also Trevor's private nurse, Janice Saunders. In soliciting, preparing for, and committing these murders, Perry meticulously employed countless of *Hit Man*'s 130 pages of detailed factual instructions on how to murder and to become a professional assassin.

Perry was not a successful contractor. He left incriminating evidence that the police gathered. He was eventually caught, and the conspiracy

41 http://ftp.die.net/mirror/hitman/4.html.
42 R. Smolla, *Deliberate Intent, op. cit.*, pp. 258–259.
43 *Vivian Rice* et al. v. *Paladin Enterprises*, 128 F.3d 233 (1997), at 239.

with Horn was revealed. The police found in Perry's possession the two books he purchased from Paladin. He was convicted and sentenced to death. Lawrence Horn was also convicted and sentenced to life without the possibility of parole.

Relatives of the three victims were not satisfied. They consider that Paladin is also blameworthy because *Hit Man* is a how-to book: how to commit murder. The families alleged that Paladin had aided and abetted Perry for the three murders. For the first time in American history, they appealed to the courts to hold that the publisher of a mass-distributed book should not be protected by the First Amendment.

The families of Horn and Saunders lost in the District Court. Judge Alexander Williams Jr argued that nothing in the book says "go out and commit murder now!" Instead, the book seems to say, "if you want to be a hit man this is what you need to do". This is advocacy, not incitement.[44] Nor does the book have a tendency to incite violence[45] (see the discussion in Chapter 6 on incitement). Applying the leading standard for American courts, set in the *Brandenburg* decision,[46] Judge Williams Jr concluded that *Hit Man* could not conceivably be considered to be incitement to imminent, lawless activity, and *contra* the families' argument it was therefore protected speech under the First Amendment:

> The constitutional protection accorded to the freedom of speech and of the press is not based on the naïve belief that speech can do no harm but on the confidence that the benefits society reaps from the free flow and exchange of ideas outweigh the costs society endures by receiving reprehensible or dangerous ideas.[47]

The families petitioned the Court of Appeal for the Fourth Circuit to overturn the decision, and won. Judge Michael Luttig, who wrote the decision in which Judges Wilkins and Williams joined, thought the record amply supported the families' allegation. The book could not be merely considered as "theoretical advocacy". Paladin had stipulated that it provided its assistance to Perry with both the knowledge and the intent that the book would immediately be used by criminals and would-be criminals in the solicitation, planning, and commission of murder and murder for hire. Thus, argued Luttig J., Paladin had stipulated to an intent, and acted with a kind and degree of intent, that would satisfy any heightened standard that might be required by the First Amendment prerequisite to the imposition of liability for aiding and abetting through speech conduct.[48]

---

44 *Rice* et al. v. *Paladin Enterprises*, 940 F. Supp. 836 (1996), at 847.
45 *Ibid.*, at 848.
46 *Brandenburg* v. *Ohio*, 395 U.S. 444, 23 L. Ed. 2d 430, 89 S. Ct. 1827 (1969).
47 *Rice* et al. v. *Paladin Enterprises*, 940 F. Supp. 836 (1996), at 849.
48 *Rice* et al. v. *Paladin Enterprises*, 128 F.3d 233 (1997), at 248.

Paladin appealed to the Supreme Court for writ of certiorari, but their petition was flatly denied, leaving Judge Luttig's opinion in force.[49] After this lengthy legal battle, on 21 May 1999, Paladin Press settled the case, giving the families of those killed by the hit man several million dollars, agreeing to destroy the remaining 700 copies of the book in their possession, and surrendering any rights they had to publish and reproduce the work. While the families were successful in damaging Paladin, they have not been successful in stifling the book. With the surrender of the publishing rights by Paladin Press, the book has entered the public domain, and was published on the Internet on 22 May 1999.[50] This is very strange. If the book has been recognized as harmful and deadly, then it should cease publication altogether. The mode of its publication, whether on paper or on the Web, should not make a difference. The current state of affairs that allows this to happen should be remedied.

Professor Rod Smolla, an American constitutional scholar who for many years has written on the importance of the First Amendment, thought that *Hit Man* constituted an exception and should not be protected as any other book. He joined, albeit reluctantly, the legal team that was hired by the families. This was not an easy decision for him to make, being in contradiction to his inherent liberal world view. After the legal proceedings were over and the case had been settled, he wrote a book about the affair. Smolla argued that Paladin knew and intended that some of its callers who ordered the book would use it as a manual to carry out contract killings: just did not know which particular book order was being made by real murderers. Paladin "knows some of the checks it is cashing are from murderers using the book to kill. It just can't separate the checks that come from killers and those that come from fantasizers."[51] That inability to match check to killer makes no moral or legal difference.

Paladin recruited many free speech and media organizations to come to their aid as *amici curiae* (including the Thomas Jefferson Center for the Protection of Free Expression, the American Civil Liberties Union Foundation of Maryland, the American Civil Liberties Union of the National Capital Area, and the American Civil Liberties Union of Colorado),[52] making briefs arguing that its murderous manual was practically no different from countless other forms of protected expression, including mystery and horror novels,[53] crime books, movies, news presentations, and televi-

---

49 *Paladin Enterprises* v. *Vivian Rice* et al., 523 U.S. 1074 (1998). See also *Paladin* v. *Rice*, petition for Writ of Certiorari, written by L. Levine et al.
50 http://ftp.die.net/mirror/hitman/.
51 R, Smolla, *Deliberate Intent, op. cit.*, p. 142.
52 *Rice* v. *Paladin*, Brief of the *Amici Curiae*, The United States Court of Appeals for the Fourth Circuit, Record No. 96–2412 (14 January 1997).
53 See Brief *Amicus Curiae* in support of Affirmance on behalf of The Horror Writers Association, *Rice* et al. v. *Paladin Enterprises*, The United States Court of Appeals for the Fourth Circuit, Record No. 96–2412 (6 October 1996).

sion programs on crime. However, a murder manual is just not the same as a Stephen King or Tom Clancy novel, or a Steven Seagal movie.[54] It is not the same in its lethal potency, in its horrifyingly detailed instructions, in its cold rationalization and encouragement to the reader become a hit man, and in its wicked, calculated intent. Paladin attempted to maximize sales by marketing to criminals and potential criminals. The case was not about merely providing information, triggering our senses or contributing to our imagination. *Hit Man* encouraged and facilitated murder.

The technical manual provided step-by-step instructions, including engineering specifications, photographs, diagrams, charts, sample maps, checklists, formulas, suggested prices, information on the selection of weapons, methods for altering weapons and ammunition, detailed and hair-raising torture and killing techniques, travel arrangements, instructions on appropriate garb, money-laundering methods, and detailed information as to how to dispose of the body. Judge Luttig contended that the list of instructions was so comprehensive and detailed that it was as though the instructor were literally present with the would-be murderer, not only in the preparation and planning, but in the actual commission and follow-up of the murder.[55] To argue that the book is abstract advocacy is untenable.[56]

The detailed information coupled with the element of encouragement is lethal. The text contains exhortation and encouragement to engage in the business of hired murder. Anything but a mere abstract teaching, the book lays before its readers a malicious, detailed, and instructive plan as to how to murder a human being and get away with it with a nice sum of money in the pocket. This reward would also apparently redeem the last stains on a guilty conscience, if such sentiments still existed after the rationalization process instructed by the author to clean the successful contractor's soul.

54 Paladin argued that like Tom Clancy's *Executive Orders*, *Hit Man* is informational in a manner removed from immediate connection to the commission of a specific criminal act. See *Rice* v. *Paladin*, Supplemental Brief of Appellee by Thomas B. Kelley and Lee Levine, The United States Court of Appeals for the Fourth Circuit, Record No. 96–2412 (May 1997), p. 10.

55 *Rice* et al. v. *Paladin Enterprises*, 128 F.3d 233 (1997), at 249; R. Smolla, *Deliberate Intent, op. cit.*, p. 225.

56 *Ibid.*, at 255. For a different perspective, arguing that the book is protected under the First Amendment, see E. Volokh, "Crime-facilitating speech", *Stanford Law Review*, 57 (2005). Volokh suggests that crime-facilitating speech ought to be constitutionally protected unless (1) it's said to a person or a small group of people when the speaker knows the listeners are likely to use the information for criminal purposes (Paladin had "little practical or ideological reason" to intend to help criminals. Volokh does acknowledge that the publisher merely knew they were helping criminals); (2) it's within one of the few classes of speech that has almost no non-criminal value; or (3) it can pose truly extraordinary harm (of the order of a nuclear attack or a plague) even when it's also valuable for lawful purpose.

Speaking of reward, I don't know how much the author received from Paladin for writing the book. Smolla reveals that the contract contained an addendum that Paladin would indemnify the author in the event of liability suits. The addendum specifically stated that this included "any litigations or censures that may arise out of the sale, use or misuse of the contents of the contracted book".[57] "The hit babe", writes Smolla, "had obviously been worried that someone might follow the instructions in *Hit Man* to kill somebody, and that she might be sued because of it."[58] This showed that Paladin was aware of the serious risk before the book was published. The publisher, Peder Lund, simply did not care. His uncaring attitude and world views are blatantly manifested in the legal deposition he gave, and his exchange with the families' attorneys.[59]

The Internet

As already stated, *Hit Man* is still available on the Internet. This new technology is now available to contest boundaries to free expression and to expand the scope of tolerance. This vast ocean of knowledge, data, ideologies, and propaganda is a wonderful, easy to use mechanism for advancing knowledge and learning across the world, for bridging gaps (educational, national, religious, cultural) and promoting understanding. The Internet contains the best products of humanity, but unfortunately also the worse.

On the Internet you may find abundant pornographic material, some of which involves child pornography, and brutal treatment of women and animals. There are more than 100,000 child pornography websites, and the numbers are growing. Hundreds of thousands of people are said to subscribe to such sites.[60] Pedophiles are using such sites to create a network of cooperation and promote their social cohesion, to cyberstalk, to seduce children and to promote their criminal activities. By showing children child pornography, abusers try to convince them that they would enjoy certain sexual acts, and that what they are being asked to do is all right and "normal".[61] For some offenders, pornographic images can be used as an aid to blackmail in order to ensure the child's silence and

---

57 R. Smolla, *Deliberate Intent*, p. 235.
58 *Ibid.* A movie was made after the book: *Deliberate Intent* (2000), with Timothy Hutton. Director: Andy Wolk.
59 R. Smolla, *Deliberate Intent, op. cit.*, pp. 240–244. See also p. 263.
60 B. Wake, "Anti-pedophile website under instant attack", *The Gazette (Montreal, Quebec)* (4 September 2001), p. A11; A. Satkofsky, "Web a playground for child porn", *The Express-Times* (25 February 2004).
61 L. Kelly, "Pornography and child sexual abuse", in C. Itzin (ed.), *Pornography: Women, Violence and Civil Liberties* (Oxford: Oxford University Press, 1992), pp. 119–120; M. Taylor and E. Quayle, *Child Pornography. An Internet Crime* (Hove and New York: Brunner-Routledge, 2003), esp. Chapter 4.

cooperation in future assaults. Threats of showing images that can, with the help of computer, be easily produced, appear to be common.[62] Further, the exchange of child pornography among pedophiles is a significant reinforcement of their urge to abuse children, providing a sense of support and legitimizing this behavior to themselves; thus it encourages continued sexual exploitation.

The Internet also provides predators with easy and anonymous access to unsuspecting kids. It promotes sex tourism and child pornography globally. It grants pedophiles another way to enter into the privacy of the home of young children and to lure them to meetings. People who pay to access these sites are injecting cash into a criminal and manipulative industry that sexually exploits and seriously damages children.[63] What I previously argued about *Hit Man* also holds true here: once the harm resulting from such material is recognized, the medium of its transmission should not make a difference. Liberal democracies should invest effort and mutual cooperation in seeing that such sites cease to exist. People who put those sites on the Web should be prosecuted and receive harsh and deterrent penalties. Internet Service Providers (ISPs) should be held liable for allowing such sites.[64]

Another concern is hate on the Internet and the potential violence it provokes. Marc Knobel, a researcher at the Council of Jewish Institutions in France, estimated the number of hate websites to be between 40,000 and 60,000. The French Foreign Minister, Michell Barnier, said that between 2000 and 2004 the number of violent and extremist sites has increased by 300 percent.[65] The International Network Against Cyber Hate (INACH), founded in 2002, monitors the Internet and publishes overviews and reports about the situation in different countries. It declares its mission to be to combat "racism, anti-Semitism, Islamophobia, Holocaust denial and discrimination on the Internet through education, monitoring, regulation, legal action and promotion of international measures".[66]

62 E. Quayle and M. Taylor, "Child pornography and the Internet: assessment issues", *British Journal of Social Work*, 32 (2002): 866.
63 L. Jarrett, "Maryland Heights detective works to protect kids from Internet predators", *St Louis Post-Dispatch* (22 March 1999), p. 5; W. Hoge, "British rock star receives lesser punishment in Internet case", *New York Times* (May 8, 2003), p. 7; A. Satkofsky, "Web a playground for child porn", *The Express-Times* (25 February 2004). For further discussion on the dangers of child pornography on the Internet, see http://www.bytescanada.com/.
64 X. Amadei, "NOTE: Standards of liability for Internet service providers: a comparative study of France and the United States with a specific focus on copyright, defamation, and illicit content", *Cornell International Law Journal*, 35 (November 2001/February 2002): 189. See also S. Hayes, "Net stalker amendments concern ISPs", *The Australian* (13 April 2004), p. C3.
65 C. Coroller, "La haine et la violence, du virtuel au reel", *Liberation* (France) (16 June 2004); http://www.liberation.fr/page.php?Article=215810.
66 See "Antisemitism on the Internet, an overview", at www.inach.net.

Some of the most graphic, industrious, elaborate, and impressive websites were created by hate-mongers, racists, and Nazi and white supremacist groups.[67] In the words of Joseph T. Roy Sr, Director of the Intelligence Project at the Poverty Law Center, the hate sites are very slick, using all the bells and whistles that technology affords them.[68] Stormfront, a white nationalist website that was launched in 1995 and is regarded as the pioneer of hate websites, is one of the most popular sites. Don Black, a former Grand Dragon of the KKK and the founder of this website, said he started the site to provide an alternative news media and to serve as a means for those attracted to the white nationalist movement to stay in touch and form a virtual community.[69] Before the Internet, Black said, people who shared his beliefs had little opportunity to try to spread them, other than through leaflets, small newspapers, and rallies. However, today a relatively inexpensive website can reach millions. Indeed, Stormfront gets more than 1,500 hits each weekday. Black owns his own computer servers and so is not dependent upon Internet service providers.[70] The thoughtful and innovative Black also founded a website especially for children, called kids.stormfront.[71] The World Church of the Creator, the KKK, the Aryan Nations, and other extremist groups have followed suit.[72]

As the Internet makes available cheap, virtually untraceable, instantaneous, anonymous, uncensored distribution that can be easily downloaded and posted in multiple places, it has become an asset for hate groups, Holocaust deniers, and terrorist organizations, who use the Internet to transmit propaganda and provide information about their aims, to

67 See, for instance, http://www.aryan-nations.org/; http://www.northernalliance.ca/index; http://info14.com/; http://club-28.com/; htmhttp://www.kkk.bz/index1.htm; http://www.resist.com/home.htm; http://izan.de/; http://www.resistance.com/; http://www.freewebs.com/ kleagle/wakeupwhiteamerica.htm; http://www.natvan.com/who-rules-america/;
   http://www.whiterevolution.com/mission.shtml. See also the hate directory compiled at http://www.bcpl.net/~rfrankli/hatedir.htm, and C. Sunstein, *Republic.com* (Princeton: Princeton University Press, 2001), p. 64.
68 Statement of Joseph T. Roy Sr, *Hate Crime on the Internet*, Hearing before the Committee on the Judiciary, United States Senate (Washington, 14 September 1999).
69 http://www.stormfront.org/; see J. Winegardner, "Is hate young and new on the web?", *Online Journalism Review*, USC Annenberg (4 April 2002).
70 M. Marriott, "Rising tide: sites born of hate", *New York Times* (18 March 1999). For more information on Don Black and Stormfront, see Prepared Statement of Howard Berkowitz, *Hate Crime on the Internet*, Hearing before the Committee on the Judiciary, United States Senate (Washington, 14 September 1999).
71 http://kids.stormfront.org.
72 Statement of Abraham Cooper, *Hate Crime on the Internet*, Hearing before the Committee on the Judiciary, United States Senate (Washington, 14 September 1999).

allow an exchange between like-minded individuals, to vindicate the use of violence, to de-legitimize and to demoralize their enemies, to raise cash, and to enlist public support.[73] Christopher Wolf, Chair of the Internet Task Force of the Anti-Defamation League, argues while providing pertinent reports: "The evidence is clear that hate online inspires hate crimes."[74]

Wolf tells the stories of two Aryan supremacists, Benjamin Smith and Richard Baumhammers, who in 1999 and 2000 respectively went on racially motivated shooting sprees after being exposed to Internet racial propaganda. Smith regularly visited the World Church of the Creator website, a notorious racist and hateful organization.[75] He said: "It wasn't really 'til I got on the Internet, read some literature of these groups that . . . it really all came together." He maintained: "It's a slow, gradual process to become racially conscious."[76] Rabbi Abraham Cooper of the Wiesenthal Center argued that the Internet provided the theological justification for torching synagogues in Sacramento, and the pseudo-intellectual basis for violent hate attacks in Illinois and Indiana.[77]

On the Web it is also possible to find extensive discussions on suicide pills[78] and "exit bags" (do-it-yourself suicide kits).[79] One site calls "[to] save

73 Cf. http://www.hizbollah.tv/english/frames/index_eg.htm; http://moqawama. org/page2/main.htm; http://eelam.com/; http://voz-rebelde.de/; see also K. R. Damphousse and B. L. Smith, "The Internet: a terrorist medium for the 21st century", in H. W. Kushner (ed.), *The Future of Terrorism: Violence in the New Millennium* (Thousand Oaks: Sage, 1998), pp. 208–224.; Y. Tsfati and G. Weimann, "www.terrorism.com: Terror on the Internet", *Studies in Conflict and Terrorism*, 25 (2002): 317–332.

74 C. Wolf, "Needed: diagnostic tools to gauge the full effect of online anti-Semitism and hate", OSCE Meeting on the Relationship Between Racist, Xenophobic and Anti-Semitic Propaganda on the Internet and Hate Crimes (Paris, 16 June 2004).

75 For information on World Church of the Creator, see http://www.volksfront-usa.org/creator.shtml; http://www.adl.org/backgrounders/wcotc.asp; http://www.reed.edu/~gronkep/webofpolitics/fall2001/yagern/creator.html; http://www.adl.org/poisoning_web/wcotc.asp; http://www.apologeticsindex.org/c171. html; Prepared Statement of Howard Berkowitz, *Hate Crime on the Internet*, Hearing before the Committee on the Judiciary, United States Senate (Washington, 14 September 1999).

76 C. Wolf, "Regulating hate speech *qua* speech is not the solution to the epidemic of hate on the Internet", OSCE Meeting on the Relationship Between Racist, Xenophobic and Anti-Semitic Propaganda on the Internet and Hate Crimes (Paris, 16–17 June 2004).

77 Statement of Abraham Cooper, *Hate Crime on the Internet*, Hearing before the Committee on the Judiciary, United States Senate (Washington, 14 September 1999).

78 http://www.saves.asn.au/resources/newsletter/jul1998/asuipill.htm; http://www.nex.net.au/users/reidgck/DOCTOR.HTM.

79 http://abcnews.go.com/sections/world/DailyNews/australia020717_suicide. html; http://www.nik.co.uk/weblog/archives/001463.php; http://members. ozemail.com.au/~deliverance/.

the planet, kill yourself".[80] It advises people to "do a good job" when they commit suicide, discussing the pros and cons of death by shooting, hanging, crashing a car, jumping, slitting wrists, drowning, freezing, over-dosing or gassing with nitrous oxide, exhaust fumes and oven gas. On the Internet you can see the horrifying pictures of people jumping to their deaths from the Twin Towers on 11 September 2001. On the Internet people exchange fantasies as to how they would like to rape violently and murder young girls.[81] Recipes regarding how to produce weapons and bombs are posted,[82] as well as manuals instructing on acts of violence, and how to build practical firearm suppressors.[83] On 23 March 1996, the *Terrorist's Handbook* was posted on the Web, including instructions on how to make a powerful bomb. The same type of bomb was used in the Oklahoma City bombing.[84] Deputy Assistant Attorney General Robert Litt, of the US Justice Department's Criminal Division, observed that only hours after the Oklahoma City bombing, someone posted directions on the Internet – including a diagram – explaining how to construct a bomb of the type that was used in that tragic act of terrorism. Another Internet posting offered not only information concerning how to build bombs, but also instructions as to how the device used in the Oklahoma City bombing could have been improved.[85]

Al Qaeda, the leading multi-national and Islamist terrorist network founded and led by the Saudi multimillionaire Osama bin Laden, relied heavily on the Internet in planning and coordinating the 11 September 2001 attacks on the United States. Members of this terrorist organization sent each other thousands of messages in a password-protected section of an extreme Islamic website.[86] In the wake of 11 September, Internet providers shut down several sites associated with Dr Sheikh Abdullah Azzam, mentor of bin Laden.[87] Until the closure of the Nuremberg File

80 http://www.churchofeuthanasia.org/index.html.
81 Cf. *U.S.* v. *Baker and Gonda* 890 F. Supp. 1375, U.S. District Court, E. D. Michigan (21 June 1995); *U.S.* v. *Alkhabaz* 48 F.3d 1220 (7 March 1995); *U.S.* v. *Alkhabaz* 104 F.3d 1492 (6th Cir. 1997). For further discussion, see J. E. Rothman, "Freedom of speech and true threats", *Harvard Journal of Law & Public Policy*, 25(1) (2001).
82 See, for instance, http://www.bluemud.org/article/11607.
83 http://www.paladin-press.com/detail.aspx?ID=134.
84 C. Sunstein, *Republic.com, op. cit.*, p. 52.
85 *Report on The Availability of Bombmaking Information*, Prepared by the US Dept. of Justice, submitted to the United States House of Representatives and the United States Senate (April 1997), available at http://www.usdoj.gov/criminal/cybercrime/bombmakinginfo.html.
86 Anti-Defamation League, *Jihad Online: Islamic Terrorists and the Internet* (2002), available at http://www.adl.org/Learn/internet/jihad_online.pdf; H. Brackman, *9/11 Digital Lies: A Survey of Online Apologists for Global Terrorism* (Simon Wiesenthal Center, 2001).
87 E. Burch, "Comment: censoring hate speech in cyberspace: a new debate in a new America", *North Carolina Journal of Law & Technology*, 3(1) (2001), p. 180.

site, operated by the American Coalition of Life Activists (ACLA), addresses, photographs, telephone and license plate numbers of doctors who practice abortion, as well as the names of their spouses and children, were published. The website said that the information would be used to prosecute abortionists when abortion becomes illegal, just as Nazi leaders were prosecuted at Nuremberg. The list of abortion providers read like a list of targets for assassination, with the names of doctors who were wounded printed in "greyed-out" letters, and those abortionists who were murdered crossed out. The website included Western-style posters, with photos of abortionists and the word "Wanted" beneath each and every one of them. Effectively, the site incited murder of the abortionists. The court held that the site constituted a true threat and was not protected by the First Amendment. The ACLA was ordered to pay over $100 million in damages.[88] Malicious content, when it knowingly and intentionally communicates a credible threat, will not be tolerated. This precedent constituted a milestone in American history as one of the few times that a court restrained speech on the Internet.

Another rare incident in which a website was shut down in the United States concerned Ryan Wilson, a white supremacist and former leader of the United States Nationalist Party, who in 1998 started a website for his racist organization, ALPHA HQ, depicting a bomb destroying the office of Bonnie Jouhari, a fair housing specialist who regularly organized anti-hate activities. Not only that, Jouhari was targeted as "race mixer" because she had a biracial child, and she was also a "race traitor" because she had had sexual relations with an African-American man, and because as a fair-housing advocate she promoted integration. Next to her picture, the ALPHA HQ website stated, "Traitors like this should beware, for in our day, they will be hung from the neck from the nearest tree or lamp post."[89] Wilson reiterated the threat in a press interview. The website referred to Jouhari's daughter as "mongrel", listed various types of guns and information where to obtain various weapons, and provided a bomb recipe under the picture of Jouhari's office. Following the Internet posting, Ms Jouhari and her daughter began to receive numerous threatening telephone calls. A known Ku Klux Klansman intimidated her by sitting outside Jouhari's office for long hours. Someone pounded on their door in the middle of the night. On another occasion, someone broke into their apartment. Jouhari and her daughter were terrified. Wilson was charged by the

---

88 http://www.cyberussr.com/adg/hitlist-san/atrocity.htm; see also *Planned Parenthood of the Columbia/Willamette Inc.* et al. v. *American Coalition of Life Activists*, U.S Court of Appeals for the Nine Circuit, 290 F.3d 1058 (21 May 2002).

89 *The Secretary, United States Department of Housing and Urban Development, on behalf of Bonnie Jouhari and Pilar Horton* v. *Ryan Wilson and ALPHA HQ*, before Alan W. Heifetz, Chief Administrative Law Judge (decided 19 July 2000), available at http://www.hud.gov/utilities/intercept.cfm?/offices/oalj/cases/fha/pdf/wilson.pdf.

Pennsylvania Commonwealth's Attorney General with threats, harassment, and ethnic intimidation. The site was removed from the Internet, and the court issued an injunction against the defendant and his organization, barring them from displaying certain messages on the Internet. The Chief Administrative Law Judge said: "The website was nothing less than a transparent call to action ... When he published the ALPHA HQ website, Wilson created a situation that put Complainants in danger of harassment and serious bodily harm."[90] The expansive and pervasive nature of the Internet calls for some regulation. Fighting speech with more speech is sometimes not the answer.

The Internet does not have any borders, but it does have limits. These vary from one country to another. Child pornography is prohibited around the globe. Virtual child pornography is viewed differently in Europe than in the United States, and so is hate. The United States allows more scope for questionable speech, but again in the United States you cannot incite to murder, and you cannot use the Internet to intimidate, threatening to kill people.[91]

The Internet is international in character, and there is a need for international cooperation to make such closure of sites meaningful. Some European countries are working together to combat cyber crime and to criminalize acts of a racist and xenophobic nature committed through the Internet.[92] The Council of Europe has adopted a measure that will criminalize Internet hate speech, including hyperlinks to pages that contain offensive content. The provision, which was passed in 2002 by the Council's decision-making body (the Committee of Ministers), updated the 2001 European Convention on Cybercrime.[93] Specifically, the amendment bans

90 *The Secretary, United States Department of Housing and Urban Development, on behalf of Bonnie Jouhari and Pilar Horton* v. *Ryan Wilson and ALPHA HQ,* p. 20. For further discussion, see "Cuomo says million dollar award sends clear message against racial discrimination on the Internet", Department of Housing and Urban Development Press Release (20 July 2000); C. Wolf, "Regulating hate speech *qua* speech is not the solution to the epidemic of hate on the internet", OSCE Meeting on the Relationship Between Racist, Xenophobic and Anti-Semitic Propaganda on the Internet and Hate Crimes (Paris, 16–17 June 2004).
91 See also *United States* v. *Machado* 195 F.3d 454 (9th Cir. 1999) involving the conviction of an expelled college student who on 20 September 1996 sent threatening e-mail message to 60 Asian students saying that he will make it his "life career to find and kill every one" of you personally. It was the first prosecution ever in the US under the Federal hate crimes statute involving threats transmitted over the Internet. Machado was sentenced to a one-year term of imprisonment, to be followed by a one-year period of supervised release.
92 See OSCE Conference on Anti-Semitism, *Consolidated Summary* (Vienna, 19–20 June 2003).
93 http://conventions.coe.int/Treaty/EN/CadreListeTraites.htm.

any written material, any image or any other representation of ideas or theories, which advocates, promotes or incites hatred, discrimination or violence, against any individual or group of individuals, based on race, colour, descent or national or ethnic origin, as well as religion if used as pretext for any of these factors.[94]

Internet providers have terms of service which often include prohibition against hate messages. When sites cross the bounds of tolerance and violate these terms, providers should enforce their rules and shut down the hate sites. In 1998, Fairview Technology Centre Ltd, an Internet Service Provider (ISP) owned by a hate-monger named Bernard Klatt whose server was located in Oliver, British Columbia and was connected to the Internet via BC Telecom, was identified as host of a number of websites associated with hate speech and neo-Nazi organizations, including the Toronto-based Heritage Front, the World Wide Church of the Creator, and the French Charlemagne Hammerhead Skinheads. At the same time, Fairview Technology provided access to local businesses, government agencies, and schools, making it extremely easy for young students inadvertently to access racist sites. The materials were written in Lyon, a center for anti-Semitism in France, and transmitted to Fairview, which put them on the Internet. The Hate Crimes Unit established by the British Columbia government was asked to examine complaints against Fairview. Scrutiny of the site resulted in the French and British authorities arresting members of the Charlemagne Skins for posting death threats against Jews. The final blow to the Fairview Technology site came when British Columbia Telephone, the local Internet access provider, required Fairview to accept full legal liability for any material available on the sites.[95] Faced with the threat, Klatt sold the Internet service to another local company.

In the United States, this model of self-regulation has meant that companies that have clear rules against hate can make a decision not to do business with people who violate these rules, and by working with Internet companies, agencies of all kinds – governmental and non-profit – can be very successful in fighting hate online.[96] The Anti-Defamation League and

---

94 J. Scheeres, "European outlaw net hate speech", *Wired News* (9 November 2002). For further discussion, see M. L. Siegel, "Comment: hate speech, civil rights, and the Internet: the jurisdictional and human rights nightmare", *Albany Law Journal of Science & Technology*, 9 (1999): 375.

95 R. Howard, "Notorious Internet Service closes; B.C. to continue probe of Klatt", *Globe & Mail* (28 April 1998); http://www.nizkor.org/hweb/ orgs/canadian/bc/fairview-technologies/press/globe-and-mail-980428.html; J. Hunter, "An Okanagan town caught in the web", *Maclean's*, 111(18) (1998).

96 B. Marcus, "Public and private partnership in the fight against racism, xenophobia and anti-Semitism on the Internet – best practices", OSCE Meeting on the Relationship Between Racist, Xenophobic and Anti-Semitic Propaganda on the Internet and Hate Crimes (Paris, 16 June 2004).

the Simon Wiesenthal Center have been monitoring the Internet and alerting against hateful websites.

Filtering is another way in which Internet providers have chosen to deal with problematic speech. Promoting the use of filters does not condemn as criminal any category of speech, and so in the United States it is the preferred solution. The potential chilling effect is eliminated, or at least much diminished.[97] Filters are a form of software that can be installed along with a Web browser to block access to certain websites that contain inappropriate or offensive material. Some of these filters are NetNanny, CyberPatrol, Cybersitter, SurfWatch and HateFilter. They block sites and categories considered to be undesirable and/or problematic. However, filtering suffers from serious inadequacies:

1   Filters can block too little, allowing problematic material to pass without hindrance.
2   Filters can block too much. The word-sensitive filters are not sensitive to content, and thus they lack precision. They block a great deal of valuable material, for instance about birth control, drug use and date rape.[98]
3   Filters can block students and researchers from accessing questionable websites for purposes of research. I had a difficult time accessing some hateful sites for the purpose of writing this book.
4   Filtering software costs money, and not every family would find it affordable or necessary to install it.
5   Filtering software depends upon parents being willing to decide what their children will surf on the Web, and to enforce that decision. In a reality when many parents are working long hours and leave their children alone at home, such supervision is not a reasonable possibility.[99]

Having said that, the wide demand for filtering raises the possibility that different versions of filtering software will be offered, corresponding to different tastes and varying levels of tolerance on the part of parents and organizations.[100] Hopefully, filtering software will be offered free of charge by governmental agencies or NGOs that care about children's education and their well being, and are willing to invest money to stop (or at least mitigate) the evils of the Internet.

---

97   *Ashcroft* v. *ACLU* 542 U.S. (2004), decided on 29 June 2004.
98   *Safer Internet*, Newsletter for Awareness Raisers in the EU Safer Internet Programme, No. 21 (January 2003), available at http://www.saferinternet.org/news/safer21.htm.
99   See Justice Breyer's dissent in *Ashcroft* v. *ACLU* 542 U.S. (2004).
100 Cf. W. D. Araiza, "Tales from the net: captive audiences, children and the home", *Loyola Law School (Los Angeles) Public Law and Legal Theory, Research Paper No. 2002–30* (October 2002).

Final word

Liberal democracies need to set boundaries to liberty and tolerance. Whatever the reader may think about the guidelines and propositions this book offers, whether the limited scope of tolerance suggested here is proper and justified, he or she needs to express an opinion and deliberate the issue. I welcome constructive debates and challenging contentions to illuminate this intriguing issue.

The United States adopts the most liberal stance on free expression. As a result of this attitude, hundreds of hate groups are active in the United States, shielded under the First (and Second) Amendments to the Constitution.[101] The Southern Poverty Law Center's Intelligence Project counted 751 active hate groups in the United States in 2003.[102] All hate groups have beliefs or practices that attack or malign an entire class of people, typically for their immutable characteristics. All of those groups have little respect for the law and governmental agencies. Some are engaged in intimidation, vandalism, and violent activities, including murder. They don't stop at speech. In 1995, twenty people were murdered in hate-motivated incidents.[103] According to the FBI, there were 7,462 hate crimes incidents in the United States in 2002. Intimidation was the most often reported offense, accounting for 35.2 percent of the total bias-motivated offenses. Destruction/damage/vandalism accounted for 26.6 percent of the total reported offenses; simple assault 20.3 percent, and aggravated assault 11.7 percent. There were eleven hate-motivated murders.[104]

Some white supremacist, anti-Semitic organizations cheered the 11 September 2001 terrorist attacks, finding common cause with the Israel-hating terrorists. They are among the many suspects in the mailing of anthrax-contaminated letters. "The people who flew those planes into the World Trade Center and the Pentagon did it because they had been pushed into a corner by the U.S. government acting on behalf of the Jews", wrote William L. Pierce, head of the neo-Nazi National Alliance in Hillsboro, Virginia. In 2001, this was the largest and most active neo-Nazi organization in the United States.[105] Pierce's book, *The Turner Diaries*,[106] is

---

101 The Second Amendment holds: "A well-regulated Militia, being necessary for the security of a free State, the right of the people to keep and bear Arms, shall not be infringed."

102 http://www.tolerance.org/maps/hate/.

103 http://www.fbi.gov/ucr/hatecm.htm.

104 http://www.fbi.gov/ucr/ucr.htm#hate. See also W. B. Rubenstein, "The real story of U.S. hate crimes statistics: an empirical analysis", *Tulane Law Review*, 78 (2004): 1213.

105 *Ibid.* See also Prepared Statement of Howard Berkowitz, *Hate Crime on the Internet*, Hearing before the Committee on the Judiciary, United States Senate (Washington, 14 September 1999).

106 Cf. http://pages.prodigy.net/aesir/ttd.htm; http://www.rotten.com/library/culture/turner-diaries/.

said to have inspired Timothy McVeigh.[107] The novel, written under the pseudonym Andrew Macdonald, describes the violent overthrow of the U.S. government and a bloody race war against blacks and Jews. It was used by McVeigh to plan the 19 April 1995 bombing, and has been linked to other hate crimes, including the 1984 slaying of Jewish radio talk show host Alan Berg.[108] I am not suggesting that *The Turner Diaries* should be banned. This book lacks the aiding and abetting explicit characteristics of *Hit Man* and, as is the case with most books, the way to fight its harmful messages is by counter-speech, by exposing their evil nature. Having said that, the United States authorities are willing to tolerate forms of speech that other democracies find too costly. The United States also espouses the most extreme liberal position because it can afford it. It is a vast, pluralistic country, and the authorities are willing to deal with manifold manifestations of hate. Other democracies feel more vulnerable in comparison to the great free-spirited superpower of today. They would not allow the existence of hundreds of militias and hate groups. Obviously they would not permit the freedom the United States allows to extreme groups, recognizing their threat but still upholding the First and Second Amendments.[109] I wonder whether the United States will be able to retain its liberal radical position in the long run.

I wish to leave you with a final thought. In his comments on a draft of this book, Geoffrey Marshall made a radical suggestion, saying that it would be a good thing to forget altogether the term "toleration". He rightly noted that tolerating people's activities just means leaving them free from restraint, so asking about toleration is no different from asking what limitations on freedom are appropriate. We would not think of asking the general question whether intolerant people should be left free. We do not have any general notion of leaving people free to do what they want irrespective of what their conduct is, or what its consequences are, and undoubtedly intolerant people do not constitute any group that requires special consideration. Once we have worked out the proper distinctions between speech and action, and the types of speech-act that are protected by the Free Speech Principle and the types that are not protected, the intolerant are bound by the rules as to speech and action as

---

107 For extensive discussion on terrorism in the United States, see C. Hewitt, *Understanding Terrorism in America: From the Klan to Al Qaeda* (New York: Routledge, 2003).

108 http://www.bet.com/articles/1,,c1gb3409-4077,00.html. See also J. Solomon, "U.S had clues before Oklahoma city bombing", *Associated Press* (12 February 2003), http:////www.religionnewsblog.com/2331-.html. See also A. Tsesis, *Destructive Messages* (New York and London: New York University Press, 2002), pp. 74–75.

109 On the militias, republicanism, and the Second Amendment, see D. J. Mulloy, *American Extremism: History, Politics and the Militia Movement* (London: Routledge, 2004), pp. 114–117, 120–123.

much and as little as anyone else. Of course, the fact that they are intolerant may be the reason why they perform more actions and engage in more speech-acts that get punished than tolerant actors and speakers, but no special theory is needed to deal with them.

The discussion, no doubt, will continue.

Index

Index of court cases

Printed in Great Britain
by Amazon.co.uk, Ltd.,
Marston Gate.